The Dead Will Arise

Author of

The House of Phalo

Before and After Shaka
(Editor)

The Dead Will Arise

*Nongqawuse and the Great Xhosa
Cattle-Killing Movement of 1856—7*

J. B. PEIRES

Senior Lecturer in History
Rhodes University
Grahamstown

Ravan Press
Johannesburg

Indiana University Press
Bloomington and Indianapolis

James Currey
London

This book is a publication of

Indiana University Press
601 North Morton Street
Bloomington, IN 47404-3797 USA
http://www.indiana.edu/~iupress
Telephone orders 800-842-6796
Fax orders 812-855-7931
Orders by e-mail iuporder@indiana.edu

Ravan Press (Pty) Ltd
PO Box 31134, Braamfontein,
Johannesburg, 2017
South Africa

James Currey Ltd
54b Thornhill Square, Islington
London N1 1BE

First published 1989
ISBN (Ravan Press) 0-86975-381-9

Manufactured in the United States of America

Library of Congress Cataloging-in-Publication Data
Peires, J. B. (Jeffrey B.)
    The dead will arise.
    1. South Africa—History—Xhosa Cattle-Killing,
1856–1857. 2. Nonqawuse, 1841–1898—Prophecies.
3. Xhosa (African people)—Religion. 4. Xhosa (African
people)—History—19th Century.   I. Title.
DT777.P45   1989   968.04   88-32799
ISBN 0-253-34338-0

British Library Cataloguing in Publication Data
Peires, J. B. (Jeffrey Brian)
    The dead will arise: Nongqawuse and the
    great Xhosa cattle killing movement of 1856–7.
    1. South Africa.Xhosa.Cultural
    processes, 1856–1857
    I. Title
    305.8'9968

    ISBN 0-85255-048-0
    ISBN 0-85255-049-9 pbk

4   5   6   7   8   9   05   04   03   02   01   00

Contents

List of Maps and Illustrations

Illustrations

The author thanks the Africana Museum, Johannesburg, the South African Library, Cape Town, and the Black Watch Regimental Museum, Perth for the following illustrations.

Between page 160 and page 161

1. Nonkosi and Nongqawuse
2. Sarhili, King of the Xhosa
3. Mhlakaza's Residence in Grahamstown

4. Sir Harry Smith
5. Sir George Cathcart
6. Colonel William Eyre
7. T. Baines, *Detachment of the 2nd or Queen's Regiment Surrounded — Fish River Bush*

FOUR BELIEVERS:
8. Sandile
9. Mhala
10. Fadana, Leader of the Thembu believers
11. Phatho

FOUR UNBELIEVERS:
12. Anta
13. Kama
14. Toyise
15. Dyani Tshatshu

16. Sir George Grey, Governor and High Commissioner
17. Colonel John Maclean, Chief Commissioner of British Kaffraria

Maps

Preface

Few people who hear the story of Nongqawuse — the young girl whose fantastic promise of the resurrection lured an entire people to death by starvation — ever forget it. Tens of thousands of Xhosa died; tens of thousands more fled their homes; hundreds of thousands of cattle were slaughtered, the pathetic victims of a beautiful but hopeless dream. And while the Xhosa nation was lying prostrate and defenceless, Sir George Grey, a self-proclaimed benefactor of the non-European peoples of the world, trampled on this human wreckage: he exiled the starving, crushed the survivors, and seized more than half of Xhosaland for a colony of white settlement. The great Cattle-Killing movement remains an open sore in the historical consciousness of most South Africans. What was it all about, people ask. Surely the Xhosa could not have believed Nongqawuse? There must be something more behind the incident, some secret story behind the story that everyone knows.

But despite the widespread interest in Nongqawuse's prophecies, the full history of that terrible period has never been written. There has never been a book on the Cattle-Killing, not even a bad one. Several historians have commenced on the topic, but none has completed it. The reason for this is that the primary sources, the evidence on which the historical account is based, are riddled with lies, both deliberate lies and self-delusions.

Most of the official documents, including almost all the printed official documents, are contaminated with references to the 'Chiefs' Plot', the theory that the Cattle-Killing was a conspiracy by the Xhosa chiefs to bring about a war with the Cape Colony. If we leave the official documents to consult the archives which are stored in the memories of the old men of Xhosaland, we get the mirror image of the 'Chiefs' Plot', namely 'Grey's Plot', the theory that the root cause of the Cattle-Killing was a trick by Sir George Grey to deceive the Xhosa into destroying themselves. Today, there is hardly a Xhosa alive who does not believe that Sir George Grey was in some way responsible for Nongqawuse's prophecies.

I started this book in 1981, feeling somewhat sceptical about both

'Grey's Plot' and the 'Chiefs' Plot'. Six years later, having examined all the evidence on the Cattle-Killing that I can find, I am more than ever convinced that there was no plot on either side. Moreover, I am convinced that we do not need a plot or a conspiracy to explain the Cattle-Killing movement. I believe, and I trust that this book will demonstrate, that the Cattle-Killing was a logical and rational response, perhaps even an inevitable response, by a nation driven to desperation by pressures that people today can barely imagine. I further believe, and I trust that the book will demonstrate this too, that the Cattle-Killing would not have been so fatal an error had it not been for the measures of Governor Grey, which first encouraged and then capitalized on the movement. In this sense, though not in the one related by the old men of Xhosaland, Grey was the true perpetrator of the *isihelegu sikaNongqawuse*, the catastrophe of Nongqawuse. That is why I nowhere use the well-known term, 'the National Suicide of the Xhosa'. The Nongqawuse catastrophe was as much a murder as it was a suicide. Probably, it was a little bit of both.

The evidence for this conclusion is set out in detail in the footnotes and in the bibliography. It is true that this evidence is partial, biased and incomplete, and that many of the secrets of the Nongqawuse period will never be told. Nevertheless, I would like to mention three crucial pieces of evidence which underpin my interpretation and lead me to hope that what I have written is not too far from the truth.

The Grey-Maclean Correspondence

GH 8/48 — GH 8/50 in the Cape Archives contain the private correspondence between Sir George Grey and Colonel John Maclean, his top subordinate in British Kaffraria. It should not be forgotten that there were no telephones in those days, and that all long-distance communications had to go by letter. While official communications should be read with scepticism, one may safely assume that a private correspondence is a frank and truthful exchange of views.

The Work of W.W. Gqoba

Two articles by W.W. Gqoba entitled 'Isizatu sokuxelwa kwe nkomo ngo Nongqause' ('The reason for the killing of cattle by Nongqawuse') are based on interviews with believers. Though Gqoba was a Christian, he was writing with the explicit intention of challenging the 'Chiefs' Plot' theories then prevalent in mission circles. Not only does Gqoba supply many details which would otherwise be unavailable, but he provides us with the Xhosa vocabulary and terminology actually used by the believers.

The Cape Journals of Archdeacon N.J. Merriman

These give us a fascinating insight into the personality of Mhlakaza, a key figure in the Cattle-Killing movement. They reveal that Mhlakaza, far from being a heathen witchdoctor, was the first Xhosa ever baptized into the Anglican Church. Once we understand Mhlakaza's background and the personal motivations which inspired his religious experiences, we realize that we have no need of the 'Chiefs' Plot' or of 'Grey's Plot' or of any other hypothesis to explain his behaviour.

Many people have helped me in the writing of this book. Special thanks are due to Professor Rodney Davenport, who organized extra study leave for me in 1981; to Professor Shula Marks, who hosted my sabbatical at the Institute of Commonwealth Studies in London in 1984-5; and to the Human Sciences Research Council, which helped to finance the research without, of course, incurring any responsibility for the results. Mike Kirkwood did much more than merely edit the manuscript. Mrs Beryl Wood introduced me to the song which opens the book, and Messrs N. Webb, R. Hulley, A. Nqamrha and M.V.S. Balfour did much to ensure the success of my research in Transkei. Mr W.O. West of Rhodes University drew the maps. The staff at the Cape Archives, the South African Library and the other institutions mentioned in the footnotes were all extremely helpful, but I should like to single out Michael Berning, Sandy Fold, Zweliyanyikima Vena and the others at Cory Library, who bore the brunt of my problems. I should also like to take the opportunity to extend warmest personal greetings to Dr R. Oelsner, who showed us a great deal more of Berlin than the Mission Archives. My parents, as always, have been a pillar of strength. *The Dead Will Arise* is dedicated to Mary-Louise and the boys, who have been compelled to endure all the innumerable prophecies and disappointments which accompanied the writing of this book.

Notes on Terminology and Pronunciation

Terminology

During the period of the Cattle-Killing, it was considered perfectly correct, even by liberal whites, to use the terms 'Kaffir' and 'Kaffirland' for 'Xhosa' and 'Xhosaland'. Rather than make pedantic use of these insulting terms, I have dropped them altogether, using square brackets in direct quotations. Hence I have written '[Xhosa]' instead of 'Kaffir' and so on.

The word 'Xhosa' itself, which is used today as a general term to describe any Nguni-speaking person from what used to be called the Cape Province, correctly refers only to one national entity, namely the subjects of Sarhili, and excludes neighbouring black nations such as the Thembu and the Mpondo. It is used here in this more restricted sense.

The Xhosa themselves were divided into various chiefdoms, grouped as follows. The *Gcaleka* Xhosa, under the immediate leadership of King Sarhili, lived mostly east of the Kei River beyond the bounds of British territory. The *Ngqika* Xhosa, under the leadership of Sandile and his brothers, and the *Ndlambe* Xhosa, under the leadership of Mhala, lived in British Kaffraria. The most important of the minor chiefdoms was that of the *Gqunukhwebe* Xhosa, led by Phatho and his junior brother Kama.

Pronunciation

The letters 'c', 'q' and 'x' are clicks. 'R' is a guttural sound like the Afrikaans 'g' or the Scots 'ch' in 'loch'. That is why 'Sarhili' is sometimes written 'Krili' in the European sources. The letter 'h' is usually an aspirate when used with another consonant. Hence the 'Ph' in 'Phatho' is an aspirated 'p' not an 'f', just as the 'th' is an aspirated 't' and not a 'th'.

Dramatis Personae

History, unlike fiction, cannot control the number of its characters or the multiplication of its sub-plots. It is hoped that the following list will serve as a convenient guide. The figure in brackets is the approximate age, where known, of the historical figure in 1856, the year when Nongqawuse's prophecies first began.

The Whites

BARRINGTON, Henry (48). Attorney-General of British Kaffraria.
BROWNLEE, Charles (35). Commissioner with the Ngqika Xhosa.
CATHCART, Sir George. Governor of the Cape (1852-4).
COTTERILL, Henry (45). Bishop of Grahamstown.
CROUCH, John (35). Trader in Sarhili's country.
CURRIE, Walter (37). Commandant of the Frontier Armed and Mounted Police.
DOUGLAS, Stair. Secretary and moving spirit of the Kaffir Relief Committee.
EYRE, Lieutenant-Colonel William. Architect of the colonial victory during the War of Mlanjeni.
FITZGERALD, Dr John (41). Founder of the Native Hospital, King William's Town.
GAWLER, John Cox (26). Magistrate with Mhala.
GREENSTOCK, William (24). Missionary with Mhala.
GREY, Sir George (44). Governor of the Cape (1854-61).
HAWKES, Robert. Magistrate with Siwani.
KAYSER, Henry. Missionary at Peelton.
KAYSER, Maximilian. Interpreter to Henry Lucas.
LUCAS, Henry. Magistrate with Maqoma and Bhotomane.
MACKINNON, George. Chief Commissioner of British Kaffraria (1848-51).
MACLEAN, John (46). Chief Commissioner of British Kaffraria (1852-64).
MERRIMAN, Nathaniel (47). Archdeacon of Grahamstown.
PORTER, William. Attorney General of the Cape Colony.

REEVE, Frederick. Magistrate with Kama.
ROBERTSON, R. Eustace. Magistrate with Anta.
SMITH, Sir Harry. Governor of the Cape (1847-52).
VIGNE, Herbert. Magistrate with Phatho and Jali.
WATERS, H. Tempest (37). Missionary with Sarhili.

The Blacks

ANTA (44). Strong Unbeliever. Brother to Sandile.
BHOTOMANE (80+). Believer. Chief of small imiDange Xhosa chiefdom.
BHURHU (76). Waverer. Uncle to Sarhili.
BULUNGWA. Strong Unbeliever. Nephew to Mhala.
DILIMA (30). Believer. Great Son of Phatho.
DONDASHE (28). Believer. Brother to Sandile.
DYANI TSHATSHU (52). Christian and Unbeliever. Chief of small Ntinde Xhosa chiefdom.
FADANA (60). Strong Believer. Former Regent of Thembuland, and leader of the Thembu believers.
FENI (18). Waverer. Nephew to Sandile.
GOLIATH, William. Name adopted by Mhlakaza while working in the Colony.
JALI (20). Unbeliever. Nephew to Mhala.
JOYI. Strong Unbeliever. Regent of the Thembu Kingdom.
KAMA (52). Christian and Unbeliever. Ranking second to Phatho among the Gqunukhwebe Xhosa.
KONA (30). Unbeliever. Son of Maqoma, ranking second to Namba.
MAKINANA (30). Unbeliever. Great Son of Mhala.
MAQOMA (58). Strong Believer. Brother of Sandile, ranking second among the Ngqika Xhosa.
MATE. Strong Believer. Son of Phatho, and leader of Phatho's people in Kama's country.
MHALA (60). Strong Believer. Senior Chief of the Ndlambe Xhosa.
MHLAKAZA. Uncle of Nongqawuse and principal interpeter of her prophecies.
MJUZA (37). Strong Unbeliever. Son of Nxele, the Prophet of the 1818-9 Frontier War.
MOSHOESHOE (70). King of Lesotho.
NAMBA (28). Believer. Great Son of Maqoma.
NDAYI. Strong Unbeliever. Councillor to Mhala.
NED. Unbeliever. Son of Maqoma. Employed in the Native Hospital.
NGUBO. Strong Unbeliever. Cousin to Sarhili.

NKWINTSHA. Strong Believer. Councillor to Mhala and uncle of Nonkosi.

NOMBANDA. Relative and fellow-prophetess of Nongqawuse.

NONGQAWUSE (15). Niece of Mhlakaza. Chief Prophetess of the Cattle-Killing.

NONKOSI (11). The Prophetess of the Mpongo River.

NXITO (75+). Unbeliever. Uncle to Sarhili.

OBA (26). Waverer. Nephew to Sandile.

PHATHO (58). Strong Believer. Senior Chief of the Gqunukhwebe Xhosa.

QASANA (38). Strong Believer. Brother to Siwani.

QWESHA (63). Strong Believer. Chief of the Ndungwana Thembu.

SANDILE (37). Senior Chief of the Ngqika Xhosa, and Senior Chief of British Kaffraria.

SARHILI (47). Senior Chief of the Gcaleka Xhosa, and King of all the Xhosa, including those in British Kaffraria.

SIGIDI. Unbeliever. Senior Gcaleka Xhosa Chief in British Kaffraria.

SIWANI (30). Unbeliever. Nephew of Mhala.

SIYOLO (44). Brother of Siwani. Imprisoned on Robben Island for the duration of the Cattle-Killing.

SMITH MHALA (27). Strong Unbeliever. Second-ranking son of Mhala.

SOGA (56). Strong Unbeliever. Councillor to Sandile.

STOKWE. Believer. Brother-in-law to Phatho and chief of the small Mbalu Xhosa chiefdom.

TOLA (40). Believer. Cousin of Bhotomane and also a chief of the imiDange Xhosa.

TOYISE (36). Unbeliever and long-time Colonial client. Cousin to Mhala.

TYHALA (55). Strong Unbeliever. Councillor to Sandile.

XHOXHO (46). Believer. Brother to Sandile.

Hayi uNongqawuse
Intombi kaMhlakaza
Wasibulala isizwe sethu

Yaxelela abantu yathi kubo bonke
Baya kuvuka abantu basemangcwabeni
Bazisa uvuyo kunye ubutyebi
Kanti uthetha ubuxoki

Oh! Nongqawuse!
The girl of Mhlakaza
She killed our nation

She told the people, she told them all
That the dead will arise from their graves
Bringing joy and bringing wealth
But she was telling a lie

CHAPTER I

Riverman's War

1. Mlanjeni the Riverman

Mlanjeni, the Riverman, was about eighteen years old in 1850, and so weak and emaciated from fasting that he could not walk about unaided.[1] The power of evil so pervaded the world, he thought, that it inhabited even the homestead of his father Kala and poisoned even his mother's cooking. In order to keep himself pure and undefiled, Mlanjeni withdrew from the society of men and spent much of his time alone. Most especially, he liked to go down to a deep pool on the Keiskamma River where he would sit up to his neck in water for hours — some said days — subsisting only on ants' eggs, water-grass and other foods of nature. He greatly feared the debilitating power of women and kept himself strictly celibate.

At first his family had remonstrated with him concerning his strange behaviour, and his father told him that uncircumcised boys had no right to speak of such things as witchcraft and disease. But Mlanjeni persisted in his sayings even after he had passed through circumcision school, and this steadfast adherence to his singular manner of life eventually gained him the credence and respect of the Xhosa of the Ndlambe district of British Kaffraria. It was clear to all that the young man had been touched by contact with the spirit world, and the people therefore believed him when he intimated to them that he had been entrusted with a special mission for the reformation of mankind.

Mlanjeni's teaching unfolded slowly and elliptically, revealing itself gradually in obscure and incomprehensible hints and metaphors. He reminded his visitors of Nxele, the giant prophet and wardoctor who had fired the Xhosa imagination some thirty years previously with his revelations concerning Mdalidephu the God of the black man, Thixo the God of the whites, and Thixo's son Tayi, whom the whites had murdered.[2] For this great crime, the whites had been thrown into the sea whence they had emerged to trouble the sinful Xhosa nation. 'Leave off witchcraft! Leave off blood!' Nxele had ordered the Xhosa. 'These are the things that are killing our people. I am sent by the Great Chief of heaven and earth and all other things to say, lay aside these two evils, so that the world can be made right again.' A great day was coming, a day on which the people who had passed away would rise again from the dead and the witches would be cast into damnation under the earth. Before the day arrived Nxele himself was dead, drowned escaping from Robben Island where the British had imprisoned him. But he had promised before he surrendered that he would come back one day, and many Xhosa were still awaiting his reappearance. They saw him repeatedly in dreams and visions and now he seemed to have returned to them in the form of this sickly youth.

Mlanjeni venerated the sun; he prayed to it and taught his followers to do likewise.

> When we were there, he [Mlanjeni] sat turned towards the sun and prayed to it. He teaches that the sun is God, and when the sun's rays break through the clouds that these are God's twigs. . . . At night God puts his cloak over us, this is the darkness. The stars are his dogs. . . .[3]

Mlanjeni led the people to believe through vague insinuations and enigmatic utterances that some great event was about to reveal itself, though he did not say exactly what it was or how exactly it would occur. In order to bring this event to fruition, however, it was first necessary to rid the world of the *ubuthi* (evil substance) which was poisoning the earth all around. It was on account of this *ubuthi* that the great drought of 1850 was burning up the country, that the baking land refused the plough, that the cattle were like skeletons from lack of grass, and that the people themselves were suffering grievously from hunger. He, Mlanjeni, was divinely appointed to purify and cleanse and to destroy *ubuthi*, which was often secretly used by Xhosa to help them find good fortune and to protect them from their enemies. 'The land is full of *"ubuthi"*!' cried Mlanjeni. 'This is the cause of so much disease and death among both men and cattle; let all cast it away, and come to me to be cleansed.'[4]

Outside his father's dwelling, Mlanjeni erected two witchcraft poles, standing as a gateway. People who wished to remove the suspicion of witchcraft walked between these poles. The innocent emerged unscathed but those who felt themselves guilty were overcome with weakness and fear as they approached. They stuck fast as if paralysed, while Mlanjeni shook and twitched and danced as well as he could. The large crowds who gathered at Kala's place — for nothing like this had ever been seen in Xhosaland before — shouted, 'He is fixed! He is fixed!' and then, while the witch writhed on the spot quite unable to move, the people would shout, 'Get out! Get out! *Bolowane!* ' to drive the witchcraft out of its victim.[5] Eventually the witch, thus purged of his or her witchcraft, staggered through the poles to Mlanjeni who gave him a small twig of the plumbago bush to protect him and keep him pure of evil. For Mlanjeni gave orders that no person was to be harmed for being a witch, since witchcraft was not a personal quality but an evil affliction which he had the god-given power to cure.

Word spread throughout Xhosaland as far as the Great Place of King Sarhili beyond the borders of British Kaffraria that any Xhosa 'having poisonous roots, all means of witchcraft, baboons [witchcraft familiars] or charms' must immediately dispose of them. In those days there was constant whispering in the homesteads concerning particular individuals suspected of evil practices, and such persons were usually glad to visit Mlanjeni to clear themselves of dangerous rumours. Everywhere people burned their charms and medicines and threw the ashes into the rivers, to the delight of themselves and their neighbours. For everyone felt in danger of being bewitched by enemies, and thus even the most innocent maintained a private arsenal of protective devices. But now that Mlanjeni, through his extraordinary powers and his witchcraft poles, had identified and disarmed the witches, there was no longer any need for anyone to dabble secretly with bewitching medicines. Freed of tension, suspicion and malicious gossip for the first time in many years, the Xhosa relaxed in an atmosphere of peace and security, waiting for the next revelation from Mlanjeni.

Rumours of the Riverman's power grew in the telling. 'He lights his pipe on the sun,' it was said; 'he heals the sick, makes the blind see, the lame walk, and the dumb speak.' When he danced, the drops of sweat falling from his body would cause the rain to fall.[6] The further away the people lived, the greater the miracles they attributed to Mlanjeni, as this report from the Phuti in the foothills of the Drakensberg shows.

> He commands the star of the morning to descend from the heavens to place itself on his forehead, and it obeys; he orders the earth to shake on its foundations, and the rocks and the mountains bow and tremble before him; he strikes the sun with his enchanted spear, and he becomes in turn a hare, a hyena or any other beast he desires; he sows the seeds of

corn with his hands, he conjures them to germinate and grow in an instant, and these seeds germinate thus, shooting out green stems and developing before one's eyes.[7]

The sun itself, his followers said, descended from heaven to touch Mlanjeni's head and passed through his body to his feet from which it arose again to appear with new brilliance in the east. And everywhere the believers saluted its rising by shouting 'He appears! He appears! Mlanjeni! Our chief!' Children exclaimed that Mlanjeni was the 'True Lord' while their parents remarked that the black man was rich by comparison with the white for, by contrast with the dead God of the missionaries, the black man's god still lived and visibly manifested his power by miracles every day.

The greatest miracle was still to come. For since the Xhosa believed that all evil, sickness and death was caused by witchcraft, and since they also believed that Mlanjeni was endowed with the power to eradicate all witchcrafts whatsoever, they therefore believed that the Riverman was possessed of the 'secret of Eternity' and could conquer death itself.[8]

2. A Surprise for Sir Harry Smith

The War of the Axe, a war fought essentially over the attempts of the Cape Colony government to abrogate a treaty it had freely signed some ten years previously, was brought to an end late in 1847 by an appropriately shabby trick.[9] Sandile, the senior Xhosa chief on the Cape frontier, was persuaded to enter the camp of the Rifle Brigade in order, so he thought, to negotiate a settlement of his grievances. Once inside he and his councillors were locked up in a small unheated room near the powder magazine, and warned that they would be fired on if they attempted to leave. Later they were transferred to an empty store-room in Grahamstown, there to await the pleasure of the Governor and, incidentally, to entertain the élite of the Grahamstown settlers who vied for the opportunity to view the captive Xhosa chiefs. For the rest of his life, Sandile 'never ceased to speak of this case as one of gross treachery' and it left him with an abiding fear and suspicion of all things British.

While Sandile was languishing in confinement, a new Governor was arriving in Port Elizabeth. This was Sir Harry Smith, the hero of Georgette Heyer's historical romance *The Spanish Bride*, and of many popular histories besides.[10] Handsome, gallant and dashing, Sir Harry was the very embodiment of the romantic ideal of the Victorian soldier. His glorious triumph at Aliwal in India had brought him not only a knighthood, but a doctorate from Cambridge University, the favour of the Duke of Wellington and the personal admiration of Queen Victoria. He possessed, moreover, considerable South African experience, having commanded the Imperial troops against the Xhosa during the Sixth Frontier War (1834-5). As Governor of the short-lived (1835-6) 'Province of Queen Adelaide', Smith had attempted to turn the Xhosa hereditary chiefs into salaried magistrates, and to 'civilize the Xhosa' by means of schools, missions and trade in money. Sir Harry had a taste for ceremony and rhetoric, and an inflated respect for the power of his own personality. He called himself the *Inkosi Inkhulu* (Great Chief), he referred to the Xhosa chiefs as his 'children', and he enjoyed holding Great Meetings at which he employed gold-topped sticks and other theatrical props to impress his ideas on a reluctant Xhosa audience. Imperial historians have tended to treat Smith's flamboyant excesses with the indulgence due, perhaps, to his good intentions. But seen from the wrong side of his boots and his riding-crop, Sir Harry's little pranks must have appeared very different. For the Xhosa, Smith's hands were always red with the blood of their beloved King Hintsa, who had entered Smith's camp in 1835 with full assurances of his personal safety and never left it alive.

Arriving in Port Elizabeth early in December 1847, Smith wasted no time in resuming his role as *Inkosi Inkhulu*, magnified a thousand times over by his vastly increased arrogance and importance. Among the many hundreds in the crowd who came to see him was his old adversary, the Xhosa chief Maqoma. Maqoma was the elder brother of Sandile but, through a complication of the Xhosa law of succession, his junior in rank. Incomparably the most brilliant and daring of the Xhosa generals, he had led the Xhosa forces which had fought Smith almost to a standstill back in 1835. Disillusioned with the failure of the colonial government to respect the treaties of that year, and embittered by the decline of his power after Sandile's coming of age in 1842, Maqoma sank into an alcohol-induced stupor from which even the War of the Axe failed to arouse him. He put up a merely token resistance to the British forces and readily accepted the colonial government's offer to keep him safely out of the way in Port Elizabeth for the duration of the war. Now this valiant Xhosa soldier, defeated more by his own failings than by the British army, was to become the first victim of Smith's return.[11] As soon as Smith saw Maqoma, he fixed him with an arrogant stare and half-drew his sword from its scabbard in a gesture of attack. Maqoma started back in surprise and the settler crowd laughed their approval of the Governor's wit and determination. But Smith was not yet finished with Maqoma. Later that day, he sent for him to come to his hotel and there, again in the presence of witnesses, he publicly humiliated the fallen chief. After storming and ranting at him and refusing to shake his hand, Smith ordered Maqoma to his knees and, placing his gubernatorial boot on the chief's neck, declared, 'This is to teach you that I am come hither to show [Xhosaland] that I am chief and master here.' Maqoma's thoughts on this occasion have been recorded by oral tradition. 'You are a dog [alluding to Smith's low birth] and so you behave like a dog. This thing was not sent by Victoria who knows that I am of royal blood like herself.' Smith was to pay dearly for his insult.

The public orgy of boot-licking which the Governor demanded from the helpless Xhosa had only begun. Proceeding from Port Elizabeth to Grahamstown, Smith confronted Sandile in his prison. Brandishing a gun, he demanded that Sandile tell him the name of the Great Chief of the Xhosa nation. Sandile, in his innocence, responded that his Great Chief was Sarhili, naming the acknowledged King of all the Xhosa, who lived beyond the bounds of British territory. Furious, Smith struck the floor with his gun and yelled out that he, Smith, was the Great Chief and the Xhosa were his dogs. Out of the goodness of his heart, but for no other reason, he was going to release Sandile. The chief offered to shake Smith's hand but was told to kiss the Governor's boot instead: the privilege of shaking hands would depend on his future conduct.

This done, Smith set off on a triumphal procession to King William's Town, deliberately choosing a route that led through the most densely populated parts of Xhosaland to enable as many Xhosa as possible to see him and to kiss his foot. On arriving in King William's Town, the capital of British Kaffraria, Smith held a Great Meeting for all the Xhosa chiefs and councillors. He made great play of two 'staffs' which he had specially devised for the purpose. The first — a common brass doorknob surmounted on a wooden tentpole — he called the 'staff of peace' and the other — an ornamental pike — he called the 'staff of war'. The beaten Xhosa chiefs were called up one by one to the central spot where Smith sat on his horse and invited them to choose between the staff of peace and the staff of war. Not surprisingly they all chose the tentpole with the doorknob on the end. The Governor then held up a scrap of paper symbolizing the Treaty of 1835, which the Xhosa still adhered to, and tore it up, shouting 'No more treaties!' The ceremony ended with the now familiar custom whereby the chiefs kissed Smith's boot and shouted '*Inkos' Inkhulu! Inkos' Inkhulu!*'

What Smith told the Xhosa in this and subsequent harangues was even more shattering and distressing than the humiliation inflicted by his arrogance. All the land between the Fish and the Keiskamma rivers, hitherto an integral part of Xhosaland, was to be annexed to the Cape Colony and given out to white settlers and the Mfengu, their African allies. The Xhosa were to be shepherded into the territory between the Keiskamma and the Great Kei rivers, now named British Kaffraria and ruled directly by the Governor and his appointees under martial law. The Governor, as Great Chief, was empowered to lay down whatever laws he liked in the cause of civilization and enlightenment.

Smith was not short of ideas on this score. British Kaffraria was to be surveyed and divided into towns and counties bearing English names. Trade was to be encouraged, and the Xhosa were to learn the value of money and the dignity of labour by working on the roads or in the Colony. The root of all evil, Smith declared, was the Xhosa love of cattle, and these were to be replaced by sheep as soon as possible. The Native Commissioners, acting as magistrates, would prevent the chiefs confiscating the cattle of their people by means of judicial fines. Any civil disputes relating to cattle would result ·in the cattle in question being shot out of hand. Bridewealth payments (referred to as 'the sin of buying wives') were prohibited. Detection and prosecution of witches and sorcerers was forbidden on pain of death. And so on.[12]

Smith's programme was far too ambitious to be practical and Colonel Mackinnon, his Lieutenant-Governor in British Kaffraria, was a nonentity and a coward, whose main preoccupation was to present his administration in as favourable a light as possible.[13] Nevertheless, the Xhosa felt harshly oppressed by the new regime. Never before had they been subjected to direct colonial rule, and they could not reconcile themselves to the experience. Chiefs and people were bossed about by alien officials whose decisions they were unable to question. They were cramped and restricted in strange territories, while their fertile land across the Keiskamma was occupied and desecrated by the white intruders. 'The whole of the land of [my] forefathers is dotted with the white man's houses and the white [surveyor's] flags,' exclaimed Sandile, adding that he would 'rather die for his country than die without a cause'.[14] Worst of all was the ban on witch-finding that, in the opinion of the Xhosa, gave the witches a free hand to work their nefarious magic and destroy the Xhosa nation from within. This explosion of witchcraft seemed to be the major cause of the terrible drought of 1850, the drought which called forth Mlanjeni the Riverman.

On 18 August 1850, the witch-finding activities of Mlanjeni were brought to the attention of the relevant colonial official, Commissioner

John Maclean. Maclean immediately sent for Mlanjeni's chief, Mqhayi, a man hitherto notable only for his dogged adherence to the British cause. To Maclean's surprise, Mqhayi defended the practices of Mlanjeni, saying that the Riverman 'was doing a great deal of good; that he was preaching what the English so often told them, that there must be no witchcraft and no murder'.[15] Maclean was not convinced. He sent for Mlanjeni and his father Kala, and when they did not appear he dispatched a detachment of police to arrest them. The police found Mlanjeni too thin and exhausted to move, and gave him five days to shift to Chief Mqhayi's Great Place, where Maclean could keep an eye on him. The Riverman failed to arrive and when the police returned they discovered that he had gone into hiding. But although the colonial authorities were unable to find Mlanjeni, his fellow-Xhosa had no such difficulty. Throughout August 1850, streams of messages passed to and fro between the people and the prophet, dispensing orders, charms, and judgements in witchcraft cases. The Riverman's pronouncements were reported far beyond the boundaries of British Kaffraria, in Thembuland, in Lesotho and in the independent territory of Sarhili, King of all the Xhosa nation. Deep within the Cape Colony, Xhosa labourers working on white farms heard the call of Mlanjeni and returned to their ancestral homesteads to prepare for they knew not what.

The colonial authorities were by now most thoroughly alarmed.[16] Although Mlanjeni had committed no crime, they decided to seize him and remove him from British Kaffraria. But they realized it would not be easy. Mlanjeni changed his residence from day to day, he slept in the bushes by night, and he had his spies constantly on the watch for the police. Lieutenant-Governor Mackinnon was uncomfortably aware that the Xhosa had noted his inability to capture the Riverman, and he was unwilling to risk an open failure. Only Governor Smith remained supremely unconcerned. 'This drought is much against us, and may enable this regenerated Mahomet to play upon the credulity of your Orientals,' he facetiously informed Mackinnon. He was very sure that Mlanjeni would soon find himself in the lunatic colony on Robben Island.[17]

Meanwhile, white settler alarm had reached such a pitch that Smith felt obliged to visit the eastern Cape to restore calm through the sunshine of his personality. Arriving on the frontier late in October 1850, he called one of his Great Meetings and reminded the chiefs how happy they were under his rule, threatening them with the most dire fate in case of war. He required them all to kiss the 'staff of peace', though he seems to have spared them his boots on this occasion. The effect of the whole was however greatly marred by the absence of the one chief whose presence most mattered. Sandile sent the excuse that he had fallen from his horse, but the fact of the matter was that he had fallen into a state 'of the most abject fear'. Smith sent Commissioner Brownlee, Sandile's magistrate, to talk to Sandile but the chief replied, 'No, I cannot come in. I dare not,' recalling the promises which had lured him into captivity during the War of the Axe. 'Sandile says that while he greatly dreads offending His Excellency, he fully believes he is to be apprehended; and with the dread of his former confinement before his eyes, he fears placing himself in a position again to lose his liberty or his life.'[18]

Though perfectly well aware that Sandile was genuinely frightened, Smith chose to interpret the chief's terror as an act of defiance. He had been considering the deposition of Sandile even before the chief failed to attend his Great Meeting, and it is probable that the governor welcomed this excuse for stern action.[19] His officials thought that the other Xhosa chiefs could be bought off with government salaries, and Smith himself believed that the Xhosa commoners, liberated and enriched by the end of chiefly domination, would rally to the colonial side. 'Every [Xhosa] who possesses anything is a supporter of the present Government,' he wrote. No sooner had Commissioner Brownlee reported that Sandile still declined to come in than Smith officially deposed the chief and appointed Brownlee himself in Sandile's place. By replacing the senior chief in British Kaffraria with a twenty-nine-year-old white official, Smith had extended drastically the scope of the Mlanjeni question and forced the Xhosa to choose between the colonial government and their own hereditary ruler. He had thrown down a gauntlet, but he did not expect the Xhosa to pick it up. He could not have been more mistaken.

Later that November the chiefs of the Ngqika section of the Xhosa — several of them bitter personal rivals of Sandile — met in secret and declared 'that as long as the Gaikas remained a nation they would always look to Sandilli as the great chief'. Next day, Sandile and sixty mounted men rode down to the Keiskamma River to seek an interview with the prophet Mlanjeni. When they returned, the chief ordered every man who wished to join his cause to slaughter one head of cattle.[20]

Although our information on the subject is very inadequate, it seems as if the Riverman ordered two distinct varieties of cattle-killing. The first order was that all dun and yellow-coloured cattle should be slain or disposed of. The settlers feared that this was because dun was the colour of the English, and that dun-coloured cattle were held to be accursed like the English. The most reliable Xhosa-language version of Mlanjeni's command — 'Remove (-*deda*) all dun and yellow cattle, for as long as they exist . . . the nation will die' — likewise seems to imply that cattle of these colours were unnatural beasts which polluted the earth.[21] In addition to disposing of the abominated beasts, people were instructed to sacrifice cattle to Mlanjeni himself.

> Men who had only two or three head, would kill one of two milch cows . . . ; to save themselves from the sight of a motherless little calf . . . the owner would kill the young creature first. Thousands more were immolated. Boys, and such as were so impoverished as to have no cattle at all, offered goats.[22]

As the sacrificer wrenched out the aorta and the dying beast bellowed forth one last great cry, the people shouted with joy, 'The victim is presented to thee, Umlanjeni; Hear; and remember us.'

Even more portentous than these sacrifices were the preparations Mlanjeni made to doctor the Xhosa for war. The Xhosa army was a citizen army. There were no regiments, no military institutions of any kind; there was no discipline. Every adult male was expected to fight under the general command of his chief and the brave men of his locality. The only preparation and central direction was that given by the wardoctor. In normal times, every chiefdom had its own wardoctor, but every now again a man arose of such exceptional talents that he directed the affairs of the whole nation, and was consulted by all the nations round about. Nxele, the prophet of 1818-9, had been such a man, and Mlanjeni was recognized as another.

By identifying witches and rooting out witchcraft, Mlanjeni had already gone some way towards 'washing' and purifying the nation, a necessary prerequisite for success in war. Now he set out to render the fighting men invulnerable. He administered medicines composed largely of the roots of the plumbago, a well-known remedy for bone fractures.[23] More original and most striking to his followers was his prescription of the fleshy purple roots of the *pelargonium pulverulentum*, known even today as the 'roots of Mlanjeni'. This pelargonium was closely related to another, commonly used to heal wounds, but it had not been recognized previously as possessing any special properties. Now, however, Mlanjeni gave out short sticks of this root for the Xhosa to wear around their necks or carry in their bags. They were to rub their bodies with juice from the root, and, on attacking the enemy, they were to chew on the stick, spit its fibres out all around them, and call on their ancestors and on the prophet, 'O! Mlanjeni! You son of Kala, help us, we are looking to [you] to come and bless us.' The guns of the British would shoot hot water, their bullets would do no harm, and their gunpowder would fail to ignite. 'Those persons who observe witchcraft will die,' warned Mlanjeni, 'but those who trust in me and observe my directions will live.'

The eruption of slaughtering, not only among Sandile's Ngqika Xhosa but also among the Ndlambe Xhosa near the coast and King Sarhili's Gcaleka Xhosa across the Kei River, together with some daring rescues of Xhosa cattle seized for trespass, frightened the colonial farmers settled on the lands Smith had recently seized from the Xhosa. Ignoring the assurances of the government that all was well, they abandoned their farms in droves. Commissioner Maclean fed his superiors a stream of alarming and accurate information until even Smith's complacency was disturbed. Less than a fortnight after his triumphal return to Cape Town, the Governor was boarding yet another ship to take him back to British Kaffraria. On 19 December, he met the Ngqika Xhosa at Fort Cox on the slopes of the Amathole Mountains, clearly intending to be conciliatory. He promised that he would send no redcoats to hunt Sandile and he appointed Sandile's mother as Xhosa regent in place of Commissioner Brownlee. But when the Xhosa asked him why he had brought so many troops with him if his intentions were peaceful, he lost his temper. Among other lamentable things, he called Maqoma a 'drunken beast' and declared that he didn't care whether that chief touched the 'stick of peace' or not.[24]

Satisfied as always with his own performance, Smith mocked the settler farmers for running away and informed a friend that 'the [Xhosa] chiefs are most submissive and obedient just now and I will try and keep them so'. The next day he sent Colonel Mackinnon and 650 men into the Amathole Mountains to make a show of British strength. It was ambushed and routed in the Boomah Pass, with the loss of twelve men killed and 3,000 rounds of ammunition captured. On their way home, Mackinnon's expedition found the dead and mutilated bodies of 16 members of the 45th Regiment, surprised on the plains of Debe Nek. On Christmas Day 1850 the Xhosa wreaked a terrible revenge on the military villagers of the Tyhume Valley, who had desecrated the grave of their late chief Tyhali. Forty white men were killed fighting to the last bullet, although none of the women or children were injured. An overwhelming force of Xhosa blockaded Sir Harry Smith inside Fort Cox and beat back Major-General Somerset's feeble attempts to relieve him. Meanwhile the 'Kaffir Police', a paramilitary body of trained collaborators, rebelled against their white officers, and the Khoi settlers of the Kat River Valley discarded their traditional alliance with the Colony to join the Xhosa in an all-out war against white domination in South Africa. The half-Xhosa, half-Khoi squatter chief, Hermanus Matroos, rang in the New Year with a pitched battle against colonial forces in the streets of Fort Beaufort. The War of Mlanjeni had begun.

3. The War of Mlanjeni (1850-3)

Mlanjeni's promises did not come true.[25] The guns of the Imperial troops did not shoot hot water, nor did the Xhosa warriors prove invulnerable to shot and shell. The squatter chief Hermanus perished in his third attempt to take Fort Beaufort, and Xhosa attacks on Fort White, Fort Hare and the town of Whittlesea failed all the sooner because the Xhosa perceived that their much vaunted protection against firearms was of no use. The battlefields were strewn with Mlanjeni's charm-sticks dyed with the blood of the true believers. Within a month the Xhosa King, Sarhili, who had not yet personally committed himself to the fighting, offered Governor Smith an honourable peace:

> We beg for peace over the whole land. Our great word is to our Father [Smith] put down the War. We intercede for the Gaikas [Sandile's followers]. Have mercy on them, and talk. Government must put down the War. We beg for them. . . . Stop the War. . . . We one and all say Stop the War. The Gaikas are also Smith's children.
> If the Governor Smith our Father does not like to send to Sandile to tell him to put down his assagais and stop the War then if Smith my Father will send to me, I will send to Sandile to tell him to put down his assagais.

Smith ignored this approach, and rejected a similar overture in March 1851. Humiliated and besieged in Fort Cox, he had issued furious orders to the settlers to 'rise *en masse* . . . to destroy and exterminate these most barbarous and treacherous savages'. 'Extermination is now the only word and principle to guide us,' he informed an old comrade of the 1835 War. 'I should be glad if the Boers would name their own commandant, under him they may go their own way and shoot as they like.' Nine months later, he was still talking privately of hanging all the chiefs after obtaining their unconditional surrender.[26]

Caught between the obduracy of Smith and the broken promises of Mlanjeni, the Xhosa knuckled down to fighting the longest, hardest and ugliest war ever fought over one hundred years of bloodshed on the Cape Colony's eastern frontier. It would be tedious and, indeed, unnecessary to give a full account of a war that consisted of an endless accumulation of minor actions, and the following short summary will have to suffice. Essentially, there were four main theatres of war. (Readers are advised to refer to the map on p.13.)

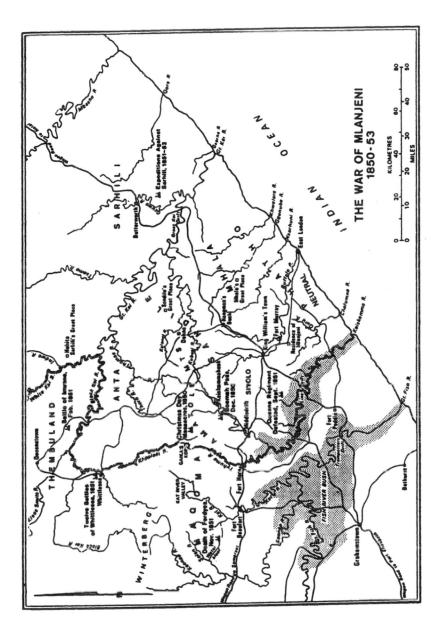

Map 1: The War of Mlanjeni (1850-53)

The Amathole Mountains

During his last, fateful Great Meeting four days before the outbreak of war, Sir Harry Smith had boasted of the shiploads of British soldiers that he could summon to his aid. 'But,' asked Maqoma, 'have you got any ships that will sail into the Amatolas?' It was an apt question. The Amathole Mountains, part of the great chain which marks the edge of southern Africa's highveld plateau, was the natural fortress of the Xhosa nation.

> Its sides are bold and precipitous; it is split and intersected with ravines; it is broken by masses of rock, and it is clothed with noble forest trees. . . . Masses of craggy rock here and there rise perpendicularly amidst these thickets, and in other parts the sides of the mountain are deeply scored by kloofs, or rocky gullies covered by rank vegetation.[27]

The overwhelming majority of the Ngqika Xhosa lived on the slopes of the Amathole, and it was there that the Great Place of their chief Sandile was situated. The war began in the Amathole, where the battle of the Boomah Pass and the Christmas Day massacre of the military villages took place. But because Sandile was no general and because he was greatly discouraged by the failure of Mlanjeni's prophecies, he was not able to exploit to the full the natural advantages which the mountains offered the Xhosa. Given their lack of firearms and inability to use them effectively, Sandile probably would have done better to abandon set-piece engagements at musket range and concentrate on hand-to-hand fighting.[28] Nevertheless, the sheer size and complexity of the Amathole range absorbed a great deal of the Imperial fighting power throughout the war, and afforded endless opportunities for bands of Xhosa warriors and their cattle to avoid capture.

The Waterkloof

The fifty or so square kilometres of mountain, valley and forest collectively known to the British as the Waterkloof formed a south-western extension of the Amathole range situated well within the borders of the Cape Colony. The Waterkloof itself was a deep valley a little over ten kilometres long, enclosed by almost perpendicular hills crowned with masses of stone and intersected by a succession of precipices and kloofs. The deeper one entered the Waterkloof, the denser the vegetation became. Gigantic yellow-wood, assegaaiwood and sneezewood trees blotted out the sky, suspending tangled masses of creepers and monkey-ropes from branches fifty or sixty metres high to merge with the dense undergrowth of acacias and other thorny bushes. The few open spaces along the only track merely served to turn the invading soldiers into standing targets for their invisible enemies. Mount Misery, the Iron Mountain and other aptly-named parts of this extraordinary complex struck fear into the hearts of the British soldiers who were compelled to enter it. This mighty natural stronghold, provided moreover with caves capable of sheltering upwards of one hundred people, was occupied around April 1851 by the Xhosa chief Maqoma and a band of Khoi rebels led by Hans Brander. The very Maqoma whom Smith had mocked in public as a 'drunken beast' had turned on his persecutor. 'I want the whole country to know that Maqoma is not mad,' he said, 'for that time of the Axe War they said I was mad.'[29] Shrugging off a decade of degradation, impotence and alcohol-inspired confusion, Maqoma stood tall and clear-eyed, the greatest military mind of his or any other Xhosa generation. Operating out of their impregnable fastnesses in the Waterkloof, Maqoma and Hans Brander burned farmhouses and raided cattle deep into the Colony, rendering large tracts of Somerset and Cradock districts uninhabitable by the white man.

For more than eighteen months the small Xhosa-Khoi force, estimated by some colonists to number no more than 200 fighting men at any one time, defied more than 4,000 of the British Army's finest troops.[30] On 4 November 1851, Colonel T.J. Fordyce, commanding the 74th Highlanders, was killed in the Waterkloof to derisive Xhosa shouts of 'Johnny, bring stretcher! Johnny, bring stretcher!'[31] This stunning disaster did not stop Governor Smith from informing his superiors in London that his generals had 'well succeeded in driving from their strongholds of the Waterkloof etc the greater portion of these numerous bandits'. But the Colonial Secretary had long ceased to believe Sir Harry:

> It is my painful duty to inform you [the Colonial Secretary wrote on receiving the dispatch in which Smith announced the death of Colonel Fordyce] that . . . you have failed in showing that foresight, energy and judgement which your very difficult position required, and that therefore . . . the Government of the Cape of Good Hope and the conduct of the war should be placed in other hands.[32]

Sir Harry Smith was recalled in disgrace, his glorious career ignominiously destroyed. Truly, the 'drunken beast' Maqoma had inflicted a terrible revenge on the 'hero of Aliwal'.

The Fish River bush

As soon as war broke out, Stokwe, Tola and a number of other minor chieftains who had been displaced by Smith's annexations returned to their own country and took up strong positions in the Fish River bush, a chaos of 'disrupted, bush hills with intervening deep and rugged kloofs and ravines'.[33] Unlike the Waterkloof, the Fish River bush was not a true forest, but consisted of thorny acacia bushes, pelargonium creepers and stunted euphorbia trees. Nevertheless, these grew so thickly upon each other that the bush was passable only by old tracks made by elephants in former years but now invisible to the unknowing eye. For those who knew the paths however, these elephant tracks provided rapid access from one part of the bush to another and linked up with similar bush along the Keiskamma, Kat and Bushmans rivers, affording easy opportunities for cattle-raiding all the way from King William's Town in the east to Alexandria near Port Elizabeth in the west and Alice/Fort Beaufort in the north. The colonial forces made several attempts to burn the acacia down, but it was too succulent to catch fire.

While Stokwe, Tola and a daring band of Khoi rebels headed by the Pockbaas brothers threatened the lines of communication between Grahamstown and Fort Beaufort, the Ndlambe Xhosa chief Siyolo planted himself firmly astride the main road between Grahamstown and King William's Town. The position of the Ndlambe Xhosa was unenviable. Their country was flat and open, the complete reverse of the Ngqika Xhosa stronghold in the Amathole Mountains, and they had taken heavy casualties during the War of the Axe. Mhala, the senior Ndlambe chief, was eager to fight but his councillors refused to permit it. His neighbour Phatho, the powerful chief of the Gqunukhwebe Xhosa, had been left to fight alone by his neighbours during the War of the Axe, and he therefore refused to join in the War of Mlanjeni. Most of the other Ndlambe chiefs, such as Toyise, Siwani and Mlanjeni's chief Mqhayi, allied themselves with the Colony. Nevertheless, declared Siyolo, Mhala's fiery nephew, 'I will fight for my country,' and he stationed his men in the 'thick thorns' of the King William's Town road to cut off the 'Government flying papers', as the military express mails were called. Siyolo's generalship was second only to Maqoma's, and Governor Cathcart did him the honour of calling him 'personally the most active, warlike and inveterate enemy we have to contend with'.[34] In November 1851, Siyolo's men, greatly aided by the cowardice of Colonel Mackinnon, cut down sixty of the inexperienced Queen's Regiment in the Fish River bush, the greatest loss of life by a British regiment in any engagement of the war. In October 1852, Siyolo was captured, like Hintsa and Sandile before him, by the time-honoured British trick of inviting him in for negotiations. The first chief to fall into British hands during this war, he was sent to a military prison in Cape Town and thence to the leper colony on Robben Island, where he remained close on seventeen years.[35]

The northern front

North of the Amathole Mountains lay the flat and open country of the Thembu chief Maphasa, much of which was annexed by Smith in 1847 and named North Victoria. North Victoria also brought the Colony into direct contact with the personal domain of Sarhili, the Xhosa King, who was still independent of colonial rule but whose political authority was recognized by all the subjected Xhosa chiefs in British Kaffraria. The flat plains of North Victoria did not lend themselves to the Xhosa mode of fighting, and as many as twelve unsuccessful attacks on the town of Whittlesea were easily repelled (January-February 1851). At the battle of Imvane (April 1851) more than two hundred Xhosa and Thembu were killed when the colonial forces managed to draw them down into open combat.[36] Disillusioned by these setbacks, King Sarhili withdrew into sullen but passive hostility, offering encouragement and refuge to fleeing Xhosa warriors and cattle. Two major expeditions (December 1851 and August 1852) were launched by the colonial government to punish Sarhili for his continued opposition to their interests. Sarhili's Gcaleka Xhosa did what they could to barricade the drifts of the Kei River by building breastworks out of rock and throwing stones at the troops, but there was a limit to what they could do with their bare hands in an invincibly flat country, and the Imperial forces got away with 30,000 head of cattle on the first occasion and more than 10,000 cattle on the second.[37]

Xhosa successes during the war were crucially dependent on the terrain where they fought. Any effort to make a stand on open ground was doomed to failure as the 200 dead at Imvane clearly demonstrated. Attempts to storm fortified positions were likewise fruitless, as the twelve battles of Whittlesea or the three attacks on Fort White ('a mere collection of wattle and daub huts erected to shelter the men from the weather') showed.[38] Given the meagre weaponry at the disposal of the Xhosa, such attempts were aptly compared by one commentator to 'shooting at Table Mountain with a pop-gun'.[39] Even the Christmas Day massacre of the military villages was possible only because the defenders ran out of ammunition. Apart from the weapons carried off by deserting Cape Corps mutineers, the Xhosa depended on inferior guns made specifically for the African trade.[40] The inexhaustible munitions and supplies of the British troops were even more vital than their enormous technical superiority. To give but one example: the

73rd Regiment was able to fire away more than 77,000 rounds of ammunition in a single day, while the Xhosa rushed out under heavy fire to collect spent bullets or bits of shell and Khoi women prostituted themselves and risked their lives to smuggle a mere 80 rounds or a cannister of powder to the Kat River rebels.[41] As far as technical inferiority is concerned, it goes without saying that the Xhosa had no artillery of their own, and no defence against the cannon of the Imperial forces.

> So at last we came to the top or den [of the Waterkloof], and such a sight I never saw before in all my life. Men, women and children that was killed and wounded by the shot and shell, some with their arms, others with their legs off. It was a terrible sight to see but such is war.[42]

Xhosaland was also used as a testing ground for the very latest in long-range weapons, the rocket and the Minie rifle.

Maqoma and Siyolo seem to have left much of the gunnery to the skilled marksmen among the Khoi rebels, while the Xhosa concentrated on the guerilla tactics they had evolved during the earlier frontier wars. The essence of their strategy was so to conceal themselves in the natural bush cover that they only engaged the British troops when they had a good chance of victory.

> Day after day officers and men tore their way through the thick jungle [of the Waterkloof] without seeing an enemy and yet as we approached or left the kloof the shots fired at us showed us they were there. Colonel Fordyce of the 74th Highlanders . . . was positive that the place was deserted. He had come through it with his whole regiment in skirmishing order without firing a shot. The next day he was killed.[43]

Often a regiment would spend the day scouring the bush with no result, only to find their rear under heavy attack as they attempted to withdraw in the dusk. The Xhosa gathered on the edges of narrow paths where the soldiers were forced to march in single file, and jumped them at a range too close to permit them to use their rifles. Sometimes the Xhosa managed to pull the soldiers into the bush by their waistbands, and in the Fish River bush, Siyolo's men trained fierce wolf-hounds to drag their enemies down. In the open, the Xhosa were vulnerable, but on their own ground they reigned supreme, daring the troops on with shouts of '*Yiz'apha! Yiz'apha!*' ('Come here! Come here!') and other taunts.[44]

Such tactics could not, ultimately, defeat the British Army, but they certainly baffled Sir Harry Smith. We have already seen how Smith, infuriated by the unexpected defiance of his Xhosa 'children,' frantically called on the settlers to 'exterminate' the savage beasts. He had daydreamed of marching triumphantly through Xhosaland at the head of a volunteer army of colonists, repeating once again his imaginary victories of 1835.[45] But the settlers did not step forward to risk their necks. 'The general feeling [among the colonists],' wrote one settler who did volunteer, 'was to rob the Government as much as possible' and to let the British Army do all the fighting.[46] Much of the heavy fighting in previous wars had been done not by settlers or troops, but by black auxiliaries, many of whom were now in open revolt. It was indeed the ongoing succession of Khoi army mutinies which kept the Xhosa war effort going through the dark period of disappointment in Mlanjeni's prophecies. In July 1851 Smith was forced to discharge his remaining Khoi conscripts for fear of further mutinies and to prevent a general Khoi rebellion throughout the Colony.[47]   When Maqoma's men destroyed 200 farmhouses, captured 5,000 cattle and cut the road to Cradock, neither Smith nor his incompetent commander-in-chief 'Old Jack' Somerset could do a thing about it.[48] All the new regiments that a worried War Office threw into the fray could not stem the tide. Many of the ordinary soldiers were sunk in despair, as this diary entry written on the first anniversary of the war clearly shows.

> This hateful drudging unsatisfactory war has lasted now a twelvemonth and God only knows how much longer it will continue, for our chiefs appear to be either unable or unwilling to do anything that may bring matters to a finish. Poor old Sir Harry is I fear too superannuated to be able to do anything now. . . .
>
> Sitting cross-legged in my little tent cursing the Colony, Kaffir War and my ill hap in being here. All the little zeal I ever had by this time quite oozed out. . . . I am sick, tired to death's door of wandering about these savage wilds, doing no earthly good. . . .[49]

A correspondent of the *Illustrated London News* did not stop short of predicting outright mutiny by the British troops. 'Many [soldiers] openly declare they will go there [the Waterkloof] no more to be butchered like cattle. . . . Courage here is of no avail; discipline and steadfastness under fire only render the men better targets for the lurking savages.'[50]

And yet, even before Sir Harry Smith had left the Cape in disgrace, the Imperial forces had effectively won the war. The man who was above all responsible for this dramatic change in fortune was Lieutenant-Colonel William Eyre, and he won the war by evolving a style of combat capable of matching the Xhosa guerilla tactics.[51] Eyre was tall, bespectacled and physically not at all a strong man. When he first arrived in South Africa, he thought it was 'both unsoldierlike and unEnglishmanlike' for British troops to lie in ambush, but as soon as a little experience had convinced him that the method was effective, he adopted it wholeheartedly. It was an article of faith with Eyre that there was no such thing as a natural obstacle. He it was who invented the technique of rolling pack-animals down hills where they could never have walked. He lost a lot of pack-animals, he stuck fast in a lot of thornbushes, he exhausted himself to such an extent that he could no longer stand up and on one occasion he very nearly drowned, but he completely changed British perceptions of what was and what was not possible. Eyre taught British soldiers to fight an African war by making them do things which had previously been dismissed as impossible. When they complained that they were tired, he burned all their blankets and made them sleep in the cold. When they feared to enter the bush, he lashed them on with a sjambok and a knobkierie. The spirit of 'yocking' (apparently a hunting term) permeated the Eyre camp. The Colonel was said to be 'as keen after cattle as any [Xhosa],' and his men shamelessly plundered whatever they did not burn. They nicknamed Eyre *Inkosi,* the Xhosa word for chief.

It cannot be imagined that such a man would treat his Xhosa enemies with compassion. 'You are too damned sensitive!' he told a subordinate who informed him that his troops had killed two unarmed Xhosa women working in the fields. No one could accuse Eyre of excessive sensitivity, as these references to his military style make clear:

> Colonel Eyre amuses himself by 'yocking' [Xhosa] and the other day his C.C. shot a poor unarmed boy, which seems a very barbarous proceeding to one but is applauded by most people in this country.

> Colonel Eyre called for the [Xhosa] guide, but he was prostrate on the ground with terror, and Eyre, who was highly excited (for there was no retreat open) ordered Mr Conway, our guide, to shoot him. Conway pretended not to hear; then Colonel Eyre ordered him to bring him his pistol out of the holster. Conway fumbled, and pretended he could not find it. 'Bring him dead or alive, Conway!' Conway dragged him along by his blanket; Colonel Eyre smashed his knobkerry on his head, and then the man pointed with his hands in the direction of the [Khoi rebel] Lager. . . .

> An unfortunate old [Xhosa] half dead with hunger was taken by the Fingoes at the drift and hanged by Eyre's orders, a piece of wanton cruelty I think. A story of his trying to steal a horse was trumped up but was I believe untrue.

Eyre, or the spirit of Eyre, wakened a new ruthlessness in British warfare. For all his talk of 'extermination', there was something in Sir Harry Smith that recoiled from the logical extremes of war to the death. He was much abused by his officers for his lenience towards

Xhosa prisoners, releasing them after only fifty lashes of the whip, and, as late as November 1851, he was still blocking proposals to burn the Xhosa crops and starve the enemy out.[53] But by January 1852, with defeat staring him in the face and his letter of dismissal already on its way, Smith yielded to Eyre and the others. A massive campaign designed to systematically eliminate the Xhosa means of subsistence was launched.

The burning of crops and dwellings had long been a part of frontier warfare. Throughout the period of Smith's command in 1851, the British troops had destroyed and laid waste wherever they had passed. What made the campaign of January-March 1852 so different was that it was a coordinated, deliberate plan aimed exclusively at the Xhosa fields and gardens. Unable to gain a straight military victory over an active and elusive enemy, the British Army now turned its attention to the exposed and immobile host of maize and sorghum located in the Amathole Mountains. The accounts of the soldiers who participated conjure up the picture far more effectively than the words of a historian:

> We are going on vigorously with the work of destruction, and I have hitherto encountered no opposition. The country appears almost abandoned. . . . The cultivation here has been most extensive but we have cut it all down — many hundred acres — with a facility and rapidity that astonished us all. . . . This will complete the entire destruction of the crops in the Keiskamma Hoek. . . . I cannot conceive that the Enemy will hold out if we persevere in this system of devastation, the practicability of which is now proved. . . . Our men are very healthy, and do not seem to dislike this work at all.

> Our two troops and three troops of Lancers with Colonel Pohl went out on a garden and kraal destroying expedition and we certainly did an immense amount of mischief. When we came to a garden, generally found three or so together, halted, formed troops and dismounted, then the work of destruction began, for some 100 men slashing away right and left with their swords make short work among mielie stalks.

> [The Xhosa] appeared to be much afraid of losing their corn and said that if we would spare their corn they would do all they could to persuade Sandilli to surrender on the 29th at 8 o'clock a.m. There being no sign of Sandilli we commenced to cut down their corn, the [Xhosa] begging on us to desist and give them some time, but no, they should either surrender at once or we would not spare their crops. . . . On the 1st February halted all day being Sunday and had divine service and washed our clothes according to instructions, we [then] marched on Patrole for the purpose of cutting all the fine vallies from the Cabousie Neck and the Thomas-Dohne mountains to the Goula valley.[54]

The destruction of the crops on the Amathole began in early January 1852 and continued to the end of February when, the Amathole being laid waste, a start was made on Siyolo's country further south. It took only one morning to cut down about 150 acres of beautiful corn, some of it growing up to two metres high.[55] As the extracts above show, the prospect of total starvation in 1852 following the partial starvation of 1851 absolutely terrified the Xhosa. They made a concerted effort to arrange a peace before the 1852 autumn harvest, getting as far as a temporary cease-fire and formal peace proposals. But Smith would accept nothing short of unconditional surrender to the clemency of Her Majesty, and the Xhosa were not yet sufficiently reduced to consider that doubtful prospect.[56] The departure of Governor Smith and the shipwreck of the *Birkenhead* which drowned 358 British soldiers bound for Xhosaland revived the Xhosa will to fight on, and the arrival of the new Governor, Sir George Cathcart, was greeted by a renewed crescendo of violence. Xhosa capacity to resist was, however, badly depleted, a shortage of basic foodstuffs replacing the shortage of firearms as their most acute problem. Significantly, their clandestine efforts were now as much concerned with smuggling corn as they had previously been with smuggling ammunition. As early as October 1851, the Xhosa had been raiding the abandoned camps of their British enemies in the hope of picking up the old bones and offal that the soldiers had discarded. Nine months later they were foraging for old bits of cowhide and leather bags to eat. In the Fish River bush they hunted tortoises. From July 1852 came reports of Xhosa fighters dead of actual starvation.[57] Those women and children who survived the final battle of the Waterkloof in September 1852 were little better off.

> All were in a most wretched state of emaciation and weakness, having been nearly starved for want of food, and subsisting entirely on leaves, roots and berries; their arms and legs were more like black sticks than human limbs.[58]

The British policy of starvation was not unconnected with the progressive dehumanization of both sides in the course of the bloody and bitter conflict. During the early stages of the war, both settlers and Xhosa had shown some recognition of their common humanity. The Xhosa released settler women and children during the Christmas Day massacre of the military villages, and continued to do so throughout the war. They also spared the life of an old white farmer named Wallace 'as he was doing them no harm'. The settlers of Fort Beaufort tended the wounds of the Xhosa injured during Chief Hermanus's abortive attacks on their town.[59] Lieutenant Bramston of the Rifle Brigade who usually called the Xhosa 'brutes', once referred to them as 'fine fellows, who are only fighting for their country as we would do in their place'. Thomas Stubbs, a settler volunteer who took no prisoners, was not incapable of reflecting on the sadness of it all.

> It is far from being pleasant to command a waylaying party. You there
> sit. You hear them coming on, perhaps humming a tune. You see them
> and almost look in their eyes and you have to give the signal for their
> death warrant. I have heard people talk very lightly about shooting
> [Xhosa], but I believe it is by those who have never experienced it. For I
> have always felt grieved that my duty compelled me to it. You certainly
> don't think much about it after the first shot is fired. But before that, and
> after the excitement is over is the time any man must feel it.[60]

Such finer feelings did not long survive the savagery of war. The
Xhosa had two magical theories which greatly disturbed the minds of
the British soldiers who witnessed their effects. They believed that war
medicines generated supernatural forces (*iqungu*) within the stomach
of a soldier. If he was killed, the *iqungu* attacked his slayer, bloating
and swelling up his body until he too died. To dissipate the *iqungu* of
the British soldiers they killed and to free themselves from the danger
of this posthumous revenge, the Xhosa ripped open the stomachs of
their dead enemies.[61] Furthermore, certain parts of the body were
believed to have magical properties which could be used to strengthen
their possessors. The liver, for instance, was held to be seat of bravery
and courage, and the skull could be used as a cup for the preparation of
war medicines. That is why the heads of certain settlers were sent to
Mlanjeni.[62] The sight of their dead comrades, usually disembowelled
and sometimes decapitated, roused the British soldiers to a pitch of
fury. They buried their dead at night and refrained from firing the
traditional final volley over their unmarked graves; nevertheless, they
often found on returning to the spot that the graves had been found,
opened and rifled. British soldiers who fell alive into Xhosa hands
suffered the tortures usually reserved for suspected witches, such as
being slowly roasted to death on red-hot stones. Lurid stories of
revolting cruelties, which have no precedent in Xhosa religion or
custom — involving, for instance, the severance of living limbs and the
tearing off of living flesh — were widely circulated and generally
believed among the British forces.[63]

Atrocities breed atrocities, and it would be wrong for the historian to
pass judgement on those who killed and tortured in this most merciless of all frontier wars. Our sources, which are mainly colonial, do not
give us graphic details of colonial misdeeds. At most, they leave us
with the dark hints implicit, for instance, in this Highland sergeant's
fine evocation of the emotions of a British soldier going into battle.

> Nervousness gives place to excitement, excitement to anger; and anger
> may be supplanted by barbarism as an infuriated soldiery rush on,

heedless of their doom. Their only thought is of victory; and when
victory is gained, it requires a masterly general to restrain the men from
deeds which cannot be named.[64]

The spirit of scientific enquiry, that glory of the Victorian age,
produced grisly consequences in the context of frontier warfare as
Stephen Lakeman, a gentleman-adventurer who raised a corps to fight
in the Waterkloof for his own private amusement, records.

Doctor A— of the 60th had asked my men to procure for him a few
native skulls of both sexes. This was a task easily accomplished. One
morning they brought back to camp about two dozen heads of various
ages. As these were not supposed to be in a presentable state for the
doctor's acceptance, the next night they turned my vat into a cauldron
for the removal of superfluous flesh. And there these men sat, gravely
smoking their pipes during the live-long night, and stirring round and
round the heads in that seething boiler, as though they were cooking
black-apple dumplings.[65]

This is not the only recorded case of the boiling off of human skulls by
colonists, which is probably related to the widespread mutilation of
Xhosa bodies to provide British soldiers with souvenirs, a feature of
Harry Smith's earlier war in Xhosaland.[66]

Yet, when all is said and done, these individual atrocities, which are
perhaps inevitable in a war, were insignificant by comparison with the
generalized incapacity of the white soldier to regard his Xhosa enemy
as a fellow human being. This is quite apparent in the following letter
home from a young Lancer.

But I could feel no compunction, do you know my dear Mother in
shooting a [Xhosa] and yet I could not shoot a dog without feeling some
pity, and yet I could feel none for this [Xhosa]. I have got his assegais
and I began to cut off his necklace but it was all Bloody.[67]

The same nineteen-year-old wrote later that 'there is no honour or
glory for anything you do out here. You have only to drive cattle and
kill [Xhosa] which is like killing rats and mice, only not quite so easy.'
And yet his letters home show quite clearly that in every other respect,
this officer was a thoroughly decent and sensitive young man. The
almost dream-like quality of mass slaughter is clearly demonstrated in
the following reminiscence of a colonial volunteer.

[The Xhosa] rose and letting their cloaks fall to the ground, started off at
a gentle run towards some thick bush about a mile distant. They made
no stand and offered no resistance, neither did they beg for mercy or
show any fear, but kept on at a steady pace while our people rode up to
them and shot them down.[68]

In such an atmosphere, the taking of live prisoners became a rarity.
The colonial sources are dotted with references to Xhosa shot dead

while asleep or feigning death, or burned alive in their dwellings.[69] On at least one occasion, Eyre explicitly told his subordinates that 'There was to be no quarter. All that were taken alive were to be hanged at the two gateways.' Settler Commandant Stubbs reprimanded one of his men for saving a prisoner's life, and told him to 'consider himself disgraced by taking a prisoner as he knew it was against orders'. Colonel Perceval, the British Commander, then intervened personally and gave the settlers to understand that they should shoot the prisoner.[70] The black auxiliaries of the colonial forces were even more ruthless in their attitude to the enemy. On one occasion, they 'hung [a captured Khoi rebel] on a yellowwood tree and practised throwing assegais at him until he was dead'. On several occasions British officers had to hold back auxiliaries who argued, 'No more women, no more Amakosa,' and sometimes they did not bother.

> We were above on the edge of the krantz and the howling and yelling were fearful at that time. After all, the women were nearly as bad as the men. . . .[71]

Settler volunteers marched about with the word 'Extermination' written on their hats, and Lakeman referred to members of his volunteer corps as 'brutally cruel . . . killing without mercy all that came in their way when engaged in a fight, young as well as old, even braining little children'.[72]

Cathcart, the new Governor, fancied himself a liberal [73] but he was very much the beneficiary of the brutal tactics pioneered by Eyre and permitted by Sir Harry Smith in the hope that final victory would soften the disgrace of his recall. In deliberate contrast to Smith's plebeian origins and populist style, Cathcart consciously played the aristocrat, holding himself aloof and coldly correct. His dandified appearance was highlighted by a pair of hip-high leather boots which he wore so incessantly that it was rumoured that he went to bed in them. The battle-hardened soldiers, who deeply resented Cathcart's contemptuous manner, called him 'Old Boots' behind his back and despised the elderly and inexperienced officers he had brought out from England. Eyre could not get along with Cathcart at all, and soon applied for sick leave.

The Xhosa hoped that the new Governor would bring a change of policy, but Cathcart's initial war aims remained identical to those of Smith, namely that Sandile's Xhosa should be permanently expelled from the Amathole Mountains and chased across the Kei River beyond the bounds of British territory.[74] When the Xhosa realized this, they intensified their efforts and the months of March and April 1852 were hot ones for Sir George. But Cathcart had brought with him from

England immense quantities of men and munitions supplied in generous profusion by a War Office anxious to give the new Governor all the tools he needed to finish the job. With these new resources, unavailable to Sir Harry Smith, Cathcart was able to build three strong new posts in strategic positions in the Amathole, the Waterkloof and Siyolo's country.

Cathcart's methods and policies were not significantly different from Smith's, and his vastly increased military means more than offset his practical inexperience.[75] Since the Xhosa and the Khoi rebels were half-starved and almost totally lacking in arms and ammunition, Cathcart's delays and hesitations were probably as effective as a more active policy might have been. The *coup de grace* was administered, appropriately enough, by Colonel Eyre who returned from leave in October 1852 with what one officer termed 'a raving commission'. 'Conflagration announced his course over the hills, and in the evening he rode into the camp with Armstrong's horse, cheered by the men.' To his already brutal and ruthless mode of fighting, he now added the extra refinement of scavenging for the bodies of dead Xhosa and then hanging the corpses up on the trees.

> The 73rd went some of them a little way down among the rocks and shot two [Xhosa] and hung these [Xhosa] in the trees as a warning to all who might pass that way, and took fifty women and children prisoners, and then we went down driving the prisoners in front like beasts, some in a wretched condition. . . .

> [The black auxiliaries of the colonial army] kept up a good fire through all the kloofs and effectually cleared it. They shot several [Xhosa] men, women and children and took women and children prisoners, but they shot more than half of them before we got down the hill.[76]

The final assault on the Waterkloof was less like a battle than a triumphal procession through a charnel house or even, perhaps, a Calvary.

> We saw two [Xhosa] hanging in the trees, just been shot as the blood was trickling from the forehead.

> The place stunk horribly from the bodies of the dead [Xhosa] that were lying about.

> As we ascended the evidences of the fight became more frequent; rolling skulls, dislodged by those in front, came bounding down between our legs; the bones lay thick among the loose stones in the sluits and gulleys, and the bush on either side showed many a bleaching skeleton. A fine speciment of a [Xhosa] head, I took the liberty of putting into my saddle-bag, and afterwards brought it home with me to Scotland, where it has been much admired by phrenologists for its fine development.[77]

Although the fighting was virtually over, the Ngqika Xhosa chiefs stubbornly refused to surrender unconditionally or to flee their country. They hid themselves in the vast expanses of the Amathole Mountains, and their very fewness in number enabled them to avoid both starvation and capture. The majority of their followers and their cattle found safe refuge in the territory of the Ndlambe Xhosa chief Mhala, who had maintained a nominal neutrality, but had exerted himself to the utmost to sustain his Ngqika brethren. Despite the urging of the settlers, Cathcart hesitated to attack Mhala and thus open a new front in a war he wanted to end before the grouse shooting season began.[78]

The impasse was broken by a wholly unexpected factor. Not content with starting a war in the eastern Cape, Sir Harry Smith had annexed the Boer territory north of the Orange River and thus embroiled himself in the Boer quarrel with Moshoeshoe, King of Lesotho. After the final clearing of the Waterkloof, Cathcart marched north with 2,500 men expecting to intimidate Moshoeshoe into paying a fine of 10,000 cattle and 1,000 horses. The Sotho ruler declared that 'there was not such a number of cattle and horses . . . in the whole of his territory'. Cathcart insisted and threatened until Moshoeshoe rose and said, 'Well, Your Excellency, you know that when a dog is kicked, he generally turns and bites.'[79] At the battle of Berea (December 1852), Moshoeshoe's Sotho cavalry overwhelmed the far smaller British force which had never previously faced such an enemy. Only a daring counter-thrust halfway up a steep mountain by the Light Company of Eyre's 73rd Regiment saved Cathcart's army from a humiliatimg defeat. (The 73rd had already made their presence felt north of the Orange by massacring some 25 Sotho women and children and, the Sotho alleged, raping a number of women.)[80] The smell of failure now hung heavily over Cathcart and he found himself staring into the same black pit of disgrace that had swallowed Sir Harry Smith. Less honest but more cunning than Sir Harry, he hastily claimed victory in Lesotho, and then returned to British Kaffraria to claim another unearned victory over the battered but still defiant Xhosa chiefs.

It will be recalled that Cathcart, like Smith, had proclaimed his intention of chasing the Ngqika Xhosa across the Kei and hence beyond the bounds of British territory. To the horror and indignation of the settler press, Cathcart devised a little charade which would enable him to claim peace with honour. The Xhosa chiefs crossed the Kei at the Governor's command, but only for a short while and only on the clear understanding that they would be allowed to return to British Kaffraria as soon as Cathcart had spoken to them.[81] The meeting (2

March 1853) lasted only half an hour and Cathcart never dismounted from his horse, but at least he did not ask the chiefs to touch the stick of peace or kiss his boots. Eyre set off for the Crimean War, promising 'to be more civilized than he was in Africa'.[82] An estimated 16,000 Xhosa had died, together with 1,400 on the colonial side.[83] The War of Mlanjeni was over.

The verbal agreements which Cathcart made with the chiefs were neither signed nor minuted,[84] but it is clear that the Xhosa made peace on the basis of two quite mistaken assumptions. Although Cathcart had informed them that they would not be permitted to return to their native lands in the Amathole Mountains, the chiefs regarded this stipulation as a mere stepping-stone on the way to a more genuine peace. They therefore set great store by Cathcart's promise that the land question would be settled by an appeal to the Queen.[85] Cathcart knew, as the chiefs did not, that this was a mere formality and that there was no real possibilty of his decisions being queried in London. And so, without waiting for the results of the appeal, on which the Xhosa laid such great emphasis, Cathcart immediátely set about re-allocating the captured territories of the horrified Xhosa. The Amathole district was renamed the Crown Reserve, and set aside for mixed settler/Mfengu occupation. Any Xhosa found in the Crown Reserve was liable to a court martial.[86] The border lands from the Crown Reserve down to the sea were parcelled out to chiefs of proven loyalty such as Kama and Toyise, partly as a reward and partly as a buffer between the Colony and the dispossessed Ngqika Xhosa, who were confined to a small and infertile reserve between the Amathole and the Kei River. The Ngqika Xhosa protested loudly against the occupation of their country by outsiders but were fobbed off with promises that Cathcart's successor would decide the matter.[87]

Cathcart also promised the chiefs that they would henceforth 'be allowed to govern their people strictly according to their own laws'.[88] Cathcart was convinced — and rightly so — that Sir Harry Smith's foolish attempt to cut down the chiefs and depose Sandile was one of the major causes of the War of Mlanjeni. His entire administrative policy was based on the principle that the colonial authorities should recognize the legal jurisdiction of the Xhosa chiefs and rule the people through them. There can be no doubt that Cathcart was absolutely sincere when he promised the Xhosa chiefs that their domestic powers would be respected. But this did not make his promise any more trustworthy, as we shall see in the next chapter.

We cannot leave the War of Mlanjeni without tracing the fate of the enigmatic individual who gave it his name. We have already mentioned that the failure of the Riverman's charms to protect the warriors from European weapons came as a great shock to the Xhosa who had trusted implicitly in his magical protection. In the wake of their disillusionment, they had attempted to make peace with the colonial government. Indeed Sandile had thoughts of capturing or killing Mlanjeni himself and then sending him to Sir Harry Smith as a peace offering. Chief Xhoxho, Sandile's brother, actually attempted to seize the Riverman but did not succeed. Even Chief Siyolo, under whose military protection Mlanjeni lived for most of the war, loudly condemned the prophet for inducing him to fight under false pretences, and did his best to make a separate peace.[89]

And yet, in spite of all the disillusionment and frustration his prophecies had called forth, the power and influence of Mlanjeni never entirely disappeared. Messengers from distant African nations — the Sotho, the Thembu, the Mpondo, the Mpondomise[90] — all sent to him for war charms or for the secret of catching witches. Many Xhosa chiefs seem to have continued to ask Mlanjeni to interpret the omens concerning specific military undertakings. Our information is scanty and we do not know enough to say for certain whether or not Mlanjeni directed the overall strategy employed by the Xhosa during the course of the war, but we do know that at some time in August 1851, he urged them to go into the Fish River bush, and that the very next month they gained a significant victory over the Queen's Regiment in that precise area. The wreck of the *Birkenhead* and the recall of Sir Harry Smith were presumably credited to his miraculous powers.[91]

Such successful prophecies, or coincidences, did much to enhance the reputation of Mlanjeni, which rose and fell with the fortunes of war.[92] When the Xhosa failed he got the blame, but when they succeeded his credibility was restored. Since we shall shortly be encountering prophecies even more wondrous and even more fatal than those of Mlanjeni, it is a matter of some importance to consider how the prophet managed to preserve the faith of his followers despite repeated disappointments. The most comprehensive contemporary statement on the subject was that of Commissioner Brownlee, who explained it as follows:[93] many Xhosa who used his charms enjoyed miraculous escapes for which they thanked Mlanjeni, while those who were killed were hardly in a position to complain. Most importantly, Mlanjeni had virtually indemnified himself against failure by giving orders which could not possibly be complied with. Many of the common people who died were alleged to have contravened Mlanjeni's orders to remain celibate during the period of preparation for battle. This injunction is remembered today and at least one descendant of

Soga, the Christian Xhosa who directed the Christmas Day attack on the military villages, still maintains that all Mlanjeni's sayings were true but that everything was spoiled by a number of young men who just could not leave the women alone.[94] We seem to be dealing here with the phenomenon described by the American psychologist Festinger who suggested that people who have staked their lives on the truth of a belief do not give it up without a struggle, and that they will renew their efforts and even resort to fresh prophecies in order to conceal from themselves the unhappy fact that their faith was mistaken.[95]

Even though Mlanjeni's reputation long survived the war, the Riverman himself did not. After the arrest of Siyolo and the collapse of the Xhosa war effort in the Fish River bush, he seems to have thrown himself on the mercy of Chief Mhala, who allowed him to take up residence near the Qumrha River in a distant corner of his domains. Mlanjeni told the people there that he had been across the sea, where he saw a great rock with a large hole in it. He entered and saw the spirits of his fathers who told him that the Xhosa had failed because the time was not yet ripe, but that the proper time would soon be upon them. Mlanjeni himself never lived to see the great day of which he had so often spoken. In August 1853, some six months after the end of the war, he died quite unexpectedly of tuberculosis. But a great deal of the Riverman's power had come from the insubstantial and enigmatic qualities which had marked him off as a being from another world, and these qualities were enhanced rather than reduced by his sudden and youthful death. It was rumoured that he said just before he died 'that he should not be buried . . . but he would go over the horizon across the sea, towards the setting sun, there to meet with [the revered and mysterious figure known as] Sifuba-Sibanzi. His last promise was that all those killed during the war would rise up again.[96]

This promise was Mlanjeni's final legacy to the Xhosa nation.

4. Goliath

The violence and bloodshed of the Frontier Wars was paralleled by a huge spiritual upheaval which resulted from the clash of Xhosa and Christian religious ideas. Xhosa religion was primarily a this-worldly religion, more concerned with guiding people's behaviour in the existing world than with abstract moral judgements or metaphysical speculations. The Xhosa had no priests as such; the Xhosa doctors (*amagqirha*) spent most of their time dealing with practical matters such as omens, medicines, witchcraft and the relationship between people and their ancestors. Ancestors were encountered mostly in terms of their earthly manifestations: they were believed to reward those who venerated them and to punish those guilty of neglect. Xhosa religion was closely associated with the other institutions of Xhosa society, a society which was ruled over by chiefs and dominated by cattle. It was not a static, unchanging world, but it was a world whose twists of fortune Xhosa religion was well adapted to explain and control.[97]

There was, however, something missing in Xhosa religion, a gap through which some of the central ideas of Christianity were able to infiltrate. Xhosa religion was deeply ambivalent about death, the most frightening of all human experiences, and the question of the afterlife. On the one hand, there was the feeling that the dead do not really die but remain with the living, that death is no more than a transition between the state of being human and the state of being an ancestor. It seems, for instance, that in very early times, the Xhosa dead were buried sitting or standing, accompanied by their weapons, their pipes and snuffboxes, and various other personal items which they would be needing in the afterworld.[98] But on the other hand, there was a contrary feeling, nurtured by the normal human fear, that death was something evil and unnatural. This contrary feeling is still expressed in a well-known folktale, which relates that in the beginning God sent the chameleon to Man with the message that he would live forever. But the chameleon delayed on the road and was overtaken by the evil lizard, which delivered instead a message that Man would die.[99] This tale reflects the instinctive feeling of most Xhosa that death was not part of God's original plan, but the unintended result of evil intervention from outside. During the precolonial period, the Xhosa greeted the advent of death with absolute terror and, especially in the case of chiefs, they often responded to symptoms of a fatal illness by desperate witchhunting.

The view of death as evil and unnatural was greatly reinforced in the middle of the eighteenth century by a terrible smallpox epidemic which struck Xhosaland about 1770. Before the epidemic, the Xhosa had buried their dead, but from that time they shrank from touching dead bodies and, as a result, the dying were carried outside and left to expire in the bush. People fled from the sight or sound of death, and in most cases the corpses were not recovered but left to the dogs and the hyenas.

> No friendly voice is heard cheering them amidst the struggles of dissolving nature; no kindly helping hand is lent to turn them from side to side; nor have their sinking spirits any the least expectation of a

deliverer. . . . The moment the spark of life becomes extinct, and sometimes before, 'ravening wolves around' feed upon their remains unmolested. In many parts of the country, by continually preying on human flesh, these animals are rendered extraordinarily fierce and very dangerous.[110]

With the collapse of ordinary funeral rituals, any comforting thought the Xhosa may have had that death was a normal and natural transition to a more exalted state must have utterly vanished.

For this reason, the Christian message of the resurrection produced an immediate and lasting impression on all who heard it, although the Xhosa did not always understand it in exactly the way the missionaries intended, as this early account shows:

When . . . [the missionary James Read] told them that woman and all mankind would rise again from the dead, it caused uncommon joy among the [Xhosa]. They said they should like to see their grandfathers, and others whom they mentioned. Congo inquired when it would happen, and if it would be soon, but Mr Read could not gratify his wishes on that point.[101]

With very few exceptions indeed, the missionaries who propagated Christianity among the Xhosa did not follow up this initial advantage. Although their sincerity is not in question, the early missionaries were very much the products of the western European civilization from which they sprang. They were horrified by what they saw as the moral shortcomings of Xhosa culture, such as polygamy, bridewealth, initiation, dress and the manner whereby the Xhosa detected witches. They were so determined to alter aspects of the Xhosa way of life which the people themselves considered natural and necessary that they completely alienated themselves from the mainstream of Xhosa society. They regarded colonial rule as a blessing to the heathen, and they did not attempt to formulate a teaching which might relieve the sufferings which the Xhosa experienced at the sharp end of that very colonialism. Although they never ceased to travel about the country and preach in the heathen dwellings, most of their attention was concentrated on the comparatively few residents of the mission stations. With the possible exception of Dr van der Kemp, the missionaries never comprehended much less tapped the vast spiritual longing which they themselves had awakened and which flourished despite, rather than because of, their efforts.

And yet the attraction of Christian ideas was manifested very early on by the appearance in Xhosaland of two extraordinary prophets whose doctrines were explicitly derived from Christianity. The first of these, Ntsikana (d. 1821), had only a marginal acquaintance with the missionaries and, appropriately for one who never personally experienced the rigours of colonialism, he preached a gospel of peace and praise. The second of these was Nxele (d. 1820), who has already been mentioned as a precursor of Mlanjeni. Nxele was brought up on a farm in the Cape Colony where he learned something of Christianity. He began to have religious visions when he was still quite young, and he came to believe that only the intervention of Christ saved him from being hanged as a madman. Later he spent many hours in conversation with the military chaplain in Grahamstown 'to elicit information in regard to the doctrines of Christianity'.[102] When the Reverend James Read visited Xhosaland in 1816 Nxele was already well established as a prophet and lived like a chief despite his humble origins. His teaching at this point, though not lacking in individuality, was mostly straightforward and orthodox. He taught of the creation, the fall of Man, the flood and the crucifixion, and he preached against witchcraft, violence and polygamy. The only unorthodox aspect of Nxele's doctrine was 'a most strange notion of his birth, as derived from the same mother as Christ'. Needless to say, the missionaries did not entertain for one moment Nxele's 'impious' notion that he was the younger brother of Christ. Whether it was this rejection or whether it was the activities of the colonial government in support of their ally, the adulterous Ngqika (the father of Sandile), it is hard to say, but for whatever reason, Nxele turned sharply against mission Christianity and evolved a revolutionary new theology in which Mdalidephu, the God of the blacks, was raised up in opposition to Thixo, the God of the whites. Christian ideas concerning the crucifixion of Christ and the resurrection of the dead were not abandoned, but were pressed into the service of the new doctrine which inspired the Xhosa during the Fifth Frontier War and was defeated with Nxele at the battle of Grahamstown in 1819.

The story of Nxele shows the extent to which Christian beliefs could feed the spiritual hunger of an exceptional man, but it shows also that such a man was unlikely to rest satisfied within the confines of mission-approved Christianity. We turn now to the story of another Xhosa, like Nxele a man whose religious imagination was fired by Christian teaching but frustrated by the harsh reality of his subordinate status in a colonial society.

In the settler city of Grahamstown this man went by the name of Wilhelm Goliath, but his real name was Mhlakaza.[103] We know that his father, who was a councillor of Sarhili, killed his mother in a fit of anger, but we do not know when or why.[104] Wilhelm must have spent several years working in the Colony, for he spoke fluent Dutch and was a baptized member of the Methodist Church in Grahamstown, where several of his relatives also lived. He was married by Christian rites to an Mfengu woman named Sarah.[105] In June 1849, he became the personal servant of Nathaniel James Merriman, the newly appointed Archdeacon of Grahamstown. It was a relationship which was to change Wilhelm's life, and the whole course of South African history with it. Merriman was newly arrived from England with the task of supervising the Anglican Church throughout the eastern division of the Cape Colony. His highly original manner of getting to know this vast domain was to walk the immense distances between the small country towns on foot, accompanied only by Wilhelm who carried his bag of clothes. Over a period of some eighteen months, the two men walked all the way from Grahamstown to Graaff-Reinet, up to Colesberg and the Orange River, and eastwards to British Kaffraria where Merriman had thoughts of starting an Anglican mission. Often the archdeacon strode ahead while Wilhelm limped behind, and the master had some sharp things to say about the laziness and improvidence of his servant.[106] Nevertheless, it seems as if this was an intensely happy period in Wilhelm's life. Merriman was clearly very fond of Wilhelm and genuinely respected his ability to manage the country and its people. Together they shared the adventures of the road, and more than once they confronted together the suspicions and prejudices of white farmers who resented the intimate and near-equal relationship of the white man and the black. But the greatest joy for both Merriman and Wilhelm was the opportunity which their long walks afforded to talk religion, and the archdeacon's journal paints a near-idyllic picture of two Christian comrades immersed together in the study of God's Word.

> Wilhelm and I as was our usual custom sometimes under the shade of the mimosa bush, sometimes in the dry channel of some river, sat and read together both in the [Xhosa] and the English Testaments, he trying to understand my language and I his.[107]

Often it must have seemed to Wilhelm that he was not a servant at all, but a partner in the great enterprise of spreading the Word of God. At some times, he sat up deep into the night talking Christianity with his fellow-blacks long after the archdeacon had retired to sleep. At other times, he delivered sermons in Xhosa to scoffing audiences, enduring the mockery and scorn of the heathen as best he could.[108]

Wilhelm Goliath was the first Xhosa ever to receive the Anglican communion, but he burned to become a full member of the Church. He despised the way the Methodist congregations 'told their hearts' in public, and he yearned for the private confessions, the beautiful robes and the old traditions of the Anglican Church. After some resistance Merriman granted him his wish, and in April 1850 Wilhelm became the first Xhosa to be confirmed as an Anglican. He could recite the creed, the Lord's prayer, the ten commandments and most of the translated Anglican liturgy in Xhosa, and he was fairly well acquainted with most of the Bible. He was deeply hostile even to the most innocent Xhosa religious practices, and he once sternly reproved a young mother for telling her child to throw a stone into the river in order to propitiate the spirits who lived there. '[Wilhelm] is moreover, I believe, a good man,' wrote Merriman. 'I had great pleasure in taking him to be confirmed.'[109]

But all idylls come to an end. Merriman could not tramp the countryside forever, and his duties confined him increasingly to the white Anglican community of Grahamstown. In October 1850, the archdeacon dismissed his faithful servant 'not a little thoughtfully and anxiously', and his journal entry displays considerable embarrassment on the subject. 'The expense of keeping him myself was becoming a serious consideration,' he began somewhat speciously, 'as the drought made living rather dear.' Then he got to the point. 'Moreover, I found naturally enough that the rest of my household did not think Wilhelm so well worth his keep as I did; and finding him regarded somewhat like the knights of King Lear . . . I dismissed him.' The statement is vague, but its general purport is clear. In Shakespeare's play, Lear's daughters force the old man to get rid of his attendant knights who amuse him but distract and inconvenience the household. Wilhelm Goliath's religious obsessions were all very well when the archdeacon was away and on the road, but they were a disturbance to Mrs Merriman's domestic peace, and so he had to go.[110]

Merriman did not simply wash his hands of Wilhelm, but found him a position teaching at the Xhosa school in Southwell, a farming district not far from Grahamstown. But with the outbreak of the War of Mlanjeni, the Xhosa school in Southwell was closed down and Wilhelm re-entered Merriman's personal service. It is not easy to piece together what happened next, for Wilhelm had clearly become a nuisance and ceased to occupy the same important and affectionate place he had formerly enjoyed in the archdeacon's journals. It is clear however that Wilhelm became unwilling to perform the menial functions of a servant, and was consequently deprived of his wages. In his last mention of 'poor Wilhelm', Merriman refers to his erstwhile comrade as 'having for some time continued too lazy to work', and having for that reason 'reduced himself' to a 'precarious subsistence'. One of Mrs Merriman's letters echoes this theme. Wilhelm, she wrote, 'was a [Xhosa] and did not like work — rather grew tired of it — and left us'.[111]

Wilhelm's reluctance to labour was associated with the increasing intensity of his religious experiences. But his desire to share these experiences with fellow-Christians fell on stony ground among the Merrimans as Mrs Merriman herself indicated.

> He [Wilhelm] was a dreamy man and I remember his once telling us about a vision that he had in connection with the spread of the Gospel . . . and I felt sorry I had laughed and made light of it.

The great desire of Wilhelm Goliath's life, wrote Mrs Merriman, was to be a 'Gospel Man'. Blocked and ridiculed by the very household which had initially promised him so much, Wilhelm quitted the Merrimans some time in 1853 and went to live near his sister's place on the Gxarha river in King Sarhili's country just beyond the borders of British Kaffraria. There he resumed his own name of Mhlakaza, and within a few years he began to preach a new Gospel of his own devising, which was to succeed — and to fail — beyond his wildest dreams.

Before he left the Colony, Wilhelm adopted a child whose mother and father had perished in the last great battles around the Waterkloof.[112] We do not know the age of the child, or even whether it was a boy or a girl. Could Wilhelm's niece Nongqawuse, the prophetess of the cattle-killing, have been this orphan of the Waterkloof? Might she have seen her mother shot dead with tens of other Xhosa women by the Colony's black auxiliaries? Might she have seen her father's body suspended on a tree, the blood still trickling from his forehead? Might she have tripped over their bones in a gully or sent their skulls rolling down the pathways as she stumbled out of the living hell of Colonel Eyre's greatest triumph? We shall never know for certain. But we certainly should not dismiss the possibility.

Notes

1. For Mlanjeni, see especially 'Nzulu Lwazi' (S.E.K. Mqhayi), 'URev Tiyo Soga, uTshaka noMlanjeni', *Umteteli waBantu*, 17 Dec. 1927; letter from Bryce Ross, 19 Dec. 1851, *Home and Foreign Record of the Free Church of Scotland*, II (1851-2), pp.267-8; A. Kropf (1891), pp.6-7; Imperial Blue Book 1334 of 1851, G. Mackinnon-H. Smith, 30 Sept. 1850 and enclosures, pp.15-19; *Grahamstown Journal*, 21 July 1855.
2. On Nxele, see Peires (1981), Ch. V and, especially, South African Library, Cape Town, Grey Collection, MS 172c, 'Kaffir legends and history' by

W.K. Kaye. For examples of sightings of Nxele after his death, see *Grahamstown Journal*, 4 Aug. 1842, *Cape Frontier Times*, 5 Jan. 1843.

3. *Berlin Missionberichte*, May 1851, p.81. Mlanjeni's emphasis on the sun is without precedent in Xhosa religion and was not taken up in subsequent Xhosa religious movements. It might support the contention of Bryce Ross (see Note 1 above) that Mlanjeni learned some of his ideas as a boy from emancipated slaves. On the other hand, it is possible that Mlanjeni's emphasis on the sun is a consequence of the felt need of the Xhosa of this time to have a 'high God' of their own. Cf. R. Horton (1967).

4. Bryce Ross, p.267.

5. Quoted from 'Nzulu Lwazi'. The term '*Bolowane*' presents some problems. I initially thought that it referred to the sacred herd of cattle among the Bomvana called '*Bolowane*' cattle. But it seems (P.A.W. Cook (n.d.), p.122) that this herd only became sacred after the Bomvana (who were nominally subject to King Sarhili) refused to sacrifice them at Mlanjeni's orders. J.H. Soga identifies '*Bolowane*' as another name for the mimosa tree (quoted in G.D. Ross, 'Sacrificial cattle', typescript, Butterworth, 10 Nov. 1924, copy in author's possession). It would seem therefore that the exclamation '*Bolowane!* ' is in some way connected with Mlanjeni's witchcraft poles, although the mimosa has no magical associations as far as I can ascertain.

6. Interview with W. Dwaba, Tshabo Location, Berlin District, Aug. 1975.

7. These reports of distant rumours concerning Mlanjeni come from the detailed letters of the French missionaries. C. Schrumpf-P.E.M.S., 13 Feb. 1851, T. Arbousset-P.E.M.S., April 1851, *Journal des Missions Evangeliques*, XXVI (1851), pp.168-176, 322-4. It might be argued that beliefs concerning Mlanjeni in the Sotho-speaking area might be very different to ideas in the Xhosa-language area, but it is clear from the letters that the Sotho leaders were in close touch with Xhosaland. The Phuti were the immediate neighbours of the Xhosa-speaking Thembu, who were strong believers in Mlanjeni.

8. Kropf (1891), p.6. Among the Phuti (Note 7), it was believed that Mlanjeni had already resurrected some of the dead.

9. For the War of the Axe, see Peires (1981), pp.119-34, 150-155. For the capture of Sandile, see Brownlee (1916), pp.293-4 and Le Cordeur and Saunders (1981), Chapter VII, esp. pp.226, 232; GH 8/25 C. Brownlee-G. Mackinnon, 2 Sept. 1854; GH 8/25 J. Maclean-W. Liddle, 4 Sept. 1854.

10. A.L. Harington (1980) goes a long way towards dissipating the popular image of Smith. But see, for example, J. Lehmann (1977). For Smith's earlier spell in South Africa and an account of the death of Hintsa, see also Peires (1981), pp.109-115.

11. For Smith's treatment of Maqoma and Sandile, and for his first Great Meeting, see Harington (1980), pp.98-109; Cory (1965), V, p.100; *S.A. Commercial Advertiser*, 22, 29 Dec. 1847, 8, 15 Jan. 1848; *EP Herald*, 25 Dec. 1847; H. Ward (1851), pp.316-8; S.E.K. Mqhayi (n.d.), p.257; Adams (1941), p. 257.

12. For Smith's policy in British Kaffraria before the outbreak of war, see Peires (1981), pp.165-8.

13. For Mackinnon's fulsome annual reports, see Imperial Blue Books 969 of 1848, 1056 of 1849, and 1288 of 1850. For his cowardice, consider his abandonment of the Queen's Regiment in the Fish River bush. Journal of

A. Holdich, Staffordshire Regimental Museum, Whittington, 12 Sept. 1851. See also C. Seymour-F. Seymour, 17 March 1853, Seymour of Ragley Papers, Warwickshire County Record Office, Warwick.

14. Imperial Blue Book, 1334 of 1851, G. Cyrus-Civil Commissioner of Albany, 15 Aug. 1850, pp.42-3. A slightly different version of this speech is given in Peires (1981), p.166.

15. The colonial authorities intervened to arrest a witch-finder who had administered a witchcraft accusation at the behest of Maqoma. See Imperial Blue Book 1288 of 1850, H. Smith-Earl Grey, 23 Aug. 1849, p.18.

16. The best source on early colonial reactions to Mlanjeni's prophecies is Imperial Blue Book 1334 of 1851. See especially J. Maclean-G. Mackinnon, 26 Aug. 1850, pp.17-8.

17. H. Smith-G. Mackinnon, 7 Oct. 1850 in *ibid*, p.15.

18. H. Smith-Earl Grey, 31 Oct. 1850 and enclosures in *ibid*, pp.38-41.

19. Mackinnon had urged Smith to depose Sandile as early as 14 October 1850. G. Mackinnon-H. Smith 14 Oct. 1850, in *ibid*, p.93.

20. J. Maclean-G. Mackinnon, 26, 28 Nov. 1850 in *ibid*, pp.102, 105; GH 8/23 J. Maclean-G. Mackinnon, 2 Dec. 1850.

21. 'Sacrificial cattle', (see Note 5 above) includes a letter from J.H. Soga giving this statement. Kropf and Godfrey (1915), p.36, record, however, that Mlanjeni commanded the people to -*bingelela* (sacrifice) dun cattle. Bryce Ross's detailed contemporary account in the *Home and Foreign Record of the Free Church of Scotland*, II (1851-2), p.268, supports Soga's version, and makes it clear that there were to be two distinct forms of cattle-killing. Dun and yellow coloured cattle were to be disposed of because they were an abomination; other cattle were to be sacrificed as a precious gift. A similar ambiguity surrounded Nongqawuse's initial orders (see below, Chapter 4(1)) and it is most probable that Mlanjeni's instructions meant different things to different people.

22. Bryce Ross, cited in Note 21.

23. For wardoctoring in Xhosa society, see J.H. Soga (n.d.), p.66. For the plants used by Mlanjeni, see A. Smith of St Cyrus (1895), pp.148-9, 170 and Kropf and Godfrey (1915), pp.410, 496. For more details on the actual charm and its use, MS 158d, Grey Collection, S.A. Library, Cape Town. Paper by Wm Kekale Kaye on the 'Koobulu of Umlanjeni'. Among many reports, mostly suspect, regarding Mlanjeni's claims that the bullets would turn to water, see Cory Interview 109. Tanco, interviewed at Kentani, 24 Jan. 1910, Cory Library, Grahamstown.

24. The best account of this crucial meeting is in Imperial Blue Book 635 of 1851, Evidence of H. Renton, pp.384-7.

25. There is no good account of the War of Mlanjeni. Harington (1980), Chapters X and XI, is probably the best treatment but is necessarily limited in scope as it is part of a biography of Sir Harry Smith. J. Milton (1983), Chapters 20 and 21, is clear and accurate but rather light on analysis. Godlonton and Irving (1851) is a compilation of newspaper reports up to June 1851. Numerous memoirs by soldiers have been published, but only W.R. King (1853), J. Mackay (1871) and T. Stubbs (1978) have much substance. There are many unpublished manuscripts of soldier's diaries and letters which will be cited in the appropriate places. Of all these sources, only the diary of L. Graham, Acc 8402-5, National Army Museum,

London, shows even the remotest sympathy for the Xhosa.

26. For the Xhosa attempts to make peace, see BK 433 W. Fynn-G. Mackinnon, 23 Jan. 1851 and Holdich Journal, Staffordshire Regimental Museum, 5, 8 March. For the text of Smith's extermination order, see Godlonton and Irving (1962), pp.89-90; for his private letter, Acc 983, Cape Archives, H. Smith-C. Andrews, 14 Jan. 1851. For his desire to hang the chiefs, Elwes deposit 2/1, VDC Elwes-Mother, 30 Oct. 1851, Lincolnshire Archives, Lincoln.

27. For Maqoma's question, see Milton (1983), p.182. The description of the Amathole Mountains is from the *Grahamstown Journal*, 29 Aug. 1846.

28. See, for example, the episode described by King (1853), pp.48-60.

29. Mqhayi (n.d.), p.112.

30. Mackay (1871), pp.178-9. There was a continuous movement of Xhosa and Khoi in and out of the Waterkloof, and Mackay might well be correct in arguing that the figure is an underestimate.

31. *United Services Magazine* (1852), I, p.592.

32. Imperial Blue Book 1428 of 1852, H. Smith-Earl Grey, 19 Nov. 1851, p.202; Earl Grey-H. Smith, 14 Jan. 1852, p.254. Grey's opinion of Smith was undermined by a series of vicious letters from W. Hogge. See Earl Grey Papers, University of Durham.

33. There is a detailed description of the Fish River bush in W.T. Black (1901). *Edinburgh Evening Courant*, 27 Jan. 1852 for attempts to burn the acacia bushes.

34. G. Cathcart (1857), pp.88-9. For Mhala's attitude, see BK 431 J. Maclean-G. Mackinnon, 10, 14, 17 Jan. 1851.

35. Imperial Blue Book 1635 of 1853, J. Maclean-'My dear General', 9 Oct. 1852, p.181. Maclean's own account of the affair shows just how unprepared Siyolo was for imprisonment, and just how underhand was the means pursued: 'He [Siyolo] evidently expected me to receive his surrender by merely handing over his gun, and that I would permit him to return to his family. . . . I therefore retired to my dresing room, and Seyolo being suddenly called to hear his statement read over, I told him that I had guaranteed his life, but that his remaining in custody was imperative . . . During this short conference I managed to get a few men to my dressing room, and he was taken off quietly. I am satisfied . . . that he would have bolted if I had acquainted him with my intention to apprehend him.'

36. Godlonton and Irving (1851), pp.268-72.

37. Cory (1965), V, pp.435, 463; *Edinburgh Evening Courant*, 16 March 1851; Imperial Blue Book 1635 of 1853, W. Eyre-A. Cloete, 6 Dec. 1851, pp.1-3.

38. S.M. Mitra (1911), p.272. During the first attack, which came as a complete surprise, Fort White was defended by only 18 soldiers and 5 civilians.

39. *Grahamstown Journal*, 6 June 1846.

40. *Edinburgh Evening Courant* 23 March 1852.

41. King (1853), pp.122-3; Holdich Journal, Staffordshire Regimental Museum, 19 Feb. 1851; *Edinburgh Evening Courant*, 20 Jan. 1852; Diary of T.H. Bramston, Greenjacket Regimental Museum, Winchester, 16 July 1852.

42. John Rich diary, Black Watch Regimental Museum, Perth, n.d. [March or April 1852]. For rockets, see MS 588, Cory Library, 23 Feb. 1852. For the Minie Rifle, see S. Lakeman (1880), *passim*.

43. J.B. Currey, 'Half a century in South Africa' (typescript), p.51.
44. Holdich Journal, Staffordshire Regimental Museum, 12 Sept. 1851; *Illustrated London News*, 22 Sept. 1851; *Nottingham Journal*, 26 Dec. 1851; Mackay (1871), p.47.
45. In fact, Smith's victory over the Xhosa in 1835 was very largely due to the treacherous capture and subsequent murder of the Xhosa king, Hintsa. As Smith's then superior, Governor D'Urban wrote to him, 'It was a fortunate circumstance, Hintsa's coming in, and so putting an end, most seasonably for us, to a sort of warfare . . . which, in our secret mind, we confessed our inability to have prosecuted further.' Quoted in Peires (1981), p.112.
46. Stubbs (1978), p.135. See also G. Cathcart (1857), p.349; C. Seymour-F. Seymour 20 Sept. 1852, 17 March 1853, Seymour of Ragley Papers, Warwickshire County Record Office.
47. Imperial Blue Book 1428 of 1852, H. Smith-Earl Grey, 17 June, 6 July 1851; J. Marincovitz (1985); Holdich Journal, 20 June 1851, Staffordshire Regimental Museum.
48. Imperial Blue Book 1428 of 1852, H. Somerset-H. Smith 16 July 1851, pp.91-2.
49. Acc. 8011, National Army Museum, London, Journal of J.C.G. Kingsley, 24, 25 Dec. 1851.
50. *Illustrated London News*, 10 Jan. 1852.
51. Among the various memoirs of Eyre, the diaries of L. Graham, National Army Museum and John Rich, Black Watch Regimental Museum, are particularly vivid. See also P.S. Campbell (n.d.), pp.59-63; Stubbs (1978), p.155.
52. Acc 8402-5, National Army Museum, Diary of L. Graham, 24 May 1852, 22 June 1852, 14 Oct. 1852; NRA 33, Black Watch Regimental Museum, Diary of John Rich, 28 Dec. 1851.
53. Elwes Deposit 2/1 Lincolnshire Archives. V.D.C. Elwes-Mother, 30 Oct. 1851.
54. MS 575, Cory Library, C. Brownlee-H. Smith, Feb. 1852; Acc 8011, National Army Museum, J.C.G. Kingsley Journal, 30 Jan. 1852; NRA 33, Black Watch Regimental Museum, 28 Jan. 1852.
55. MS 584, Cory Library, J. Michel-n.a. 18 Feb. 1852.
56. The extensive correspondence on the peace proposals is printed in Imperial Blue Book 1635 of 1853, H. Smith-Earl Grey, 16 Feb. 1852 and enclosures, pp.23-37.
57. DDHV/73/23 Humberside County Record Office, Beverley, Letters of H. Robinson. H. Robinson-Mother, 30 Oct. 1852; King (1853), p.131; *Grahamstown Journal*, 12 Feb. 1853; Royal Greenjackets Regimental Museum, Winchester, Diary of T. H. Bramston, 20, 22 July.
58. King (1853), p.265.
59. Godlonton and Irving (1851), I, p.174; Mackay (1871), pp.63-4.
60. Stubbs (1978), p.155.
61. J.H. Soga (n.d.), pp.76-7; Mackay (1871), pp.41, 151, 221; NRA 33, Diary of John Rich (reference to the War of the Axe).
62. Brownlee (1916), p.158; King (1853), p.119; Holdich Journal, Staffordshire Regimental Museum, 29 March 1851; Acc 8402-5, Diary of L. Graham, National Army Museum, 7 April 1852.
63. The story of the horrible death of the Bandmaster Hartung was particularly

notorious. King (1853), pp.92-3. See also Lakeman (1880), p.104.

64. Mackay (1871), p.44. See also Mellish of Hodsock Manuscripts, University of Nottingham, [Captain Roopes] — n.a., 9 Feb. 1853. 'Not but that some things done [by the British soldiers] were bad enough, I should not like to say all I have seen and known and suffered when possible but great excuse is due when you consider on a white man falling into their hands, they not only kill, but torture him, and treat his remains with the most wonderful brutality.'

65. Lakeman (1880), pp.94-5. For another similar case, see Stubbs, p.176.

66. Peires (1981), p.112. For Smith's personal participation in these horrors, see PR 3563, Cory Library, autobiographical manuscript of H.J. Halse, p.20 in which Smith sends a pair of ears to one of his subordinates as a joke.

67. Elwes Deposit 2/1, Lincolnshire Archives. V.D.C. Elwes-Mother, 11 Feb., 13 March 1852.

68. Currey, (1986), p.49.

69. Mackay (1871), p.136; *Cape Frontier Times*, 16 Jan. 1853; Godlonton and Irving (1851), II, pp.78-9.

70. Stubbs (1978), pp.161, 169.

71. Mackay (1871), p.152; DDHV/73/23, Humberside Country Record Office, H. Robinson-Uncle, 12 April 1853; H. Robinson-Mother, 16 March 1852.

72. Mackay (1871), pp.218-19; Lakeman (1880), p.103.

73. For Cathcart's liberal pretensions, see his conversation with Commissioner Brownlee, Brownlee (1916), p.124 and the private letter in which he says, comparing settlers and Xhosa, that 'the [Xhosa] is much the finer race of the two.' Cathcart (1857), p.349. For the negative attitude of his men, see for example, DDHV/73/23, Humberside County Record Office, H. Robinson-Mother, 9 May 1852, Acc 8108, National Army Museum, Journal of Lieutenant W.J. St John, 9 Dec. 1852; Acc 8402-5, National Army Museum, L. Graham Diary, 1 May 1852.

74. Cathcart (1857), p.41.

75. Most of the army felt, after the event, that the recall of Smith had probably prolonged the war. This is probably correct, but it should be pointed out that, in a war of attrition, Cathcart's dilatory methods were probably as effective as Smith's energetic ones — and probably cost less lives. For examples of pro-Smith sentiment, see DDHV/73/23, Humberside Country Record Office, H. Robinson-Mother, 9 May 1852, 4 June 1852; Acc 8402-5, National Army Museum, Journal of J.G. Kingsley, 6 March 1852.

76. Mellish of Hodsock Papers, University of Nottingham, Diary of Private E.G. Richards, 3 Nov. 1852.

77. *Ibid*; King (1853), p.271; J. Fisher-Mother, Greenjackets Regimental Museum, Winchester.

78. Cathcart (1857), pp.41, 107-8; Acc 8402-5, National Army Museum, Diary of L. Graham, 18 Feb. 1853.

79. Mackay (1871), pp.252-4.

80. H. Pearse, 'The Kaffir and Basuto campaigns of 1852 and 1853,' *United Services Magazine* (1898) and, for the massacre, Acc 8108, National Army Museum, Journal of W.J. St John, 23 Dec. 1852.

81. *Grahamstown Journal*, 5, 8 March 1853; *Cape Frontier Times*, 8 March 1853; Seymour of Ragley Papers, Warwickshire County Record Office,

C. Seymour-F. Seymour, 17 March 1853; GH 19/8 C. Owen-G. Cathcart, 11, 16 Feb. 1853.

82. Acc 6807/231, National Army Museum, L. Graham, Diary of the Crimean War.

83. *Cape Frontier Times*, 8 Nov. 1853.

84. GH 8/28 C. Brownlee-J. Maclean, 24 Jan. 1856.

85. They were encouraged in this illusion by memories of the retrocession of Queen Adelaide Province in 1835 (see Peires (1981), p.115) and by rumours that the influential liberal, Sir A. Stockenstrom, had appeared before a committee of the House of Commons.

86. Acc. 8402-5, National Army Museum, Diary of L. Graham, 15 March 1853.

87. Cathcart (1857), pp.189-215; BK 69 C. Brownlee-J. Maclean, 14 July 1853; *Cape Frontier Times*, 26 May 1853.

88. GH 8/28 J. Maclean-W. Liddle, 15 Feb. 1856; GH 8/28 C. Brownlee-J. Maclean, 24 Jan. 1856.

89. Holdich Journal, Staffordshire Regimental Museum, 3 Feb., 12 July 1851; Imperial Blue Book 1428 of 1851, Deposition of Toyise, 3 Aug. 1851; *Edinburgh Evening Courant*, 3 Feb. 1852.

90. CO 4386 Statement of Qotshi, 5 Dec. 1851; CO 4386 J. Thomas-J. Appleyard, 10 April 1851; Holdich Journal, Staffordshire Regimental Museum, 30 March 1851; Imperial Blue Book 1428 of 1852, H. Smith-Earl Grey, 18 Sept. 1851, pp.148-9.

91. Holdich Journal, Staffordshire Regimental Museum, 4 Sept. 1851; MS 2783, Cory Library, J. Ross-Mrs Paterson, 16 June 1852; W. Hogge-Earl Grey, 4 Sept. 1851, Earl Grey Papers, University of Durham.

92. Imperial Blue Book 1428 of 1852, H. Smith-Earl Grey, 18 Sept. 1851, pp.148-9; Earl Grey Papers, University of Durham, W. Hogge-B. Hawes, 17 Sept. 1851; Holdich Journal, Staffordshire Regimental Museum, 3 Feb. 1851.

93. As recorded by L. Graham in his diary for 24 June 1853. Acc 8402—5, National Army Museum.

94. Interview with M. Soga, Kobonqaba Location, Kentani District, 25 Aug. 1983. The same point was mentioned by oral historian W. Nkabi, interviewed Bulembo Location, King William's Town District, 24 Aug. 1975. A letter by the Paris Missionary C. Schrumpf, 1 June 1851, *Journal des Missions Evangeliques*, XXXVI (1851), pp.369-70 describes the aftermath of battle as follows: 'At least [ten] blacks were killed, but the rest gave thanks to Mlanjeni for the victory. They do not worry about those who were killed, they say they must have neglected some part of the ceremony.' For Mlanjeni's excuses to Sandile, see Holdich Journal, Staffordshire Regimental Museum, 29 June 1851.

95. L. Festinger, H.W. Riecken and S. Schachter (1956).

96. Imperial Blue Book 1969 of 1855, G. Cathcart-Duke of Newcastle, 3 Sept. 1853, p.14; *Grahamstown Journal*, 22 Oct. 1853; 'Nzulu Lwazi', 'URev. Tiyo Soga uTshaka noMlanjeni', *Umteteli waBantu*, 17 Dec. 1927.

97. For an overview of Xhosa religion from a historical perspective and for all references not cited, see Peires (1981), Ch.V. For an excellent ethnological account of the Mpondo, a people very close in respect of religion to the Xhosa, see M. Hunter (1936).

98. S. Kay (1833), p.194.

99. J. Chalmers (1878), pp.356-8. This version is heavily overlaid by Christian ideas of God and the Devil. It is followed by another tale, which also describes the introduction of Death as an accident. For a discussion, see J. Hodgson (1983), pp.32-8.
100. The quotation is from S.Kay (1833), p.192. Further confirmation may be found in H. Lichtenstein (1812-15), I, p.319; L. Alberti (1810), p.21; H. Dugmore (1858), pp.157-8. For the link with smallpox, see J.W.D. Moodie (1835), II, p.271.
101. J. Campbell, q. Peires (1981), p.68.
102. Peires (1981), Ch. V; C. Stretch (1876); J. Read (1818); 172c Grey Collection, South African Library, J. Brownlee, 'On the origins and rise of the prophet Nxele'.
103. Almost all the information we have on Wilhelm Goliath/Mhlakaza comes from one source, Merriman (1957). Merriman does not of course mention that his erstwhile protege was to become Mhlakaza, and this link has not previously been noticed by historians. It is, however, irrefutably established by LG 396, G. Cyrus-R. Southey, 4 Aug. 1856, and is also noticed in the *Graaff-Reinet Herald*, 9 Aug. 1856. Governor Grey also stated at one point that Mhlakaza had worked in the Colony, where he caused his employers trouble from visions he claimed to have seen, though he is too tactful to name the employers GH 23/26 G. Grey-H. Labouchere, 16 Aug. 1856. Although Mrs Merriman was at pains to deny that her former servant was Mhlakaza (see Note 111) she does admit that he disappeared into Xhosaland shortly before the Cattle-Killing and was never seen again. I must record my sincere thanks to Mr Michael Berning and Mrs Sandy Fold of the Cory Library for the interest and energy with which they have assisted me in this section.
104. Merriman (1957), p.224.
105. *Ibid.*, pp.52, 116, 152. MS 15 899/1, Cory Library, the Register of Baptisms and Marriages of the Methodist Church in Grahamstown, mentions the baptism of a 'Kaffir' (that is, a Xhosa as distinct from a Mfengu) named Goliat on 26 Sept. 1841, which seems just about right. There is no record of a marriage between a Wilhelm Goliat and a Mfengu woman named Sarah in this volume. A Karel Gola or Goliat is mentioned in the volume as being married in the Magistrate's Court in December 1836.
106. Merriman (1957), 52, 62, 70-2, 77, 108, 112, 117, 120-1, 123.
107. *Ibid.*, p.65.
108. *Ibid.*, pp.93, 123.
109. *Ibid.*, p.106.
110. *Ibid.*, p.127. Archdeacon Merriman does not mention his wife but since his eldest son was only nine years old at the time, it is difficult to see who else he might have meant. Mrs Merriman was consistently hostile to her husband's inclinations and she frustrated his sincere desire to become a missionary himself. *Ibid.*, p.214.
111. One of Merriman's acquaintances in the western Cape wrote in a memoir that Wilhelm was 'the same that became famous as the witchdoctor who instigated his tribe to rise in the war, I think, of 1849'. J. Baker, 'Some personal recollections of the late Bishop Merriman,' *Cape Church Monthly*, IV (1896). Mrs Merriman responded with two letters, asking Baker to correct this 'misstatement'. MS 16, 690, GDA 284-5, Cory

Library, Mrs J. Merriman-J. Baker, 20, 30 Oct. 1896. Baker did of course get the details wrong (not surprisingly, forty years on, and considering that he had never lived in the eastern Cape). The correspondence is, however, exceptionally interesting for the extra light it sheds on Wilhelm's character, and, contrary to Mrs Merriman's expectations, it confirms rather than refutes the hypothesis that Wilhelm was Mhlakaza. The Merrimans were away in England throughout the period of the Cattle-Killing. I owe these references to Dr Mandy Goedhals's impeccable research on the life and work of N.J. Merriman. See M. Goedhals (1984).

112. Merriman (1957), p.205-6, states Wilhelm found the orphan 'near his hut [in Grahamstown] a homeless wanderer'. In Cape Parliamentary Paper G 38 of 1858, 'Deposition made by Nonquase, a Kafir Prophetess', Nongqawuse states only that 'Umhlakaza was my uncle. . . . My father's name was Umhlanhla, of Kreli's tribe. He died when I was very young.' As we shall see, Grey doctored everything he had published and would have suppressed any embarrassing items. The deposition is certainly injected with inferences conducive to Grey's theory of a chiefs' plot to make war on the Colony (see Chapter 7 below for a full discussion). Nevertheless, there is no reason to doubt this particular statement, which contradicts Merriman's implication that the orphan arrived at Wilhelm's place by accident. On the other hand, Wilhelm was not staying anywhere near the Waterkloof and one may legitimately ask whether the orphan did not deliberately make its way to him. (We know that Mhlakaza's sister lived near him from BK 14 'Examination, before the Chief Commissioner of Unqula, brother of Nombanda'.)

One must state frankly that there is no more than a chance that Nongqawuse was the orphan of the Waterkloof. Nevertheless the impact of the orphan's experiences would have surely been felt by all in Wilhelm/Mhlakaza's household.

CHAPTER 2

Crooked Like a Snake

1. The Artful Dodger of Governors

'To those who have studied [Sir George Grey],' wrote one eminent historian of New Zealand, 'his conduct is a never-failing source of astonishment. Such a mixture of greatness and pettiness, breadth of intellect and dishonesty, is rarely met with.'[1] Grey was indeed a giant among colonial Governors, and comparison with any of the clapped-out ex-soldiers who had previously governed the Cape only makes him seem more gigantic still. A man of great intellectual distinction himself, Grey counted some of the foremost minds of Victorian England as his personal friends, among them Carlyle, Darwin, Lyell the geologist, and Babbage, the inventor of computing. His own interests included botany, zoology, entomology, geology, linguistics and folklore, and he patronized and befriended men of science, besides making small but significant contributions to human knowledge in all these fields. He was an avid collector of books and found time, even in the midst of acute political crises, to collect Xhosa grammars and medieval manuscripts, creating one of the finest libraries of the Victorian age.[2] Few other colonial Governors shared his interest in the cultures of the conquered peoples of the British Empire, or his conviction that all men were inherently equal. A regular church-goer and an ostentatious reader of the Bible,[3] Grey was the intimate of bishops and the patron of missionaries. Education and health care were among his public passions, and wherever he went he established and endowed schools and hospitals for indigenous people. In South Africa especially, Grey's reputation still rides high. For the old Cape liberals as well as for more recent analysts, Grey's governorship was a lost Golden Age, a glorious period in which a wise and humane

Governor briefly demonstrated the value and the possibility of harmonious racial integration.[4]

But there was a dark, even a sinister side to Grey's personality. The Governor was driven by what Professor Dalton, the New Zealand historian, has called a 'ruthless egotism to which he would sacrifice anything and anybody'.[5] Beneath the polished veneer of charm and intelligence, there lurked a deeply insecure personality, which was selfish, vindictive and almost paranoid. Grey dreamed of absolute power and seriously maintained that despotism was the best possible system of colonial government. He shared the Victorian tendency to divide men into two categories, heroes and ordinary mortals. 'To find your ablest man and then give him power, and obey him' was regarded by many Victorians as 'the highest act of wisdom which a nation can be capable of'. Or, as Grey's friend and admirer, Thomas Carlyle, phrased it, 'if people will not behave well, put collars round their necks. Find a hero and let them be his slaves.'[6]

Grey identified himself at once as a hero, but it was no easy matter to secure a dictatorship in Victorian England. He turned therefore to the obscure British colonies of the southern hemisphere, where he found fresh fields to dominate and to exercise his absolute sway. Once established as a colonial Governor, Grey stopped at nothing to remove the least check or restraint on his absolute power. His public letters and dispatches were monuments of prevarication and deceit, exalting himself, traducing others and threatening the Colonial Office with war and bloodshed if he did not have his way. He destroyed his European rivals with lies and smears, and his non-European victims with court martials, transportations, summary justice and even, as we shall see, mass starvation. For all his rhetorical concern for the welfare of indigenous peoples, no Governor did more to break the independence and steal the land of the Maori and the Xhosa than Sir George Grey.

Despite his peculiar genius, Grey should not be seen as an extra-ordinary individual who grabbed History by the scruff of the neck and moulded it according to his own desires. He was a great colonial Governor, but his greatness lay in his ability to implement successfully the established objectives of early Victorian imperialism: to extend the territories of the British Empire and found colonies of settlement for its surplus population, while at the same time paying lip service to the moral commitments which the Victorians had inherited from the anti-slavery movement. Grey's despotic inclinations and paranoid obsessions would certainly have involved him in failure and ridicule had he remained in England as a politician or an army officer. But as a colonial Governor, these very same personality disorders fuelled his extraordinary capacity for crushing and subjugating indigenous peoples, while loudly and sincerely proclaiming that he was doing so in their own best interests.

The young Grey burst upon an unsuspecting world in a suitably spectacular and inauspicious manner. His pregnant mother was sitting idly on the verandah of her hotel in Lisbon one spring day in 1812 when she overheard two army officers saying that her husband, George Grey senior, had been killed in the storming of Badajoz. The shock sent her into labour, bringing on the premature birth of her first child, the future Sir George. Mrs Grey remarried, and the young George grew up in the house of his stepfather, a baronet turned clergyman at Bodiam, near the Royal Military College of Sandhurst. Here he imbibed the values and attitudes of the English minor gentry and acquired the social connections so necessary to upward mobility within the aristocratic upper strata of English society.

Like many other young men of good social standing but limited means, Grey entered Sandhurst as a 'gentleman cadet'. He was commissioned at the age of seventeen and posted to Ireland, where he spent the next six years enforcing English laws against the resistance of an increasingly rebellious Irish peasantry. Grey's Irish experiences made an indelible impression on him. He seems to have realized that there was no way of alleviating the sufferings of the poor within the confines of the British Isles without challenging the hidebound and oppressive social system of which he himself was a product and a defender. He began to see emigration as the solution to Britain's chronic problems, and he turned his attention to the yet uncolonized lands of the southern hemisphere as a possible site for the creation of a new and better society. With the approval and financial support of the Colonial Secretary, Grey embarked in 1836 on an expedition to explore the hitherto unknown corner of far northwestern Australia.

It was a fiasco from the very beginning. Their first day ashore, the party found no water, collapsed from sunstroke, nearly got lost, and narrowly escaped being killed by Australian aborigines. On the fourteenth day Grey himself was speared three times and developed a severe abcess in his wounded hip, which he kept at bay with laudanum until his deteriorating health brought the expedition to a premature end. Grey was to complain of this wound all his life, blaming it for the severe bouts of depression which totally incapacitated him from time to time, and giving rise to some historical speculation that his extraordinary patterns of behaviour were inspired to some extent by opium or some other drug.[7]

The failure of his first expedition did nothing to dampen Grey's fierce desire to rise from obscurity and achieve something for his country and for himself. Ten months later, he set sail a second time for northwestern Australia. With incredible shortsightedness, he landed his expedition on an island which turned out to have no water. After a month of fruitless shuttling between the islands and the mainland, the expedition began to face the very real possibility of death by exposure and starvation. Grey insisted on attempting the journey home by sea, but his boats were dashed to pieces, stranding the party nearly 500 kilometres from Perth. After a week of slow progress, Grey decided to leave his weaker companions to their own devices and push on as fast as he could. He reached Perth a fortnight later, but it was another 25 days before the last of the stragglers was rescued. Fortunately for Grey's reputation, only one man had actually died.

Grey had thus mismanaged two expeditions, abandoned his subordinates, and decisively failed to found the new colony of which he had dreamed. Nevertheless, it was not difficult for him to pass himself off as an intrepid explorer. He had named ten rivers and discovered two new mountain ranges, clashed with aborigines and reported on their customs, besides collecting numerous specimens of hitherto unknown shrimps, shellfish, butterflies and insects. His carefully written *Journals of Two Expeditions of Discovery in North-Western Australia* became an instant classic of Australiana.[8]

Grey was offered a temporary position as magistrate at Albany in Western Australia. Here he married Lucy Spencer, the daughter of his predecessor, and acquired some practical experience of governing Australian aborigines. His ideas on the proper line of policy to be pursued towards aboriginal peoples by colonial governments were fast maturing, and he took advantage of the long sea voyage back to England to write these up in a memorandum. As these ideas were to form the basis of Grey's future policies in New Zealand and at the Cape, it is necessary to pause in our narrative and look at them in some detail.[9]

Grey began by attacking the premise on which all official colonial policy towards indigenous peoples had hitherto been based, namely that 'so long as they only exercised their own customs upon themselves . . . they should be allowed to do so with impunity'. Leaving the 'natives' to indulge in their 'barbarous' customs was well meant, Grey thought, but it was a mistake. He professed great respect for the natural capabilities of the aborigines. 'They are as apt and intelligent as any other race of men I am acquainted with,' he wrote. 'They are subject to the same affections, appetites and passions as other men.' And yet, in spite of this natural aptitude, they remained sunk in barbarism and savagery. Grey thought that the reason for this was that those aborigines who wished to adopt English civilization were trapped by the laws and customs imposed on them by the barbarous older generation.

> To believe that man in a savage state is endowed with freedom of thought or action is erroneous in the highest degree. He is in reality subjected to complex laws, which not only deprive him of all free agency of thought, but, at the same time, by allowing no scope whatever for the development of intellect, benevolence or any other great moral qualification, they necessarily bind him down in a hopeless state of barbarism, from which it is impossible for man to emerge, so long as he is enthralled by these customs. . . .

Grey had no doubt that any aborigine given the freedom of choice would choose the British version of civilization rather than his own. He could see no saving grace whatsoever in the indigenous cultures of the Polynesian and African peoples he encountered. Although he made very real contributions to the study of Maori linguistics and folklore, Grey had nothing but contempt for his subject matter. Maori traditions were 'puerile' and Maori religion was 'absurd'. He estimated that savage customs had caused the deaths of no fewer than four million Maori, not counting the victims of infanticides and witch-beliefs. The only reason for studying such worthless cultures, he maintained, was to communicate more effectively with the Maori chiefs and to destroy the illusion that the intellectual systems of barbarous races were in some way worthy of respect.[10]

Instead of tolerating the savage customs which kept their adherents bound in eternal thrall, Grey argued, colonial Governors should push ahead as fast as possible with the imposition of English law in the place of the 'bloodthirsty' aboriginal law. The cause of civilization would be further advanced by establishing native schools and by providing aborigines with well-paid employment on public roads. Aborigines who, by their labour, proved themselves 'serviceable members of the community' should be given grants of land on individual tenure. Aborigines should not, however, be allowed to congregate together and keep up their old bad habits, but should be scattered and distributed all over settler country.

Grey's ideas were very much in keeping with the Utilitarian spirit of the early Victorian age. Utilitarianism owed something to the Evangelical Christian doctrine that human nature was intrinsically the same in all races, but it exalted government and law above religion and education as the main engine of social improvement.[11] For many years, the Utilitarian school of political economy had been attacking the policies of the English East India Company which ruled India. Writers such as Jeremy Bentham and James Mill argued that by freeing the individual Indian from the tyranny of Indian customs and Indian government and giving free scope to the interplay of labour and capital, British law might stir Indian society out of its centuries-old stagnation and set it moving along the road of progress. During the administration of Lord William Bentinck (1828-35), the British government in India embarked on an extensive campaign to suppress Indian customs, introduce English legal procedures into Indian courts, and impose English language and education into areas where Sanskrit and Islamic learning had hitherto been tolerated.

Grey's ideas were more attuned to contemporary thinking than the philanthropic attitudes of the Colonial Office which still sought to protect indigenous peoples by keeping them strictly separate from intrusive settlers. By 1840, however, it was apparent even to Sir James Stephen, the philanthropically minded Permanent Secretary at the Colonial Office, that this policy of segregation was not viable, and that colonists and aborigines alike were tearing down the frail barriers which kept them apart, involving the British government in expensive wars which it did not want.[12] Grey's approach came as a welcome escape from the Colonial Office dilemma of reconciling its conflicting obligations to settlers and indigenous peoples. Far from being antagonistic, Grey maintained, the interests of settlers and indigenes were in fact complementary, so long as the latter were given the opportunity of acquiring the skills and education necessary to survival as equals. Far from trying vainly to segregate the conflicting races, the Colonial Office should throw all its efforts into trying to amalgamate them as quickly as possible. Not only did Grey thus conjure up a picture of progress and harmony particularly pleasing to the Victorian taste for order and rationality, but he couched it in the humanitarian terms most likely to appeal to the old veterans of the anti-slavery crusade. Through the good offices of an old patron, Grey was introduced to Sir James Stephen at the Colonial Office. He turned on his magical charm and, at the exceptionally youthful age of twenty-eight, found himself appointed Governor of South Australia.

This is not the place to enter into a lengthy discussion of Grey's governorships of South Australia (1841-5) and New Zealand (1845-54). Suffice it to say that his reputed successes were achieved by a lethal combination of brute force and barefaced lies. The Maoris of New Zealand suffered most. Through Grey's agency, they lost six million acres of the disputed North Island and all South Island's thirty million acres. Other victims included Henry Williams, a saintly missionary, and Charles Sturt, the discoverer of South Australia. Grey was a fake humanitarian and a fake explorer who did not relish being shown up by the real thing.

Even more repulsive was his treatment of Te Rauparaha, a powerful but neutral Maori chief, whom Grey accused — again falsely — of conspiring to kill settlers and rape white women. Te Rauparaha was released only after his subjects agreed to surrender three million acres for white settlement. Other Maoris were not so lucky. One Christian convert was tried and shot by court martial without benefit of defence counsel, and his companions were illegally transported to Australia. All these little tricks — conspiracy theory, false accusation, court martial and wholesale transportation — became part of Grey's stock-in-trade, and were utilized by him in South Africa.

Admittedly, Grey's policy in New Zealand included more constructive measures such as schools, hospitals, and public works. And, in contrast to his policy at the Cape, he refrained from interfering too aggressively with Maori chiefs or Maori law. But neither Grey's aggression nor his restraint really succeeded, and, even before his departure, some of the more perceptive Maori chiefs began to canvass the idea of a Maori king who would unite the Maori people to resist white encroachment.

Grey was aware of this movement but took care to conceal the information from his successor and from the Colonial Office in London. He 'was anxious to wind up his governorship in a blaze of glory,' writes the historian Alan Ward, 'and bombarded London with despatches, compounded of purblind optimism and deliberate deceit, about the progress of the amalgamation policy.' The Colonial Office was completely taken in. They credited Grey with a 'singular ability in dealing with the savage races' and they rewarded him with a knighthood and the governorship of the Cape of Good Hope.[13]

As we have seen, Grey was not nearly as unique as he liked to pretend. His ideas of imposing British law, breaking the power of the chiefs and civilizing the natives through the intellectual discipline of hard work were not in fact very different from those which had brought disaster and disgrace to Sir Harry Smith. That Grey succeeded where Smith failed was due not to any special virtues but to Grey's peculiarly serviceable personality defects. Grey was an authoritarian, even dictatorial individual, so convinced of the superiority of his own judgement that he was ruthless to the point of vindictiveness in pursuit of his goals. His contempt for truth and his habit of sending lying and self-serving dispatches designed to present his behaviour in the best possible light confused the Colonial Office and make it extremely difficult even now to get at the facts. As one New Zealand historian has put it:

> Grey set forth on a policy of trickery and deceit. So difficult is it to find one important subject about which Grey did not lie or, the most favourable view, which he did not misrepresent, that the impact of Grey must be judged from what he did and not what he said he did. Grey was untruthful from the moment he arrived [in New Zealand], and so practised in this art that it is difficult to believe that he had ever been otherwise. . . . In short he lied when misrepresentation appeared to suit his immediate ends . . . the Colonial Office always gave him the benefit of any doubt. In this way . . . he earned himself, in London, a brilliant reputation that time has scarcely dimmed.[14]

Grey built his entire reputation on the lie that the interests of the settlers and the indigenous peoples could be rendered complementary and harmonious. When dealing with the natural Maori opposition to the colonial attempt to steal their land and ram civilization down their throats, Grey resorted to scapegoating and conspiracy theory, as his treatment of Te Rauparaha clearly shows. Whereas other lesser Governors bogged down in a morass of contradictions, Grey was supremely indifferent to all practical and moral difficulties. For all his grand talk of civilization and benefiting the native, he never hesitated to go for the jugular.

It is possible to see Grey's addiction to conspiracy theory as the natural refuge of his deeply insecure and highly self-righteous personality when faced with the unpleasant consequences of his own actions. But those who suffered at the Governor's hands had a less charitable explanation. One New Zealand politician called him 'the Artful Dodger of Governors'. The Maori compared him to a 'rat that burrows underground out of sight, and would come up in their midst when and where they least expected'. One of the Sturt family wrote that the Maori said of Grey, 'Guv'ner, when him want something, him no go straight like a bird, him always go crooked like a snake.'[15] The story must be apocryphal, for there are no snakes in New Zealand. Nevertheless it accurately sums up Sir George Grey's peculiar style of colonial government.

2. Changing Enemies into Friends

Blessed with great gifts but cursed with an obsessive self-pride, Sir George Grey exploded on the South African scene, half Superman and half Devil. If an Elizabethan dramatist had written the life of Grey as a variation on the theme of Faust — and no comparison could be more appropriate — the Governor's administration of the Cape would have appeared as Act Four, the magnificent victory just prior to the tragic denouement of Act Five. For Grey's entire career as a Governor was played out on the brink of an abyss, and the same extraordinary qualities which secured his success in South Africa wrought his downfall in the years which followed. But no man who lived through Grey's South African triumphs could possibly have suspected that the Governor's magic charm would ever fail.

Sir George Grey was a great Imperialist. His ambitions stretched beyond the narrow confines of the Cape Colony to embrace South Africa as a whole, which he aimed to make 'a real power, which may hereafter bless and influence large portions of this vast continent'.[16] He sought to add the Boer Republics and the independent black states of the subcontinent to the existing British dependencies, and he patronized David Livingstone's expeditions in search of fresh fields to conquer. But Grey was not so shallow as to conceptualize such a new colony purely in territorial terms, nor did he think that such a domain could be created purely by military means. Grey's talk was always of spreading 'civilization', by which he meant more than just the conquest of new territories, the subjugation of indigenous inhabitants and the capture of natural resources. By the spread of 'civilization', Grey meant the amalgamation of the disparate Boer and African societies into a single integrated whole, modelled on Victorian Britain — English by culture, Christian by religion and capitalist by economic structure.

The 'civilizing' of British Kaffraria was the critical first stage of Grey's whole grandiose plan. Although the Xhosa inhabitants of British Kaffraria were the only African people in South Africa under the direct administration of Britain, they were still, in a very real sense, independent of it. The Xhosa were militarily defeated, they had lost their best land, their best cattle and their best young men. Their economy had become dependent on colonial markets and their world-view had become clouded by mission Christianity. And yet, in spite of all this or even, paradoxically, because of it, the Xhosa remained an identifiably distinct nation, socially, economically and politically distinct from the Cape Colony and in no way subsumed by it. Defeated though they had been in the War of Mlanjeni, they had at least forced Sir George Cathcart to reverse those measures of Sir Harry Smith which had been designed to integrate them into the colonial system. This continuing self-sufficiency was recognized by Chief Commissioner Maclean when he wrote, in 1855:

> The [Xhosa] contented like the North American Indian with his barbarous state, and apathetic as to improvement, has in addition to

these other characteristics, that he clings tenaciously to his old customs
and habits, is proud of his race, which he considers pure and superior to
others, is therefore eminently national, is suspicious, and holds aloof
from others; and while considering the white man as a means of
obtaining certain articles which the despised industry of the latter
supplies would yet prefer their absence.[17]

It was arms and ammunition and nothing else which kept British
Kaffraria British. Take away colonial military power, and British
Kaffraria would instantly have reverted to Xhosaland again. True,
some of its inhabitants might profess Christianity, and most of them
might depend more or less on colonial products, but the underlying
political and economic integrity of the precolonial Xhosa social
formation was still intact, right up to the time of Sir George Grey. To
this extent, Grey was quite correct in terming the situation on the
Cape's eastern frontier at the time of his arrival as nothing better than
an 'armed truce'.[18] It was the Governor's task to smash the organic
structure of Xhosa society and integrate its remnants into the brave
new colonial world.

Grey's South African policies were conceived long before he arrived
at the Cape and clearly stated within three weeks of his arrival
(December 1854).[19] They were, predictably, an amplification of the
principles he had enunciated as a young explorer and then tried to
implement in New Zealand. Starting from the assumption that 'human
nature was not confined to the whites'[20] and that the interests of Xhosa
and settlers were complementary and not antagonistic, he proposed a
complete blueprint for the harmonious amalgamation of the conflicting peoples of South Africa. The Xhosa should not be segregated from
the white colonists and left to manage their own affairs as best they
could. This was only storing up trouble for the future, since as long as
the Xhosa lived in a state of 'barbarism', they would inevitably remain
hostile towards the Cape Colony and European civilization generally.
Instead, Grey proposed to extend his influence peacefully by schools,
by hospitals, by public works, by new institutions of government, 'and
thus to change by degrees our at present unconquered and apparently
unreclaimable foes into friends who may have common interests with
ourselves'.[21]

South Africa was not New Zealand, however, and the policies which
Grey had worked with some success in one colonial setting were
bound to fail in the other. This had nothing to do with the cultural
differences between Maori and Xhosa, and everything to do with the
respective exposure of the two peoples to colonial pressure. British
rule in New Zealand was less than ten years old when Grey arrived,

and the Maori people, on the whole, still looked to the British government for protection against the land hunger of the New Zealand Company. Grey was able to exploit this Maori goodwill, and he managed to achieve many of his aims, including land purchase and the extension of British law, through the help of those Maori chiefs whose friendship he had won. This close personal association with individual Maoris tempered Grey's iconoclastic zeal and lent him discretion with regard to many established Maori customs and practices.

The Xhosa, on the other hand, had grown up in the shadow of British colonialism. They hated it and they had fought against it as long as they could. They did not attach much importance to the distinction between British settlers and the British government, which had deprived them of most of their best land in the years between 1812 and 1853. When Grey arrived, the Xhosa were just emerging from the catastrophic defeat of the War of Mlanjeni which dwarfed in death and starvation anything the Maori had yet experienced. The only thing which the Xhosa had salvaged from the wreck of Mlanjeni was the right to govern themselves according to their own laws, and it was precisely this right which Grey was now proposing to withdraw. It would have been beyond the scope of any diplomacy to persuade the Xhosa to renounce their remaining privileges voluntarily, but Grey did not even have the opportunity to exert his famous personal magnetism on the Xhosa chiefs. Through no fault of his own, he was based in Cape Town, more than one thousand kilometres away from British Kaffraria, and his occasional visits to the frontier could not possibly create close relationships of the kind he had enjoyed with the friendly Maori chiefs who buzzed around his home in Auckland. Far more isolated from the Xhosa than he had ever been from the Maori, Grey applied his 'civilization' policy with a rigour untempered by sympathetic restraint.

But back in December 1854, none of this was yet apparent. Grey's major concern was not so much deciding on a course of action — as we have seen, that was all preconceived — but in finding the means of paying the bill for the expensive measures which he contemplated. In all probability he had hoped to winkle the necessary funds out of the Cape Colony's legislature, but when he arrived in Cape Town he found that a much better opportunity had presented itself.

Ever since their victory in the War of Mlanjeni, the minds of the settlers and the colonial administration had been greatly exercised by the problem of the Mfengu people. The Mfengu had fought alongside the colonists during the frontier wars and had been rewarded with some of the best land taken from the Xhosa. Many settlers were deeply aggrieved by this and they were further offended by the Mfengu belief that, as loyal subjects of Queen Victoria, they were entitled to equal rights with their white fellow citizens. Governor Cathcart had admired the Mfengu and advanced their cause, but once Cathcart had departed anti-Mfengu agitation reached rabid proportions in the eastern Cape, where it took the typical frontier form of a war scare.[22] Rumours of a supposed Mfengu-Xhosa alliance panicked the commander of the colonial troops, Sir James Jackson, a doddering old veteran of the Napoleonic Wars who had served alongside Grey's father long before the Governor was even born.

Ever receptive to conspiracy theories, especially when they served his purpose, Grey enthusiastically embraced these rumours of a 'Fingo alliance' against the Colony. He dashed off a letter to the Colonial Office in London in which he greatly exaggerated the threat of a frontier war and pointed out that the last one had cost the British taxpayer more than one million pounds. Never fear, Grey continued, he had a plan which would prevent the war but it needed to be put into effect immediately. It involved putting the Xhosa to labour on public works, establishing schools and hospitals for their benefit and introducing new forms of administration into British Kaffraria. It would only cost £40,000 a year, and since the matter was so urgent and £40,000 was such a small sum by comparison with £1,000,000, Grey felt he should just go ahead and spend the money immediately, leaving the Colonial Office to cope with the small detail of getting the funds approved by Parliament.[23]

The 'Fingo alliance' war scare could not have suited Grey better if he had engineered it himself. He continued to harp on the danger of war until the money was safely in his treasury. As Professor Rutherford put it, the war scare lasted two months longer in Grey's dispatches than it did in the Colony itself. In time to come, Grey's habit of predicting war and bloodshed if he did not get his way became something of a joke in the Colonial Office, but in 1854 they were still mesmerized by Grey's image as a man uniquely able to deal with natives. Even Sir William Molesworth, who was more cynical than the rest, conceded that there could be little harm in allowing Grey to try out his scheme.[24]

After a month's visit to the frontier, Grey was ready to act. He announced his intentions in a speech to the Cape legislature (March 1855) that must surely rank as one of the finest ever made in South Africa. Even a historian conscious of Grey's ethnocentric bias cannot but be struck by the soaring idealism of his words and by the transient beauty of his portrait of a South Africa united in harmony and common purpose.

I would rather that we should, with full but humble confidence, accept the duties and responsibilities of our position, that we should admit that we cannot live in immediate contact with any race or portion of our fellow men, whether civilized or uncivilized, neglecting and ignoring our duties towards them, without suffering those evils which form the fitting punishment of our neglect and indifference; that we should feel that if we leave the natives beyond our border ignorant barbarians, shut out from all community of interest with ourselves, they must always remain a race of troublesome marauders, and that, feeling this, we should try to make them a part of ourselves, with a common faith and common interests, useful servants, consumers of our goods, contributors to our revenue; in short, a source of strength and wealth for this colony, such as Providence designed them to be.

We should, I think, use our time of strength, when our generosity cannot be misunderstood, to instruct and civilize — to change inveterate enemies into friends, alike from interest and increased knowledge — destroyers of our stock and produce into consumers of our goods and producers for our markets.[25]

The references to economic integration with its clear implication of black subordination to white domination will, even in these moving passages, have set warning lights flashing in the minds of many readers. But worse was to come. Grey was a great proponent of colonization, and he maintained that there was plenty of space in the 'fertile' land of British Kaffraria to accommodate 5,000 British ex-soldiers 'of a class fitted to increase our strength in that country'. Grey's vision of a future British Kaffraria was very much that of a mixed settlement colony.

Should this plan be carried out, our ultimate frontier defence would be a fertile and populous country, filled with a large population, partly European, partly native; the Europeans, reared in the country, acquainted with its inhabitants, and their mode of warfare; the natives, won by our exertions to Christianity, trained by us in agriculture and in simple arts, possessing property of their own and a stake in the country, accustomed to our laws and aware of their advantages, attached to us from a sense of benefits received, respecting us for our strength and generosity.

The Governor never got the settlers he wanted, not least because his promise of a cottage and an acre of land did not sufficiently appeal to the British ex-soldier. But he was to be given unexpected opportunities to fill British Kaffraria with settlers of another sort, as we shall see.

For the first few months of his administration, Grey busied himself with the more straightforward aspects of his civilization policy. Public works got off the ground almost immediately. Charles Brownlee, the Ngqika Xhosa Commissioner, was an enthusiast for irrigation and he soon got his men busy cutting water channels, but for the most part the public works consisted of labour on roads through the Amathole Mountains and other hitherto inaccesible parts of Xhosaland. Roadbuilding had a military and strategic relevance beyond its purely economic significance. As Grey boasted to the Colonial Secretary, 'They have in our pay, and organised by us, completely opened up their country by roads made by their own hands — so that the greater part of it can now be traversed by a Military force in any direction.'[26] Even Brownlee's water courses were not without economic significance, as some of Sandile's councillors pointed out, saying that to accept irrigation works in the country of their exile was tantamount to recognizing that they would never regain their old lands in the Amathole.[27]

Wages paid were between 6d and 1s per day, depending on the rank by merit of the worker. Average pay for similar labour within the Colony ranged from 2s to 3s 6d per day, and the prosperous Mfengu refused to work for Grey's low wages. The Xhosa, who were being refused passes to seek work in the Colony, were in no position to complain about the rate of pay. The war and the lungsickness epidemic had impoverished most of the homestead heads, and as soon as word of the 'public works' got out, many Xhosa began eagerly to volunteer. Brownlee was soon turning away hundreds of applicants, and the speed of recruitment was limited only by the lack of available white supervisors. Grey was delighted by the success of his scheme, having anticipated a great deal of trouble from the alleged barbarous laziness of the Xhosa. In fact, the Xhosa had always been willing to work in return for adequate incentives. That they were turning out for his public works only because they had no other alternative to destitution never occurred to Grey. He thought it was a sign that they were becoming civilized already.[28]

Grey's plans for Xhosa education were not exactly new. Sir Harry Smith had something similar in mind in 1848 when he invited suggestions 'to inspire in the [Xhosa] a desire to cultivate their lands by ploughing and to induce them to follow habits of industry, the first steps to civilization.'[29] Robert Gray, the Bishop of Cape Town, had been advocating industrial schools and hospitals since the late 1840s. Governor Cathcart had supported such proposals but lacked the £1,000 a year he thought necessary. Grey, on the other hand, had £40,000 a year, and he was prepared to spend a large percentage of it on education. He toured the mission stations of the eastern Cape on his first visit to the frontier, accompanied by a Maori evangelist, who assured his awe-struck Xhosa hearers that the Maori had been cannibals until they were saved for civilization 'through the Missionaries, and [pointing to Grey] the kindness of this man'.[30] Grey himself was optimistic and excited, selecting the sites of the buildings he wanted erected and sketching out the plans for them himself. For the missionaries, long starved of official encouragement, Grey was a Moses and his £40,000 a year manna from heaven. Grey's major worry was that the existing missions were 'too bookish', and, though he was prepared to concede that the main purpose of the missions should remain the training of teachers and evangelists, he was concerned to create industrial schools for the better promotion of his 'useful servants' economic policy. Five missions were selected and set to work teaching the Xhosa the 'more useful mechanical arts' such as masonry, tailoring, carpentry, shoemaking and waggon-making. Girls were taught needlework and domestic skills. Grey was unusually concerned with female education, not because he was a feminist but because, as a social engineer, he was concerned that his new breed of Europeanized black males should have correctly educated wives and mothers to provide a proper degree of civilization in the home.[31]

Grey's hopes for self-sufficient industrial schools soon degenerated into meaningless hard labour. The 'pupils' at one of the schools found that their 'industrial education' took the form of three hours work a day on the mission farm, while those at another school found that the teacher's income depended on selling the items which they produced. Except for the Presbyterian Mission at Lovedale, none of the 'industrial schools' managed to survive the withdrawal of the British government subsidy in the 1860s.[32]

Grey also wanted to create an elite school for chiefs' children in Cape Town, where they might learn to appreciate the extent of Britain's wealth and power, grow up in a fully 'civilized' environment, and become entirely divorced from their own culture and its attendant habits. But none of the chiefs with whom Grey discussed the matter were prepared to consider giving up their children. Not yet.[33]

Grey's health programme was perhaps the one unqualified success of his policy, and, as far as the Xhosa were concerned, its one unqualified benefit. The Governor was, of course, aware of the important part played by the Xhosa doctors (*amagqirha*) in supporting the political authority of the chiefs, and he laid particular stress on their role in accusing witches and confiscating property. Emphasizing this aspect but ignoring the very positive role played by Xhosa doctors in the social, psychological and, indeed, medical spheres, Grey naturally believed that the visible proof of the power of European medicine would concretely demonstrate the material superiority of

European science over Xhosa superstition. In Dr J.P. Fitzgerald, who followed him from New Zealand, Grey possessed a disciple who shared all his high ideals but lacked his deviousness and his egotism. Fitzgerald was soon treating fifty patients a day, examining a total of 6,000 or more in his first ten months. He had been trained in opthalmic surgery, and his cataract operations gave him the reputation among the Xhosa of a man who could restore the sight of the blind. The Xhosa doctors were sufficiently impressed to visit Fitzgerald's practice, and Fitzgerald himself was sufficiently broad-minded to treat his Xhosa equivalents as fellow practitioners. Inasmuch as the Xhosa were able to swallow Fitzgerald's medicine without in any way giving up their beliefs in the powers of the Xhosa doctors, the great contest between science and superstition which Grey had envisaged never occurred. On the other hand, Fitzgerald's personal influence on those Xhosa who worked for him as assistants was profound, and was largely responsible for keeping Ned and Kona, Chief Maqoma's sons, out of the Cattle-Killing.[34]

Grey was also eager to alter land tenure arrangements in British Kaffraria in order to introduce 'individual tenure' and thus give the Xhosa homestead head a 'stake in the country' independent of his chief. Like so many of Grey's other proposals, this was nothing new and had been implemented already by Governor Cathcart at the instigation of certain missionaries. Measures were initiated among the Mfengu to define private plots and lay them out in villages. But even Grey appreciated the explosive consequences of premature interference in Xhosa land rights and held his fire on the subject for the time being.[35]

3. Cutting Down the Chiefs

Grey knew, and so did everybody else, that his measures concerning health, education and public works could only be effective in the long term, and that the £40,000 a year he had extorted from the British government required tangible results almost immediately. Something needed to be done to reduce visibly the power of the Xhosa chiefs in British Kaffraria, in particular to remove their capacity to launch another frontier war.

This was not going to be easy. It was the assault on Sandile's chieftainship that had precipitated the War of Mlanjeni, a fact that even Sir Harry Smith realized, for within a week of its outbreak he ordered Commissioner Maclean to inform all those chiefs who had not yet entered the war that he would henceforth allow them to 'govern

Above
Nonkosi. Nongqawuse. Sarhili, King of the Xhosa.

Below
Mhlakaza's residence in Grahamstown.

4

6

5

Above
Sir Harry Smith
Below
Sir George Cathcart

Right
Colonel William Eyre
Opposite page
Detachment of 2nd or Queen's Regiment
surrounded — Fish River Bush by T. Baines

Four believers

Above
Sandhile. Mhala.

Below
Fadana, leader of the Thembu's believers.
Phatho.

12

13

15

Above
Anta. Kama.

Below
Toyise. Dyani Tshatshu.

14

Four Unbelievers

16   17

Left
Sir George Grey, Governor and High
Commissioner.

Right
Colonel John Maclean, Chief Commissioner of
British Kaffraria

Above
Charles Brownlee, Gaita Commissioner. Walter
Currie, Commandant of the Frontier Armed
and Mounted Police.

Below
Major John Gawler, Magistrate with Mhala.
Captain Frederick Reeve, Magistrate with
Kama.

Above
Xhosa Chiefs on Robben Island.

Below
(left to right) Maqoma, Siyolo, Xhexho after
their release from Robben Island in 1869.

their people according to their own laws and customs'. After Smith's dismissal, Governor Cathcart asked Maclean to repeat these assurances in his name and 'to express his [Cathcart's] determination not to interfere with their native laws and customs'. Cathcart viewed Smith's 'absurd' interference with Xhosa custom as the main cause of his downfall, and based his entire administrative policy on the principle of government through the chiefs. When peace was made in March 1853, Cathcart 'formally stated to [the Xhosa chiefs] that henceforth the chiefs should be allowed to govern their people according to their own laws'. 'Do not let us revert to the old policy of lowering the chief in the eyes of his people,' he cautioned Maclean. 'We must on the contrary support him [the chief] and govern the people through him.'[36]

So unwilling was Cathcart to upset the chiefs, that he bluntly informed the missionaries that the government would do nothing to help them. Even when Chief Mhala executed some of his followers for witchcraft shortly after the peace of 1853, Cathcart did not flinch.

> As to witchcraft and chiefs eating their people up — we really must not attempt to alter the customs of the people unnecessarily, and when we have not the power. — Witchcraft was punished in England, and recognized by law as late as the time of James Ist, and even much later, suspected old women were hardly dealt with in England.—
>
> We must not get back into the old attempt to weaken the power of the chief, and set up his own people against him, we have seen enough to teach us that this will not do.[37]

These principles and these promises, Grey now proceeded to trample underfoot.

Inevitably, relations between Grey and the Xhosa chiefs got off to a bad start. The Ngqika Xhosa longed for the lands they had lost through the War of Mlanjeni, and hoped against hope that they might get them back. Governor Cathcart had promised, at the peace conference, to send on their supplications to Queen Victoria, and although the British treated this as a mere formality, the Xhosa set great store by it. They still remembered that a change of British government policy in 1836 had returned to them the lands they had lost through the Frontier War of 1834-5,[38] and they hoped that somehow the miracle might be repeated. Grey naturally brought no such good news, and was thus bound to disappoint Xhosa expectations no matter what he did. Advised by the local officials to avoid the great public meetings in which Sir Harry Smith had so foolishly indulged himself, Grey adopted a policy of never formally meeting with the chiefs as a group. The Ngqika Xhosa chiefs were obliged to wait at a military post for five days to see the Governor as he passed by, and when he eventually did appear he had nothing positive to tell them. Grey declined even to discuss the land issue with the anxious chiefs, pleading his ignorance of the matter, and insisting on receiving their request in writing. The message, sent in Sandile's name, spoke for all the chiefs.

> Sandile says: am I not your child? Why when I am punished am I deprived of my people? Why am I severed from the grave of my father? The inheritance of a chief is not cattle, it is lands and men, saying this, I pray to you my father to whom I have been given. I have no other word. I ask alone for land.[39]

Far from considering how best to restore the Xhosa to their mountain strongholds, Grey was busy devising a method which would still further break down their resistance. After much thought and enquiry, he correctly identified the material basis of the Xhosa chiefs' power as the legal fees and fines which they collected in their judicial capacities as arbiters of Xhosa law.[40] Not only did this source of private revenue render the chiefs economically independent of colonial pressure but, Grey argued, it encouraged witchcraft accusations by means of which the wealth of the alleged witches passed into the hands of the chiefs and their immediate associates.

> No sooner, therefore, does a person grow rich, than he is almost certain to be accused of this offence, and is, at least stripped of all he possesses.
> It is impossible that people subjected to such a system can ever advance in civilization, or long persevere in attempting honestly to acquire property, of which they are almost certain ultimately to be stripped at the caprice of the chief and his counsellors.

While it might have been true that witchcraft accusations inhibited the development of a class of small capitalists such as Grey desired to see arising among the Xhosa, it should be remembered that executions for witchcraft, though spectacular, were of comparatively rare occurrence in Xhosaland. There had been only two such occasions in British Kaffraria since the peace of 1853, and whole years might pass by without a single witchcraft death.[41] Grey was, as usual, exaggerating for the benefit of the Colonial Secretary in London. The thrust of Grey's policy was, however, quite in accordance with the principles he had consistently argued since his youthful memorandum of 1840, that no non-European race could ever progress as long as their ancient customs remained in force, and that the imposition of British law was necessary to free the progressive individual from the chains of the precolonial social structure and enable him to adopt the British version of civilization.

Grey now proposed, in his own words, to 'gradually undermine and destroy' Xhosa laws and customs by replacing the Xhosa chiefs' rights to judicial fees and fines with a fixed monthly income in colonial money which would, again in Grey's words, make the chiefs financially 'dependent on the Government of the country'. The councillors, who assisted their chiefs in return for a share in the judicial fines, would likewise receive salaries and would thus likewise become dependent on the government rather than on their chiefs. The chiefs and their councillors would still judge legal cases, but they were to be 'assisted in their deliberations and sentences' by a British magistrate, specially chosen from 'the ablest [white] men this country affords'.

> European laws will, by imperceptible degrees, take the place of their own barbarous customs, and any [Xhosa] chief of importance will be daily brought into contact with a talented and honourable European gentleman, who will hourly interest himself in the advance and improvement of the entire tribe, and must in process of time gain an influence over the native races, which will produce very beneficial results.[42]

The existing situation in British Kaffraria, Grey wrote, was no better than an 'armed truce' which must sooner or later dissolve in another war. Only a complete revolution in Xhosa thought and government offered the stable basis of common interests necessary for a lasting peace.

Chief Commissioner Maclean protested in vain that Grey's new system broke Cathcart's promise to respect chiefly prerogatives and threatened the peace of the country.[43] The friendly Mfengu were conceivably ready for Grey's suggested measures, but the Xhosa were unwilling to be 'civilized' and they were not yet sufficiently conquered in body or in spirit to permit the colonial government to impose its wishes by force. However much the Xhosa commoners might resent individual chiefs, they nevertheless clung to the political institution of chieftainship 'as a power which is of and which represents themselves and their race'. Maclean concluded by strongly recommending that the Governor defer his proposed innovations to some future time.

Grey swept these objections imperiously aside. Every argument which he heard in contradiction of his cherished plans only served to reinforce his belief in their essential rightness.[44] He wanted them adopted as soon as possible. He told Maclean, quite untruthfully, that his official dispatch was already sent off to England, and that the Chief Commissioner's objections 'put a rope around his [Grey's] neck'. 'You [Maclean] must endeavour to induce [the Xhosa chiefs] one by one to adopt the proposed system,' he ordered bluntly.

The Xhosa chiefs did not, in fact, put up the stiff resistance to Grey's system that Maclean and the other local officials had expected.[45] They were naturally reluctant to give a flat refusal to any proposal of government, they temporized, and they were lost. Instead of contesting the central principle of the new proposals, they contested minor details such as the disposition of fines for murder. Instead of refusing a magistrate outright, they agreed to the suggestion but asked that it be a person of their own choosing. Instead of taking the responsibility on themselves, they procrastinated, each waiting to see what the other chiefs would do. Maclean and his subordinates were able to play on these internal divisions, and by getting some chiefs to accept the system, isolated others who wished to oppose it. Some of the more cunning chiefs seem to have thought that they could manage to keep the money but contrive to evade the interference of the magistrate. The generous salaries (£96 per year for Sandile, for example, and £180 per year for his councillors) were great inducements to many chiefs, whose revenues had suffered from the impoverishment of their followers and who had, moreover, acquired a taste for alcohol satiable only through colonial money. Both Sandile and Maqoma 'were anxious to finger the silver as soon as possible', according to Commissioner Brownlee. It was the councillors, not the chiefs who raised the most pertinent objections.

> [Old Soga, Sandile's councillor] was particularly strong in his opposition to the measure, as breaking down the customs of the [Xhosa], depriving the chiefs of the concession which Sir George Cathcart had made them of governing their people according to their own laws, that the receipt of money would bring the chiefs into trouble . . . .
>
> It was also asked why the Governor wished to change the present system, who had complained of it, and if he could change what Sir George Cathcart had conceded to them why cannot he change what the former Governor had done with regard to the land, and restore their country to them.[46]

Unfortunately for the Xhosa, this sort of forthright opposition on principle was the exception rather than the rule. The chiefs' petty objections were overridden one by one, and the first of the new magistrates took up their posts in November 1855.

British Kaffraria now hovered on the brink of the great catastrophe with which this book is primarily concerned. Before we proceed, let us take advantage of this pause, while Grey's magistrates are, as it were, riding out to meet their chiefs, to introduce the main actors in the forthcoming drama.

Grey could have had no more ideal subordinate in British Kaffraria than its Chief Commissioner, John Maclean, a Highland Scot who had

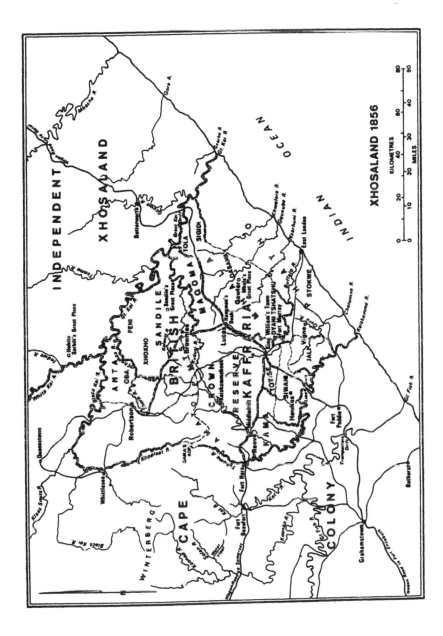

Map 2: Xhosaland, 1856

served in the eastern Cape since 1835. It was largely through Maclean's adroit management that almost all the Ndlambe Xhosa remained neutral during the War of Mlanjeni, and Governor Cathcart rewarded him in 1852 with the Chief Commissionership. Sharing as he did Cathcart's view that the power of the Xhosa chiefs should be respected, Maclean received Grey's instructions for the 'better management' of British Kaffraria with horror and resentment. Aware, however, that he would bear the blame for any failure, Maclean worked hard to make Grey's system a success.[47] As the events of 1856-8 unfolded, revealing that Grey was no woolly philanthropist but a ruthless imperialist, the Chief Commissioner warmed to his task. Maclean was no liberal; he never liked the Xhosa and he never learned to speak their language. But he had an intimate and shrewd appreciation of Xhosa politics and personalities, which enabled him to direct Grey's blows where they would hurt most. Moreover, he was infinitely loyal and obedient to the Governor, qualities which were very important to Grey.

The next most senior official in British Kaffraria was the Ngqika Commissioner, Charles Brownlee. The son of a missionary, Brownlee had grown up among the Ngqika Xhosa and spoke their language fluently. His reputation as a great administrator, which rests mainly on the continuing popularity of his book, *Reminiscences of Kaffir Life and History*, is greatly exaggerated. Brownlee was a passionate advocate of the advance of European civilization, and he did not understand the Xhosa nearly as well as he thought he did. His intimate knowledge of the personal and political affairs of most Ngqika Xhosa earned him their resentment rather than, as he ingenuously thought, their love. Nevertheless, Brownlee was, by the standards of his time and place, a humane and liberal official, who genuinely liked the Xhosa and sincerely wanted to see them happy. Maclean despised him for being 'soft' on the Xhosa and resented his superior knowledge of the Xhosa world, but could not do without his assistance. Brownlee's role under Sir George Grey personifies the dangerous trap which the liberal government official poses to a colonized people. On the one hand, Brownlee's advice was disregarded by Grey and Maclean while, on the other hand, his obviously genuine sympathy and concern were most effective in getting the Xhosa to accept policies which neither he nor they liked or wanted.[48]

Brownlee naturally fitted into Grey's new dispensation as the magistrate with Sandile, the highest ranking Xhosa chief in British Kaffraria. Chief Sandile was neither particularly clever nor particularly brave, he had a dread of making decisions or taking responsibility, and he had a club foot. But for all that, he was deeply respected by his people and was possibly the best loved of all the Xhosa chiefs. Sandile was extremely amenable to popular feeling and exceptionally generous with his cattle.[49] He never took a decision without consulting all his councillors and, as far as possible, all his people as well. His word, when it finally came forth, was usually at one with the popular will. Although Sandile's proceedings were thus democratic in the extreme, it is not unfair to say that when confronted by challenges such as Grey's new system or the Cattle-Killing which followed hard on its heels, Sandile failed to give his people the sort of lead that they required, and simply drifted from crisis to crisis, inevitably running aground on the rocks and getting the worst of all possible worlds. Besides Sandile, Charles Brownlee also acted as magistrate for his brother Xhoxho and his nephew Feni, both of them chiefs of little weight.

Second in rank to Sandile among the Ngqika Xhosa was Maqoma, the hero of the Waterkloof and the greatest fighting general the Xhosa ever produced. Maqoma was everything that Sandile was not — brave, intelligent, strong-minded and decisive. He was also more than twenty years older than Sandile, but through the lower rank of his mother, he was inferior by birth to his despised younger brother. As a young man, Maqoma had shown some interest in Christianity and English culture, but these inclinations had been quickly killed off by the colonial authorities, who expelled him from his native valley in 1829 and chased him out of his refuge near Fort Beaufort in 1853. Frustrated thus in every direction, Maqoma's behaviour became increasingly erratic, which greatly reduced his popularity among the ordinary Xhosa. Lieutenant Henry Lucas, the young officer appointed as magistrate to Maqoma and his neighbour, the eighty-year-old Bhotomane of the small imiDange chiefdom, was contemptuously ignored by both chiefs and exerted no influence whatsoever on either of them.[50]

Anta, the other of Sandile's brothers to get a magistrate, was a capable man, but of low rank on account of the low status of his mother. Anta had formerly lived with Sandile and had been his close associate up to the time of Mlanjeni. The brothers had quarrelled during the war, and Anta had become bitterly disillusioned with Xhosa traditions on account of the failure of Mlanjeni's promises. After the peace of 1853, he took up residence high in the Windvogelberg in the extreme north of the Ngqika country. He welcomed his magistrate, a Scottish officer named Eustace Robertson, because it accorded him a status he did not possess by birth. Near Anta lived his nephew, the young chief Oba.[51]

The Gqunukhwebe Xhosa chief Phatho who had resided with Maclean throughout the recent war, a semi-hostage for his people's good behaviour, and the young Ndlambe chief Jali were placed in the hands of Herbert Vigne, a young gentleman from the western Cape and the only one of Grey's appointees who was not a military officer. Vigne was not incapable and he worked himself hard, but Phatho was a very popular chief and too skilled in the art of dissimulation to permit him any measure of control. With Phatho lived his brother-in-law, Stokwe, chief of the small amaMbalu chiefdom, who had lost all his lands and most of his people in the Fish River bush. Phatho's younger brother, the model Christian chief Kama, received the Ngqika Xhosa lands around Middledrift as a reward for his pro-colonial stance. He and his immediate followers were fiercely loyal to the British government, but there were too few of them to fill up the whole of their vast district and their ranks were augmented by large numbers of Phatho's land-hungry followers, headed by his son Mate and his brother Lama. The magistrate at Middledrift was Captain Frederick Reeve, a tough product of Colonel Eyre's dreaded 73rd Regiment.[52]

The Ngqika Xhosa chiefs had all lost their lands on account of the War of Mlanjeni. The Ndlambe Xhosa, under Maclean's guiding hand, had remained neutral and thus in possession of their lands — with the sole exception of Siyolo, now expiating his error on Robben Island in the far western Cape. Siwani, Siyolo's unpopular senior brother and a long-time colonial client, had his own magistrate, Major Robert Hawkes. Toyise, a usurper dependent on colonial support, and Dyani Tshatshu, a Christian chief much distrusted by Maclean, lived close to King William's Town and were cared for part-time by two British Kaffraria officials. The key to the Ndlambe district was Mhala, the senior Ndlambe Xhosa chief. A man of lowly birth, Mhala had risen to eminence by cunning and deceit. He was an enthusiastic prosecutor of witchcraft cases and an acquisitive predator of his followers' cattle. Among colonial officials, Mhala was renowned for never giving a straight answer to any question and for his bad habit of feigning illness in awkward situations. Mhala was very nearly killed during the War of Axe, and had a deep and bitter hatred of the colonial government and all its works. He had strongly urged his followers to join in the War of Mlanjeni, but was frustrated by some of his senior councillors and by the influence of Maclean.[53] In Major John Cox Gawler, Colonel Eyre's former adjutant, Mhala found a magistrate worthy of his steel. The battle between them was to be of titanic proportions and of profound importance to the future of British Kaffraria.

This section would not be complete without a reminder to the reader that not all of Xhosaland belonged to Great Britain. Colonial domination was confined to British Kaffraria, that is the territory west of the Great Kei River. All the chiefs of the Ngqika and the Ndlambe Xhosa who inhabited British Kaffraria were descendants of the Chief Rharhabe, who died in 1782, and therefore junior in rank to the descendants of Rharhabe's senior brother Gcaleka (d. 1778) who lived and reigned in independent Xhosaland across the Kei. Sarhili, great-grandson of Gcaleka and King of all the Xhosa, lived at Hohita just beyond the borders of British territory. Sarhili's influence over the Xhosa chiefs in British Kaffraria was enormous in theory though limited in practice. He was the great judge of the Xhosa nation, the arbiter of disputes between the chiefs and the ultimate authority on all matters relating to Xhosa custom and religion. He even had the right, though only in theory, to call out the whole Xhosa nation for the purposes of war.[54] In precolonial times, the powers of the Xhosa King had been resisted by the Ngqika and Ndlambe Xhosa chiefs. But now, suffering as they were under the sway of colonialism, the eyes of the Xhosa of British Kaffraria turned increasingly for guidance to Sarhili, their King across the river Kei.

4. The Russians are Coming

The arrival of Grey's magistrates passed off without undue difficulty. Sandile and the other Ngqika Xhosa were accustomed to Commissioner Brownlee, who eased the transition to the new system by giving Sandile the councillors' salaries to distribute as he pleased. Anta, pleased to have his autonomy recognized, humoured Magistrate Robertson's attempts to make him wear the Highland kilt.[55] Kama, Siwani, Toyise and the other pro-government chiefs settled down without difficulty. Maqoma and Bhotomane protested vigorously but too late. Maqoma claimed that he had only accepted a magistrate on condition he got his old land back, and Bhotomane was suspicious of the bribe offered in the form of colonial money. 'I have known you for many years,' the old chief said to one colonial official. 'Tell me truly, is there nothing will come after we have taken the money?' Mhala was similarly recalcitrant, insisting again and again on his right to choose his own magistrate. Magistrate Gawler was forced to wait nearly two months at a nearby mission station until Mhala, isolated by the capitulation of the other chiefs, finally agreed to receive him.[56]

But it was probably the reaction of Chief Phatho, of all the chiefs, that was most significant. Phatho and his people did not want a magistrate, but they were too distracted by another and seemingly more potent threat even to notice the arrival of Magistrate Vigne. 'I tried to introduce Mr Vigne to them,' reported one official, ' but all they could talk about was lungsickness.'[57]

This dreaded cattle disease, which already had killed off hundreds of thousands of cattle in Europe, was brought to South Africa in September 1853 by a Dutch ship carrying Friesland bulls to Mossel Bay, a small port between Port Elizabeth and Cape Town. Starting off as little more than a dry, husky cough, lungsickness slowly tightened its grip on the hapless beasts it destroyed, bringing to them a lingering and uniquely horrible death. The cough gradually increased in severity, forcing the animals to stretch forward with their front legs wide apart, their heads extended and their tongues protruding, gasping for air. Yellowish fluid crept over their lungs which stuck to their ribs, and as the disease spread, the cattle putrefied from the inside out, becoming first constipated and then diarrheoatic. In their final agony, the beasts were unable to move or lie down at all. Their nostrils dilated for lack of air, their muzzles frothed with saliva until, unable to eat, they wasted away and died mere skeletons.[58]

The Cape government hurriedly issued regulations to check the spread of the disease, but there was no stopping it. Farmers who were only too eager to shoot other people's lungsick cattle did their best to hide the fact when lungsickness appeared in their own herds. No one could tell whether it was endemic or infectious, or whether innoculation halted it or helped it spread. Bleeding, the normal treatment for lung ailments, only made it worse.[59] It was difficult to diagnose the disease with any certainty until a beast was so far gone that the rest of the herd were likewise infected. Worst of all, the virtually invisible lungsickness bacteria could lodge for very long periods in the lungs of a beast without manifesting themselves. Secretly infected cattle thus mingled freely with uninfected animals and, in some cases, laid whole herds low some eighteen months after the owners believed that the danger was past. It was thus impossible to control the disease, or even to know where or when it would strike next.

Lungsickness spread like an evil fire as infected oxen transported it along the waggon roads of the Cape Colony. By March 1854 it had reached Uitenhage, whence a Mfengu travelling with five cattle brought it to Fort Beaufort on the borders of Xhosaland. From Fort Beaufort it passed through Chief Kama's territory on its way to King William's Town, the capital of British Kaffraria (March 1855). From King William's Town it spread through the coastal territories of Chiefs Phatho and Mhala, and along the waggon road to Natal, passing Maqoma's and reaching Butterworth in King Sarhili's country in

January 1856. Last to be affected were the Ngqika Xhosa under Chiefs Sandile, Xhoxho and Feni, protected by their distant location north of King William's Town. High up in the Windvogelberg in the extreme north, Chief Anta was lucky enough to escape the disease altogether (see Map 4 on p.167).[60]

The Xhosa could see the disease coming and took all the precautions they could to escape from it. They drove their precious cattle to mountainous and secluded places. They quarantined all strange and colonial cattle within their borders and prohibited the introduction of others. They fenced kilometre after kilometre of pasturage, and burnt the grass all around the perimeter until the night sky was illuminated by the reflection of the flames. Infected carcasses were buried deep in the ground, and most Xhosa refused to eat the meat. King Sarhili and the other chiefs executed men caught infringing these regulations, but there were always some individuals who hoped that their lungsick cattle might yet recover and thus contributed to the further spread of the disease.[61]

Xhosa losses from lungsickness ran at about 5,000 cattle a month, and in some areas approximately two out of every three cattle died. Some homesteads escaped relatively lightly, but others lost absolutely everything they had. Reliable figures from Phatho's chiefdom give us some indication of the catastrophe. The chief himself lost 2400 out of 2500 cattle, his Great Son Dilima lost 60 out of 70, his brother Kobe 130 out of 150, and his brother-in-law Stokwe all of 110. A passing official described the scene in Phatho's country, later a stronghold of the Cattle-Killing movement.

> The utmost destitution prevails throughout the country we traversed; they have lost nearly all their cattle. . . . Those who have a few cattle are slaughtering them rather than run the risk of losing them by lung-sickness.[62]

To make matters even worse, the maize was blighted by a species of grub which penetrated the roots and destroyed the stalks before the corn was edible. Excessive rains rotted many of the surviving fields, and even the birds were more destructive than usual that season.[63] Truly, it seemed as if nature herself was in league with the enemies of the Xhosa.

Nothing like this had ever happened before. The Xhosa subsided into a mood which one observer described as 'depression and a sense of great loss'. Their thoughts turned naturally towards the possibility that the disease might have been caused by malevolent witchcraft. Sarhili put more than twenty witches to death across the Kei river but even these harsh measures failed to halt the epidemic.[64]

Despair often lapses into apathy and inactivity, but a little hope can ignite it with an explosive force. That hope was supplied to the Xhosa people early in November 1854 when the luck of 'Old Boots' Cathcart, the somewhat fortunate victor of the War of Mlanjeni, finally ran out. Having charged out in the wrong direction during one of the battles in the Crimean War, Cathcart suddenly found himself virtually alone and utterly surrounded by the Russian army. 'I fear,' he said with fine understatement, 'we are in a mess.' A moment later he was dead.[65]

The death in battle of their former Governor spread among the Xhosa with a speed that few Europeans could credit. The Xhosa had never heard of Russia; much less did they understand the obscure causes of the Crimean War. All they knew was that these mysterious 'Russians' had killed Sir George Cathcart and put the British army on the defensive. Who were these Russians? What weapons did they fight with? What colour were they? The colonial answer that the Russians were white like themselves and that the British were winning was received with polite scepticism.[66] Two runaway settlers who fled to independent Xhosaland to escape their creditors were rumoured to be deserters from the defeated British army. The Russians, it gradually came to be believed, were not a white nation at all but a black one, the spirits of Xhosa warriors who had died fighting in the various wars against the Colony. For months after the news of Cathcart's death, the Xhosa posted lookouts on the higher hills to watch for the arrival of the Russian ships.[67]

In Sarhili's country across the Kei, Mjuza, the son of the prophet Nxele, announced that his father had not drowned escaping from Robben Island but was leading the conquering black army across the sea. Mlanjeni, too, was believed to have risen from the dead.

> [Sarhili's people] firmly believe that . . . the sickness among the cattle was predicted by the prophet [Mlanjeni], and that he can bring all their cattle to life again, that there has been a general resurrection of the [Xhosa] killed in the last war, and that the nation we are now fighting with are not Russians but [Xhosa].[68]

By the summer of 1855, more than five prophets had sprung up within British Kaffraria itself, asserting that they were in contact with the black nation across the sea, who were on their way to help the Xhosa. In the meantime, the people should refrain from cultivating and should kill cattle. The most renowned of these early prophets was the wife of Councillor Bhulu in Kama's chiefdom.

> [The wife of Bhulu] predicts that at the Tabendoda [mountain] will be provided an inexhaustible supply of skins of wild animals prepared for wearing as well as ornaments of every description . . . . [She] exhorts

the [Xhosa] to lay aside their witchcraft in order that the good time may come, and she has dug a trench round her hut into which will fall those who are guilty of witchcraft.[69]

Another prophetess, the daughter-in-law of Petsheni, ordered the Xhosa to kill cattle, as more would be provided, and to buy new axes to build new cattle enclosures which would be filled with cattle at the appointed time. All the early prophets were vigorously anti-white, saying, 'Do not align yourselves with the whites because they crucified His son, and you will be punished if you join them.'

Chief Phatho, who had lost 96 per cent of his cattle by lungsickness, heeded these prophets and declined to cultivate in the spring of 1855, and so did many of the people of the worst affected districts.[70] By March 1856, however, the excitement seemed to be subsiding. The wife of Bhulu was unwise enough to set a date for the great day, and her influence declined when it passed without event. The Russians made peace with Britain, and the Crimean War came to an end.

But all the elements of the great Cattle-Killing movement were already in place. Everywhere in Xhosaland, the homestead heads gazed at their favourite cattle, wondering whether to slaughter them before the plague of lungsickness rendered them utterly useless. At the Great Places of the chiefs, Sir George Grey's magistrates took up their positions, visible symbols of colonial domination and concrete warnings of further oppression to come. The minds of the people were filled with ideas of a mysterious black race across the sea, newly resurrected from the dead.

And then, one day in April 1856, down by the Gxarha River in the country of King Sarhili, a young girl went out to the cultivated fields to scare the birds away from the standing corn. Her name was Nongqawuse. Her parents were dead. She lived with her uncle Mhlakaza, once known as Wilhelm Goliath, the former servant of Archdeacon Merriman.

Notes

1. Sinclair (1961), p.33. The standard biography, that of Rutherford (1961) is detailed and helpful but bends over backwards to present Grey in a favourable light. The early biographies, Rees (1892), Milne (1899) and Henderson (1907), are frankly idolatrous. One must turn to the specialist studies of periods in New Zealand's history for a more critical view. See especially Dalton (1967), Wards (1968) and Ward (1974). Australian

historians such as Clark (1973) are even more critical.

2. Rutherford (1961), p.303; Thornton (1983).

3. For example, Milne (1899), p.57; Rutherford (1961), p.276.

4. For example, Merriman (1969), p.63; Stanford (1958), pp.102-3; Brookes (1974), pp.25-8.

5. Dalton (1967), p.259.

6. For Grey's reference to Carlyle, see Rutherford (1961), p.283, and for his close friendship with Carlyle and his fellow hero-worshipper, Froude, see Milne (1899). For an excellent discussion of hero-worship in Victorian England, see Houghton (1957), Ch. 12, from which the quotations cited have been taken. In fairness to Grey, it should be said that he did not share Carlyle's racist views, and that most of his ideas were taken from Utilitarians such as Bentham and J.S. Mill, who were anathema to the Romantic Carlyle. But on the subject of the absolute rule of the ablest man, there can be no doubt of Grey's standpoint.

7. The main direct evidence bearing on this point is Grey's advice to a subordinate in New Zealand, 'Whenever you feel downhearted in your work, a little medicine would always set you right.' Gorst (1908), p.226. The rest is conjecture, based on Grey's clearly erratic behaviour.

8. Rutherford (1961), Ch. 2; *Australian Dictionary of Biography* (1966), pp.476-80.

9. Imperial Blue Book 311 of 1841, pp.43-7.

10. Grey (1841), pp.217-8; Grey (1855), pp.xii-xiii. Thornton (1983), pp.86-7, argues that Grey sought a clue to the nature of creation through his ethnological researches. But he does not mention the introduction to Grey (1855), nor has he come to terms with Grey's practice as opposed to Grey's rhetoric.

11. The link between Grey and Utilitarianism is fascinating and the resemblance between Grey's personality and that of the Victorian reformer Edwin Chadwick is startling, but these details cannot be explored here. On India, see the admirable work by E. Stokes (1959).

12. Ward (1974), pp.34, 62.

13. Ward (1974), pp.89-90.

14. Wards (1968), p.391.

15. *Australian Dictionary of Biography* (1966), p.479; Gorst (1908), p.168; Waterhouse (1984), p.6.

16. Imperial Blue Book 1969 of 1855, Grey's Speech to the Cape parliament, enclosed in G. Grey-G. Grey, 17 March 1855, p.56.

17. Imperial Blue Book 2096 of 1856, J. Maclean-W. Liddle, 4 Aug. 1855, p.18.

18. Imperial Blue Book 1969 of 1855, G. Grey-G. Grey, 22 Dec. 1854, pp.36-8.

19. Grey wrote to Cathcart as early as October 1852, suggesting to him that the schemes he had introduced in New Zealand be applied at the Cape. Du Toit (1954), p.238. For Grey's first dispatches to the Colonial Office outlining the policies he intended to follow, see Imperial Blue Book 1969 of 1855, Grey-Grey, 22 Dec. 1854, pp. 36-8 and for his speech to the Cape parliament, see Note 16 above.

20. In a comment to the pro-settler Civil Commissioner of Fort Beaufort. T. Stringfellow-R. Godlonton, 3 Dec. 1858, Godlonton Papers, University of the Witwatersrand.

21. Imperial Blue Book 1969 of 1855, G. Grey-G. Grey, 22 Dec. 1854, pp.36-8.

22. The whole scare was based on the marriage of Sandile, the senior Ngqika Xhosa chief, to a daughter of the Mfengu chief Njokweni, and on some drunken comments made by Njokweni at a beer drink. For a full report on the matter, see the special report by H. Calderwood, 22 Jan. 1855, enclosed in Imperial Blue Book 1969 of 1855, G. Grey-G. Grey, 29 Jan. 1855, pp.42-51.
23. Imperial Blue Book 1969 of 1855, G. Grey-G. Grey, 22 Dec. 1854, pp.36-8.
24. Rutherford (1961), pp.304, 311.
25. Imperial Blue Book 1969 of 1855, Address to the Legislative Council and the House of Assembly at the Opening of the Second Session of the Colonial Parliament, enclosed in G. Grey-G. Grey, 17 March 1855, pp. 56-9.
26. GH 23/27 G. Grey-H. Labouchere, 19 Jan. 1857.
27. Imperial Blue Book 2096 of 1856, C. Brownlee-J. Maclean, 30 May 1855, p.19.
28. BK 24 J. Ayliff-J. Maclean, 15 March 1856; BK 70 C. Brownlee-J. Maclean, 20 May 1855; *Grahamstown Journal*, 1 March 1856; Imperial Blue Book 1969 of 1855, J. Maclean-W. Liddle, 26 March 1855, pp.65-6, and 2096 of 1856, G. Grey-J. Russell, 19 July 1855, p.8.
29. H. Smith, quoted in Du Toit (1954), p.233. For a convenient summary of progress in this area during the time of Smith and Cathcart, see Du Toit (1954), Ch. 15. For references to specifically industrial training, see Dodd (1938), Ch. 1.
30. Healdtown (1955), p.12.
31. This point has been well made by Weldon (1984), p.41.
32. Dodd (1938), Ch. 1.
33. J. Hodgson (1979), pp.127-8.
34. Fitzgerald's fascinating correspondence has been preserved in BK 100. For an example, see J. Fitzgerald-J. Maclean, 6 Dec. 1856.
35. For early moves with regard to land tenure, see Du Toit (1954), pp.105, 262-8. For Grey's early interest in the subject, see his speech to the Cape parliament (Note 16 above), p.57.
36. For Cathcart's policy see GH 8/28 J. Maclean-W. Liddle, 15 Feb. 1856, and the many documents enclosed therein, particularly G. Cathcart-J. Maclean, 12 April 1853.
37. GH 8/28 G. Cathcart-J. Maclean (private), 12 April 1853.
38. Peires (1981), p.115.
39. For Grey's first meeting with the chiefs, see Imperial Blue Book 1969 of 1855, G. Grey-G. Grey, 14 Feb. 1855, pp.52-3. For the chiefs' response, see BK 70 C. Brownlee-J. Maclean, 5 Feb. 1855.
40. For Grey's statement of the matter, see Imperial Blue Book 2096 of 1856, G. Grey-W. Molesworth, 18 Dec. 1855, pp.14-5. For another analysis (which owes nothing to Grey!) see Peires (1981), pp.31-9. Once again, one should note how close Grey's ideas on this point were to the disastrous experiments of Sir Harry Smith.
41. The one at Chief Mhala's already mentioned, and another at Chief Toyise's in 1855. For the incidence of witchcraft more generally, see Peires (1981), p.206 (Note 83).
42. Imperial Blue Book 2096 of 1856, G. Grey-J. Maclean, 17 Sept. 1855, G. Grey-W. Molesworth, 18 Dec. 1855, pp.15-16, 24-5.

43. Imperial Blue Book 2096 of 1856, J. Maclean-W. Liddle, 4 Aug. 1855, pp.18-19.
44. For example, Grey's minute, 21 Aug. 1855, in GH 8/27 J. Maclean-W. Liddle, 14 Aug. 1855.
45. Imperial Blue Book 2096 of 1856 has a great deal on the chiefs' reactions. See for example, J. Maclean-G. Grey, 3 Nov. 1855, pp.25-6.
46. Imperial Blue Book 2096 of 1856, C. Brownlee-J. Maclean, 27 Sept., 9 Oct. 1855, pp.27-9.
47. For interesting references to Maclean's personal reactions, Wilmot (1856), p.67; GH 8/27 J. Gawler-J. Maclean, 17 Nov. 1855.
48. For Maclean's contempt for Brownlee, see Acc 611/7 J. Maclean-J. Bissett, 19 March, 4 June 1860; J. Maclean-R. Southey, 18 March 1860. Gawler considered Brownlee 'a good and conscientious though weak man'. J. Gawler-Earl Grey, 14 Nov. 1873, Earl Grey papers, University of Durham.
49. Imperial Blue Book 2096 of 1856, C. Brownlee-J. Maclean, 8 Aug. 1855, p.22, gives the following figures: Sandile had received 300 cattle in fines during the past two years, but his own personal herd never amounted to more than 120. Of 100 cattle he had received in gifts he kept only ten. Of 80 cattle confiscated from a certain Qontshi, he kept only five.
50. For the early expulsion of Maqoma from the Kat River, see Peires (1981), pp.89-91. Lucas was very much a third choice — two other officers had been approached and refused before Lucas accepted. GH 8/16 J. Jackson-G. Grey, 14, 28 Feb., 23 March, 12 April 1856. Maclean thought to make Lucas more acceptable by giving him for his interpreter Maximilian Kayser, son of Maqoma's old missionary. But the young Kayser was very unpopular with the Xhosa chiefs who specifically asked for his removal. BK 140 Maqoma and Botman-G. Grey, 27 April 1856.
51. BK 85 R.E. Robertson-J. Maclean, 20 Aug. 1856.
52. For the situation in Kama's country, see Reeve's informative dispatches in BK 86, for example, 27 Nov. 1856.
53. For example BK 431 J. Maclean-G. Mackinnon 10, 14, 17 Jan. 1851. Maclean (1858), p.126; Merriman (1957), p.100; Brownlee (1916), pp.185-6.
54. For the history of Gcaleka and Rharhabe, and for the relationship between the King and the other Xhosa chiefs, see Peires (1981), pp.26-31, 46-7.
55. For a marvellous description of Brownlee's first pay-out to Sandile, see Wilmot (1856), pp.61-2, 75. For Anta, Gh 8/49 J. Maclean-G. Grey, 24 Nov. 1856.
56. BK 82 J. Ayliff, Minutes of an Interview, 22 April 1856; BK 140 Maqoma and Botman-G. Grey, 27 April 1856; GH 8/27 J. Maclean-W. Liddle, 23 Nov. 1855; Uncatalogued MS, Cory Library, Diary of Clerk to Colonel Maclean, Fort Murray, 13, 19 Jan. 1856; MS 2984, Cory Library, J. Ross-R. Ross, 2 Feb. 1856.
57. GH 8/28 J. Ayliff-J. Maclean, 26 May 1856.
58. I would like to thank Dr Stuart Rivell for helpful discussions on lungsickness. For an early account with some historical background, see D. Hutcheon (1905).
59. The spread of lungsickness among the herds of white farmers is extensively chronicled in the colonial newspapers. See, for example, *Grahamstown Journal*, 18 March, 29 July, 5 Aug. 1854.
60. On the spread of lungsickness: GH 28/70 J. Jackson-G. Grey, 5 Feb. 1856;

GH 8/28 C. Brownlee-J. Maclean, 6 Feb. 1856; E. Robertson-J. Maclean, 30 July 1856; Acc 793 J. Gawler-F. Reeve, 7 July 1856; *Grahamstown Journal*, 24 March 1855; MS 7639, Cory Library, B. Ross-J. Ross, 8 May 1854; Merriman (1957), p.215.

61. On Xhosa precautions, see *Grahamstown Journal*, 10 Feb., 24, 26 March, 4 Aug., 8 Sept., 17 Nov. 1855; Gqoba (1888), Part II; *Anglo-African*, 1 March 1855.

62. *Grahamstown Journal*, 26 March 1855; Imperial Blue Book 2096 of 1856, W. Shaw-J. Jackson, 16 May 1855, p.9; GH 23/26 G. Grey-H. Labouchere, 20 Sept. 1856; Imperial Blue Book 2352 of 1857, G. Grey-H. Labouchere, 3 Oct. 1856; GH 8/28 J. Ayliff-J. Maclean, 26 May 1856.

63. *Cape Monitor*, 9 Feb. 1856; GH 8/29 J. Maclean-G. Grey, 17 July 1856; BK 81 J. Gawler-J. Maclean, 13 May 1856.

64. Merriman (1957), p.216.

65. Hibbert (1961), pp.177-8.

66. Merriman (1957), p.215.

67. GH 8/31 Schedule 417, Information communicated to Lieut-Gen. Jackson, 4 Apr. 1856; BK 70 C. Brownlee-J. Maclean, 14 Feb. 1856; Scully (1913), p.310.

68. GH 8/27 J. Maclean-J. Jackson 16 Oct. 1855, enclosing C. Canham-B. Nicolson, 30 Sept. 1855.

69. GH 20/2/1 Information received from a shrewd and trustworthy native, 14 Oct. 1855; BK 70 C. Brownlee-J. Maclean, 11 May 1856.

70. BK 70 C. Brownlee-J. Maclean, 11 May 1856; BK 86 F. Reeve-J. Maclean, 4 June 1856; GH 8/28 C. Brownlee-J. Maclean, 5 Apr. 1856; Berlin Mission Archives, Kropf and Liefeldt, Report for the first half-year, 1856.

CHAPTER 3

Nongqawuse

1. Down by the Gxarha

It is impossible to walk along the banks of the Gxarha as it threads its way through the rugged and broken country along the Indian Ocean coast just east of the Great Kei River. A small stream, no more than 20 kilometres in length, the Gxarha sometimes drops down waterfalls and sometimes deepens into pools but mostly runs through a narrow cutting between high precipitous cliffs. So abrupt are the Gxarha's twists and plunges that from some vantage points a slight turn of the head is enough to change a panoramic view of the river beneath one's feet into a sheer rock face or an impenetrably wooded thicket. Near its mouth, the Gxarha widens and the steep cliffs flatten out into receding green hills, stretching the visitor's field of vision far beyond the distance which his voice might carry or his ears might hear, and allowing his eyes to see objects which he could not reach on foot in an hour or more of hard travelling. Tall reeds and leafy clumps of strelitzia line the edges of the river, casting giant shadows which mingle at dusk with the small islands that dot the stream to form curious shapes in the shallow water. Southwesterly winds often blow the mist off the sea into Gxarha mouth, and, although a sandbar now blocks the estuary, it is possible that in the nineteenth century the schools of dolphin then common on the coast swam into the river mouth. The Gxarha mouth's blend of sea, bush, cliffs and river was by no means unique in Xhosaland, but it was striking nevertheless and it included most of the natural elements which usually inspired the Xhosa with awe and foreboding.[1]

On a certain day in April 1856, two young girls left Mhlakaza's homestead on the Gxarha to frighten the birds away from the cultivated fields. The elder was Nongqawuse, an orphan girl of about fifteen living with her uncle Mhlakaza. The younger was Nombanda, Mhlakaza's sister-in-law, then aged about eight or ten. As they stood in the fields guarding the crops, Nongqawuse heard her name called by two strangers standing in a small bush adjoining the garden. After giving her their names, they entrusted her with the following singular message:

> Tell that the whole community will rise from the dead; and that all cattle now living must be slaughtered, for they have been reared by contaminated hands because there are people about who deal in witchcraft.
>
> There should be no cultivation, but great new grain pits must be dug, new houses must be built, and great strong cattle enclosures must be erected. Cut out new milksacks and weave many doors from buka roots. So says the chief Napakade, the descendant of Sifuba-sibanzi. The people must leave their witchcraft, for soon they will be examined by diviners.[2]

Nongqawuse and Nombanda returned home and related what had happened but no one would believe them. The next day they went again to scare the birds and again the strangers appeared to them. The strangers asked whether their message had been delivered and how it had been received. 'They only treated it like a joke,' replied the girls. 'Nobody listened. They said we were telling fairy-tales.' The strangers were not to be put off. They ordered Nongqawuse to go to her uncle Mhlakaza.

> Say to him we wish to see him, but that he must first kill a beast, wash his body clean and, having thus prepared himself to appear before us, come to us in four days time.[3]

Nongqawuse told her uncle that one of the strangers had enquired most anxiously about him, and from her description Mhlakaza realized that this stranger was none other than his young brother, Nongqawuse's late father. He purified himself according to the instructions of the strangers and four days later went off to the fields with a party of companions. The strangers did not reveal themselves to him in person but spoke to him in voices that only Nongqawuse could hear.

> They told him that they were the people often spoken of in former days by [Nxele] and Umlanjeni, as being a strong people, who would in the course of time render the [Xhosa] the assistance they required in driving the white men out of the land, that they had been sent by their great chief Sifubasibanzi, who is likewise the Great Chief of all the [Xhosa] to their help, and in order that this may be carried into effect, they must prove themselves deserving by acting up to their commands, which are,

first, to throw away all bewitching matter — second, to kill all their cattle, so as to be stocked with others that are free from any disease.[4]

Mhlakaza lost no time in communicating these instructions to the chiefs and the Xhosa people generally. The rapid spread of lung-sickness seemed to prove the strangers' words that existing cattle were rotten, 'bewitched' and 'unclean', and encouraged the people to destroy these in the hope of getting 'a fresh supply of clean and wholesome' beasts. 'They have all been wicked,' implied Mhlakaza, 'and everything belonging to them is therefore bad.' The old cattle were tainted and polluted and the new cattle would be contaminated by them. 'The cattle [the new people] bring with them may not mix with those of men, and they themselves cannot eat the food of men.' For this reason, all cattle had to be killed, all corn destroyed, and all magical charms given up. All their copper rings, all their clothes, all their cooking pots, all their hoes and other implements, everything they had, was contaminated and should be destroyed or sold. They themselves were impure and they should purify themselves by secluding themselves for three days and offering up certain sacrifices.[5]

Mhlakaza said that the new people had many cattle and horses, and wore blankets and garments made of the skins of wild animals. They knew all the Xhosa who came to see them, even those who came from far away. They brought with them a whole new world of contentment and abundance. 'Nongqawuse said that nobody would ever lead a troubled life. People would get whatever they wanted. Everything would be available in abundance.' 'All the people who have not arms and legs will have them restored, the blind people will also see, and the old people would become young.' 'There would rise cattle, horses, sheep, goats, dogs, fowls and every other animal that was wanted and all clothes and everything they would wish for to eat the same as English people eat and all kinds of things for their houses should all come out of the ground.'[6] It was a sharp contrast to the impoverishment and despair experienced by those who had lost their land, their livelihoods and, most recently, even their cattle.

The great chiefs of Xhosaland despatched high-ranking emissaries to investigate. King Sarhili sent his brothers Ndima and Xhoxho, and Sarhili's uncle Bhurhu sent his sons Qwabe and Xhoseni. These chiefs did not actually meet with the strangers who, Mhlakaza assured them, were absent on an expedition against the Colony, but they never-theless became convinced of the truth of the prophecies and immediately began to kill their cattle. Qwabe slaughtered two oxen on the day that he got home, and Xhoseni sent orders that cattle should be sacrificed for all his wives who had small children.[7]

King Sarhili sent four head of cattle as a gift to Mhlakaza. He sent his councillors Kinco and Gxabagxaba to officially notify the chiefs under British jurisdiction that, their existing cattle being all bewitched, 'they must sacrifice them for others which will be obtained from the new people'. The response was immediate in the coastal areas, stricken by drought and lungsickness, which had listened to the wife of Bhulu and the other early prophets. Chiefs Phatho and Mhala sent men to investigate. The minor chief Tabayi visited Mhlakaza himself and returned greatly enhanced in reputation, declaring that he had seen the new people and believed the prophecies to be true.[8]

The great slaughter had begun but it was still very tentative. Wondrous rumours were heard of the marvels seen at the Gxarha, but many visitors were shown nothing at all, and returned in a state of uncertainty. Many homesteads killed some of their cattle, but then desisted pending further news. The fate of the Cattle-Killing movement hung in the balance until, on or about 10 July 1856, Sarhili arrived at the Gxarha to see the new people for himself.[9]

2. The Python that Encircles Hohita

Sarhili, King of all the Xhosa, was at the height of his power. He was a tall, somewhat gangling figure, saluted *A! Ntaba!* (Mountain!) on account of his great height. Now 47 years old, Sarhili had reigned over Xhosaland for more than twenty years. He had survived three colonial invasions of his Gcaleka Xhosa territory and had managed to preserve almost all his lands intact without in any way compromising his political integrity or his duty to the other Xhosa chiefs. He had waged successful war against the neighbouring Thembu kingdom despite its alliance with the colonial government, and had established a new Great Place, Hohita, in the heart of the disputed territory. Immensely wealthy, he owned several thousand cattle scattered for their health and safety at stations and outposts throughout his huge domains. The praise poet sang:

> His eyes are as the sun, his body is as large as the earth, his people are as numerous as the spires of grass; and the milk of his cattle is like the ocean.[10]

A master of the Xhosa style of oratory, etiquette and court ceremonial, celebrated for his knowledge of custom and precedent, Sarhili was respected by all the other chiefs, who were guided by him in matters concerning law and ritual, and who regarded him as the very epitome and model of Xhosa chieftainship. By the force of his personality and the subtlety of his diplomacy, Sarhili imparted a certain degree of unity and coherence to the vast, decentralized Xhosa kingdom, curbing the ambitions of his brothers and other important chiefs 'who act', wrote one colonial newspaper, 'like the haughty Barons of old did in our own country'.[11] The Rharhabe Xhosa chiefs, groaning under the political yoke of the British Kaffrarian government, were on that very account more inclined than ever before to heed the word of the Great House.

Above all, Sarhili was a king who was loved by his people. Unlike his father Hintsa, who had won respect through fear, cunning and manipulation, Sarhili enjoyed the spontaneous loyalty and affection of his subjects. He was an accessible ruler, unfailingly pleasant and courteous. His judicial decisions were renowned for their fairness and tact, and he made a point of softening a harsh judgement with words of humour and sympathy. Sarhili enjoyed his beer, he played simple practical jokes on his councillors, and his praises celebrate his prowess as an uninhibited lover of women. He was the last true King of independent Xhosaland, and the complete embodiment and person-ification of all that was best in the old order.

But beneath the polished surface of Sarhili's royal persona ran deep scars which seriously affected his perceptions and his judgement. Since his early youth he had been in the hands of magicians and diviners. As a boy he had been so weak mentally and physically that he was not expected to live. As a youth, he was cut off from his father Hintsa by the latter's quarrel with his mother. Shortly after the reconciliation of father and son, Hintsa was shot dead by colonial forces and the young King was left alone to face external attacks from the Thembu and internal challenges to his authority from the chiefs and councillors of his father's generation. Sarhili leaned on the advice of doctors and rainmakers throughout these troubled years, though the relationship was often a stormy one and he had at least two of the doctors killed.[12]

Sarhili's fortunes began to improve about the time that a trader named King shot a huge python in the Manyubi forest. This python was the first of its kind ever seen, and its skin and bones were sent to the Great Place, where they were ground into a powder with which the King and his closest relatives were doctored. Not long afterwards, Sarhili's forces won a notable victory over the Thembu and his mounting success as a ruler was thereafter indelibly associated with the python, which is featured in the best-known lines of his praises:

> He is the great python which encircles Hohita.
> He who wakes too late will have missed it.
> For he will not have seen the python uncoiling itself.[13]

The name of the doctor who ground the python's bones to powder and infused it into the incisions he made in Sarhili's back was Bomela.[14] Bomela became immensely powerful and wealthy on account of his magical skills but, being credited with the successes of the 1840s, he was unable to escape responsibility for the failures of the early 1850s. Even more bitter to Sarhili than the military catastrophes of the War of Mlanjeni was his failure to produce a male heir to his kingdom. He had at least five wives, but he seemed unable to beget a healthy son. First his son Gobandolo died, then Dabamfana, and then Feni. The greatest blow came last, in June or July 1853, when his Great Son Nonqano, a boy of twelve, died as well. Such a malign series of sudden deaths was clearly the result of witchcraft and, instigated by Sarhili's Great Wife Nohute, the councillors bypassed Bomela and called in a Thembu diviner named Janyawula.

Janyawula blackened the left side of his face and whitened the right side. He took five spears in his left hand and two in his right. Then he cried, 'I see you, Bomela. . . ! You took the bones of the python.' 'No,' returned Bomela, 'I did not.' 'I'm not interested in your words,' replied the diviner, 'but I want the people to hear [what you have done].' At this point in the proceedings, Sarhili's uncle Bhurhu intervened, and asked Janyawula whether he had actually seen Bomela taking the bones of the python. 'I am not done yet,' said Janyawula furiously and he stalked off and secluded himself in a small dwelling nearby.

When he emerged, Janyawula declared that he had 'seen' Bomela take earth from a patch of land struck by hail and he had 'heard' the sound of the *ichanti* (a malevolent water creature) which Bomela kept as a familiar. Bomela had mixed the earth of the hailstorm and the poison of the *ichanti* and the bones of the python and made medicine with which he had 'cut' each of Sarhili's four sons. 'Seize, seize Bomela,' cried Janyawula, 'and kill him. Bring him to his house and compel him to produce the three things . . . if he will not, call for me and I will find them.'

Bomela was taken a prisoner to his own place, but he denied he possessed any bewitching matter. He was tied to the ground near a fire, so that his flesh slowly roasted while cold water was sprinkled over him to prevent him actually catching fire. Nevertheless, he refused to confess. The next day the torturers broke up an anthill and threw black ants all over him. Still he maintained his innocence. On the third day he was again tortured with the ants, but equally to no avail. Then Sarhili arrived in person, accompanied by Janyawula. 'Kill me,' said Bomela, 'for I have nothing to bring out.' 'We have been two days here,' said the chief torturer, 'and nothing has come out. Bring out the things yourself, Janyawula.'

Janyawula threw off his blanket and flourished his spear. He bit from a large root carried by his servant, spat on his chest and then rubbed the spittle all over his face. At the entrance to Bomela's homestead, he found a small bundle containing, so he said, a piece of leopard skin, a piece of Hintsa's blanket, some hair from Sarhili, some excreta from Sarhili's dead children and other similar items. 'That is not my bundle,' said Bomela, 'but Janyawula's.' Janyawula found various charms, including the skull of a British officer killed in the War of the Axe, hidden in secret places about Bomela's dwelling. These were not unexpected, considering that Bomela was a publicly professed wardoctor and master of secret mediums. But where was the poison from the hail, the python and the *ichanti* so precisely described by Janyawula? After a last look under the gateposts, the Thembu doctor declared that these must have been removed by Tshono, one of Bomela's councillors.

At this, Sarhili rounded on Janyawula. 'You have smelt out Bomela not Tshono,' he pointed out. 'Shall I kill all my people?' The other chiefs were, however, impressed by the number of charms and magical devices which Janyawula had found and they told Sarhili to heed the doctor's words. 'Why should I keep still?' asked Sarhili, 'Shall I kill all my men?' 'But,' the chiefs said, 'we have long told you that you cannot keep children.' Unable to respond but unwilling to take direct responsibility for Bomela's death, Sarhili rode silently away. The next day, he was told that Bomela had died of his wounds. In fact, he had been strangled by the chiefs, who feared to release him lest he take revenge for his sufferings.

Sarhili was deeply affected by the death of Bomela, a man who had served him well and whom he had abandoned in the face of the opposition of the other chiefs. He returned a portion of the confiscated cattle to Bomela's children as a sign of his belief in Bomela's innocence. It was rumoured that while Bomela was being burned he had cried out, 'Don't burn me alive, but kill me outright. If you continue to torture me thus, a great misfortune will befall you.' Sarhili was to have cause to remember these words.

Nor could Sarhili ever forget that terrible day more than twenty years previously (April 1835) when he had accompanied his father Hintsa as he rode proudly into the camp of Governor Sir Benjamin D'Urban.[15] Hintsa was given assurances of his personal safety, but he was never to leave the camp alive. D'Urban disarmed Hintsa's retinue, placed the King under heavy guard and threatened to hang him from the nearest tree. Hintsa was held hostage for a ransom of 25,000 cattle and 500 horses, 'war damages owed to the Colony. He tried to escape but was shot down, and after he was dead his ears were cut off as military souvenirs.

This was Sarhili's first introduction to his colonial neighbours. He never forgot and he never forgave. 'Where is my father?' he asked his councillors when the War of the Axe broke out. 'He is dead. He died by the hands of these people. He was killed at his own house. He died without fighting. . . . Today we all fight.' The Gcaleka Xhosa were not as battle-hardened as the Rharhabe, and the open country around Queenstown (the only place where Sarhili's territory adjoined the Colony) was not conducive to the Xhosa style of guerilla warfare, but Sarhili committed all his resources to the Wars of 1846-7 and 1850-3. The Gcaleka were heavily savaged by colonial firearms — over 500 killed at the battle of Imvane (1851) — and they were forced to pay heavy war indemnities but their geographical position to the rear of the Rharhabe preserved them from the huge territorial losses suffered by Sandile and his people.

Even worse than the colonial enemy at the gates was the colonial enemy within. Even before the death of Hintsa, Gcaleka suspicions of British intentions had been roused by the activities of the Reverend John Ayliff, the Wesleyan missionary at Butterworth. Ayliff had espoused the cause of the Mfengu refugees, clients to the Gcaleka, whom he saw as potential converts to Christianity. Ayliff sheltered Mfengu refugees from their Gcaleka masters and when the Imperial column crossed the Kei in 1835 he encouraged them to switch their allegiance to the British Crown. This seemed to Hintsa, and to Sarhili after him, to be an act of rank treachery on the part of a man living on his land, by his permission and under his protection. This double betrayal of Xhosa good faith by both the secular and the spiritual arms of Western civilization left a deep mark on Sarhili. He became implacably opposed to the colonial presence and he instinctively shrank back into a fierce attachment to the old Xhosa methods and the old Xhosa beliefs.

It was partly to get away from the Wesleyan mission that Sarhili moved the Gcaleka Great Place up north to the Hohita.[16] Butterworth Mission was burned down in the War of the Axe and again in the War of Mlanjeni. Indeed the Wesleyans regarded their prospects in Gcalekaland as so hopeless that they did not replace the Reverend Gladwin who fled for his life in 1851. This left the field clear for the United Society for the Propagation of the Gospel, and in September 1855, St Mark's Mission was established near Hohita with the Reverend H.T. Waters as its first missionary.

Sarhili was reluctant to accept the mission and his first response to Waters was to tell him that there was no ground to spare, that he had come too near the Great Place, and that he must fall back. 'The horrible suspicion that that I am a government agent annoys me at every step,' wrote the missionary. But when Sarhili called at St Mark's to pay a courtesy visit, he was struck despite himself by a picture of the Crucifixion:

> He enquired minutely into a history of Our Lord, which I gave him through the Interpreter, and a large Pictorial Bible. He was most taken with the Crucifixion, Christ walking on the sea, and St Thomas' unbelief.[17]

One can only wonder whether these strong visual images of Christ walking on the water and rising from the dead, and of doubting Thomas, flashed through Sarhili's mind when Nongqawuse and Mhlakaza pointed to the sea, showed him the resurrected ancestors, and asked him to believe.

The anxieties arising out of Bomela's death and out of the continuing colonial intrusion were compounded from the beginning of 1855 by the spread of lungsickness across the Kei and into Sarhili's country.[18] As in British Kaffraria, lungsickness was followed even before Nongqawuse by prophecies of a resurrection:

> The Galekas firmly believe that Umlanjeni has risen from the dead — that the sickness among the cattle was predicted by the prophet and that he can bring all their cattle to life again.

Sarhili put more than twenty people to death for witchcraft or for breaking the quarantines established on the movement of cattle, but he could not check the spread of the disease. By February 1856, it was reported that many cattle had died of lungsickness in the lower part of Sarhili's country where Nongqawuse lived. In April, the very month that she began to prophesy, lungsickness broke out among the homesteads bordering on Sarhili's Great Place. By August, at the very latest, the king's own herds were affected.

It must be said that despite all his admirable qualities, Sarhili was in some respects a very limited ruler. His tenacious attachment to the old Xhosa traditions which was the source of much of his strength was also the source of his greatest weakness. He had neither the will nor the ability to devise original solutions to the new problems which confronted him. In the depths of his perplexity, Sarhili was an easy mark for the prophecies which, although in essence radically new, were expressed in a familiar religious idiom.

Thus occurred one of the saddest ironies in Xhosa history, that a man who loved his subjects so dearly and by his good qualities so deserved their love became the chief instrument of the traumatic disaster which was soon to overwhelm them.

3. Seeing is Believing

Saddened by the loss of his sons, guilt-ridden over the death of Bomela, helpless in the face of the lungsickness which was decimating his cattle, his imagination fired by the stories he had heard of the wonders at the Gxarha and also, perhaps, by the images in the 'large pictorial Bible', Sarhili undertook the long journey from the Hohita to the sea in a spirit of hope and expectation. On or about 10 July 1856, he arrived at Mhalakaza's residence.[19] What exactly happened over the next few days will probably never be known for certain. Our most reliable oral source informs us that 'the same voices that spoke to Nongqawuse spoke to him as well', and, given the King's emotional state, this may well be true. In addition, Mhlakaza and Nongqawuse showed Sarhili certain things which he believed to be a fresh ear of corn, a fresh pot of beer, a favourite horse lately dead, and best of all his dead son, now alive and well. He asked whether the promises could not be fulfilled without the destruction of the existing cattle, but when he was told that this was impossible, he bowed to the prophecies, asking only for three months space to give him time to kill his immense herds.

He issued formal commands (*imiyolelo*) to the Xhosa nation, ordering them to obey the instructions of Mhlakaza, and as a public sign of faith he commenced the slaughter by killing his favourite ox, a beast renowned throughout Xhosaland.

After Sarhili's declaration, hundreds more Xhosa made their way to the Gxarha. Here they were received by Mhlakaza, who urged all 'who had any respect for departed relatives' 'to kill their cattle as they had heard the bellowing beneath the ground of thousands of cattle that will replace those that are killed'. The enquirers were introduced to Nongqawuse.

> A girl of about 16 years of age, has a silly look, and appeared to me as if she was not right in her mind. She was not besmeared with clay, nor did she seem to me to take any pains with her appearance.[20]

Nongqawuse was still seeing the strangers often. Sometimes they came to her in the homestead after dark. Eventually she became too 'ill' (presumably too confused and disorientated) to talk, and her place was taken by her young relative Nombanda, who was preferred by many visitors, including the chiefs.

Many of the enquirers were anxious to see and hear the new people,

and Mhlakaza and Nongqawuse were obliged to try and satisfy their
wishes up to a point. Not all the visitors received the same treatment.
The most privileged were taken to see the new people, though not to
speak to them. Other visitors witnessed the sight of Nongqawuse or
Nombanda talking to the spirits, though they saw and heard nothing
themselves. A large number of visitors, probably the majority, saw and
heard nothing at all and had to be content with assurances. Let us look
a little more closely at the available evidence.

W.W. Gqoba, whose narrative of the Cattle-Killing is based on oral
traditions collected from believers, conveys something of the
emotional impact of Nongqawuse's performance. He describes a party
of chiefs following Nongqawuse towards the Gxarha river. Their
throats are dry with fear, and when they reach the river, they kneel
down and drink.

> Then they heard the crashing of great stones breaking off the cliffs
> overlooking the headwaters of the River Kamanga [i.e. Gxarha],
> whereupon the men gazed at one another wondering for they were
> seized with dread for it seemed as if something was going to explode in
> the cliff. While they stood wondering, the girl was heard saying, 'Cast
> your eyes in the direction of the sea.'
>
> And when they looked intently at the waters of the sea, it seemed as if
> there were people there in truth, there was the bellowing of bulls and
> oxen, and there was a black mass coming and going, coming and going
> until it disappeared over the horizon, there in the waters of the sea. Then
> the people began to believe.
>
> This army in the sea never came out to meet the chiefs. Even their
> speech was not heard by anyone except Nongqawuse.[21]

Gqoba's account probably describes an actual visit paid to Nongqawuse during the early part of November 1856. Two independent
versions of the same event survive, both recorded shortly afterwards.
The first is from Dilima, the Great Son of Chief Phatho, and the second
is that of an official delegation from the Ndlambe chiefdom.

> He . . . saw sundry black things in the water rising to the surface
> either singly or in numbers appearing as it were as a cloud in the water —
> these were playing in the water, rising and disappearing. He says he was
> anxious to go and speak to them but he was not allowed to do so . . . He
> never saw cattle but . . . he saw things he could not account for in the
> water — which he says are called these strange people who have risen
> from the dead.

> The day of their arrival and the next two days, the prophetess would not
> talk to them. On the third day, they were told that they should see all
> that they should see. There was a mist over the water — the girl went
> from them to the distance of about a mile and a half — they presently saw
> figures but of what they could not tell. They requested to be allowed to

Map 3: The Scene of the Prophecies

talk to the people and see them closer, but they were told to go home, destroy their corn and their cattle and then they would be allowed the privilege of speaking with the new people.

These three accounts agree on the main points, namely that the chiefs saw black shapes in the water, rising and falling in the distance but so far away that it was impossible to see them clearly. A similar experience was described by other eyewitnesses, who saw 'the lower parts of the bodies of these men [the new people] but . . . the wizards raise a mist about their bodies which conceals their heads and the upper parts'. Many Xhosa who saw such sights attempted to get closer, but were pushed back by Mhlakaza on one pretext or another.

Other enquirers, although not privileged to see the new people, were permitted to watch Nongqawuse conversing with them. Even Mhlakaza depended on the prophetess as a medium of communication.

> She [Nongqawuse] withdraws to a distance from others in her spiritual operations, and there seems to hold converse with the unseen under the ground. She reveals it to [Mhlakaza] who announces it again to the nation. He says 'Usifuba' and 'Unopakade', the two great chiefs in the unseen world, have commanded him to tell the people, high and low.

> Mhlakaza went with a party of men, but these [strangers] did not appear. They spoke with Nongqawuse, and were heard only by her and the other girl, who interpreted what they were saying.[22]

Similar proceedings were also reported by Commissioner Brownlee, who wrote that 'though no sound is heard in answer to the questions put, she gives forth the responses of the oracle'. Oral tradition places much emphasis on the auditory and visual qualities of the prophetic scene at the Gxarha. The oral historian Ndumiso Bhotomane, whose father was often Sarhili's personal emissary to Nongqawuse, was positive that both Sarhili and his father actually heard voices coming out of the reeds and he explained this as follows:

> The place was close to the cliffs, and when people spoke there, the cliffs echoed. Thus it was that people believed.

In addition to the thickly vegetated banks of the Gxarha, Nongqawuse also took visitors to a cave and to aardvark holes where lowing sounds might be heard. Another favourite location remained the bush adjoining the cultivated field where she first met the strangers.

> The party retired to the haunted bush, the chiefs, counsellors, sight seers and newsmongers sat outside. Miss Umhalakaza [Nongqawuse] entered and after a short absence returned and said she had been to a great hole in the bush and looked in and she had seen there numbers of people long since dead quite alive and an incalculable number of new cattle for the true Believers.

Nombanda has left her own description of what occurred.

> I frequently accompanied Nonqause to a certain bush where she spoke with people — And although she frequently informed me when I was with her at this bush, that she saw people and heard them speak to her — I neither saw them nor did I hear them speak till after I had constantly visited the bush with her.[23]

The confidential nature of Nongqawuse's communications with the new people might have disappointed the enquirers present, but would not have surprised or disillusioned the majority of them. Spirits often manifested themselves in the form of *imilozi* (voices), which spoke a strange whistling kind of language that only the privileged could understand. Most Xhosa who were 'called' by the ancestors to become doctors underwent experiences similar to Nongqawuse's, as this account of a doctor's initiation makes clear.

> [The initiate's] whole manner becomes strange and like that of an insane person, and his speech is often incoherent and ambiguous. . . . This is the period of inflation. He is indulging strange ideas and indescribable fancies; and sometimes startles the people by seeming to converse with invisible and unknown beings on some strange and incomprehensible subjects.[24]

There is much in this description which fits Nongqawuse, and other aspects of her behaviour, such as her dishevelled appearance, likewise resemble that of an initiate undergoing *thwasa*. To question Nong-qawuse's methods would have been to question the entire Xhosa system of divination and thus, by extension, the whole of Xhosa religious belief. In 1856 very few Xhosa were prepared to go that far.

The most common response of Mhlakaza and Nongqawuse was, however, to turn the enquirers aside without showing them anything at all.

> The people who have come from the sea are invisible, being the spirits of departed brave men.

> Pato's men have returned and say that they should each bring a head of cattle before they could be introduced to the new people.

> People recently returned said Umhlakaza told them that the army had gone to attack the amaBai [whites of Port Elizabeth] but would return shortly.

> I asked Umhlakaza for a sight of them but he said that lately none were privileged to see them, except the Gcaleka royal family. I saw the place where they were in the habit of appearing, but not the new people themselves.[25]

These refusals did not rouse the suspicions of the disappointed visitors. On the contrary, they reinforced the prestige of Mhlakaza,

Nongqawuse and all who were said to have met the new people. Most of the enquirers had come prepared to believe and were, in any case, afraid to go to the place where the strangers were said to be seen.[26] The journey to and from the Gxarha was usually sufficient in itself to generate experiences which seemed to confirm Nongqawuse's prophecies. Many of the visitors came from very long distances, often on foot. Some had never seen the sea. We may imagine that they were excited and buoyed up by the stories they had heard and the marvels they expected to see. We may further imagine that their anticipation mounted as the journey progressed and reached fever pitch when they finally arrived at the very place where, every night, the spirits came to meet their chosen ones.[27] There were many enquirers at Mhlakaza's place and they passed the time feasting, drinking and swopping rumours. Finally, the prophets would appear in person and exhort them to kill their cattle so that the good time might come. In some cases, Mhlakaza would actually present his visitors with cattle, saying that these were a gift from the new people. There would have been noises in the bushes, wind in the reeds, shadows in the water, sounds from the sea, murmurings at night, memories and dreams of long-lost loved ones. Is it surprising that many people also heard the lowing of cattle, the clashing of horns and the voices of their forefathers?

> At Mhlakaza's place one might see wonderful things. Hundreds had heard there at night, in the air, the old Xhosa heroes parading by in a wild army.[28]

We do not have any first-hand accounts by believers of their experiences at Mhlakaza's residence, but the following unique description of an all-night vigil in British Kaffraria by a young girl who actually participated, conveys something of the atmosphere of such occasions and provides a vivid illustration of the power of suggestion.

> They were to go down to Phatho's land to a place which she pointed out, where there were two little hills — one a little higher than the other. On the one there were some thorn bushes and a few other bushes. The other rise was clear. It was on the bare hill that they were to go. . . .
> We ate and danced till after midnight until we were all quite tired and sleepy. When one of the Chiefs said that the hour was come, we were all to get up. We got up and as we were sitting and looking in the direction of the hill where the bushes were [we were told that] we would see the Cattle moving about in the bushes. So we sat looking for some time when the men began one and then another to say: 'Do you see them?' Others would say: 'That is them.' One could see one thing and another another thing. My father scolded me and said, 'Now do you believe it. . . . Can you not see the things on the side of that hill?' 'No. I can see nothing but thorn bushes.'

He said it was not bushes but I thought that the men had eaten too much corn and meat and drunk too much of [Xhosa] beer to know what they saw. But the [Xhosa] would see whether there was anything to be seen or not. I could see nothing but bushes. So my father got very angry with me: he told me if I dared to say it was bushes again he would kill me. But I saw nothing else. But some of the men ran for their horses and galloped off to the spot to see what they were: for some of the people could see their old friends that had been dead for so many years. So some of them galloped off to see and before they got there, they said that the things had disappeared.[29]

Nongqawuse's demonstrations were only effective when shown to those already converted in their hearts. They completely failed to convince sceptics such as Sarhili's first cousin, the powerful Chief Ngubo who went down to the Gxarha specifically to confront the prophetess.

[Nongqawuse] went to the place, and said they refused to see him [Ngubo] as he had not killed his cattle or destroyed his corn. . . . This did not satisfy him, so he went to the place and said that he insisted on seeing them and talking to them himself. The girl told him he would die if he did, on which he beat her and called her an impostor.[30]

Very few Xhosa had the courage or the authority to confront Nongqawuse openly, as Ngubo did. But there were other lesser figures who returned quietly to their homes, reflected on what they had seen — or failed to see — and determined on a course of resistance.

A man named Yekiwe returned from Umhlakaza saying that he could see nothing strange and that, having thus satisfied himself that all was false . . . whatever others might do or say, he would stay quietly at his kraal, and cultivate his gardens, and he advised his friends to do likewise.

It was such men who eventually formed the nucleus of an active party of unbelievers.

Unfortunately for Xhosaland, however, most of the visitors were suitably impressed by Mhlakaza and Nongqawuse and their tales grew in the telling so that the majority of Xhosa who never left home received the most exaggerated reports which were apparently confirmed by the returning enquirers. For there were few who would admit that they had seen nothing when all their friends had seen marvels.

The workings of rumour are well illustrated by the case of Sarhili's brothers Ndima and Xhoxho who, it might be remembered, accepted the truth of the prophecies but admitted that they had seen nothing.[31] By the time the news of their visit to Mhlakaza had reached British Kaffraria it was being reported that they had seen the long-deceased kings Phalo (d.1775) and Khawuta (d.1793). About the same time Bulungwa, a minor chief and a vocal unbeliever, began to suffer from a scrofulous swelling about his testicles, ending in an abscess. It was therefore spread about that he had been cursed for his unbelief and that his man's genitals had turned female. T.B. Soga, the grandson of a leading unbeliever, described the process as follows:

> It happened like this: the fear and anxiety of waiting for this thing to be fulfilled increased the false things that were said. It was often said in conversation, 'So-and-so saw his deceased father, and the cattle of his homestead from long ago.' Even when a group of men gathered together and made, as usual, a shadow on the hillside, they would run to it and it would disappear. Then they would say, 'we saw something disappearing over that hillside'.

Thus every piece of news or unusual report was inflated by the expectations of the believers until it too became exaggerated enough to serve as a validation of Nongqawuse's prophecies.

4. The First Disappointment

> Tidings of the marvellous sights witnessed near Mhlakaza's village filled the country. The horns of oxen were said to be peeping from beneath the rushes which grew round a swampy pool near the village of the seer; and from a subterranean cave were heard the bellowing and knocking of the horns of cattle impatient to rise. . . .
>
> There were those who said they had actually seen the risen heroes emerge from the Indian Ocean, some on foot, some on horseback, passing in silent parade before them, then sinking again among the tossing of the restless waves. Sometimes they were seen rushing through the air in the wild chase as of old. Then again they were marshalled in battle array. . . .

The news from the Gxarha was quite enough to convince most ordinary Xhosa as they sat in their homesteads.[32] The official sanction of King Sarhili removed the last doubts of those who wanted to believe. 'The movement seems peculiarly to have been one of the common people,' wrote Commissioner Brownlee.[33] Many of the chiefs opposed it, and those who did not oppose it permitted rather than encouraged it. Certainly no Xhosa chief could have enforced the demands which the people accepted readily when commanded by the prophet. They cut new poles and collected thatch to rebuild their houses. They greatly enlarged their cattle kraals in anticipation of the marvellous new cattle which they expected. They threw away their old hoes, spades and knives, and bought new ones. They parted with their copper rings and their brass necklaces and other precious ornaments. Hundreds of Xhosa labourers and roadworkers abandoned

Grey's famous public works because it was said that if they made a noise in the ground with picks it would disturb the cattle and delay their appearance. Finally — although there is no direct evidence on this point — we may safely assume that most of the Xhosa secretly rid themselves of their charms, their medicines and all their other magical objects.

Most important of all, the believers zealously commenced the work of destruction. They dug out their corn from the insulated safety of the grainpits where they had stored it up for the hungry winter months. Some of it was sold off at half its normal price, but most of it was left carelessly scattered on the cornfloors where two or three days damp weather was enough to make it inedible. Ardent believers, too impatient to wait for nature to take its course, deliberately wasted their corn by boiling it.[34]

Hundreds of cattle were killed every day.[35] The believers were ordered not to eat the meat of any cattle killed the previous day, so that every day fresh cattle were slaughtered and yesterday's remaining meat thrown away. Rotten flesh lay putrefying around the homesteads. All along the road to East London Magistrate Vigne observed 'large numbers of skeletons lying in the veldt'. It is clear that such cattle had been summarily killed, rather than ritually slaughtered. The emphasis of the Cattle-Killing at this point was not on sacrifice but on getting rid of the impure beasts.

Those Xhosa who preferred to sell their cattle drove them to the markets of King William's Town and East London, or sold them to the firmly unbelieving Mfengu.[36] Cattle which previously would have realized £3 or £4 were sold for less than the value of their hides. In some cases 11 shillings was taken for a cow and 15 shillings for a full-grown ox. One Xhosa drove 15 or 16 oxen into East London and offered them for sale 'at a nominal price' but was unable to dispose of them (even at such low prices, the threat of lungsickness made many buyers hesitate). Instead of taking them elsewhere, the Xhosa simply drove them to a neighbouring hillock where he slaughtered the lot, flayed the carcasses and sold the hides. Bishop Gray reported the mood in King William's Town on the eve of the First Disappointment: 'They sell an ox for 10 shillings or 12 shillings. When they cannot sell them, they kill them. Goats they sell for two shillings or 3 shillings. Chickens for 2*d* or 3*d*. Mealies they throw away.'

The chiefs reacted more slowly than their subjects. Those who normally followed the lead of the colonial authorities moved first. Toyise forbade his followers to kill their cattle. Siwani confiscated some cattle which Mhlakaza had given to some of his subjects. Kama, the most Christian chief in British Kaffraria, called a meeting of his subjects to put down the movement. Freely invoking the name of his deceased father Chungwa, shot dead by British troops in 1812, Kama attempted to crush the Cattle-Killing belief not by reasoned discussion but by weight of his chiefly authority.

> What kind of men are they, thus to despise their chiefs? Can mercy be shown to those who would break up and scatter the tribe of Chungwa? Why, I ask has Gweleta 'washed'? And you too Qogo! (I only call on those who were presented to me by my father, and whom I expected would be true to me.) Why are you, Qogo, slaughtering your cattle? Have you also seen Chungwa, and has he told you to despise his son?[37]

Kama's closest associates weighed in with spirited attacks. 'Have not [deceased chiefs] Hahabe, Tshaka and Chungwa been seen by Umhlakaza?' asked Sityi. 'You who believe what Umhlakaza says have you seen these chiefs? Have they told you, common people, to raise yourselves in pride above our born chief, and thus try to kill him?'

'Speak now,' jeered Hashe. 'You have always been boasting in your houses, at your kraals, and in the absence of your chief, of Umhlakaza. Has he told you that when you assemble before your chief you are to leave your faith in him in your houses, that you keep your mouths shut?'

The believers quailed before the onslaught. None of them attempted to defend the prophecies. They shuffled and evaded, offering only transparent denials and excuses. Phatho's son Mate, who would eventually become the leader of the believing faction in Kama's country, attempted to shield them. 'Do not pour down your anger on your dog,' he asked Kama, 'but tell us what you require of us.' The chief irritably brushed him aside.

> I have one word. It is this — these reports must not be believed by those who live in this country. Why should such a step be taken first by common people?. . . You who believe on him, go to Umhlakaza. I will not allow you to break my power. . . .
>
> Until the Queen or her Representative tells me that Umhlakaza's sayings are true, I will never believe them. I will ever risk my life in opposing him, and I call on God to be my judge that I would then be doing what is right. . . . Let those who believe what Umhlakaza says leave me and go and live with him; though they are Chungwa's subjects I will not prevent them. I would rather they would do this at once than remain with me.

A week later Mani, Kama's Great Son, and a party of armed men burned down the homestead of a leading believer named Xola.[38] But however much Kama and the other pro-Government chiefs threatened their subjects and fired their houses, they could not stop the growth of the movement.

The uncommitted chiefs were slower to come to a decision. They were exposed to the retribution of the colonial authorities, and they knew and dreaded Maclean's heavy hand. They remembered the prophecies of Mlanjeni, who had promised them much, but failed them in the end. Lungsickness came late to the Ngqika Xhosa district, and the impetus towards cattle-killing was therefore somewhat delayed. Sandile, the senior chief in British Kaffraria, was unwilling to take a lead but, typically, waited on events. Pressed by Commissioner Brownlee, he issued orders forbidding his subjects to kill but did little to enforce them.[39] His full brother Dondashe inclined towards the movement and killed some cattle. The overall effect of indecisiveness at the Great Place slowed but did not seriously impede the impact of Nongqawuse's prophecies.

In contrast with the Ngqika district, those areas hit the hardest by crop failure and lungsickness took up the Cattle-Killing almost immediately. Maqoma, the hero of the Waterkloof, was now fallen to the status of a minor chief. Although he said little in public about the prophecies, both he and his neighbour, the eighty-year-old Bhotomane, supported the Cattle-Killing from a very early stage.[40] Another foremost believer was Phatho, chief of the Gqunukhwebe Xhosa. Phatho had lost the sight of one eye and was going blind in the other. His chronic stomach ulcers were aggravated by heavy drinking, and his family life was racked by tensions between himself and his Great Son, Dilima. Phatho was greatly embittered against the colonial government, which had neglected to reward him for his valuable services during the War of Mlanjeni though it had granted an extensive territory to his younger brother, the Christian chief Kama. Phatho had lost, moreover, 96 per cent of his 2500 cattle through lungsickness, and most of his close associates had lost an equivalent number or even more. Phatho had been chief of the Gqunukhwebe for more than thirty years. He had fought for the Colony and he had fought against it, and nothing he had done had ended well. 'In other wars,' he said, 'he was rich and had reason for remaining at peace but now being poor he wishes for change.'[41]

On the surface Phatho professed to ignore the prophecies. He told his Resident Magistrate that his people were killing their cattle because they were hungry and that his people would cultivate their ground as soon as it rained. Secretly he sent his brother Kama a formal message accusing him of witchcraft, 'which has been the means of making you a great chief, though not the son of the Great Wife', and ordering him to kill his cattle.[42]

The Ndlambe Xhosa chief Mhala, ranking second after Sandile in

British Kaffraria, was in a difficult position. He himself was strongly inclined to believe the prophecies, but his leading councillors, Ndayi and Gqirana, were strongly opposed, and his Great Son Makinana came out violently against them, saying that 'he would believe the report when he saw his grandfather Hlambi and not till then, and that he would cut the throat of any fool in his kraal who commenced killing or selling his cattle'.[43] Mhala was warned by his fellow believer Maqoma that he should not move openly lest his support for the prophecies become known to the government. He therefore temporized, saying 'it was a foolish thing that he should not trouble his head about', but endeavoured to strengthen the position of the believers in his chiefdom by putting them forward for colonial salaries.[44] Whle Mhala was still hesitating, the faith of the believers was shaken by the First Disappointment.

It is unlikely that Nongqawuse and Mhlakaza took the initiative in setting a date for the great day of resurrection. They had rather stressed that the prophecies would come true as soon as all the orders of the new people had been complied with. However, they were under pressure to produce results and many Xhosa expected the resurrection as early as the full moon of June 1856.[45] When this date passed without consequence many of the believers became seriously disturbed. Sarhili called a meeting at his Great Place. All the principal men of the Gcaleka Xhosa were present, and the prophets were harshly criticized. 'The Xhosa were finishing all they had,' said the sceptics. A great deal of time had passed but nothing had happened. Mhlakaza must be forced to demonstrate the truth of his sayings by producing the new people and the new cattle. At first, Mhlakaza attempted to evade this demand, saying that the new people had gone off to their unknown stronghold, but finally he was compelled to name the next full moon (mid-August) as the 'moon of wonders and dangers'.[46]

On the great day, two suns would rise red in the sky over the mountain of Ntaba kaNdoda where they would collide and darkness would cover the earth.[47] There would be a great storm, which only the newly built and thatched houses would be able to withstand. Then the righteous dead — not those who had been killed by God for their wickedness through snakebite or drowning — and the new cattle would rise out of the earth at the mouths of the Kei, Kwenxurha, Tyhume and Keiskamma rivers. They would be wearing white blankets and new brass rings. The English and their collaborators ('all who wear trousers' in one account) would retreat into the sea, which would rise up in two walls to engulf them and open a road for them to return to the Uhlanga (place of Creation) whence they came.

No believer slept that night. The young people danced and revelled, while the older men sat about in silent groups or nervously paced about the huge cattle folds, which had been prepared for the new cattle. But nothing happened. If anything, the promised day of darkness was particularly bright.[48] The effect on the believers can only be guessed at, but it would seem that the initial result was bitter disillusion. Sarhili dispatched orders to all the Xhosa chiefs, prohibiting the further slaughter of cattle. He sent messengers to Mhlakaza, and it was widely reported throughout Xhosaland that Mhlakaza had denied ever uttering prophecies, that he had laid the whole blame on Nongqawuse, even that he had shown the messengers his own cattle unslaughtered in their kraal. Commissioner Brownlee wrote:

> The frenzy and excitement which prevailed during the whole of last month are somewhat lulled and subsiding; the people appear to think they have performed their part, and are looking to the prophet for some evident and convincing manifestation of his power. Many of the firmest believers are growing doubtful; and those who, though unbelievers, had been carried away with the stream, are beginning to speak out.[49]

It semed as if the whole Cattle-Killing movement must collapse. And indeed, had it collapsed in August 1856, relatively little damage would have been done. For all the talk of destroying every living head of cattle, most of the Xhosa believers had slaughtered only a few of their cattle and then stopped pending confirmation of the prophecies.[50] Travelling in the heavily affected coastal districts, Magistrate Vigne had seen 'large numbers of skeletons of cattle lying in the veldt', but he had also seen 'considerable numbers of cattle left alive'. 'Some' Xhosa had killed the only two or three cattle which had survived lungsickness and 'more than one' had killed all his cattle, but these were clearly a small minority. In Kama's country, another stronghold of the Cattle-Killing, a 'large number' of cattle still remained, and several stock owners retained herds of 50-60 head. Thousands of cattle had been killed, wrote Commissioner Brownlee, but 'there are still sufficient cattle and corn left to prevent want'. Few or none of the Ngqika Xhosa had killed more than two or three head.[51]

But it was precisely the continued survival of so many cattle which made the further continuation of the Cattle-Killing movement possible. So long as the believers failed to obey the injunctions of Nongqawuse to the letter, so long could she claim that the fault lay not with the prophecies but with the failure of the people to heed them properly. Had not Sarhili himself said that it would take him three months to kill all his cattle? The flame of hope once kindled was very difficult to extinguish. Even as the first prophecies failed, rumours arose at the Kei that the new people had appeared at the Kwelerha.[52] The fate of the Cattle-Killing hung in the balance. And then, for the second time, King Sarhili went down to the Gxarha.

Notes

1. Description from a visit to the Gxarha in August 1983. I would like to take this opportunity to thank Mr N. Webb and Mr R. Hulley, who assisted me on this occasion.
2. There are three main sources for Nongqawuse's vision. Gqoba (1888) is excellent, but suffers from the fact that he telescopes his entire narrative into eight days. The statements recorded in February 1858 by some of the key participants, including Nongqawuse, Nombanda and Nombanda's brother, Nqula, are suspect because of the circumstances in which they were taken, and I have used them only to a very limited extent, mainly to elucidate the relationship between Nombanda and Mhlakaza. The third source is to be found in the reports made by police spies before the colonial authorities had grasped the magnitude of the movement or decided to turn it to their advantage. The most important of these is in GH 8/29 Information communicated to the Chief Commissioner, 4 July 1856. Where the statements conflict, I have relied on the spies' reports. The text of the strangers' message quoted here is taken from Gqoba (1888).
3. GH 8/29 Information communicated to the Chief Commissioner, 4 July 1856.
4. *Ibid.*
5. MS 9063, Cory Library. N. Falati, 'The story of Ntsikana'; Acc 793 J. Gawler-J. Maclean, 25 July 1856; GH 8/29 Information communicated to the Chief Commissioner, 1 July 1856; *King William's Town Gazette*, 14 Aug. 1856. Berlin Mission Archives, Abt. III, J. Rein-Berlin Missionary Society, 28 Aug. 1856.
6. S.A. Library, MSS African, uncatalogued, 'The frontier': anonymous, but certainly written by Dr J. Fitzgerald; Interview with Masiphula Ngovane, Mahlahlane Location, Willowvale District, Oct. 1975; J. Goldswain (1946-9), Vol. 2, p.191 (I have amended Goldswain's eccentric spelling and punctuation); GH 8/29 C. Brownlee-J. Maclean, 29 June 1856; GH 8/29 Information communicated to the Chief Commissioner, 4 July 1856.
7. GH 8/29 C. Brownlee-J. Maclean, 29 June 1856.
8. GH 28/71 Information communicated by a trustworthy Native, 2 Aug. 1856.
9. GH 8/29 C. Brownlee-J. Maclean, 13 July 1856.
10. T. Smith (1864), p.63. The only detailed treatment of Sarhili is in J.H. Soga (n.d.), Ch. 6, but like all Soga's work, it presents only a partial picture. On Sarhili's early life, see Peires (1981), pp.115-7. For Sarhili's praises, see Rubusana (1906), pp.228-9.
11. *Grahamstown Journal*, 22 Oct. 1853.
12. Peires (1981), p.116. Also Brownlee (1916), p.158.

13. Rubusana (1906), p.228.
14. For details on the python, *Cape Frontier Times*, 12 June, 31 July 1845. The story of Bomela was recorded in great detail at the request of Governor Grey because he thought he might be able to use it as ammunition against the Xhosa King. BK 70 'Death of Bomella, Chief Priest of the AmaGalekas in 1856 as stated by Kaffirs of Kreli's tribe' recorded by H.T. Waters n.d. (1858). Valuable details are added by *Grahamstown Journal*, 26, 30 July, 2, 6 Aug. 1853. For Bomela's curse, see Cory Library, Cory Interviews, Tanco and Somana, Kentani, 24 Jan. 1910.
15. For the death of Hintsa and the Mfengu exodus, see Peires (1981), Ch. 8 (1).
16. Peires (1981), p.116.
17. For the early years of St Mark's Mission, see Journal of Rev. H.T. Waters, United Society for the Propagation of the Gospel, Microfilm 96723/1/1 172/2, Reel 1, Cory Library. The quote is taken from the entry for 1 Jan. 1856. See also 14-15 Sept. 1855.
18. On lungsickness in Gcaleka territory, *Anglo-African*, 1 March 1855; *Grahamstown Journal*, 8 Sept. 1855; Merriman (1957), p.216; GH 8/26 M.B. Shaw-J. Maclean, 3 April 1855; GH 8/49 J. Maclean-G. Grey, 31 Oct. 1856; GH 8/28 C. Brownlee-J. Maclean, 5 April 1856; GH 28/70 5 Feb. 1856; BK 70 C. Brownlee-J. Maclean, 25 Aug. 1856. The quotation is from GH 8/27 C. Canham-B. Nicholson, 30 Sept. 1855, enclosed in J. Maclean-J. Jackson, 16 Oct. 1855.
19. Imperial Blue Book 2352 of 1857-8, C. Brownlee-J. Maclean, 16 Aug. 1856, p.18; C. Brownlee-J. Maclean, 13 July 1856; GH 28/71 C. Brownlee-J. Maclean, 30 July 1856; Berlin Missionary Archives, Abt. III, J. Rein-B.M.S., 28 Aug. 1856; Interview with Chief N. Bhotomane, 16 Dec. 1975; a letter from Brownlee to Maclean dated 23 July 1856 which apparently gives details of the visit is missing from its place in GH 8/29 Schedule 297.
20. BK 89 Secret Information, 20 June 1856; Acc 793 J. Gawler-J. Maclean, 25 July 1856; BK 89 Information . . . communicated by a reliable secret service man, 18 Oct. 1856; GH 28/71 C. Brownlee-J. Maclean, 30 July 1856. For the role of Nombanda, see BK 14 Statement of Umjuza, 24 Feb. 1858; BK 14 Statement of Nombanda, 28 Feb. 1858; Examination of the prophetess 'Nonqause', 27 April 1858.
21. Gqoba (1888); BK 81 J. Gawler-J. Maclean, 22 Nov. 1856; BK 140 H. Vigne-J. Maclean, 17 Nov. 1856; BK 89 Secret Information, 20 June 1856; Abt. III, Berlin Mission Archives, A. Kropf and T. Liefeldt, Report for first half-year, 1856.
22. Gqoba (1888); Scully (1913), p.309; GH 8/31 C. Brownlee-J. Maclean, 4 Jan. 1857; Acc 793 J. Gawler-J. Maclean, 25 July 1856; Interview by J. Peires with Chief N. Bhotomane, Ramntswana Location, Kentani District, 16 Dec. 1975; J.H. Soga (n.d.), pp.163, 169.
23. BK 14 Statement of Nombanda, 28 Feb. 1858.
24. W. Shaw (1860), p.447. See also Maclean (1858), pp.82-3.
25. GH 8/29 J. Maclean G. Grey, 3 July 1856; GH 8/29 Information communicated to the Chief Commissioner, 4 July 1856; BK 89 Information communicated to the Chief Commissioner, 18 Oct. 1856.
26. GH 8/29 C. Brownlee-J. Maclean 29 July 1856.
27. GH 8/29 C. Brownlee-J. Maclean 8 July 1856.
28. *Berlin Missionberichte*, 1858, p.38.

29. Goldswain (1946-9), Vol. 2, pp.192-3.
30. GH 8/49 J. Maclean-J. Jackson, 30 Oct. 1856 (Ngubo) ; BK 89 Secret Information, 10 Aug. 1856 (Yekiwe).
31. Compare letter cited in Note 7 above with GH 8/29 J. Gawler-J. Maclean, 9 July 1856; BK 70 C. Brownlee-J. Maclean, 11 Aug. 1856; T.B. Soga (n.d.), p.164.
32. Brownlee (1916), pp. 126-7.
33. GH 20/2/1 C. Brownlee-J. Maclean, 25 Aug. 1856; GH 8/29 J. Maclean-G. Grey, 3 July 1856; GH 28/71 J. Maclean-G. Grey, 11 Aug. 1856; GH 28/71 C. Brownlee-J. Maclean, 30 July 1856; *King William's Town Gazette*, 14 Aug. 1856; *Grahamstown Journal*, 2 Aug. 1856; GH 28/71 H. Vigne-J. Maclean, 9 Aug. 1856; R. Gray, 'Journal', *Church Chronicle* (Grahamstown), Vol. 2 (1881), p.330.
34. 7s 6d per muid rather than the usual 13s or 15s. BK 70 C. Brownlee-J. Maclean, 22 Aug. 1856; MS 2990 Cory Library, J. Ross-R. Ross, 13 Sept. 1856.
35. At the height of the excitement preceding the first disappointment, 800 hides a day were being brought into King William's Town. *King William's Town Gazette*, 14 Aug. 1856; BK 109 H. Vigne-J. Maclean, 20 Aug. 1856; CO 2935 R. Giddy-R. Southey, 15 Aug. 1856; GH 28/71 C. Brownlee-J. Maclean, 30 July 1856; Acc 793 J. Gawler-J. Maclean, 25 July 1856,
36. As in 35. Also R. Gray, 'Journal', *Church Chronicle*, Vol. 2 (1881), p.330.
37. For Siwani, see *Grahamstown Journal*, 13 Sept. 1856. The text of Kama's meeting was secretly noted down by the court interpreter with Kama's approval and published in full on pp.56-8 of Imperial Blue Book 2202 of 1857/1. I have slightly rearranged the sequence of the speeches in order to make the whole more readily comprehensible.
38. BK 86 F. Reeve-J. Maclean, 10 Aug. 1856.
39. GH 28/71 C. Brownlee-J. Maclean, 30 July 1856; BK 70 C. Brownlee-J. Maclean, 9, 31 Aug. 1856; GH 8/29 J. Maclean-G. Grey, 17 July 1856.
40. GH 28/71 H. Lucas-J. Maclean, 1 Aug. 1856; BK 70 C. Brownlee-J. Maclean, 9, 11 Aug. 1856.
41. Maclean (1858), p.131; GH 8/49 J. Maclean-G. Grey, 28 May, 22 Dec. 1856; GH 8/23 J. Maclean-W. Liddle, 18 Aug. 1854; G. Grey-H. Labouchere 3 Oct. 1856. Imperial Blue Book 2352 of 1857, p.35 for Phatho's cattle losses; Acc 793 J. Gawler-J. Maclean, 30 June 1856 for his adherence to pre-Nongqawuse prophets; BK 70 C. Brownlee-J. Maclean, 30 June 1856 for quote.
42. GH 8/29 F. Reeve-J. Maclean, 11 July 1856.
43. GH 28/71 J. Gawler-J. Maclean, 2 Aug. 1856; BK 70 C. Brownlee-J. Maclean, 9 Aug. 1856.
44. GH 8/29 J. Gawler-J. Maclean, 14 Aug. 1856; GH 18/6 J. Gawler-J. Maclean, 15 Aug. 1856.
45. GH 28/71 Information communicated to the Chief Commissioner, 6 Aug. 1856; GH 28/71 Information received from a trustworthy Native, 2 Aug. 1856.
46. It is difficult to fix the exact date of the First Disappointment. The strongest rumours seem to have clustered around 9 and 14 August. See *King William's Town Gazette*, 14 Aug. 1856; *Grahamstown Journal*, 9 Aug. 1856; Bishop Gray's 'Journal', *Church Chronicle* (Grahamstown), Vol. 2 (1881), p.330.
47. GH 28/71 C. Brownlee-J. Maclean, 30 July 1856; GH 8/29 F. Reeve-

J. Maclean, 2 Aug. 1856; *Grahamstown Journal*, 9, 16, 19 Aug. 1856; GH 20/2/1 C. Brownlee-J. Maclean, 25 Aug. 1856; R. Gray, 'Journal', *Church Chronicle*, Vol. 3 (1882), p.238; GH 28/71 Memo by J. Maclean, 4 Aug. 1856; GH 8/29 Information communicated to the Chief Commissioner, 4 July 1856.

48. *Grahamstown Journal*, 19 Aug. 1856; J. Macdonald, 'Manners, customs, superstitions and religions of South African tribes', *JRAI*, 19 (1890), pp.280-1.

49. C. Brownlee-J. Maclean, 15 Aug. 1856, Imperial Blue Book 2352 of 1857-8, p.17; GH 8/49 J. Maclean-G. Grey, 28 Aug. 1856; BK 89 J. Crouch-J. Maclean, 12 Aug. 1856; GH 28/71 J. Maclean-G. Grey, 21 Aug. 1856; GH 20/2/1 'Information communicated . . . by a man just returned from a visit to Umhlakaza', 18 Aug. 1856; BK 81 J. Gawler-J. Maclean, 30 Aug. 1856.

50. For examples, see BK 89 Secret Information, 10 Aug. 1856; Acc 793 J. Gawler-J. Maclean, 9 July 1856.

51. BK 70 C. Brownlee-J. Maclean, 22, 25, 31, Aug. 1856; BK 109 H. Vigne-J. Maclean, 20 Aug. 1856; *King William's Town Gazette*, 25 Sept. 1856.

52. BK 81 J. Gawler-J. Maclean, 30 Aug. 1856.

CHAPTER 4

'There is a Thing Which Speaks in My Country'

1. The Revival of the Prophecies

After the disappointment of 16 August, the flame of the Cattle-Killing flickered, but it did not go out. No sooner had the prophecies conclusively failed to materialize at Kei mouth than it was rumoured that the new people were wandering about the wooded country near the Qora River or had been seen at the mouth of the Kwelerha. Less than two weeks after the First Disappointment, the order to kill was reiterated.[1]

Mhlakaza had an explanation ready for the failure of the prophecies: the people should have slaughtered their cattle instead of selling them off. Nongqawuse explained that even though the people were quite at liberty to buy and sell the meat of the slaughtered cattle, they should carefully preserve the *umpefumlo* ('breath' hence 'soul') of the beasts, so that they could rise again. As for the Englishman's money, it would change into fire and destroy all who possessed it.[2]

It will be remembered that the initial motivation for the Cattle-Killing movement came from the perception that existing cattle were tainted, infected, lungsick beasts which could not be permitted to mix with the perfect cattle of the new people lest they contaminate them. Selling was certainly as effective a means of getting rid of existing cattle as slaughtering them, but it was unable to relieve the deep feelings of guilt or to satisfy the desire to propitiate the ancestors which had inspired the movement in the first place. To make the world right again, it was necessary to kill cattle in the ritual manner, that is to sacrifice them.

Sacrifice was recognized by the Xhosa as the only effective method of communicating with the spirit world.[3] They looked forward especially to the great bellow made by the dying beast when its windpipe was severed. That cry was, they believed, the last breath of the animal going up to the place of the ancestors, and when they heard it, the crowd at the sacrifice would all shout 'Camagu!' meaning something like a combination of 'Amen' and 'Be satisfied, O Great Ones!' It was to this cry that Nongqawuse probably referred when she said that the umpefumlo should be preserved. The other functions of sacrifice were, as we have already seen, to please the ancestors, who were known to be very fond of cattle, and to allow the beast to absorb, through its quality of innocence, the evil which polluted the homestead and thereby restore its initial purity. 'Without the spilling of blood,' wrote T.B. Soga, 'there can be no forgivenesss from sins or propitiation of the ancestors of the home.' It would not, therefore, have seemed strange to Sarhili that the sale of cattle was insufficient to satisfy the spirits who were about to bring so great a blessing on the world.

Mhlakaza's explanations concerning the First Disappointment were immediately accepted by Sarhili who at once set guards on all the roads leading out of his territories in order to prevent the further sale of cattle.[4] Shortly after the beginning of September, he paid his second visit to the Gxarha. Once again, little is known about this visit except that the King saw something and that it was enough to satisfy him.[5] According to one usually reliable source, Mhlakaza told Sarhili and his councillors that he would show them the shadows of the new people. They were to sit down and keep their eyes firmly fixed on the ground and not, on any account, to look up. They did so, and when shadows duly passed in front of their eyes, they were convinced. An official messenger named Sixaxa told the Ndlambe chiefs that Sarhili had seen numbers of men 'playing' on a hill. He could not say how far away the hill was, 'but they were seen'. 'Where the people have landed,' he said, 'is a large place with a broad ditch round it inside of which a number of houses have sprung up. Not [Xhosa] houses or brick houses, but houses forced up like hills out of the earth.' Sarhili himself told a white trader that he had seen something in the sea, something like a small speck. None of these reliable sources state that the King had any conversation with the new people.

But like all stories of visits to the Gxarha, the tale grew in the telling and less than a month later one Gcaleka reported that he had heard Sarhili saying:

> I have seen [my father] Hintza face to face. I went to Umhlakaza's and
> met my father one night among the wild mealies . . . he gave me the
> assegai which was buried with him — I have it now.[6]

Another report, clearly an elaboration of earlier, more accurate statements, was that a great host of new people had appeared in boats at
the mouth of the Kei and told Sarhili that they had come to establish
the independence of the blacks and that he must send messages to all
the black nations. In the meantime, the Xhosa must continue to kill
their cattle.

The importance of these rumours and reports lay not so much in
their actual content as in the fact that they bore the authority of the
Xhosa King. As the Ngqika Xhosa put it, 'a chief in Kreli's position
would not send the message he has sent unless he was fully convinced
of the truth of Umhlakaza's assertions'. Time and time again, just as it
seemed as if the Cattle-Killing was about to lose its momentum, Sarhili
drove it relentlessly forward. 'The whole movement [was] Krieli's,'
said Ganya, an elderly Gcaleka councillor who unwillingly slaughtered
580 out of his 600 cattle, 'and so resolute was he that he would not
permit anyone to reason with him on the subject.'[7]

In accordance with the orders of Mhlakaza, the most important of
Sarhili's neighbours were officially informed of the prophecies and
asked to join the movement. The highest-ranking of the Thembu chiefs
were firmly allied to the Cape Colony and the Regent Joyi dismissed
the prophecies with contempt.

> What folly is this that you are being guilty of? [Joyi asked the Thembu
> believers.] Did anyone ever hear of people rising from the dead? Let the
> greybeards come forward and speak. Let them show me Zondwa; let
> them show me Ndaba; let them show me my father Ngubencuka, that I
> may believe!
> What will become of us now the greybeards have gone astray? Who
> will instruct the children and teach them wisdom, now that the old men
> have become fools? What is this I hear? What fools have you become,
> thus to pour out your beauty [cattle] on the ground![8]

Nevertheless the Cattle-Killing evoked a huge response among those
Thembu who lived on the Colony's northeastern border, especially
among the subjects of the late Maphasa, who had lost both their chief
and their lands during the War of Mlanjeni. Tyopo, Nonesi, Yeliswa
and other Thembu chiefs sent messengers who visited the Gxarha and
returned with magical tales of supernatural horsemen and other
wonders. Most of the leading Thembu chiefs remained hostile but the
large number of commoner believers found an energetic leader in the
ex-Regent Fadana, who seized his opportunity to emerge from fifteen

years of political obscurity. Fadana was joined by Maqoma's father-in-law Qwesha, the ex-chief of the Ndungwana Thembu, who had been deposed for fighting against the Colony during the War of Mlanjeni.

The Cattle-Killing movement had less success in Mpondoland despite a personal visit — so said the believers — from the spirit Napakade himself. Sarhili did his best to induce his old rival King Faku to join him, returning stolen horses and personally accompanying an official Mpondo delegation down to the Gxarha to meet the new people. The Mpondo were not convinced, however, and they returned home saying that they had seen nothing. Faku ordered his people not to kill their cattle, commenting that Mhlakaza was no better than the false prophets Nxele and Mlanjeni.[9]

The Sotho King Moshoeshoe had been in close communication with Sarhili ever since the year 1852, when both kings found themselves facing Imperial troops. The Sotho victory over Governor Cathcart at the Battle of Berea profoundly impressed the Xhosa, and Sarhili's brother Xhoxho made a special visit to Lesotho to collect some of the medicines which had enabled the Sotho to defeat the British. There is some evidence that Moshoeshoe made some enquiries concerning the Cattle-Killing in August 1856, but it was only after he had received Mhlakaza's instructions that Sarhili sent his messenger Matomela to lay the prophecies formally before the Sotho King. Around the beginning of October, an official embassy from Moshoeshoe arrived at the Hohita

> to see if it was true that the [Xhosa] were killing their cattle, and if it was true what Umhlakaza was telling their people. . . . Moshesh was very anxious to know what it all meant, as he (Moshesh) wished to make himself ready for anything that might happen.[10]

Grey and Maclean chose to read sinister implications into Moshoeshoe's behaviour, but it is unlikely that the Sotho King wanted to do anything more than 'make himself ready for anything which might happen'. Neither he nor any of his people killed their cattle.

Even more ambitiously, Mhlakaza suggested that the white settlers should also kill their cattle, destroy their crops and put away their witchcraft. For, he said, 'the people that have come have not come to make war but to bring about a better state of things for all'.[11] He invited the whites to come to the Gxarha to hear and see for themselves. 'The word to kill is for all people,' reported Magistrate Gawler, '[Xhosa], English and Dutch.' Reverend Henry Kayser of Peelton was warned that it was not enough for him to be reading from the Book — he must throw away his bewitching matter as well.

No whites ever accepted Mhlakaza's invitation, and there is no evidence that the believers made any serious attempt to convert them. There was a general assumption among the Xhosa, which even the words of Mhlakaza could not break, that the whites had come out of a different *uHlanga* to their own, or, in other words, that they were an entirely different species of humanity. It was the whites not the blacks, thought the believers, who had killed Christ.[12] But Christian Xhosa were a different matter. The prophecy of resurrection had its roots in Christianity, and the believers spared no effort to win over the mission residents by stressing the similarities between the teachings of Mhlakaza and those of Christ. The head of the new people was identified with Adam, 'our first father', and one passage from missionary Ross's letters vividly suggests the kind of heated debates which occurred over the mission fences:

> The doctrines of the atonement and that of sanctification were represented as justifying cleansing by standing on the smoke of burning fat. All that was said or done was in the name of God, or that His Word says so. It was as profusely as it was vainly used.

Few mission residents were converted by these arguments, though three old ladies did flee Knapps Hope Mission by stealth some time in October.

At the same time that Mhlakaza was seeking fresh fields for conversion, he was stepping up his campaign against the unbelievers. In the original prophecies it was enough to state in general terms that they would receive divine punishment, that they would be swept away by whirlwinds or that they would be swallowed up by the sea. By September, however, the idea was beginning to take shape that the failure of the prophecies was due in part to the selfishness of the unbelievers, and an increasing spate of rumours related the horrid punishments inflicted on stubborn unbelievers. Satan, it was said, had been let loose in the country to watch those who dared to disobey the orders of the new people and to take them to himself.[13]

2. Grey Intervenes

In his attempts to revive the Cattle-Killing movement, King Sarhili found one ally as effective as he was unexpected: Governor Grey himself. To understand how this came about, it is necessary to go back a little and consider the colonial reaction to the events just described.

The ranking Imperial official in British Kaffraria was of course its Chief Commissioner, Colonel John Maclean. Maclean was a cautious man who had succeeded to high office largely on account of his capacity to avoid the mistakes of others. He had built up an excellent network of spies and informers which he set in motion as soon as the prophecies began to take effect on his side of the Kei. As details of the Cattle-Killing movement began to filter through to his head-quarters at Fort Murray, Maclean found himself torn between the hope that nothing untoward would happen and the fear that he might be caught unprepared for any crisis which might occur. Thus he tended at first to discount the importance of the movement, dismissing the reports of cattle-killing as exaggerated rumours of measures taken by the Xhosa as a result of lungsickness.[14] Gradually, however, as he became increasingly unable to construct a satisfactory explanation of these strange events from the facts at his disposal, Maclean turned quite naturally to the assumption that the key to understanding the Cattle-Killing lay in information which was being concealed from him. Like his master Grey, Maclean possessed a good measure of the paranoia born of authoritarianism and, once again like Grey, he found conspiracy theory a congenial means of damning his opponents and justifying himself. Ever since Moshoeshoe's victory over Governor Cathcart at the battle of Berea, Maclean had seen the Sotho King as the potential mastermind of a united black combina-tion against white domination in southern Africa. Now, seizing on some evidence of Moshoeshoe's interest in Xhosa affairs, Maclean jumped to the remarkable conclusion that Mhlakaza was 'merely a secondary instrument in the hands of the Great Chiefs [Sarhili and Moshoeshoe] working on the superstition and ignorance of the common people'.[15]

On the basis of these deductions, Maclean wrote Sarhili a warning letter threatening him with a colonial invasion unless he put an end to the Cattle-Killing. 'If Kreli cannot stop him [Mhlakaza], I will be very ready to help him.' The letter was never delivered, but Grey was furious. He wrote Maclean a savage letter of reprimand, reminding the Chief Commissioner that that he, Grey, was the Governor and the person responsible for the peace of the country. Sadly chastened, Maclean apologized and left all future initiatives to Grey.[16]

The only other official in British Kaffraria with recognized status and experience regarding Xhosa affairs was Charles Brownlee, the Ngqika Commissioner. Brownlee cared for the well-being and prosperity of the Xhosa in a way that Grey and Maclean did not, and he could communicate with the people in their own language. Although the Xhosa always regarded Brownlee as first and foremost a man of *uRhulumente*, they always felt him to be a 'man of the Government' that one could talk to.

When the Cattle-Killing erupted, Brownlee was less concerned with its consequences for his reputation than with staving it off, and above all with keeping Chief Sandile, his immediate responsibility, out of it. Everybody knew that Sandile's decision, whether to kill or not to kill, was crucial, for it was certain that the great mass of uncommitted Xhosa would follow him. Sandile was often regarded by colonial officials as weak and stupid, and indeed he entirely lacked the bravery of Maqoma, the cunning of Mhala or the regal presence of Sarhili. But Sandile did have one great quality: he took his position as the senior Rharhabe Xhosa chief very seriously and he did his best to act up to the responsibilities of that position. If he was indecisive — and he often seemed so — it was because he was often placed in a situation where it was impossible to decide what was the best thing to do. The Cattle-Killing was just such an occasion.

> [Sandile said] that he would call a meeting of his councillors and would adopt their decisions. He was now in the midst of two evils, dread of the wrath of the people who have appeared, and dread of famine. Should he direct the people to cultivate their lands, and they should therefore be destroyed, the blame would be his, and likewise should he direct them not to cultivate and a famine ensue, the blame would be his. He did not wish to take the responsibility in this matter.[17]

Paradoxically, Sandile's very indecisiveness inclined his people to follow his word. When he eventually did come to a decision, they felt sure that it must be the right one. Brownlee thus knew that if Sandile killed his cattle all the other Ngqika would follow suit, and he therefore devoted all his energies to making sure that the chief played a public part in putting down the movement.

At first it seemed as if Brownlee's strategy was working well. Lungsickness had not yet made great inroads into the relatively isolated Ngqika territory, and Sandile was not yet under any great pressure to kill. In accordance with Brownlee's wishes, he ordered his people to ignore the prophecies and threatened to fine anyone he caught killing cattle. But as enthusiasm for the Cattle-Killing spread among the commoners Sandile became increasingly doubtful.

In the midst of this uncertainty, Brownlee received a message from an unexpected source. King Sarhili himself sent to say that he was very anxious to see him and asked him to come up to the Hohita as soon as possible. Brownlee was enthusiastic.[18] 'I have known him [Sarhili] long and am on friendly terms with him,' he wrote, 'I also thought that [Sarhili] had gone so far that he was ashamed to draw back, even though he saw his error, and that he might be glad of the opportunity afforded by our friendly advice of undoing what he had done.' He proposed to take Sandile with him, hoping thereby to get that chief to commit himself irrevocably against the Cattle-Killing. Sandile jumped at the idea, and wanted to set off as soon as possible but Brownlee had other commitments. It was a fatal delay. Maclean, who resented Brownlee's influence among the Xhosa, disapproved of the proposed visit and, needless to say, Governor Grey was equally hostile to any good suggestion that he had not thought of himself. As he had reprimanded Maclean for trying to send Sarhili a message, he now reprimanded Brownlee for trying to visit him. 'Were it not for the zeal with which he [Brownlee] discharges his duties,' wrote Grey, 'I should really have felt exceedingly annoyed with him.'[19] From the colonial point of view, the Governor had just missed a possible opportunity of stopping the Cattle-Killing in its tracks. If Sarhili was genuinely uncertain about what to do next — and his invitation to Brownlee seems to indicate that he was — then the very presence of a government man at the Gxarha might have provoked a confrontation between the prophets and the Xhosa King which could have wrecked the movement. Such an opportunity was never to return.

Having thus rejected the suggestions of both his top subordinates and having made it very difficult for either of them to take the initiative again, the onus now devolved on Grey to devise a colonial response to the escalating crisis of the Cattle-Killing movement. He left Cape Town towards the end of August, and after spending several days in Grahamstown, he arrived in King William's Town on 2 September with a new administrative policy already in his pocket.[20] Quite typically, this new policy was based not on any practical experience of the situation, but on Grey's own abstract logic and his memories of New Zealand.

Far from delaying his innovations until the Cattle-Killing crisis had passed, Grey seized the opportunity to tighten the screws on the chiefs yet further. They would continue to receive their salaries as before, but the money previously allocated to their councillors was to be taken for the pay of 'headmen' directly appointed by the government. The main duty of these headmen was to organize an unpaid police force in each district, which would be responsible for maintaining order and restoring stolen property. Effective control in the districts would thus pass from the chief to the magistrate, and Grey correctly anticipated that he would 'get a much firmer hold on the country' than ever before. The new system, though rationalized in terms of the disorders expected to follow the Cattle-Killing, was not in fact a reaction to the movement at all but a stubbornly consistent decision to pursue his policies as if nothing extraordinary was happening.

The demonic energy which drove the Governor during this visit may have originated in an exalted emotional 'high', one of the characteristics of the extraordinary mental condition which Grey always blamed on the wound he had received from the Australian aborigines. It is a remarkable fact, and it cannot have been a coincidence, that each of the three visits Grey paid to British Kaffraria during the height of the Cattle-Killing was undertaken in a state of heightened nervous anxiety, which might account for his manic activity while on the frontier.[21] The historical significance of these fits is, however, open to question since his personal instability was more than compensated for by the clarity and consistency of his goals.

We know remarkably little about the month or so that Grey spent on the frontier before he suffered a nervous collapse and returned prostrate to Cape Town. He saw the chiefs privately, each in his own district, avoiding showy public meetings à la Sir Harry Smith and leaving no written records of his proceedings. It seems as if he warned the chiefs against killing their cattle and urged them to cultivate their fields. The chiefs were clearly anxious to placate the Governor, and several issued strong statements condemning the Cattle-Killing movement.[22] But Grey's main purpose was not to suppress the Cattle-Killing but to impose his new administrative system on the reluctant Xhosa. He explained this to the chiefs and gave them to understand that they had no option but to accept it. Then he rode away thinking, perhaps, as he informed the Secretary of State in London, that he got along well with the Xhosa, and that they were not in any way hostile to the colonial administration.[23]

But Grey had got it wrong again. His visit was the very reverse of a success. Far from damping down the Cattle-Killing, his dictatorial new measures only fanned the flames of resentment which fed the growing movement. No sooner had he left Sandile's meeting than a party of latecomers arrived and asked the assembled councillors to tell them what had happened.[24] The unbelievers expected Sandile to praise the Governor politely according to the conventions of Xhosa oratory, to reassure them that nothing was wrong, and to take the opportunity to exhort his followers to resist the Cattle-Killing. Instead Sandile, advised by the believers, refused to say anything at all. Since it was inconceivable that Sandile would make a public attack on the Governor, his silence signified that this was a serious matter which could not be discussed openly but would have to be dealt with more discreetly. Certainly, the mood of the meeting was hostile to the Governor and to Mhlakaza's opponents. Sandile's brother-in-law, one of the leading unbelievers, left the Great Place in despair and all the unbelievers were desperately cast down.

Three days later Sandile, who — whatever his private thoughts — had consistently opposed the Cattle-Killing in public, informed Brownlee that he would not cultivate, that he was afraid, that a Mfengu who tried to cultivate had been rooted to the spot, unable to leave it. Brownlee called a group of labourers off the public works and made them cultivate in front of the chief and, even though none of them was rooted to the spot, Sandile nevertheless insisted that he was afraid, conceding only that he would cultivate if all the other Xhosa cultivated as well. The net effect of Grey's intervention therefore was to turn the most important chief in British Kaffraria from a passive opponent of the Cattle-Killing into an active though secretive believer.

Even in the pro-colonial chiefdoms of Anta, Oba and Kama, the new system was received with reluctance and suspicion, and the chiefs were astounded and shocked by the fact that their opinions were neither requested nor desired.[25] After six weeks of attempting to implement the new system among Anta's and Oba's people, Magistrate Robertson confessed that he was still 'laying the foundations'. Magistrate Reeve, in Kama's country, found that faithful ally's 'vacillating disposition requires much management and patience before I can get him to understand any new arrangement, and that I have to give him time'. Old Chief Bhotomane's attitude of feigned stupidity obliged Magistrate Lucas to come to him three days running and on each day Bhotomane claimed he had forgotten everything he was told the day before. In the end Lucas was forced to try and make all the new arrangements on his own.

The strongest resistance of all came from Chief Phatho whose territory straddled the vital road link between King William's Town and the port of East London.[26] Phatho had gone into the Cattle-Killing from the beginning and had driven his luckless magistrate, Harold Vigne, close to despair. Vigne was never told about Phatho's law cases or any of Phatho's doings 'except in false versions made for my ears'. Phatho's councillors would not even speak to him, except in the chief's presence. It was clear that Phatho was not going to fall in with Grey's plans. He would not send his men to the stations appointed for the road police. There was no food for them, he said. They would quarrel with each other. Many of the people who lived along the road were properly the subjects of his brother-in-law, not of himself. What would the government do if he did not accept the plan? Would the government fight? Vigne did his best to meet all these objections, but he got nowhere with the new system. The councillors demanded coffee, sugar, tobacco and extra pay. They mocked Vigne to his face and they refused his orders outright. They did not go to their stations.

The reaction against Grey's visit was still in full swing when the flames of the Cattle-Killing were fanned even higher by the arrival of Kapu, a messenger from Sarhili. About 19 September the Xhosa King had held a great meeting attended by all his principal men.[27] This had endorsed Sarhili's renewed enthusiasm for the Cattle-Killing and ordered messengers sent to all the chiefs in accordance with Mhlakaza's instructions. Kapu informed Sandile, somewhat untruthfully, that Sarhili had seen the new people at the mouth of the Kei, that he had spoken to them, that they had ordered him to kill all his cattle, finish his corn, throw away his charms and tell all the chiefs under him to do the same. Having thus delivered his message to Sandile, Kapu moved off south to inform the chiefs Mhala and Phatho.

Probably because he realized that the whole matter would have to come out into the open eventually, Chief Mhala decided to treat Kapu's message in a formal manner. He called a public meeting and he sent his Great Son Makinana to inform Magistrate Gawler.[28] Grey, who was still in King William's Town, was pleased by this sign, as he thought it, of Mhala's loyalty and sent him a friendly letter urging him to oppose the Cattle-Killing. He sent to Sandile asking him why he had not reported Kapu's presence.

To Sarhili, Grey sent a harsh and threatening communication. After warning the King that continued cattle-killing would cause starvation and disorder, the Governor demanded that he stop it forthwith. He wrote:

> I shall consider you as the guilty party and will punish you as such. You have seen that I have been a good friend to you and your people, and I desire to continue so — But if you force me to take a contrary course you shall find me a better enemy than I have been a friend, for your conduct has been most unprovoked.[29]

Sarhili was unhappy to see the government messenger and, even before he knew what Grey's letter contained, he was very reluctant to receive it. He had long been worried about the colonial reaction to the Cattle-Killing, and although Mhlakaza had told him that the English would be tamely acquiescent 'like a stabled horse', the King must have had his doubts. He had not expected Mhala to disclose his message to the colonial authorities and he was angry about this new and unwanted distraction.[30]

But once Sarhili had received the Governor's letter, he knew that he had to reply. He called a meeting of his councillors and together they considered their formal response. They understood that Grey was threatening them, but since they could not please the Governor without giving up the prophecies, they decided to temporize. Sarhili sent a representative named Xoseni to King William's Town 'to know from Maclean's mouth whether these really are the Governor's words, and wants to know why the Governor says he will at once bring trouble upon Kreli, What wrong has he done?' Xoseni emphasized that Sarhili did not want a war, and said that even if the English sent an army into his country Sarhili would not resist them. Maclean replied that even as they were speaking, a new messenger from Sarhili was visiting the British Kaffrarian chiefs. 'I have no word for Kreli, except the Governor's letter,' he concluded.[31]

Xoseni was accompanied home by a settler named John Crouch who traded in Sarhili's country and spoke Xhosa fluently. Inasmuch as Sarhili trusted any white man, he trusted Crouch, but it was a misplaced confidence. Crouch was the government's chief agent in the transKei, supplying Maclean with detailed information on Sarhili and his people, and not hesitating, as we shall see, to conspire against the person of the King himself. Now Crouch was to be the bearer of Sarhili's reply to Grey.

> I Kreli came to this place today to have the Governor's letter properly explained to me. — I am astonished the Governor should send to me about this thing, before he first heard from me.
>
> I now understand his letter, my answer is this — I wish Crouch to report to the Governor, that there is a thing which speaks in my country, and orders me and my people to kill all our cattle, eat our corn, and throw away all our witchcraft wood, and not to plant, and to report it to all the chiefs in the country — in reporting this to the other chiefs to kill their cattle, I was ordered to do so by the thing which speaks in my country.[32]

It was a straightforward reply, restrained but uncompromising. Sarhili did not recognize the right of Governor Grey to interfere in Xhosa affairs without being invited to do so. Sarhili did not recognise the right of Governor Grey to prohibit his communications with the Xhosa chiefs living under British jurisdiction. Sarhili would abide only by the word of that thing which spoke in his country. The Xhosa King defied the British Governor. Grey was never to forgive him for it.

3. The Cruise of the Geyser

Censured by Grey for failing to report the presence of Sarhili's messenger, Sandile and his brother Xhoxho called a public meeting to oppose the Cattle-Killing. The unbelievers mustered their full strength under the leadership of Tyhala, Sandile's second-ranking councillor.

'Let us learn to eat grass,' he mocked the believers, 'for we must eat that when we have killed our cattle.' Kemhle, another unbeliever, urged his chief 'no longer to listen to the lies of every passer-by but to consult with the Government'. The believers were silent — theirs was not a case to be made in the open. Sandile contritely announced that he would start to cultivate on the following day but in his heart he did not wish it.[33]

Phatho, another chief in disgrace for receiving Sarhili's messenger, also held a public meeting to clear his name with the government. He made good use of the troubles of the road police to avoid any mention at all of Nongqawuse's prophecies. 'My word is that this thieving must stop,' he declared piously.[34] After this loyal demonstration, Phatho and his Gqunukhwebe Xhosa went home and resumed the killing of their remaining cattle. The power of the colonial authorities in British Kaffraria was enough to furnish the government with as many public declarations as it liked, but these were quite hollow at the core. In the end, the government's hard line against the Cattle-Killing only succeeded in driving it underground.

After an exceptionally dry winter, rain began to fall steadily and abundantly. The trees were covered with leaves, the grass shot up and the soil awaited the sower. Nature itself set a timetable which made the question of cultivation more urgent even than the killing of cattle. Under normal circumstances, planting began in British Kaffraria towards the end of August when the early rains wet the soil and enabled the Xhosa to break it up. Sowing might begin a little late without serious consequences, but it had to be completed by the middle of December at the very latest to give the crops time to ripen before the end of the rains the following April. Since the rains came late that year of 1856, the believers realized that if they could stave off cultivation for only two months more, all the Xhosa would be committed to the prophecies whether they liked it or not. Conversely, the unbelievers and the colonial authorities were eager to get cultivation going as quickly as possible.[35]

The believers threw their spades into the rivers, and unpleasant rumours began to circulate throughout Xhosaland concerning the fate of some who had been foolish enough to cultivate.

> Those who attempt to cultivate will be fixed to the ground and unable again to leave their work.
>
> A man who was burning grass to cultivate his garden was tossed into the air, he knew not by what.
>
> All the women who are sowing will be carried into the sea with a strong wind when the mimosa blossoms.

> A woman went to sow and there she became fastened to the spot, picking up the ground without making any progress, unable to go home.

> A man went to cut bushes for a fence to his garden. He got up on a tree but could not come down nor did he make his work advance. [36]

Such rumours were especially widespread among Xhosa women, who performed most of the agricultural labour, and many women refused to cultivate despite pressure from their husbands. Commissioner Brownlee wrote:

> The women are now the strongest supporters of the delusion, most of the men who have cultivated have had to break up their ground themselves, and when the husbands have insisted that their wives should take a part, they have left and gone to their parents. [37]

The cornfields were an easy target for the believers inasmuch as they were very vulnerable to attack. They could not be hidden or removed as cattle could, nor could they be defended. It was easy for the believers to reap what the unbelievers had sown or trample down their gardens with cattle. Furthermore, the Xhosa did not feel the same emotional attachment to their gardens as they did to their cattle, and it was much easier for the believers to persuade the uncommitted to passively desist from cultivating than it was to put them through the emotional ordeal of slaughtering their cattle.

Ultimately the decision to cultivate rested with the chiefs, the nominal owners of the land, who normally regulated the agricultural cycle on behalf of the community and whose 'word' was required before sowing could commence. When rain finally fell towards the end of September 1856, all eyes turned in their direction.

The role of Sandile was clearly going to be crucial. Not only was he the senior chief in British Kaffraria, but he was, as we have seen, the focal point for the average uncommitted Xhosa. All parties therefore looked to Sandile to give them a lead, but this was precisely what Sandile did not want to do. On the one hand, he was profoundly afraid of the colonial government and its local agent, Commissioner Brownlee. Tyhala and Soga, his venerable councillors, were strongly opposed to the Cattle-Killing, and six influential younger unbelievers took turns, unknown to the chief, to stick close by him at all times. But Sandile was also coming under pressure from believers such as his chief councillor Vena, his full brother Dondashe, his father-in-law Tobi and two anti-colonial firebrands named Baba and Mlunguzi. His mother, Suthu, urged him to join the Cattle-Killing.

> It is all very well for you Sandile. You have your wives and children but I am solitary. I am longing to see my husband; you are keeping him from rising by your disobedience to the command of the spirits. [38]

Sandile was also worried about his political standing among his fellow Ngqika chiefs. Although he was the undisputed Great Son of his late father Ngqika (d.1829), he was in constant competition with his elder brother Maqoma, whose skill with words and courage in battle Sandile could never hope to match. Maqoma was urging his fellow Ngqika chiefs to throw off their allegiance to Sandile and to place themselves directly under the rule of King Sarhili.[33] Sandile himself did not like the idea of disobeying Sarhili whom he had always respected and heeded. He was well and truly caught in the middle.

In deference to Brownlee, Sandile permitted the unbelievers to cultivate his gardens and those of his mother Suthu and his Great Wife Noposi but he never fenced them and they soon spoiled. The chief also made life so unpleasant for those unbelievers who had been delegated to watch over him that they were forced to quit the Great Place. About the middle of October, Sandile began to kill his cattle, though he did so at night to hide this from Brownlee. He received messengers from Sarhili at night, alone with his mother and his brothers.[40]

The confidence of the believers was however undermined by their continuing uncertainty with regard to the date on which the prophecies were to be fulfilled. After a flurry of expectation towards the end of October, a reaction against the Cattle-Killing set in throughout the Ngqika district. Sandile called a meeting on 19 November and promised, with apparent sincerity, to cultivate. He even broke up a large patch of ground with his own hands. The wavering majority thronged Commissioner Brownlee with requests for seed. Though it was too late in the season to yield full crops, enough might still have been put into the ground to produce some kind of harvest.[41]

Everywhere else in British Kaffraria, the chiefs were forced to make a decision with regard to cultivation. Where the unbelieving chiefs were popular rulers and moved carefully, they were able to carry the majority of their people with them. Chief Anta called a meeting, from which his magistrate was excluded, in order to allow his people to air their thoughts freely. They decided to plant. Chief Dyani Tshatshu, who was more of a Christian than Chief Commissioner Maclean was willing to admit, set an example by cultivating himself, and most of his followers did the same. Chief Toyise stopped his followers from performing any other kind of work until they had their fields ready. Most of them cultivated though two of his brothers, including the rightful heir whose chieftainship Toyise had usurped, believed the prophecies and left the chiefdom. The young chief Jali, dominated by an old councillor of his late father named Mgwagwa, ploughed, though his elder brother Tabayi did not.[42]

The unbelieving Chief Siwani, deeply unpopular in his chiefdom for his violent authoritarianism and aggressively pro-colonial stance, peremptorily ordered his subjects to cultivate and not to listen to the 'lies' going about the country. But Siwani's determination cut no ice with his people, most of whom killed their cattle, refused to cultivate and regarded Bangayi, the son of the imprisoned Siyolo, as their real leader. Siwani survived at least one assassination attempt and chose not to visit homesteads in his own chiefdom for fear that he would be mobbed and killed.[43]

The gentle Christian Kama was unable to enforce the stern warnings he had given at his August meeting. Kama's country had experienced cattle-killing prophecies even before Nongqawuse. Many of the people were facing their second season without corn, but this did not in the least abate their commitment to the movement. They survived on the corn they purchased from their Mfengu neighbours in the Crown Reserve.[44] A high proportion of Kama's people were not his followers at all, but had settled in the large country given him by Governor Cathcart in 1853. They found their natural leader in Mate, the son of Kama's senior brother, Phatho. Mate acknowledged Kama's authority, and had acquiesced in Kama's strong stand against the Cattle-Killing, but he remained the son of his father. Phatho taunted Mate with cowardice and urged him to kill his cattle.[45]

Kama was not equal to the challenge of the believers. He was by nature a man of withdrawn and uncombative disposition, and preferred to stay at home rather than ride about enforcing unpopular decisions. He was, moreover, resentful of Grey's new administrative system which he professed not to understand. Reeve, his energetic magistrate, took Kama on a tour of his district and was distressed to find how few of the people had cultivated, and how many either received their chief coldly or avoided him altogether. Only Kama's long-standing followers cultivated, and Reeve foresaw trouble when their corn ripened and the believers were hungry. By December 1856, Kama was forced to admit that the southern half of his country was completely ungovernable. The attitude of his own Great Son, Mani, was also very much open to doubt.[46]

Only Maqoma, his natural truculence unrestrained by his weak magistrate Lucas, openly admitted to supporting the Cattle-Killing. When the rains finally came in late September none of his people cultivated. He declared that neither he nor his people would sow again in the lands of their exile, 'nor would they listen to anything the Government had to say . . . as long as they are living where they now are.' It was 'useless' to cultivate since the new people would destroy all the standing crops when they arrived. 'There appears to be a sullen determination amongst them to say and do nothing,' wrote Lucas. Maqoma issued an unambiguous order, forbidding cultivation in his territories and threatening those who had already planted. There was to be no individual choice in the matter of sowing. Kona, Maqoma's favourite son, worked on in his gardens although threatened by his father and abandoned by his mother until he was forced to quit the chiefdom and join his unbelieving brother Ned, who worked for Dr Fitzgerald at the hospital. In the end, not a single field was planted in Maqoma's chiefdom, and only one in that of his neighbour, Chief Bhotomane.[47] Phatho and Mhala, the most powerful chiefs in British Kaffraria after Sandile, were both ardent supporters of the Cattle-Killing. Phatho was greatly loved by his people and had managed to frustrate completely the efforts of Magistrate Vigne. 'Never in one instance,' complained Vigne, 'did I ever get any truthful information from a councillor and no councillor allowed himself or was permitted to listen to me and plant, or save his cattle.'[48] Yet even Phatho was too wary to come out into the open and admit that he supported the Cattle-Killing. In Vigne's presence, he urged his people to cultivate. He promised that he would do so himself as soon as the rains came. When the rains did come, he promised again to plough, but said he had no oxen. Magistrate Vigne stocked up with oxen, yokes and ploughs only to find that Phatho was claiming that there was no one in his country who knew how to use a plough. It was only when Vigne named three men who were able and willing to plough for the chief that Phatho was forced to admit that he had no intention of cultivating. Late in December, however, he was at it again, promising to cultivate at the first opportunity — which never quite arrived. Meanwhile, the stocks of seed corn lay rotting in Vigne's offices, with only five takers over a period of more than two months.

Mhala's problems were far more complex than those of Phatho: not only did he have an exceptionally tough magistrate in Major John Cox Gawler, but he faced considerable opposition from within his chiefdom, including his two senior sons, Makinana and Smith, and his powerful councillors, Ndayi and Gqirana. Mhala himself never doubted the truth of the prophecies but he nevertheless required some sort of concrete evidence if he was to carry his people with him. He sent several delegations to the Gxarha, the first as early as July 1856, but none of them returned with any conclusive proof. In public, Mhala refused to commit himself, saying that the Cattle-Killing was 'a foolish thing that he should not trouble his head about', but discreetly he attempted to substitute reliable believers for the unbelieving councillors on the government payroll. It was only with the visit of Sarhili's second messenger Sixaxa at the beginning of October that Mhala came out into the open and issued a formal order not to cultivate, threatening to confiscate the cattle of any who disobeyed. His confidence in the prophecies grew to the point that he felt able to challenge the government openly:

> The English tell us to cultivate and not to kill our cattle but how can we obey them when they have taken and killed our chiefs, Hintza, Seyolo etc, and we have done them no harm.[49]

Of all the unbelievers in Mhala's chiefdom only one man, Bulungwa, Mhala's nephew and a chief in his own right, dared to cultivate.

The story of Mhala will be taken up again in Chapter 6. Here we must summarize the position as it stood at the beginning of November 1856. Sandile, the most senior chief in British Kaffraria, was declining to cultivate but he was under pressure from Commissioner Brownlee. The unbelieving chiefs Anta, Oba, Toyise, Jali and Dyani Tshatshu were trying with some success to keep their people in line. Their fellow unbelievers, Chiefs Siwani and Kama, were failing to contain the believers in their chiefdoms. Maqoma publicly supported the Cattle-Killing and his fellow believers Phatho and Mhala were slowly coming out into the open. The overwhelming majority of ordinary Xhosa commoners were inclining towards the movement.

On the other hand, there was continuing uncertainty with regard to the actual date of the manifestation of the new people, and many believers were growing anxious about the lack of tangible results. The leading chiefs of the Thembu, the Mpondo and the Mpondomise had all made known their opinion that Mhlakaza was a 'fool', and five leading chiefs of Sarhili's own Gcaleka Xhosa had told the prophet that if he did not produce the new people forthwith they would cut him to shreds.[50] Chief Ngubo, Sarhili's highly respected cousin, had beaten Nongqawuse and called her a liar to her face. The Cattle-Killing movement was growing, but it was very fragile. Predictably, it was Governor Grey who gave it another boost.

As early as August, Grey had considered making some sort of naval demonstration at the mouth of the Kei River near the Gxarha.[51] He approached the captain of the *Castor* who pointed out that a visit to Kei mouth might prove counter-productive if the Xhosa thought that troops wanted to land but were unable to do so. This was sound advice, but Grey did not take it. In mid-October, he engaged *HMS Geyser* en route from Natal to Cape Town to call in at Kei mouth and see if it was possible to land men and supplies there (November 1856).

It was never a good idea to send the *Geyser* into Kei mouth without a very precise conception of the effect its presence was supposed to produce, but the plan miscarried to a truly spectacular extent. The acting commander was drunk and he did not stop at East London to pick up the pilot he required. The Geyser entered the Kei by the wrong channel. After sailing a little way up the river, it sent out a boat which promptly overturned, nearly drowning the five men in it. One of these, a Mr Upjohn from Cape Town, flatly refused to get back in the boat and walked all the way back to East London.

As soon as the Geyser entered the river, the Xhosa sounded the war cry and gathered in great numbers. They had no way of knowing that the ship was instructed only to make a survey and, given the very recent hostile exchange between Grey and Sarhili, they naturally presumed that the Geyser had come to attack them. When the boat capsized and the Geyser sailed tamely away without apparently achieving anything, the Xhosa were deeply impressed. The news soon spread that the new people had destroyed a ship, leaving only one man (Mr Upjohn) alive to carry the tidings home. As the rumour circulated, it grew in stature until it was commonly believed that Sarhili's father, the martyred Hintsa, had destroyed the Geyser with a wave of his hand, or that Mhlakaza had driven the troops on board mad, and sent them running wildly along the Kei road firing away their powder and ammunition.[52]

The news of the 'destruction' of the Geyser caused a great sensation among the Xhosa who greeted it with 'joy and avidity'. Many who had started to cultivate now stopped, and the only fields that were eventually sown were those of the original unbelievers. Cattle were killed 'more madly than ever' and within two weeks of the Geyser incident their numbers had visibly decreased. The believers, who were getting hungry, expected the Great Day to occur very soon, although there were some among them who felt that the new people were waiting for another ship so that they could demonstrate their power by again destroying it.

4. The Central Beliefs of the Xhosa Cattle-Killing

The stunning magnitude and seeming incomprehensibility of the Cattle-Killing have brought forth explanations as fantastic as the movement itself. Governor Grey and colonial historiography blamed the Cattle-Killing on a conspiracy by the Xhosa chiefs to foment war. Most Xhosa today blame the movement on a plot by Grey to fool their simple forefathers.[53] We need to look rather more closely at the central beliefs of the movement if we are to understand how and why the

Xhosa came to believe in the message of Nongqawuse. Merely to talk of 'superstition' and 'delusion' explains nothing at all. We have to try and understand why beliefs which seem to us — and to all Xhosa now living — patently absurd and impossible seemed logical and plausible to the Xhosa of 1856. As the explanation is not a simple one and will take some time and patience, readers who are eager to find out what happened next are encouraged to skip the remainder of this section, and proceed immediately to Chapter 5.

One reason why most explanations of the Cattle-Killing are so inadequate is that they are based on inadequate information. Historians and anthropologists have contented themselves with the order to kill cattle and with the prediction that the dead would rise, and have thus begged a great many questions. Who were the spirits who appeared to Nongqawuse? Were the cattle to be sacrificed or merely killed? Where did the idea of the resurrection come from? Which dead exactly were going to rise? What was supposed to happen after the resurrection? It is necessary to define the practices and the expectations of the believers in much greater detail before one can begin to explain the logic which underlay their actions. In doing so, it is very important to recreate as far as possible the Xhosa-language vocabulary used by the believers. Many of the most relevant concepts of the Cattle-Killing movement either do not translate directly into English, or are translated by English words which lack the weight and connotations of their Xhosa equivalents and thus hide from the English reader associations and connections which would be immediately apparent to a Xhosa.

In this section, I advance three propositions which will, I hope, clear up some of the existing misconceptions concerning the Cattle-Killing and explain why beliefs and practices which seem bizarre and irrational to us appeared natural and logical to the Xhosa of the 1850s.

(a) The form which the movement took, namely the killing of cattle, was suggested and determined by the lungsickness epidemic of 1854.

(b) The resurrection of the dead was only an aspect of a much wider event which the Xhosa believed to be in prospect, namely the regeneration of the earth and the re-enactment of the original Creation.

(c) The movement was by no means a 'pagan reaction', but one which combined Christian and pre-Christian elements fused under the heroic leadership of the expected redeemer, the son of Sifubasibanzi, the Broad-Chested One.

Nothing which follows should be interpreted as meaning that the Cattle-Killing movement was possessed of a fully articulated orthodox ideology. There were many uncertainties and ambiguities in the prophecies and instructions, and there was, in any case, plenty of room in the Xhosa world view for a variety of not necessarily consistent beliefs. The Cattle-Killing did, however, have a widespread and spontaneous appeal for the overwhelming majority of Xhosa. It cut right across the spectrum of divergent interests in Xhosa society. Its programme of action seemed necessary, credible and effective. This would not have been the case had it not been compatible with bedrock common beliefs which most Xhosa of the time shared but which are not obvious to us today.

(a) Lungsickness and cattle-killing

The lungsickness epidemic was a necessary cause of the Xhosa Cattle-Killing. Without it, the movement could never have occurred. This is not to say that lungsickness was a sufficient cause in itself, for it spread all over Africa without producing the same effect anywhere else. But at its very first stop, in Xhosaland, it encountered an exceptionally battered and divided society, demoralized by the frustration of a long series of military defeats; by the social insecurity of expulsion from natal lands and pastures; by the material sufferings of migrant labour and of resettlement in cramped and ecologically deficient locations; by the new wealth of those who had climbed on the military-commercial bandwagon of settler expansionism. Such conditions fed and sustained a belief which would have starved on the scepticism of a population enjoying economic abundance and social opportunity. The movement was further encouraged by contingent factors such as Grey's new policies and the hopes raised by rumours of British defeat in the Crimean War. But ultimately it was lungsickness which determined the form of the Cattle-Killing.

We have already seen that the early cattle-killing prophets, such as the wife of Bhulu, were inspired to dreams of resurrection by the outbreak of lungsickness. Nongqawuse's own prophecies were similarly linked with the epidemic. Information reaching Chief Commissioner Maclean indicated that the Xhosa had been ordered to 'kill all their cattle, so as to be stocked with others that are free from the disease', and that 'the cattle at present possessed by the Kaffirs are bewitched and that they must sacrifice them for others'. According to the Ndlambe Xhosa, Mhlakaza ordered them 'to get rid of their cattle . . . and the reason he has assigned is that they have all been wicked and everything belonging to them is therefore bad'. The Xhosa King Sarhili, whose enthusiastic support was crucial to the success of the movement, initially preserved his corn,

> but is killing his cattle faster than the flesh can be consumed he says it is because the lungsickness has broken out among his flocks, but from whatever cause it may be, I believe his slaughtering is confined to the flocks in which the disease has shown itself.[54]

Everywhere lungsickness went in Xhosaland, cattle-killing followed. This cannot have been a coincidence.

When, despite all their efforts, lungsickness broke out everywhere, the thoughts of the Xhosa turned naturally to the ultimate source of the disease. They recognized a category of minor illness, *umkuhlane*, but beyond *umkuhlane* lay *isifo*, or disease proper. 'In those days,' wrote the historian E.G. Sihele, 'there was no person who became sick just so. Being sick was caused by a reason.' Xhosa doctors of the time openly boasted of their power to 'raise plagues of all sorts, and inflict sores and different kinds of leprosy'. Major disasters such as drought or smallpox were usually blamed on malevolent sorcery, and there is some evidence that several people were executed as witches in the early attempts of the Xhosa to halt the spread of lungsickness. But since executing witches failed to stop the disease, the Xhosa were forced to look elsewhere for the sort of explanation which could serve as the basis for effective action.[55]

An alternative explanation for misfortune was that it was due to one's own shortcomings and derelictions of duty. The spirit world, as the guardians of the moral order, were responsible for punishing both individual and collective misbehaviour. Sickness in cattle was a common mark of divine displeasure as two texts, more than one hundred years apart, both demonstrate. Andrew Smith, writing in the 1820s, reported:

> When many cattle die at a kraal the sorcerers affirm that they see and talk with the *shologoo* (ghost or apparition) of some person deceased, and they affirm that the destruction of the cattle . . . is the result of the vengeance of the angry *shologoo* for the neglect of some arrangement relative to the cattle or people.[56]

And Chief Ndumiso Bhotomane, the distinguished oral historian, said in 1968:

> At times the cattle die. At times you expect to have good maize, but you don't get maize. Yes, sometimes you break a bone. You are being told about something, but you are stubborn. You are repeatedly told to do certain things, but you don't do them. That is why your thing is broken.[57]

This condition was referred to by Chief Bhotomane as *umzi ungalungi* (the homestead is not right), and the process of putting it right again is called *ukulungisa*. '-Lunga' in Xhosa combines the twin meanings of 'right' in English, namely the concept of order and the concept of justice. The term 'homestead' used by Chief Bhotomane might refer either to the residence of an individual or to the whole Xhosa nation, which was conceptualized in many contexts as one great family. Thus Nxele, the prophet of 1818-9, called on the Xhosa to leave evil ways so that the earth might be made 'right' (-*lunga*) again. Nongqawuse herself said that the spirits told her that they had come to 'put the country to rights'.[58]

The moral wrong for which the Xhosa had incurred the punishment of lungsickness was expressed in terms of 'witchcraft'. The injunction to give up witchcraft, little noticed in English secondary sources, is emphasized in both the Xhosa texts and in the original colonial accounts. According to Gqoba, the spirit who first appeared to Nongqawuse explained his order to kill by referring to the 'witchcraft' of the people:

> All those [cattle] now living must be slaughtered for they have been herded by defiled hands, for there are people about who are handling witchcraft.[59]

The spirit repeated his warning against witchcraft just before he disappeared, and Nongqawuse herself mentioned witchcraft on three occasions in Gqoba's relatively short text. Commissioner Brownlee reported that the 'ancestors' had told the Xhosa that 'before anything could be done for them, they were to put away witchcraft', and Chief Commissioner Maclean noted that 'all charms are to be given up'. The believing chief, Mhala, 'considered a man's killing his cattle a proof that the man either used no witchcraft or that he put it away now altogether'.[60]

Witchcraft, in the narrow sense of malevolent sorcery, was undoubtedly widespread in Xhosaland. Writing in the late 1850s, Agent Warner claimed that 'there is not the slightest doubt that the [Xhosa] do frequently attempt to bewitch each other; and for which purpose they practise a great number of villanous tricks'. And since all good or bad fortune was attributed to witchcraft, people believed it to be even more prevalent than it actually was. Thus the believing chief, Phatho, gave the following order to his upstart brother, Kama: '*Bulala ubuthi* [Kill your witchcraft] which has made you a great chief though not the Great Son.'[61]

Witchcraft was also associated with any sort of morally wrong behaviour which, being evil, constituted a polluting and harmful force in the naturally good and harmonious universe. This broader, more pervasive sense of witchcraft is apparent in Gqoba's phrase 'herded by defiled (*ezincolileyo*) hands', which he later amplifies as follows:

> They [the cattle] were reared by dirty hands that were handling witchcraft and other things such as incests and adulteries.[62]

One of these incests was the remarriage of widows, previously regarded as perfectly legitimate, but now forbidden by the prophetic group. However, by 'incests and adulteries', Gqoba is probably referring less to specific misdeeds than to sexual indiscretions generally — a category of behaviour, like witchcraft, so broad that few Xhosa could have denied its existence.[63]

Another cause of pollution was defeat in war, and it is easy to believe that the military disasters of the War of Mlanjeni (1850-3) not only filled the Xhosa with thoughts of loved ones recently dead but left them exposed to feelings of self-doubt and vulnerability, a state of mind associated with yet-to-be-cleansed impurity. Though there is no hard evidence of this, it is strongly suggested by the following evocative lines from the Xhosa poet and historian S.E.K. Mqhayi (d.1945), which explicitly link military defeat and consequent pollution to dreams of heavenly salvation:

> But this land is defeated and captured.
> All who live in it are become as prisoners.
> Man is defiled and polluted.
> It is now that the heavens fight and resound with war.[64]

Embracing as it did the admitted evils of sorcery, sexual misconduct and military defeat, the idea of witchcraft thus provided an interpretation of events which all Xhosa could accept and few contradict.

Existing cattle, being polluted by witchcraft, endangered the pure, undefiled cattle of the new people, which might 'not mix with those of men'. This made it necessary for the Xhosa to dispose of their cattle before the resurrection took place, and there are indications that in the initial stages Nongqawuse and Mhlakaza attached more importance to getting rid of the tainted cattle than to the method adopted in doing so. There are several reports before September 1856 of believers *selling* their cattle. Magistrate Gawler wrote that the message of the prophet was 'to get rid of their cattle either by slaughtering or by sale'. Bishop Gray, noting the low prices paid for Xhosa cattle, remarked that 'when they cannot sell them they kill them'.[65] This initial assumption of the believers, that the mere physical disposal of existing cattle would be sufficient to bring about the fulfilment of the prophecies, was modified as a result of the First Disappointment. From September 1856, cattle were sacrificed rather than disposed of at random.

Another implication of cattle killing is suggested by J.J.R. Jolobe in his poem on Nongqawuse, where he refers to it as *urumo*. The idea of *ukuruma* is based on the Xhosa concept of reciprocity, that one must give something oneself when one is expecting some gift or privilege. Thus a Xhosa would *ruma* a rainmaker if he wanted rain, or the river people if he wanted to cross a river, or a homestead if he wanted to attend a sacrificial feast. By so doing, the giver established a claim to the benefits he anticipated, and it is in this sense that we should interpret the following phrase from the colonial records: 'in order that this [prophecy] may be carried into effect, they must prove themselves deserving by acting up to their commands'. The millennium was thus not initially meant for all Xhosa indiscriminately, but only for those who showed themselves worthy by paying their dues and thus gaining access to the community of believers and their share of the great feast to come.[66]

The mass killing of cattle stemmed directly from the lungsickness epidemic, but soon acquired wider symbolic significance. Mysterious and unpredictable, lungsickness was far beyond the power of the Xhosa stock owner to control, and overwhelmed his natural reluctance to slaughter by the near certainty that his cattle were going to die anyway. The concept of sacrifice naturally suggested by the killing of cattle clothed the act in symbolic significance and associated it with the usual religious practices observed during a time of divine affliction. In addition, the killing of cattle was a due, paid to the 'new people' in appreciation of their imminent arrival bearing a 'happy state of things to all'. It is to the nature of these new people and the content of this 'happy state' that we now turn.

(b) Starting all over again

Although the lungsickness epidemic gave rise to the Cattle-Killing, it cannot explain all the features and beliefs of the movement. For the Cattle-Killing was not merely negative, not merely concerned with the elimination of pollution and diseased cattle. It also incorporated positive expectations. The most important of these, obviously, was 'that the whole nation will rise from the dead'. This was not as abrupt a transition as one might think. For the Xhosa, as for many other African peoples, death was not a definite and conclusive departure from this earth. The dead lived on, though in a somewhat altered state. As one Xhosa expressed it in 1858, 'Even though dead, he [the departed one] is still alive.' Death does not sever all links 'because, it is said, that although he has today become a Great One, those who remain are [still] his family'. William Philip, the son of Cattle-Killing believers, referred to burial as the 'hiding' rather than the disposal of the body. At the funeral of a chief, the mourners cried out:

> Look upon us you who have gone to your vantage point.
> Look upon the family of your house.[67]

The image of the vantage point (imiboniselo) is especially striking. It implies that the dead have gone off not to a different place but to an elevated position, in the world but not of it, where they can see but not be seen.

The presence of the dead constantly manifested itself in the lives of the living. They were responsible for good health and prosperity as well as for bringing misfortune upon the guilty. 'Our daily life depends on him,' said Chief Bhotomane, 'even though he is no longer present.' The dead occasionally communicated directly with the living through the medium of dreams. And if, as Harriet Ngubane has recently maintained, sleep is a kind of miniature death, then death, like sleep, might be regarded as a normal and transient state. The idea that the dead might rise (the Xhosa word for 'rise', *vuka*, being the usual term for 'get up in the morning') was thus not in itself a startling or surprising one. The following comment by William Philip clearly shows that the prophecies of Nongqawuse operated well within established and accepted Xhosa beliefs concerning the powers and capabilities of the ancestors:

> The idea that a person does not die was an original belief of we black people. When, therefore, the girl spoke of the rising up, she was [merely] setting a spark to things that were already known concerning the ancestors.[68]

Although no Xhosa person then living had ever seen a mass rising of the dead on the scale envisaged by Nongqawuse, all were aware that the doctors whom they regularly consulted had experienced death and rebirth in the course of acquiring their special powers of communication with the invisible world.

> It is remarkable that the word [*thwasa*] used to express this state of initiation [as a doctor] means 'renewal', and is the same that is used for the first appearance of the new moon, and for the putting forth of the grass and buds at the commencement of spring. By which it is evidently intended to intimate that the man's heart is renewed, that he has become an entirely different person to what he was before, seeing with different eyes and hearing with different ears.[69]

There are enough important parallels between the process of *thwasa* and the Cattle-Killing movement to warrant us examining the former in more detail. After receiving his supernatural call, the initiate cut himself off from normal society. He refused to eat food cooked in the usual manner, cast aside his old garments, and lived off the pure and undefiled fruits of the field. He heard strange voices and seemed 'to converse with invisible and unknown beings on some strange and incomprehensible subjects'. If this behaviour was accepted by established doctors as a genuine call from the ancestors then certain ceremonies, including cattle-killing, would be performed which would enable the candidate to re-enter normal life in his reborn state as a qualified doctor.

During the Cattle-Killing, the believers refused to eat their usual food and they disposed of their personal ornaments. They sacrificed their cattle as a prelude to a future rebirth. Unfortunately, we do not know if the ordinary believer experienced mystical visions though Gqoba's account of one group at the Mpongo river is highly suggestive.

> [They] used to see abakweta [circumcision initiates] dancing on the surface of the water, and they thought they heard the thudding of the oxhide, accompanied by a song to which the abakweta danced. Truly, the people were so deluded that they went so far as to claim that they had seen the horns of cattle, heard the lowing of milk cows, the barking of dogs, and the songs of milkmen at milking-time.

Visitors to Nongqawuse's place are reported to have 'heard there at night, in the air, the old Xhosa heroes parading by in wild array'. It would be impossible to assert on the basis of limited evidence that the generality of believers experienced some kind of collective thwasa, but the turmoil, the frantic activity, and the suspension of usual routines and occupations must certainly have suggested a rite of passage from the old world to the new.[70]

In awaiting the rising of the dead, the Xhosa were clearly expecting the resurrection of their parents, grandparents, spouses and friends. Chief Mhala, for instance, 'believed that he should be restored to youth and see the resurrection of his father and all his dead relations'. Nevertheless, it is curious that the colonial sources seldom use the well-established English equivalents of Xhosa words such as izinyanya (ancestors) or imishologu (spirits). They almost invariably refer to the expected deliverers as 'the new people', a term which does not correlate directly with any phrase in the surviving Xhosa-language texts. The operative term, however, no matter what the expression used, would certainly have been -tsha, a common Xhosa word translated in the standard Xhosa dictionary as 'new, young, healthy'. This hypothesis is supported by Gqoba's reference to the reborn ancestors appearing 'selematsha' ('all new') and by Chief Bhotomane's narrative of the Cattle-Killing, in which he refers to new ('ezintsha') cattle and 'new' ('ngokutsha') food.[71]

The word 'tsha' is significant in that it associates the idea of newness with the idea of youth and health. The Xhosa linguist A.C. Jordan translates the phrase 'selematsha', which I have rendered 'all new', as 'fresh and strong', and his translation is equally valid.[72] 'New' in Xhosa does not have its English connotation of novelty or originality, but rather implies freshness and rebirth. The Xhosa idea of newness is rooted in their perception of the cyclical recurrence of natural phenomena and, ultimately, the cyclical nature of time itself.

Without entering into so vast a topic as African concepts of time, I wish merely to observe that the following assessment by Benjamin Ray seems to apply to the Xhosa:

> Instead of a linear unitary conception of time, there are a variety of 'times' associated with different kinds of natural phenomena and human activities. Time is episodic and discontinuous. . . . There is no absolute 'clock' or single time scale.[73]

The Xhosa did have a conception of linear time, expressed through genealogies and the succession of *iziganeko* (significant happenings) which men used to date events in their personal lives. Nevertheless, the annual cycle of stellar constellations, associated as these were with the changing of the seasons and the pattern of agricultural production, accustomed the Xhosa to expect every year the return of the circumstances of previous years. The rites of passage concerning birth, maturation and death represented human life not as an irreversible aging process but as a repetitive cycle comparable to the repetitive cycles of seasonal and agricultural change. One example of this, already mentioned, was *thwasa*, the association perceived betweeen the rebirth of a person as a diviner and the re-emergence of the new moon and the spring buds. Similarly, chiefs were buried standing or sitting upright, surrounded by their spears, their pipes and all the other personal possessions they would require in their new life.[74]

Nongqawuse did not, however, confine herself to prophesying the rebirth of the past and the regeneration of the present. She promised nothing less than the re-enactment of the act of Creation itself as expressed in the concept of *uHlanga*, by which the Xhosa meant both the Creator god and the source of creation. King Sarhili informed his people that uHlanga had appeared at the Gxarha River. Fadana, the leader of the Thembu believers, was said to be a man favoured by uHlanga. The believers thought that the settlers and the Christian Xhosa would return to the uHlanga when the prophecies were fulfilled. Uhlanga was even confused on occasion with the biblical story of Creation, as when it was rumoured that 'Adam our first father has come upon the earth accompanied by God and two sons of God, together with a numerous new people.'[75]

Uhlanga was believed to be the very place where God brought forth man and cattle upon the earth. It was pictured as a marsh (which appears to be solid but yet is not) overgrown with reeds which hid the entrance to a huge cavern in the centre of the earth from which the uHlanga sent forth all living things. Almost any river or deep pool potentially harboured an opening to the uHlanga. It was well known that spirits dimly connected with the ancestors and called 'river people' lived on the dry land which was to be found under the water in most rivers and pools.

The Xhosa did not regard the Creation as a one-off, never to be repeated event. According to Lichtenstein, who travelled in Xhosaland in 1805:

> It is a current belief among them, that far to the north of their country, there is a vast subterraneous cavern, from which their horned cattle originally came, and that cows and oxen might still be procured from it in great abundance, if the entrance of the cavern could again be found, and a proper bait silently laid there. The cattle would then come forth, when they might be taken, and they would bring a blessing upon the possessor.[76]

Nxele, the prophet and wardoctor of 1818-9, claimed to originate in the uHlanga, and he predicted on one occasion that the Xhosa 'would see all who had long been dead come forth alive from beneath the rock, and then all the people who possessed powers of witchcraft would be seized and placed in a cavern under the rock'.[77]

Nongqawuse's followers believed that these long-promised expectations would be fulfilled.

> The horns of oxen were said to be seen peeping from beneath the rushes which grew around a swampy pool near the village of the seer; and from a subterranean cave were heard the bellowing and knocking of the horns of cattle impatient to rise.[78]

The prophetess's residence on the Gxarha River was thus invested with all the attributes of the long-lost cavern of the uHlanga.

Most of the subsidiary rituals of the movement were associated with the general theme of regeneration, and echoed existing Xhosa practices regarding birth and death. The new houses and new milk sacks ordered by Nongqawuse followed the custom whereby a dead man's sons abandoned his old homestead and cut open his old milk sacks before starting afresh elsewhere in a new homestead with new milk sacks. The sale of old ornaments and the purchase of new ones followed customs relating to mourning and celebration. The *buka* roots, with which Nongqawuse bade the believers weave their new doors, were normally administered to young women to make them pregnant and prevent miscarriages.[79] The new houses, new grain pits and new cattle enclosures, untainted by the sins and failures of the past, were a representation in miniature for each homestead of the bright new order about to be reborn on earth.

The ban on cultivation was naturally associated with the destruction of old food stocks and the expected dawning of a wholly new era. Blight and wet had devastated the Xhosa sorghum just as the lungsickness had devastated their cattle. Just as the new cattle might not mix with those of men, so too the new people 'cannot eat the food of men'.[80] Phatho's men refused to cultivate that spring, but they bought new spades and hoes to till the ground in the new time coming. Cultivation had long been considered a human interference with the earth and the believers felt that it would 'disturb' the ground. Long before the Cattle-Killing, it was forbidden to cultivate the day after uHlanga had shown his displeasure by striking a homestead with lightning. When rainmakers asked uHlanga for rain, they forbade the people 'to take either pick-axe or seed-bag, to dig or plant during the day; lest the lowering clouds should be thereby driven away'. Xhosa labouring on the roads during the Cattle-Killing abandoned their jobs lest the noise of their picks disturb the cattle and delay their appearance.[81]

There was little room in the Cattle-Killing movement for whites and other peoples who lacked a place in the Xhosa cosmology. The movement owed part of its momentum to hatred of the colonial intruders and the expectations raised by rumours of the Crimean War, but it is unlikely that the initial talk of whites swept into the sea was anything more than a convenient way of disposing of an anomalous element who had no place in the indigenous Xhosa scheme of things. However, after the First Disappointment, the believers seem to have reached the conclusion that they had erred in excluding the whites and the Christian Xhosa. Orders went out that the whites should also kill their cattle, and the believers initiated dialogues with the mission converts in an attempt to persuade them that Nongqawuse's message was the fulfilment of biblical prophecy. The new offensive was short-lived and half-hearted and soon faded in the light of colonial antagonism and the need to find fresh scapegoats for continued failure. The whites, having killed the Son of God, were declared ineligible for salvation. Nevertheless the brief Christian offensive is significant inasmuch as it demonstrates that the main concern of the believers was not the expulsion of the settlers but the advent of a 'happy state of things to all'.[82]

The millennium was to be absolute and total. The future was seen through a haze of white, the colour of purity.[83] Not only were there to be new people, new cattle and eternal youth for all, there were to be no unfulfilled wants and desires of any kind. The new people would come ashore at designated places, mostly at the mouths of rivers. Their leader, according to Gqoba, was named Napakade, son of Sifuba-sibanzi. It was in the person of this figure that the strands of pre-Christian thought discussed in this section merged with the new teachings of the Christian missionaries.

(c) The Broad-Chested One

The noted anthropologist Monica Wilson called the Cattle-Killing movement a 'pagan reaction' to the pressures of colonial and Christian influence. But far from being a retreat into a pre-Christian shell, the Cattle-Killing owed its very existence to biblical doctrines. As the Bishop of Cape Town put it, 'it is curious to observe how much this false prophet Umhlakaza borrows from Christianity and the Bible'.[84] We, who know that Mhlakaza was no heathen witchdoctor but a converted Anglican, a man who could recite the Creed, the Lord's Prayer, the Ten Commandments and most of the liturgy, do not find it so surprising, but it is nevertheless necessary to explain why so many ordinary Xhosa found certain aspects of Christianity extremely appealing.

Mission propagation of Christianity had been proceeding continuously in Xhosaland since 1817, and, despite the small number of formal conversions, elements of Christian teaching had spread far and wide. The concept of resurrection in particular had gained strength from the disruption of funeral rituals after the smallpox epidemic of the 1770s. Despite the efforts of the early Xhosa prophets to reintroduce the custom of burial, the majority of Xhosa continued to drive out their dying relatives in order to evade the religious necessity of abandoning a homestead where a death had occurred. By 1850 some homesteads had been in the same locality for two or three generations.[85] The picture is one of an increasingly overcrowded population unhealthily squeezed together in a rapidly deteriorating environment. The spiritual effect of such material conditions may easily be imagined. Overcrowding collapsed the spatial distinctions which separated the world of the dead from that of the living. No longer were the dead safely 'sent home' to a distant place of the ancestors. No longer were their deserted homestead sites clearly distinguishable from the occupied homesteads of their descendants. Instead, the living residents of a site must have been constantly disturbed by thoughts of their ancestors roaming the homestead that was once their own. Perhaps in no other respect did colonial dispossession contribute more directly to the Cattle-Killing movement.

Nxele, who prophesied between 1816 and 1819, did much to popularize some of the more apocalyptic Christian ideas. Long before

Mhlakaza, he had fused the new Christian doctrines with established Xhosa ideas to create a new religious synthesis which was to exert a powerful influence on the Cattle-Killing movement. He taught of a white God and a black God, and of God's son, who had been murdered by the whites. Nxele maintained that he had been sent from the uHlanga to *lungisa* (put right) the world. He denied the finality of death. 'People do not die,' he said, 'they go to that chief [of Heaven and Earth].'[86] He ordered people to abandon witchcraft, to slaughter all red cattle and to destroy stores of corn. He predicted that the ancestors and new herds of cattle would rise from the dead, and he attempted to resurrect them out of a cavern below Gompo rock.

After the defeat of the Xhosa in the Fifth Frontier War (1818-9), Nxele was imprisoned on Robben Island. He was drowned in an attempt to escape, but right up to the Cattle-Killing, the Xhosa never abandoned the expectation of his return and he was repeatedly seen in dreams and visions. It was believed that he was the leader of the Russian army which was defeating the British in the Crimea, and when the new people appeared to Nongqawuse they said 'that they were the people often spoken of in former days by Lynx [Nxele] and Umlanjeni'.[87] The figure of Nxele would doubtless have played a leading part in the prophecies but for the vigorous rejection of Nongqawuse by Mjuza, his son and heir. Nevertheless, it was to Nxele that the Cattle-Killing owed many of its beliefs concerning uHlanga, sacrifice, the *lungisa* of the earth and the resurrection of the dead.

A new and revolutionary brand of Christianity was introduced to the Xhosa by the Khoi rebels who fought alongside them during the War of Mlanjeni. Mission products all, the Khoi read their Bibles regularly and they prepared themselves for battle by the devout singing of hymns. A commissariat messenger by the name of David Lavelot incited mutiny among the Cape Mounted Rifles in the course of daily prayer meetings, and the mutineers were characterized as men 'of a peculiarly religious turn of mind, or . . . under the influence of a species of fanaticism'. The following letter by one of their leaders displays an unmistakably millenarian turn of mind:

> Trust, therefore, in the Lord (whose character is known to be unfriendly to injustice), and undertake your work, and he will give us prosperity — a work for your mother-land and freedom, for it is now the time, yea, the appointed time, and no other.[88]

This was a version of Christianity very different from that taught by the missionaries and in places like the Waterkloof, where Maqoma's Xhosa lived cooped up with Khoi rebels for more than eighteen months, it could hardly have failed to make some impact on Xhosa beliefs.

The experiences of the first Christian missions to be established with King Sarhili and Chief Mhala, the two foremost supporters of the Cattle-Killing, show that these notoriously heathen rulers were surprisingly interested in certain aspects of Christianity. We have already seen how impressed Sarhili was by the 'large Pictorial Bible' which the missionary Waters showed him. More than a year later, in the midst of disappointment and starvation, Sarhili visited Waters again and impressed him by his knowledge of the story of Lazarus, who rose from the dead. Ten years after the Cattle-Killing, the embittered and fiercely anti-Christian king could still be 'electrified' by a discussion on the immortality of the soul, and raise pertinent questions concerning the death of the son of God.[89]

More than five years before the Cattle-Killing, Chief Mhala, who 'did not seem much interested' in the other aspects of Christianity, asked a visiting Bishop several 'questions about the soul coming back after death to revisit those still in the flesh' and got 'so much excited that the perspiration ran down his naked body'. Greenstock, the missionary working among Mhala's people, found that they were constantly asking questions on religious subjects. The origin of evil was a great favourite, and they wondered what people ate in heaven. Mhala felt that the Cattle-Killing doctrines were quite compatible with Christianity. 'Why should not cattle rise as well as human beings?' he asked. 'They have spirits and were created on the same day with man.' Many Xhosa thought that parts of the Bible were far more improbable than the ideas of Nongqawuse. They doubted that God had exhausted all His Wisdom when he gave 'His Book' to man. 'Might He not still have another revelation to make?' they asked. Mhala's Great Son felt that it was only out of prejudice that the whites refused to accept the Cattle-Killing prophecies. 'Why should you English set down the [Xhosa] as fools?' he asked. 'You certainly have great skill in arts and manufactures but may not we surpass you in our knowledge of other things?' The believers felt not only that Christianity was compatible with Cattle-Killing beliefs, but even that Christianity positively corroborated Nongqawuse.[90]

The Christian element was an essential component of the identity of the spirits who appeared to Nongqawuse and promised to send forth new people and new cattle upon the earth. William Gqoba rendered the name of the first spirit as 'Napakade, son of Sifuba-sibanzi' and the same two names occur, together with uHlanga, in the colonial records, although 'Napakade' or 'UnguNapakade' ('Eternal One') is usually given precedence over 'Sifuba-sibanzi' ('Broad-Breasted One'). The introduction of two new figures rather than one probably reflects the Christian dichotomy between God and Christ, and Xhosa uncertainty regarding the relative status of the two probably reflects the problems they had in defining a relationship in which God/Napakade is senior but Christ/Sifuba-sibanzi is more active. The following quotation, describing the attempts of a Cattle-Killing prophetess to account for the failure of her prophecies demonstrates this confusion:

> She [Nonkosi, a prophetess in Mhala's country] talked of Sifuba-sibanzi, that is the broad-breasted one . . . and Ungunapakade, the eternal one. The Broad-Breasted One will manifest himself to the Eternal One, and the Eternal One will invite the Broad-Breasted One to rise from death and he will do the same. And the latter [Napakade] will make it known to the other [Sifuba-sibanzi] that he must wait for his arising so that he [Sifuba-sibanzi] can follow him [Napakade]. But Sifuba-Sibanzi said that he had spoken of a rising first so he wanted to arise first.[91]

It is difficult to be sure when these two names originated. It has been argued that Sifuba-sibanzi, which is today a universally recognized praise name for Jesus Christ, was originally a Khoi name for God, and certainly it fits in well with the more anthropomorphized Khoi view of the Deity. Most Xhosa, however, associate the name with the teachings of the Xhosa Christian prophet Ntsikana (d.1822), who was a contemporary of Nxele. The Xhosa historian S.E.K. Mqhayi, writing in the 1920s, said that Mlanjeni predicted just before he died that he was going across the sea to meet Sifuba-sibanzi. Yet Chief Commissioner Maclean, who was usually well-informed, referred to the name as a 'new creation', and several contemporary reports link the name Sifuba-sibanzi to the Russians,[92] whose supposed victory in the Crimea produced the spate of millenarian prophecies immediately preceding those of Nongqawuse.

The origin of the name 'Napakade' (Eternal One) is even more obscure. However it is clear that both 'Broad-Chested One' and 'Eternal One' are typical of the sort of heroic apostrophe which fits in as well with Xhosa praise poetry as with Christian moral tales in the vein of Pilgrim's Progress, which have been immensely popular in Xhosaland. The fusion of Xhosa and Christian prophecies, united in the figure of Sifuba-sibanzi, created an apocalyptic tradition which outlasted the Cattle-Killing and remained potent well into the twentieth century.

> Then at last there will be a general rising in which a mother will quarrel with her own daughter-in-law; the son will rise against his father, and friend against friend. Men will stab each other's shoulders, and there

will be such a crossing and recrossing as can only be likened to ants gathering stalks of dried grass. But these things are only as travail pains of child-birth. Then the end will come — the beginning of peace for which there had been no pre-concerted council or arrangement of man. The reign of BROAD-BREAST (Sifuba-sibanzi) will commence and continue in the lasting peace of the Son of Man.[93]

These late nineteenth-century prophecies relating to migrant labour (the ants crossing and recrossing, bearing heavy loads) and to the collapse of social ties and family life aptly epitomize more than a century of Xhosa history — and help to explain the millenarian thread which preceded and actually survived the disaster of the Great Cattle-Killing.

Conclusion

The Xhosa Cattle-Killing movement, suggested in the first instance by the lungsickness epidemic of 1853, tapped a deep-seated emotional and spiritual malaise resulting from material deprivation and military defeat. By blaming the epidemic on witchcraft and proposing to cleanse the earth of its taint, Nongqawuse's prophecies provided an explanation for current circumstances and a rationale for future action. The ideology of the Cattle-Killing movement combined old and new ideas, both of which were equally necessary to its credibility. Familiar beliefs concerning sacrifice, Creation and the ancestors rooted the movement in a conceptual world which the Xhosa understood and trusted. As the Reverend Philip said, 'When . . . the girl spoke of the rising up, she was merely setting a spark to things that were already known.'[94] The new concepts of an expected redeemer and an earthly resurrection, unwittingly disseminated by the missions via the prophet Nxele, seemed to provide a possible means of escape from the hopeless and desolate situation in which the Xhosa found themselves. Even the Bible, a book which the colonial intruders themselves claimed to be the truth, appeared to confirm Nongqawuse's prophecies. The central beliefs of the Xhosa Cattle-Killing were neither irrational nor atavistic. Ironically, it was probably because they were so rational and so appropriate that they ultimately proved to be so fatal.

Notes

1. BK 70 C. Brownlee-J. Maclean, 25 Aug. 1856; BK 81 J. Gawler-J. Maclean 30 Aug. 1856.
2. Imperial Blue Book 2352 of 1857-8, J. Warner-W.G.B. Shepstone, 23 Sept. 1856, p.26; Gqoba (1888) Part I; GH 8/37 Information received from Umjuza, 10 Feb. 1859.
3. The best account of Xhosa sacrifice is in Kropf and Godfrey (1915), pp.77-8. See also W. Shaw (1860), pp.449-50; J.H. Soga (n.d.), Ch. 8; T.B. Soga (n.d), pp.129-30; H. Scheub, interview with Chief N. Bhotomane (1968); J. Peires, Interviews with N. Qeqe, Shixini Location, Willowvale District, October and November 1975.
4. GH 28/71 J. Maclean-G. Grey, 21 Aug. 1856; GH 8/49 J. Maclean-G. Grey, 28 Aug. 1856.
5. BK 70 C. Brownlee-J. Maclean, 2 Oct. 1856; BK 81 J. Gawler-J. Maclean, 7, 25 Sept., 1 Oct. 1856; BK 89 Secret information 18 Sept. 1856.
6. Acc.793 Statement of Yosi 3 Nov. 1856. Kashe, the bearer of the quoted statement, gave out that he was an official messenger of Sarhili. But Sarhili had an official messenger, Sixaxa, in British Kaffraria already and it is unlikely that he would have sent another. Whoever Kashe actually was, there is no reason to doubt that this sort of statement was widely reported and generally believed in British Kaffraria. The second statement is a version of an official message as understood by Chief Xhoxho, Sandile's somewhat slow-witted brother. BK 70 C. Brownlee-J. Maclean, 24 Sept. 1856.
7. BK 70 C. Brownlee-J. Maclean, 4 Oct. 1856; BK 71 C. Brownlee-J. Maclean, 21 Feb. 1857.
8. For Joyi's speech, CO 2949 J. Warner-R. Southey, 24 Feb. 1857. I have taken a liberty with historical truth here. Joyi only made this speech after the Cattle-Killing. But his attitude was consistently hostile throughout. For the Thembu, see Imperial Blue Book 2352 of 1857-8, J. Warner-W.G.B. Shepstone, 23 Sept. 1856, p.26; BK 89 Secret Information 18 Sept. 1856. There is a great deal of information on the Thembu which I have been unable to treat in detail. See J. Warner's dispatches in CO 2949-CO 2951. For more on Fadana, see Ch. 9/1.
9. BK 89 Information communicated to the Chief Commissioner 13, 26 Oct. 1856.
10. All the details of Moshoeshoe's dealings with Sarhili were painstakingly assembled by Maclean and enclosed in his lengthy despatch to Grey, 25 March 1856, printed in Imperial Blue Book 2352 of 1857-8, p.72 ff. Reading Maclean's report, one finds it hard to believe that they were able to draw such far-reaching conclusions from such a small amount of evidence.
11. BK 81 J. Gawler-J. Maclean, 25 Sept. 1856; MS 3328 Cory Library, J. Ross-J. Laing, 11 Oct. 1856; King William's Town Gazette, 16 Oct. 1856.
12. MS 9043 Cory Library, J. Laing Diary, 1 Oct. 1856; LMS papers, SOAS, Box 30 F.G. Kayser-LMS, Oct. 1856; MS 3236 Cory Library, J. Ross-A. Thomson, 24 Nov. 1856; BK 89 Information communicated by Jan Tshatshu, 15 Oct. 1856; Chalmers (1878), p.355.
13. BK 89 Information communicated by Jan Tshatshu, 13, 15 Oct. 1856.

14. See, for example, some of Maclean's early despatches, such as GH 8/29 J. Maclean-G. Grey, 17 Aug. 1856; BK 373 J. Maclean-W. Liddle, 4 Aug. 1856.
15. BK 373 J. Maclean-W. Liddle, 18 Aug. 1856.
16. GH 8/29 J. Maclean-Sarhili, 15 July 1856; GH 30/4 G. Grey-J. Maclean, 24 July 1856; GH 8/49 J. Maclean-G. Grey, 31 July 1856.
17. BK 70 C. Brownlee-J. Maclean, 24 Sept. 1856.
18. Imperial Blue Book 2352 of 1857-8, C. Brownlee-J. Maclean, 16 Aug. 1856, p.18; BK 70 C. Brownlee-J. Maclean, 6, 11 Aug. 1856.
19. GH 8/29 Marginal note by Grey on Schedule 306, 14 Aug. 1856.
20. GH 30/4 G. Grey-J. Maclean, 28 Aug. 1856.
21. Grey's mysterious illness, which was always blamed on his 'wound', was characterized by abrupt and sudden changes of mood, great waves of enthusiasm and frantic scheming alternating with deep lows of lethargy and depression, during which he was too weak even to receive visitors or write letters. The evidence on Grey's health, which is very limited, can be found in: GH 30/11 C. Boyle-H. Cotterill, 16 May 1857; GH 23/27 G. Grey-H. Labouchere, 6 June 1857; GH 8/16 J. Jackson-G. Grey, 16 May 1857; Acc. 611/7 R. Rawson-R. Southey, 11 Jan. 1858.
22. For example, Maqoma and his Great Son, Namba. GH 8/29 H. Lucas-J. Maclean, 27 Aug. 1856.
23. Imperial Blue Book 2352 of 1857-8, G. Grey-H. Labouchere, 20 Sept., 24 Oct. 1856, pp.24-5, 52-3.
24. BK 70 C. Brownlee-J. Maclean, 21 Sept. 1856.
25. BK 85 R. Robertson-J. Maclean, 15 Sept., 27 Oct. 1856; BK 86 F. Reeve-J. Maclean, 7 Sept. 1856; BK 82 H. Lucas-J. Maclean, 29 Sept. 1856.
26. BK 140 Memorandum of a meeting, 29 Sept. 1856; BK 140 H. Vigne- J. Maclean, 3, 10 Nov. 1856.
27. BK 89 Secret information, 18 Sept. 1856; BK 70 C. Brownlee-J. Maclean, 24 Sept. 1856; GH 28/71 C. Brownlee-J. Maclean, 26 Sept. 1856.
28. BK 81 J. Gawler-J. Maclean, 25 Sept. 1856; GH 30/12 G. Grey-Umhala, 27 Sept. 1856.
29. GH 30/12 G. Grey-Sandile, 27 Sept. 1856; GH 30/12 G. Grey-Kreli, 27 Sept. 1856.
30. GH 8/29 C. Brownlee-J. Maclean, 20 Oct. 1856; BK 89 Secret information, 27 Oct. 1856.
31. 20/2/1 Memorandum by J. Maclean, 12 Oct. 1856.
32. BK 140 Statement of Kreli in reply to H.E. the Governor's letter, 3 Nov. 1856.
33. Imperial Blue Book 2352 of 1857-8, C. Brownlee-J. Maclean, 27 Sept. 1856, Memorandum of a meeting, 29 Sept. 1856, pp.32-3; A.W. Burton (1950), p.31; BK 70 C. Brownlee-J. Maclean, 29 Sept. 1856.
34. BK 140 Minutes of a meeting at Pato's Great Place, 26 Sept. 1856.
35. Grahamstown Journal, 7, 11 Nov. 1856; GH 8/30 C. Brownlee-J. Maclean, 7 Dec. 1856; MS 2990 Cory Library, J. Ross-R. Ross, 13 Sept. 1856; GH 8/49 J. Maclean-G. Grey, 13 Oct. 1856.
36. BK 70 C. Brownlee-J. Maclean, 21 Sept. 1856; BK 81 J. Gawler-J. Maclean, 1 Oct. 1856; MS 3328 Cory Library, J. Ross-J. Laing, 11 Oct. 1856; MS 3236 Cory Library, J. Ross-A. Thomson, 24 Nov. 1856; Mission Record (United Presbyterian Church), 12 (1857), Letter from J. Cumming, 3 Dec. 1856.
37. GH 8/30 C. Brownlee-J. Maclean, 7 Dec. 1856. See also BK 373 J. Maclean-

G. Grey, 3 Nov. 1856; BK 81 J. Gawler-J. Maclean, 17 Oct. 1856; GH 8/49 J. Maclean-G. Grey, 11 Dec. 1856.
38. Brownlee (1916), p.134; BK 70 C. Brownlee-J. Maclean 28, 31 Aug., 19 Oct. 1856. For further details on the composition of the believing and unbelieving parties, see Ch. 4/4.
39. Brownlee (1916), pp.146-7; MS 8981 Cory Library, C. Brownlee-P. Wodehouse, 19 June 1866.
40. BK 70 C. Brownlee-J. Maclean, 13, 19 Oct., 2 Nov. 1856; Acc 793 J. Gawler-J. Maclean, 24 Oct. 1856.
41. GH 8/29 C. Brownlee-J. Maclean, 22 Oct. 1856; BK 70 C. Brownlee-J. Maclean, 2, 19 Nov. 1856.
42. BK 71 C. Brownlee-J. Maclean, 28 May 1857; BK 85 R. Robertson-J. Maclean, 30 Oct. 1856; BK 89 R. Fielding-J. Maclean, 14 Oct. 1856; GH 20/2/1 John Ayliff (jnr)-J. Maclean, 11 Oct. 1856; BK 140 H. Vigne-J. Maclean, 25 Oct., 20 Nov. 1856; GH 8/49 R. Tainton-J. Maclean, 29 Dec. 1856.
43. BK 140 Information communicated to the Chief Commissioner, 8 Oct. 1856; GH 8/31 R. Hawkes-J. Maclean, 17 March 1857; CO 2935 T. Stringfellow-R. Southey, 14 Sept. 1856; *KWT Gazette*, 4 Sept. 1856.
44. BK 86 F. Reeve, Diary, 27 Sept. 1856.
45. BK 89 Secret information, 19 Sept. 1856.
46. BK 86 F. Reeve, Diary 7 Sept., 15 Oct., 27 Nov. 1856; BK 86 F. Reeve-J. Maclean, 12 Dec. 1856.
47. BK 82 H. Lucas-J. Maclean, 26 Oct., 29 Nov. 1856; GH 8/29 H. Lucas-J. Maclean, 27 Sept. 1856; BK 70 C. Brownlee-J. Maclean, 19 Oct. 1856; GH 8/49 J. Fitzgerald-J. Maclean, n.d. (Dec. 1856).
48. BK 83 H. Vigne-J. Maclean, 16 Sept. 1856; BK 140 H. Vigne-J. Maclean, 10, 20 Nov. 1856; GH 28/71 H. Vigne-J. Maclean, 9 Aug. 1856; GH 8/49 J. Maclean-G. Grey, 27 Oct. 1856.
49. GH 18/6 J. Gawler-J. Maclean, 15 Aug. 1856; BK 81 J. Gawler-J. Maclean, 1, 14 Oct. 1856; GH 8/49 J. Gawler-J. Maclean, 11 Oct. 1856.
50. Acc 793 J. Gawler-J. Maclean, 24 Oct. 1856; *KWT Gazette*, 13 Nov. 1856.
51. On the *Geyser*, see GH 22/8 H. Trotter-G. Grey, 15 Aug. 1856; GH 8/49 J. Maclean-G. Grey, 16 Oct., 10, 20 Nov. 1856; GH 30/4 G. Grey-J. Maclean, 18, 28 Oct. 1856; BK 81 J. Gawler-J. Maclean, 17 Oct. 1856; *Gtn Journal*, 28 July 1857.
52. On the Xhosa reaction to the *Geyser* incident: BK 70 C. Brownlee-J. Maclean, 11 Dec. 1856; BK 81 J. Gawler-J. Maclean, 20 Nov. 1856; GH 8/30 R. Robertson-J. Maclean, 23 Nov. 1856; GH 8/30 C. Brownlee-J. Maclean, 7 Dec. 1856; *Argus*, 3 Jan. 1857.
53. The most perceptive accounts thus far, those of Wilson (1969, 1977) and Zarwan (n.d.), have pointed out some of the more obvious components of the Cattle-Killing belief but fall far short of providing a satisfactory explanation. Wilson, for example, writes that 'the insistence on purification, renouncing witchcraft, and sacrifice was all part of the traditional pattern', while Zarwan thinks that 'the cattle-killings were traditional in form and the leaders were diviners of the traditional pattern'. This emphasis on 'tradition' is wholly misleading. Although various forms of purification, divination, sacrifice and witchcraft were practised in Xhosaland long before the Cattle-Killing, these practices were far too

diverse and far too liable to change over time to be fossilized conceptually as 'traditional patterns'. Whatever 'traditional patterns' may have existed in Xhosaland before 1856, they certainly did not include mass destruction of basic subsistence needs or the expectation of an imminent resurrection of the dead.

In their well-meant attempts to show that the Cattle-Killing was not entirely devoid of logic, Wilson and Zarwan have missed the crucial element of innovation in the movement. Despite their sympathetic approach, the Wilson-Zarwan view that 'the pagan reaction . . . was to seek supernatural aid' is not very far removed from the opinion of previous writers that the Xhosa relapsed into 'superstition' and 'delusion' when confronted with repeated military defeats.

54. BK 70 C. Brownlee-J. Maclean, 25 Aug. 1856; GH 8/29 Information communicated to Chief Commissioner, 1, 4 July 1856; Acc 793 J. Gawler-J. Maclean, 25 July 1856.
55. E.G. Sihele, 'Ibali labaThembu', uncatalogued MS, Cory Library, Grahamstown; Lakeman (1880), p.141; Merriman (1957), pp. 215-6.
56. Andrew Smith, 'Kaffir notes', South African Museum, Cape Town, p.373.
57. Interview with Chief Ndumiso Bhotomane, conducted by Professor Harold Scheub, Kentani District, 1968.
58. MS 172c Grey Collection, South African Library, 'Kafir legends and history by Wm. Kekale Kaye'; GH 8/33 Schedule 69 of 1858, 'Examination of the Kafir prophetess Nonqause before Major Gawler', 27 April 1858.
59. Gqoba, 'Isizatu', Part I.
60. GH 8/28 J. Maclean-G. Grey, 17 July 1856; GH 8/29 C. Brownlee-J. Maclean, 29 June 1856; BK 81 J. Gawler-J. Maclean, 14 Jan. 1857.
61. J. Warner in Maclean (1858), p.89; GH 8/29 F. Reeve-J. Maclean, 11 July 1856. Also W. Shaw (1860), p.446.
62. Gqoba, 'Isizatu', Part II.
63. It is worth noting that the failure of the wardoctor Mlanjeni's promise to turn bullets into water was attributed by him to the failure of certain young warriors to heed his ban on sexual intercourse before battle. Interview with W. Nkabi, Bulembu Location, King William's Town District, 24 Aug. 1975; Interview with M. Soga, Kobonqaba Location, Kentani District, 25 Aug. 1983.
64. S.E.K. Mqhayi, 'A! Sifuba-sibanzi!' in Imibengo, ed. W.G. Bennie (Lovedale: Mission Press, 1935), pp.189-90. I am indebted to Professor Wandile Kuse for drawing this to my attention and helping me with the translation.
65. MS 9063 Cory Library, N. Falati,'The story of Ntsikana' (1895); Acc 793 J. Gawler-J. Maclean, 14 July 1856; BK 109 H. Vigne-J. Maclean, 20 Aug. 1856; Bishop R. Gray's Journal in 'Missions to the heathen', The Church Chronicle, Vol. 2 (Grahamstown, 1881), p.330; KWT Gazette, 14 Aug. 1856.
66. J.J.R. Jolobe, Ilitha (Johannesburg: A.P., 1959), p.57; Kropf and Godfrey (1915), p.375; GH 8/27 Information communicated to the Chief Commissioner, 4 July 1856.
67. MS 172c and 172d, South African Library, Cape Town, 'Kafir legends and history by Wm Kekale Kaye'; W. Philip, letter to Isigidimi samaXosa, 2 July 1888.
68. Philip, in Isigidimi; Bhotomane, interview; Ngubane (1977), p.115.

69. Warner, in Maclean (1858), p.82.
70. Gqoba, 'Isizatu', Part I; *Berlin Missionberichte*, 1858, p.38.
71. CO 2950 J. Warner-R. Southey, 29 July 1857; GH 8/29 Information communicated to the Chief Commissioner, 4 July 1856; Bhotomane, interview; Gqoba, 'Isizatu', Part I.
72. Jordan (1973), p.74.
73. Ray (1976), p.41.
74. Kay (1833), p.194.
75. CO 2950 J. Warner-R. Southey, 29 July 1857; LG 410 J. Warner-R. Southey, 14 July 1857; GH 8/29 F. Reeve-J. Maclean, 2 Aug. 1856; BK 89 Information communicated by Jan Tshatshu, 15 Oct. 1856; GH 8/29 C. Brownlee-J. Maclean, 22 Oct. 1856.
76. H. Lichtenstein (1812-5), Vol. 1, p.314.
77. W. Shaw (1972), p.103.
78. C. Brownlee (1916), pp.126-7. A report in the *Grahamstown Journal*, 9 Aug. 1856, stated that the new people were expected to rise 'out of a pit or cave in the mouth of the Kei river'.
79. J.H.Soga (n.d.), p.324; Kropf and Godfrey (1915), p.46.
80. MS 9063, Cory Library. N. Falati, 'The story of Ntsikana'.
81. MS 15,413, Cory Library, R.F. Hornabrook, 'Cattle killing mania'; Kay (1833), p.208; C. Rose, quoted in J.W.D. Moodie (1835), Vol. 2, p.331; GH 28/71 J. Maclean-G. Grey, 11 Aug. 1856; GH 8/71 H. Vigne-J. Maclean, 9 Aug. 1856.
82. BK 81 J. Gawler-J. Maclean, 25 Sept. 1856; MS 8295, Cory Library, C. Brownlee-n.a., 18 Oct. 1856; MS 3328 Cory Library, J. Ross-J. Laing, 11 Oct. 1856; London Missionary Society Archives, School of Oriental and African Studies, London, Box 30, F.G. Kayser-L.M.S., Oct. 1856; MS 9043, Cory Library, Diary of J. Laing, 1 Oct. 1856.
83. It was rumoured among the believers that Chief Kama had seen a vision of 'white tents', MS 3328 Cory Library, J. Ross-J. Laing, 11 Oct. 1856; GH 28/71 Memo by J. Maclean. The 'great man' rumoured to have appeared to believers was dressed in a white blanket. On colour symbolism among the Nguni, see Ngubane (1977), Ch. 7.
84. Journal of Bishop Gray, 11 Aug. 1856, *Church Chronicle*, Vol. 3 (Grahamstown, 1882), p.238.
85. Maclean (1858), p.153. See also A. Smith, 'Kafir notes', p.372, South African Museum, Cape Town.
86. MS 172c, S.A. Library, 'Kaffir legends and history by Wm Kekale Kaye'. For more on Nxele, see Peires (1981), Ch. 5. There is further important evidence on Nxele's prophecies in MS 157 f, S.A. Library, G. Cyrus-R. Graham, 10 Jan. 1857.
87. GH 8/29 Information communicated to the Chief Commissioner, 4 July 1856; BK 14 Statement made . . . by Umjuza, 24 Feb. 1858.
88. For the Khoi rebellion, see T. Kirk, 'Progress and decline in the Kat River Settlement, 1829-54', *JAH*, 14 (1973). For the quotations, see Imperial Blue Books 1428 of 1852, W. Uithaalder-A. Kok, 11 June 1851, p.152, and 1380 of 1851, H. Smith-Earl Grey, 17 March 1851, p.21. See also S. Lakeman (1880), p.60.
89. United Society for the Propagation of the Gospel, Cory Library Microfilm 172/2, Journal of H.T. Waters, 15 Nov. 1855, 1 Jan. 1856, 7 July 1857; T. Soga

in *Monthly Records of the United Presbyterian Church,* 1 March 1867, N.S., Vol. 1, Part 15; MIC 172/2, Cory Library, U.S.P.G. Archives, Journal of W. Greenstock, Nov. 1856; BK 81 J. Gawler-J. Maclean, 7 Sept. 1856; MS 3236, Cory Library, J. Ross-A. Thomson, 24 Nov. 1856; BK 89 Substance of statements made to the Chief Commissioner, 5 Feb. 1857; C.N. Gray, *Life of Robert Gray* (London: Rivingtons, 1883), p.133.

91. Abt. 3, Berlin Missionary Archives, J. Rein-Berlin Missionary Society, Report for second half year, 1857.

92. Nzulu Lwazi, 'URev Tiyo Soga'; Kropf and Godfrey (1915), p.106; J. Hodgson, *Ntsikana's Great Hymn* (Cape Town: University of Cape Town, 1980), pp.37-9. Berlin Missionary Archives, Abt. 3, Report of Kropf and Liefeldt for first half year, 1856 and BK 71 C. Brownlee-J. Maclean, 12 Dec. 1856, both specifically link the name Sifuba-sibanzi with the Russians. The suggestion that the name may be of Khoi origin comes from M. Mabona, 'The interaction and development of different religions in the eastern Cape' (Religious Studies essay, School of Oriental and African Studies, 1975), p.107. Although I find Mabona's general argument convincing, I consider that his specific citation (to a Latin source of 1691, in which the Khoi describe their God as 'grandi eundem esse et deducto in latitudinem corpore') too general to refer specifically to a 'Broad-Chested One'.

93. J.K. Bokwe, *The Story of Ntsikana* (Lovedale Mission Press, 1914), pp.23-4. Similar prophecies may be found in MS 9063 N. Falati, 'The story of Ntsikana' (1895), and in contemporary oral tradition.

94. *Isigidimi,* 2 July 1888.

CHAPTER 5

To the Bitter End

1. Waiting for Nxito

The early months of the Cattle-Killing were happy times for the believers as they wandered through their uncultivated fields or sat in the shade of their deserted cattle kraals, boasting of the powers of Mhlakaza and dreaming of a better world to come. 'The people are led by a strange infatuation,' reported Commissioner Brownlee. 'In the midst of their ruin they are happy and contented and in the confidence of the fulfilment of their expectations they now no longer make a secret of what was at first so carefully concealed.' 'I have seldom felt more depression of spirits than after my ride through Umhala's location,' wrote the stony-hearted Maclean. 'Everywhere I found the people cheerful, although the neglected fields spoke plainly of the woeful and calamitous hereafter — starvation and death — I spoke to several, but they merely smiled.' Chief Mhala's optimism was such that his goodwill embraced even his hated magistrate, Major Gawler. 'His former dull and frequently sullen and uncivil demeanour towards me has lately changed,' Gawler commented. 'He is now very civil, high-spirited and witty.' In October, the prophets ordered the people to adorn themselves beautifully in celebration of the coming of the new day 'and withered old hags who had discontinued painting and ornaments for years, though tottering with age and want are found covered with red clay and ornaments, hoping soon to have youth restored and an abundance of food'. The Xhosa on the public works cheerfully mocked their white overseers and frequently burst into song until they abandoned their labour altogether to prepare for the great day.[1]

The euphoric moods which seized hold of the believers when fulfilment seemed at hand alternated with spells of doubt and depression as hope was continually deferred. 'The supposed destruction of the Geyser has put their backs up,' wrote Brownlee in December, 'but they are going down again.'[2] Maqoma and Phatho were both heavy drinkers and Mhala, too, began to hit the bottle hard during the long months of waiting.[3] Even Sarhili admitted at one time that he had had doubts but that having started with this thing, he was determined to see it through.[4] As time passed, the believers were left with little to do but to sit 'in apathy regarding their fate, still deluding themselves in the hope that the time of their delivery is at hand'.[5]

For, by December 1856, most of the believers were getting very hungry. The worst conditions occurred in those parts of Xhosaland where drought and lungsickness had come earlier and where early prophets such as the wife of Bhulu had instigated the killing of cattle nearly a year before Nongqawuse. In Maqoma's country and in Phatho's, the spring of 1856 was the second sowing season to pass by without any attempt being made by the people to plant their crops. Many common people had already 'reduced themselves to a state of the greatest destitution' as early as August 1856, and survived only by going to the places of those who continued to kill their cattle and sharing their feasts. In late September, the first direct victim of the Cattle-Killing — the son of a diviner who had killed his cattle and refused to plant in 1855 — died of actual starvation near Peelton mission. Old people and children fainted from hunger and the very dogs were so deprived that they were too weak to rise and bark at the sight of strangers. People tightened their 'hunger belts' (special girdles fastened around the stomach) and women and children, still refusing to plant, were busily at work digging up roots and stripping mimosa trees of their bark, 'eking out a miserable subsistence, and anxiously looking for help from Umhlakaza'. Down by the coast they were reduced to eating shellfish and many old people and children died of dysentery.[6] Increasingly, those who had not stole from those who still had. The believers saved their milk cows till last — five or six were enough to feed a homestead — but as the prophetic exhortations continued, these too fell under the spear. Even the funeral herds of the deceased chiefs, consecrated at their burials and never slaughtered under normal conditions, were not to be spared. 'Hunger,' wrote Brownlee in early December, 'is fast closing upon its victims, and though there should be no war their sufferings will far exceed anything which they have hitherto experienced.'[7]

In their distress, the believing chiefs turned to Sarhili, the one man who, above all others, had taken the responsibilty of the Cattle-Killing upon himself. Prematurely aged and almost blind, the entire product of his thirty-five years' chieftainship now staked on the great gamble of the Cattle-Killing, the Gqunukhwebe chief Phatho called vainly on his King:

> This is the second year that I have not ploughed. The lung-sickness destroyed the most of my cattle. Some time since I saw some people from Krieli's country, they informed me that some new people had arrived in Krieli's country and they ordered the destruction of the cattle. I therefore killed those cattle which had been left over by the lung-sickness. My people are now in want. . . . Disappointment and shame come over me that I should receive no formal announcement from Krieli. . . . Krieli is our great chief and we look for his word.[8]

Maqoma, the greatest military commander in Xhosa history and now leading his brother Ngqika Xhosa chiefs into mass destitution, also sent messengers to Sarhili saying that the Ngqika were dying and that the promises should be fulfilled without further delay.

Disaffection was likewise spreading among Sarhili's own Gcaleka Xhosa. Nyoka, one of the King's councillors, was sent to Mhlakaza to collect the spoil taken from the *Geyser*, but returned saying that the reports of its destruction were false. The unbelieving chiefs and councillors led by the sceptical Ngubo mustered their strength and demanded that the new people be made to appear forthwith. Their wives and children would starve on account of Mhlakaza's falsehoods, they said, and if the prophecies remained unfulfilled they would cut the prophet and all he possessed into little strips. When Sarhili's uncle, Bhurhu, a late convert to the Cattle-Killing but now fully committed to it, urged his followers to complete the slaughter of their cattle, many of them refused angrily, saying 'that they had already killed most of their cattle, and before killing more, they want to see Umhlakaza's people and the cattle and other things promised'. A rumour began to spread to the effect that Sarhili had been bewitched by the Thembu chief Mqanqeni for putting away his Great Wife, Mqanqeni's sister, so that he saw things which no one else could see.[9]

No definite date had been set for the rising of the new people and the new cattle since the disappointment of August and the believers were growing impatient and restless. Sarhili would have liked to force the pace, but the matter was quite out of his hands. For several months, Nongqawuse and Nombanda had been demanding the return of Nxito, their chief, to his native place near the Gxarha.[10] We do not know enough about Nxito to be sure why it was that Nongqawuse was so insistent on seeing him. Certainly, the fact that he was her chief must have played its part, and his return to his late father's grave was very appropriate to the general Cattle-Killing theme of bringing the living and the dead together again. Perhaps Nxito's advanced age — he was well over seventy, perhaps well over eighty, and he belonged to the fast fading generation of Sarhili's grandparents — had something to do with it. Moreover, Nxito's lineage, the amaTshayelo, was equal in antiquity though junior in status to the two great lineages of Rharhabe and Gcaleka which dominated British Kaffraria and transKeian Xhosaland respectively. But whatever the reason, the return of Nxito came to dominate the fantasies of these two young girls on whose slightest word the fate of thousands of Xhosa now depended. The new people would show themselves, Nongqawuse said, when Nxito returned to the Kobonqaba river and took up residence near the grave of his father Lutshaba.

Despite this evident desire to honour him, Nxito remained an unbeliever. Perhaps he knew Mhlakaza and Nongqawuse too well to take their prophecies seriously. For several months he refused to move from the safe isolation of his distant residence to the eye of the storm at the Gxarha. Finally, in November 1856, Nxito yielded to intense pressure from the believers and returned. He went to see Mhlakaza who told him that the chiefs no longer wished to communicate through a common black man like himself but through a chief of high rank, namely Nxito. The new people would appear to him soon, and when they did so he was to summon all the chiefs and all the believers to assemble together and await the fulfilment of the promises.

News of Nxito's arrival home circulated rapidly among the believers and it was widely but wrongly reported that he had been converted from his unbelief. The return of Nxito, together with the supposed destruction of the *Geyser*, led the believers to expect that the rising would take place at the next full moon, and the tempo of slaughtering increased accordingly. The night of 11 December was wet and misty and the believers were consequently unable to see whether the moon was full or not. But nothing happened on the next day, or on the day after that. Once again, the Cattle-Killing faltered. Stalwart believers like the 'disappointed and dejected' Maqoma began to reconsider their position, and Dilima, the Great Son of Phatho, almost decided to plough.[11] Sarhili grew weary of waiting and departed for the Gxarha, leaving orders that he would kill anybody who still possessed a living beast by the time he returned. He halted at his father's old capital of Butterworth, halfway between the Hohita and the sea, prevented by the rains from going further (about 17 December 1856). There Nxito met him and told him publicly that Mhlakaza had nothing to show and that he, Nxito, refused to believe any of the prophecies.[12]

Sarhili was not to be put off. He returned home and killed 40 cattle — nearly a quarter of his remaining stock — on the day of his arrival. He was further encouraged by some rumours from Lesotho, which stated that the promises had already been received in Moshoeshoe's country, to the accompaniment of great thunder and lightning, and that most of the unbelievers and their cattle had been swept into the sea. Within a week, Sarhili received a further message from the Gxarha saying that Sifuba-sibanzi, the chief of the new people, had arrived and was waiting to see him.[13]

Sarhili hastened down but was stopped again at Butterworth by alarming intelligence (about 24 December 1856). Nxito had long been urging Mhlakaza to formally summon all the chiefs to show them the people who had risen, but the prophetic group had demurred and stalled his requests. Eventually Mhlakaza had yielded and agreed to arrange a meeting between Nxito and the new people, but the old chief, wary of deception, had sent one of his men, a firm unbeliever named Makombe, to spy out the designated place and guard against trickery. Unfortunately for Nxito, Makombe's presence was discovered and Mhlakaza announced that Nxito had insulted the new people by placing an unbeliever in their road. They therefore refused to have anything further to do with him. Moreover, it was being rumoured that the new people had decided not to rise as a result of the intercession of the unbelievers' ancestors, who feared that their descendants would be damned for refusing to kill their cattle.[14]

Sarhili sent Ndima and Bhotomane, two high-ranking Gcaleka chiefs, down to the Gxarha to investigate the truth of these reports. At sunset, they found two of Nxito's men who told them that they had watched all day and seen nothing, nor had they received any answers to their questions. They spoke next to Mhlakaza, who told them that Nxito had insulted the new people and that they had therefore gone off in a fury to the mouth of the Fish River. It was all Nxito's fault: if he had obeyed his orders, the new people would have risen already. But if Sarhili himself came down in six days' time, the new people would speak to him. Mhlakaza admitted that he was no longer in communication with the spirits and that all his information came via Nongqawuse. Ndima and Bhotomane attempted to engage the new people in conversation but they heard no sound in reply to the questions they put, only the voice of Nongqawuse interpreting the responses. They left gravely disappointed and on their return (about 28 December) they made it quite clear that they felt that the whole story of new people and new cattle was a fraud and a deceit.[15]

Sarhili and his councillors, gathered in Butterworth, were deeply disturbed by the news. Sarhili proposed that all the chiefs and leading believers of the the Xhosa and the Thembu should publicly proceed to the Gxarha and confront the prophets 'as it was time . . . something definite should be accomplished'. The old councillor Gxabagxaba urged caution, saying that the new people had asked for Sarhili alone, and a mass confrontation might offend the new people or else give Mhlakaza an excuse for the failure of his prophecies. Doubts and hesitations began to appear for the first time among the inner circle of believers. But Sarhili took courage from the promise of a resolution in six days' time, and he sent a messenger named Nonxwayi to the British Kaffrarian chiefs telling them that the prophecies had already been fulfilled in Moshoeshoe's country, that the time was ripe, and that all remaining cattle and goats must be slaughtered.[16]

Six thousand Xhosa gathered at Butterworth to await the great day, and on or about 3 January 1857 Sarhili and a large body of councillors went down to the Gxarha according to Mhlakaza's promise. But Mhlakaza and Nongqawuse had vanished, leaving only a message to the effect that the new people had left out of indignation at the conduct of the unbelieving chiefs. If the next full moon (10 January 1857) should rise blood-red, Sarhili and his people should return to the Gxarha, 'for that is a sign that the spirits are merciful again'. If not, they should wait until the full moon of February.[17]

The news of yet another postponement shattered the joyous mood of the expectant gathering at Butterworth, and for the first time Sarhili found himself faced with open criticism and reproach. The King was downcast, humiliated and unable to answer or evade the furious questions of the angry crowd. The meeting became increasingly stormy until it broke up in complete disorder. Sarhili began to see the abyss beneath his feet and somewhere along the long lonely road back to his Great Place — the road he had travelled down so full of expectation — he tried to kill himself. His councillors were obliged to remove all knives, spears and sharp objects from his reach and to watch him carefully. On 6 January 1857, he arrived back at Hohita.[18]

2. The Great Disappointment

'There can be no recovery now,' wrote Commissioner Brownlee on the last day of 1856.[19] It was true. By January 1857, the time had long since passed for sowing and planting to be any use. So many cattle had already been killed that there was no longer any sense in holding the slender remainder back. It was this total absence of any alternative that drove the Cattle-Killing onwards during its last frenzied months. By this time, the possibility that the prophecies might be at fault was simply too horrific to consider and since the believers had no way back, they were compelled to go forward, stifling their doubts. Thus it was that the more the evidence mounted that they should give up hope the more the believers clutched at every straw, and the more that logic demanded that they slacken their pace the more they redoubled their efforts to slaughter every last beast that walked and to eliminate the small band of unbelievers who had refused to share their hopes and their tribulations.

This protracted agony was in a large measure due to the unwilling-ness of many genuine and sincere believers to kill all of their cattle. Even though Nongqawuse's order that every last head of cattle was to be slaughtered was from the first clear and unambiguous, this did not extinguish the feeling among many Xhosa that a more restricted sacrifice would be enough to convince the new people of their commitment and their repentance. Many, especially on the Gcaleka Xhosa side, killed most of their cattle immediately in proof of their good faith, but decided to hang on to the rest until they received some concrete manifestation of the promised new cattle.[20] Time after time, as every new moon approached its fullness, the orders went out to kill every last walking beast; and yet, every time, even the strongest believers held some back. King Sarhili himself did not complete the slaughter of his immense herds until the middle of January 1857, and convinced believers such as Phatho, Mhala and Maqoma all retained some cattle right up to the very eve of the Great Disappointment. As late as 5 February 1857, the average Ngqika believer still retained three or four cattle. Maqoma still had three and Sandile had ten.[21]

The waverers were caught in the middle. On the one hand they killed a number of their cattle to earn a share in the deliverance to come, but on the other they tried to retain some cattle in case the prophecies failed. The arch-waverer, Sandile, killed some of his cattle as soon as he received the formal order from Sarhili, but he was quite perplexed when the King demanded the sacrifice of the rest. In order to hedge his bets and keep in with all sides, Sandile ended up slaughtering half his cattle in secret for fear of the government and concealing the rest beyond the borders of Xhosaland for fear of the believers. As the numbers of their cattle declined, the believers slowed down the rate of slaughter for fear of starvation, leaving their milk-cows until last.[22] But such pitiful delays and subterfuges could not resist the pressure of the movement's internal logic. So long as the Xhosa held their cattle back, this logic insisted, they could not reasonably expect the rising of the new people or blame Nongqawuse and Mhlakaza for the failure of the prophecies. The Cattle-Killing could only come to an end when, as Magistrate Gawler sardonically put it, it finally ran out of victims.[23]

Sarhili's message of 1 January produced a spate of slaughtering throughout British Kaffraria. Commissioner Brownlee, touring the country, found cattle killed at every homestead, with most people killing three or four. A man named Madayi killed nine cattle on the day he heard Sarhili's message, and eight more cattle and twenty goats the following day. Cattle were killed furiously and recklessly with such speed that neither the hungry believers nor even the vultures had time to eat them. Their hides were carelessly stripped off and sold while the decomposing carcasses lay rotting on the ground, or hanging on the thorn fences of the kraals. The stink of putrefying flesh filled the air all the country round for days afterwards. When the full moon failed to rise blood-red on the night of 10 January, the believers were shattered and dejected. Many declared that they had given up hope but, in truth, it was all they had left.[24]

Meanwhile Sarhili, whose unbounded confidence had driven the Cattle-Killing forward when all others were filled with doubt, found himself hesitant and apprehensive just when all his people believed with the perfect faith of desperation. He often stated that he himself had seen the wonders that were shortly to appear, but it seems as if his words were meant more to reassure himself than to convince others.[25] The missionary Waters, who saw him the day after his attempted suicide, described him as 'unusually gloomy, but kind'. There was no news, he said, but 'people were mad for following Mhlakaza'. Waters told Sarhili what the King already knew very well, that his people would starve; and added, in attempted sympathy, that his heart was very sore. Why should the missionary's heart be sore? demanded Sarhili, flaring up briefly. *He* would not be hungry. With remarkable lack of tact, Waters suggested that Sarhili send some of his daughters to a charitable lady named Mrs Douglas. He mentioned Tangiza, 'nine years old and very pretty'. 'No! No!' cried the King, hugging his breast defensively as if he foresaw the ruin of everything he held dear, 'She is the child of my bosom. I cannot part with her.'[26]

Stormy meetings followed at Sarhili's Great Place. There seem to have been attempts by some of the foremost believers, including Sarhili himself, to throw the blame on others. There was talk of what might be done if the prophecies failed. There was mention of raiding cattle from the Thembu, the Mfengu, the unbelievers, indeed anybody who still had cattle. On 17 January, Sarhili loosened up a little at a beer drink, and his words do much to reveal his state of mind as the Cattle-Killing approached its climax:

> I have undertaken a thing of which I now entertain certain doubts, but I am determined to carry it through. . . . No one opposed me when I first undertook what I have undertaken, I consider therefore that they have approved of what I have done. I have sent to Sandille, Macoma, Pato and Umhala, and our views are one. I have now no cattle left, but I cannot starve, there are still cattle in the land, and they are mine. I will take them when I require them.[27]

'I have done nothing against the British Government,' he continued and, in a spirit of bravado rather than menace, added, 'but should the Governor attempt anything against me, I have dogs that will bite.' Little did he realize that this idle boast would be reported to Sir George Grey and little could he guess the uses to which it would be put.

About the middle of January 1857, Sarhili summoned all the believing chiefs or their representatives to a Great Meeting in Butterworth. Some Xhosa thought that the King was trying to force the issue, determined either to see the new people or to abandon the movement. But in public, at least, Sarhili brimmed with confidence. He announced that Mhlakaza had sent for him, saying that the moment had come for the chiefs to fix a date for the final destruction of all cattle and goats, so that a definite time could be set for the rising of the new people and the new cattle. All the unbelievers were to be finally cast off. None might communicate with them, and they were forbidden to attend the Great Meeting. The infidel Nxito was expelled from the neighbourhood of the Gxarha.[28]

On 18 January, Sarhili's confidant, the Gcaleka chief Bhotomane, arrived at Butterworth to make the arrangements for the Great Meeting. Sarhili came down slowly, accompanied by Maphasa, the Great Son of his uncle Bhurhu. As they proceeded, they were joined by large numbers of believers, giving their leisurely six-day journey the air of a triumphal procession. At Butterworth, they were joined by the remainder of the great chiefs and councillors of the Xhosa nation, five thousand men in all. Mhala sent his brother Nowawe. Phatho, Maqoma and Bhotomane sent their Great Sons. From Thembuland came Maramncwana and Philip, the Great Sons of Fadana and Qwesha, who led the Thembu believers. Unbelievers were strictly excluded.[29]

On 30 and 31 January, the assembly considered accusations of unbelief levelled against some of their number, and three of Sarhili's brothers were among those hounded out of the Great Meeting. On 1 February Pama, the believing son of Nxito who now acted in his father's place, arrived hotfoot from the Gxarha. He announced that he had seen men down by the sea, some clothed, some on horseback with new saddles and guns. All the believers were to return home immediately and kill their cattle, even the cattle they were retaining to provide milk for their children, and they were to use the hides to make doors to keep out the thunder and lightning which would precede the great day. There would be two days of darkness, said Pama. The sun would rise in the west, the sea would dry up and recede, the sky would descend until it might be touched by the head, and then there would be a great earthquake during which the new people and the new cattle would appear. Pama declared that he was prepared to stake his life on the truth of his assertions. The chiefs might kill him if they did not believe him for, if they did, he would soon be rising with the others. Sarhili alone should remain with a few of his followers, such as had no witchcraft about them. He should seclude himself for four days, and on the fifth go down to the Gxarha where Mhlakaza would show him all and everything.[30]

The ordinary believers were disappointed and not a little suspicious at being sent home so abruptly. Sarhili himself was 'somewhat dispirited': he had clearly hoped for something more than another delay. Nevertheless, he put a brave face on it. He announced that he was staying on to see his father's Great Place and his father's cattle rising again at Butterworth, where once they stood. He asked the local traders to sell his people candles to light up during the great darkness, and he secluded himself as instructed.

Four days later, the King again went down to the Gxarha. It was a disconcerting and disappointing experience. Maqoma's Great Son Namba, who accompanied Sarhili, said later that they were called to see something, but neither he nor anyone else had seen anything. The Gcaleka chiefs were taken over the hill to see something, but he and the other Rharhabe chiefs were not allowed to go. Mhlakaza was disclaiming responsibility for the whole movement, and the management of everything was in the hands of Nongqawuse. Dilima, the son of Phatho, arrived a little later. He said that he heard the new people speak, though he and his companions were not allowed to go to the spot where the new people were. Only Nongqawuse and two or three young men went there.[31]

As for Sarhili, he left his retinue at a quarter of an hour's distance from Mhlakaza's residence. They waited there, while he went in. The King spoke for a long time to Mhlakaza and Nongqawuse 'and when he came back, one could read the annoyance on his face'. Nevertheless, he told the assembled people that he had seen wonderful things and had heard men talking under the earth. The new people ordered that the Xhosa must kill all they possessed, except one cow and one goat, within eight days of his return to Hohita. On the eighth day — certainly before the end of the ninth day — the resurrection would take place. The sun would rise late, blood-red, and set again, upon which it would be as black as night. A terrible storm would follow, with thunder and lightning, and then the dead would rise. . . .[32]

But in his heart Sarhili knew that it was all a lie, and that nothing was going to happen on the eighth day, nothing at all. He told a trader named Conway that he had been deceived, and that he was anxious to explain the whole thing to the Governor personally, as he did not want a war.[33] Despite these internal misgivings, the King pressed ahead with preparations for the great day. He drove his unbelieving brothers out of the Great Place. There was more killing than ever: cattle, goats, even chickens. All who had not killed were accused of some crime and forced to save themselves by slaughtering.[34]

The intense pressure on the unbelievers during this final climactic period of the Cattle-Killing finally cracked the resistance of those chiefs and people who had tried to hold to a middle course, notably Chief Sandile and his close associates, Chiefs Xhoxho and Oba. Still a young man in his early twenties, Oba had initially followed the lead of his neighbour, the strongly unbelieving Anta. Five of his leading councillors were strong supporters of the movement, however, and they did their best to persuade the chief to change his mind. In the middle of January, his mother and his wives packed up their belongings to return to their paternal homes for fear of the consequences of his unbeliefs. Oba killed two cattle to persuade them to stay, and from then on his fall was irreversible.[35]

The position of Sandile, as senior chief in British Kaffraria, remained crucial to believers and unbelievers alike. He had been forced to move to a site near Brownlee's post and, with the help of the unbelievers and the threat of military action, the Commissioner had managed to keep some semblance of cultivation going at Sandile's Great Place. Sandile was trapped between two devils. He was too afraid of Brownlee to attend the Great Meeting in Butterworth, but when he received messages that the assembled chiefs had seen immense flocks of cattle and sheep waiting for the true believers, he was too afraid of the consequences of unbelief to deny the prophecies any longer. Maqoma's son Namba sent to say that two deceased councillors of Sandile's late father Ngqika had appeared and warned the chief to 'rise out of the dust' and return to his Great Place. The spirits were angry with Sandile for hesitating so long. 'He was a fool and throwing away his authority and chieftainship. . . . He was holding with both hands [at once] instead of adopting a straightforward and decided course.' Sandile should immediately rid himself of the influence of the unbelievers and kill the rest of his cattle. That very day, Sandile killed ten of his remaining 35 cattle, and within a week he had killed twenty more.[36] Brownlee was met with fear-stricken silence, as Sandile haltingly explained that he wished to leave his new residence as 'his mother and his wives would no longer stay at the village, and were determined to return home because the huts they occupied were uncomfortable and small, and there was a scarcity of firewood'. That night the chief fled from Brownlee's neighbourhood, and resumed possession of his old Great Place, finally and after many twists and evasions an open believer.

The ensuing confrontation between the believers and the unbelievers, now expelled from the royal presence, has been recorded by Commissioner Brownlee. Although Brownlee probably exaggerates his own role in the deliberations, his account is a vivid depiction of the final scene in the eight-month battle for Sandile's allegiance.

> On arriving at [Sandile's Great Place] I found between four and five hundred people assembled, all armed, under the leadership of Umlunguzi and Baba, two councillors. I was received in solemn silence and scarcely saluted. On the hill just above Sandile's village, Tyala and his party were assembled and joined me immediately on my arrival, taking up their position about twenty paces from Umlunguzi and Baba's party.
>
> After I had spoken to Sandile, reproaching him for having brought this trouble upon his country against my advice, Soga arose and pointing to Umlunguzi and Baba said:— 'There are the men who have brought this trouble into the country. Sandile is not to blame; he has been misled by them.'
>
> Tyala then, in a stentorian voice shouted: 'No! Soga, you are wrong. There is the offender (pointing to Sandile.) Put the rope round his neck. He is no longer a child to be led by Baba and Umlunguzi. He is responsible for the troubles which are over the land.'
>
> At this Umlunguzi jumped up and approached brandishing his assegai, exclaiming, 'Traitor! Dare you accuse our chief in our hearing?' Tyala replied: 'Yes, I do! and I repeat that he is the guilty person.'
>
> As the two men were about to fall upon one another, I rushed between them; took Tyala by the arm and told him to sit down. . . . Turning to Baba and Umlunguzi I said: This is your work. How have you discharged the trust committed to you by Sandile's father, who left Sandile an infant in your care? . . . I have done. I came to save Sandile, and those who had gone into the cattle-killing movement. I have failed. Your counsels have prevailed against mine. You have led Sandile into trouble. I leave you to get him out of it as best you can. I can do nothing more for him.'

Baba then arose and said: 'Why do you trouble with us? You tell us
that hunger will destroy us — we will see, — and if it does it will be your
testimony against us. Leave us alone and do not trouble any more with
us.'

I replied: 'Baba, I will record your words in my book, and the day will
come when I shall remind you of them. It is not for you that I now feel,
but for the helpless women and children, who in a few days will be
starving all over the country.' At this point my feelings were too strong
for me, and I sat down and covered my face with my hands and wept. [37]

The eight appointed days sped by as the believers stifled their
doubts and their hunger with a multitude of last-minute tasks.[38] There
were new milk-sacks to be sewn, new doors to be made, and courtyards to be scrubbed thoroughly clean. The dwellings of the believers
were carefully rethatched to prevent the entry of fiery rain or noxious
beasts during the terrible storm which would precede the fulfilment of
the prophecies. Remarried widows deserted their husbands and
returned to the abandoned homesteads of their late first loves.
Chieftainness Sutu, the mother of Sandile, passed the days smoothing
out her wrinkles with infinite patience in preparation for her reunion
with Ngqika, her long-dead husband. Remaining stocks of corn were
scattered in the dirt or put to the torch. Slaughtering was not as intense
as on previous occasions, for there was not much left to slaughter.
Nevertheless heaps of carcasses were visible in every direction,
accompanied by their inevitable companions, the vultures and the
carrion crows. Cattle, goats and chickens all had to go, and many
steadfast believers killed at the last minute in order to avoid the charge
of witchcraft.

Though the people were already beginning to suffer the pangs of
hunger, they remained 'cheerful, living by faith and hourly expecting
the new cattle to rise'.[39] Some climbed high hills or stood for hours on
their rooftops, hoping for an early sight of the new people. Others lit
signal fires for fear that their homesteads might be passed by.
Sensational rumours — that Nongqawuse had ordered the killing of
old people, or the destruction of colonial money — were avidly discussed and repeated.

On 16 February 1857, the long-awaited eighth day, the sun rose as
usual about six o'clock, neither late nor blood-red.

The sun rose just like any other sun. The believers withdrew into their
houses all the day, fastened tightly behind their many doors, peeping
outside occasionally through little holes in their dwellings until the sun
disappeared. Meanwhile those who had never believed or done any of
the things prescribed went about their usual work.[40]

'Now the hopes of the poor people were thrown onto the ninth day.

Probably no eyes have greeted a morning light with so much longing as those eyes of the [17th] of February. The morning light came as always, the longed-for freedom it did not bring.'[41] As one believer recalled many years later,

> I sat outside my hut and saw the sun rise, so did all the people. We watched until midday, yet the sun continued its course. We still watched until the afternoon and yet it did not return, and the people began to despair because they saw this thing was not true.

For several days thereafter, the people sat in rows in front of their homesteads watching the progress of the sun. Some widows and widowers went to sit by the graves of their late husbands and wives. On the 21st, there was a great thunderstorm, and the people rushed to their houses and secured themselves inside, convinced that the great day had arrived at last. But it did not come, not that day, not ever.

3. The Agony of the Unbelievers

The catastrophic failure of 16-17 February stunned the chiefs and the believers. Sarhili, in particular, was described as 'very much disconcerted and does not know what to do with himself'.[42] On receiving a routine message from an old adversary, J.C. Warner the Thembu agent, the King was moved to a grief-stricken response:

> I have been a great fool in listening to lies. I am no longer a chief.
> I *was* a great chief, being as I am the son of Hintza, who left me rich in cattle and people, but I have been deluded into the folly of destroying my cattle and ordering my people to do the same; and now I shall be left alone, as my people must scatter in search of food; thus I am no longer a chief. It is all my own fault; I have no one to blame but myself.[43]

Nevertheless, Sarhili was furious with the unbelievers, whom he blamed for their treachery, and he placed guards on the drifts to prevent them escaping with their cattle.

Chameleon-like as ever, Chief Sandile removed to the neighbourhood of his unbelieving councillors, saying that he was not bound to Sarhili, who had induced him to ruin himself and his people. Xhoxho, Sandile's brother, visited Commissioner Brownlee 'sad and downcast'. 'The [Xhosa] are ruined, and their chieftainship is gone,' he said. Sandile, Xhoxho and Feni all begged the Governor to give employment to their people.[44] Old Phatho submitted himself at last to his magistrate, Vigne, 'in low spirits'. His people were leaving him, he said, they had listened too much to Mhlakaza. He, Phatho, wished he had listened to Vigne rather than to Sarhili's messages. He would go to Fort Murray and work to check thieving. Now he came to borrow money to save his children from starvation. Once, he said wistfully, remembering the days before lungsickness when he owned 2,500 cattle, *once* he had had plenty of cows to provide thick milk for everyone, but he had killed them all. He hoped the government would pity him and let him have his salary back.[45]

The colonial authorities, for reasons we have yet to discuss, were no longer interested in the chiefs and were not prepared to let them have their salaries or anything else. Mhlakaza and Nongqawuse were equally unhelpful. Reports from the Gxarha after the Great Disappointment are contradictory, but the prophets seem to have informed the believers 'that the new people say they do not want to be troubled with the importunity of the [Xhosa], and will make their appearance when they think fit'.[46] Rejected by the government and forsaken by the prophets the believers had yet one resource available to them: the cattle of the unbelievers. Even as those of Sarhili's councillors who had managed to preserve their stock fled from him, the stricken chief vowed that he would kill them all. For it was they who had caused the prophecies to fail. Perhaps he still remembered his words of mid-January: 'I cannot starve, there are still cattle in the land, and they are mine. I will take them when I require them.' In Phatho's country, the believers boasted that they would soon kill the unbelievers and take their cattle. At Sandile's they declared that they would soon reduce everyone to their own level.[47]

Fury against the unbelievers had been mounting gradually ever since the spring campaign against cultivation. Then the unbelievers had been threatened by rumours of supernatural punishments and abandoned by believing mothers and wives. As early as September 1856, believing Gcaleka chiefs had been raiding their cattle. By November, it was becoming difficult for unbelievers to travel about the country, for the believers refused them food even while they regaled themselves on sacrificed cattle. In the wake of the December disappointments, Mhlakaza pointed an accusing finger squarely at the *amagogotya*, blaming them for the failure of the prophecies. Napakade had been ready to rise, he said, with six hundred cattle, but the ancestors of the unbelievers had begged for a delay, pleading that their children had not killed their cattle and that they would be consigned to Satan if the others rose too soon. The January failure was likewise blamed on the unbelievers, whose stubbornness had caused the new people to depart in anger, saying, 'We said that all your cattle were to be killed, you have not done so — we leave you in disgust.'[48]

The believers insisted that until all existing cattle were destroyed, the new cattle could not come out of the earth. The unbelievers were killing them by their stubborn and selfish refusal to slaughter. Chief Mhala 'considered a man's killing his cattle a proof that the man either used no witchcraft or that he put it away now altogether. . . . These people [the unbelievers] are not only guilty of witchcraft but they have stopped the new cattle of the faithful from coming forth and disgusted the new people.'[49] The believers shrank from any contact with the impurity of the unbelievers. They would not eat, drink, smoke or even off-saddle near their homesteads, and if an unbeliever so much as stopped at a believing homestead, he might hear the women cry out, 'He is an unbeliever! Let us go and wash and cleanse ourselves!' Wives who spoke to unbelievers might be repudiated by their husbands. As time passed, the believers rushed off to purify themselves if they so much as passed an unbeliever on the road by accident. Busakwe, the son of one of Sandile's councillors, administered an emetic to members of his homestead who had mistakenly eaten the food of unbelievers. In Mhala's country, the believers shaved off their eyebrows to avoid being mistaken for unbelievers.[50]

Even when the doubtful finally capitulated to social pressure and killed their cattle, their previous resistance was held against them and they might hear the believers calling out to them, mocking and triumphant, 'We knew you would yield, your holding out was useless. Pass on! You are unbelievers and unclean. Don't come near and defile us.' Or they might shout angrily to the dwindling bands of diehard unbelievers, 'Go on, you liars and deceivers! You may now ride your horses, but soon you will ride to the devil on them.'[51]

The hatred of believers for unbelievers ripped whole families apart. Fathers turned on their sons and wives deserted their husbands. In Sandile's chiefdom, a believer named Qongo tried to murder his son who was an unbeliever, and several other fathers were likewise guilty of violently persecuting their unbelieving children. Conversely, several cases were recorded of grown-up sons expelling their aged fathers from the homestead for refusing to kill, or butchering the family cattle without their fathers' consent.[52] Many wives left their husbands for fear of their unbelief, and many women 'cried and howled' as Chief Jali's mother did in her efforts to get her son to kill his cattle.[53] The most curious case was that of a husband and wife, both deaf-mutes, who 'took different views about the cattle killing, but how they came to understand the subject, I do not know'.[54]

The leading unbelievers had more than scorn and mockery to worry about. The cattle they had so carefully tended and the gardens they had so painfully cultivated through the longest of seasons were in grave danger, and, as the climax of the movement approached, their very lives seemed at risk. Those that could manage it joined the unbelieving chiefs, especially the resolute Anta, but there were many who were only too aware that their every move was watched and that any attempt to remove their cattle from the territory of their chiefs was, according to established custom, liable to the penalty of seizure and confiscation.

The unbelievers in British Kaffraria looked anxiously to the colonial government for protection. They were greatly encouraged by the example of Magistrate Gawler, who had saved an unbeliever named Bulungwa from certain death by intervening in a witchcraft hunt that had already smelt him out. But Bulungwa's life owed more to Gawler's personal bravery than to colonial policy and his request that Bulungwa should be allowed to settle in the Crown Reserve to ensure his future safety was ignored by Maclean.[55] The Crown Reserve, confiscated by the government after the War of Mlanjeni and still virtually empty, was set aside for white occupation, and no Xhosa, unbelievers or otherwise, were to be allowed to settle there.

In early December 1856, Ndayi, the leader of the unbelievers in Mhala's country, approached Gawler saying that he was hated by all and asking for assurances that he would be physically protected. But the magistrate was unable to give the desired response either to this request or to the many that followed it.[56] In Sandile's country, the unbelievers made a secret compact to band together for mutual protection when the crisis came, and in early January they sent a secret delegation to Commissioner Brownlee asking that the government should fix a place for them where they might be free from the 'oppression of the overwhelming number of believers' under whose authority many were compelled to kill their cattle without hope of escape. Brownlee advised them to gather together for protection (which they were doing already, in any case) and warned Sandile against forcing anyone to kill cattle. But he could not point out a place where they would be safe.[57]

The cruel fact of the matter was that Maclean and Grey had made a definite decision to offer no concrete assistance to the unbelievers. The most they would do was warn the believing chiefs against harming the unbelievers and admit refugees to the shelter of their forts if there was no alternative. 'We could not send parties throughout Kafirland to defend each person who might be attacked,' minuted Grey. The best construction that the historian can place on this decision is that Grey and Maclean truly believed that Moshoeshoe and Sarhili were plotting a war against the Colony and did not want to give them a pretext for attacking. The worst is that Grey and Maclean did not care what happened to the unbelievers so long as they stayed off land earmarked for white settlement. A more forward policy in defence of unbelievers might well have preserved many Xhosa from the disaster of the Cattle-Killing.

> Many have told me also that were they certain of protection they would not kill or leave their gardens uncultivated but without such protection they would only be keeping their cattle and cultivating their gardens for the benefit of others who would rob them.[58]

Maclean was less concerned with helping the unbelievers than with keeping them where they could be of maximum use to him, that is back in their own chiefdoms where they could act as a brake on the chiefs and disrupt the plans of the believers. The elderly councillor Mgwagwa, who had worked hard to keep his young chief Jali out of the Cattle-Killing, discovered this when he arrived at Fort Peddie towards the end of December quite certain that his life was in danger for cultivating. Maclean felt that he could not afford to lose Mgwagwa's influence with Jali and forced the old man to return, accompanied only by vague promises of government protection.[59]

Another to suffer from Maclean's indifference to unbelievers was Kona, Maqoma's Right-Hand (second-ranking) son. Unlike his father or his senior brother Namba, Kona was an unbeliever. Although he had once been the centre of a celebrated witchcraft case, Kona had recently spent a great deal of time with his brother Ned, who was the interpreter at Dr Fitzgerald's Native Hospital, and had been deeply impressed by the power of Western medical science. Kona's conversion was, one would think, just the sort of thing Grey had been aiming at when he set up his hospital to demonstrate the superiority of European civilization. When the rains began in late September, Kona found himself virtually isolated in Maqoma's chiefdom and cultivating in spite of his father's orders. His mother was so angry at this that she left him. By November he was desperate to get out of Maqoma's country and move to some safe place under the colonial government. A former superintendent of the Kaffir Police offered Kona a place on his farm. Alternatively, he could have joined Kama who, hard pressed by Mate and the believers in his chiefdom, would have been glad to receive him. Even Kama's magistrate thought this was a good idea. But Maclean, supported by Grey, refused Kona's application because he thought it might be a trick of old Maqoma to sneak back to his former country. It would set a bad precedent. Kona had not been as badly persecuted as he made out. Dr Fitzgerald protested against the decision and offered Kona his own house, but was told that he did not understand politics and should mind his own business. It took another two months before Maclean became sufficiently convinced of the genuineness of Kona's predicament to permit him to take temporary refuge near Fort Murray.[60]

The small group of unbelievers in Sandile's territory attempted to retain the nominal support of the chief by cultivating his gardens and maintaining a presence at his Great Place. But Sandile was under pressure, especially from Maqoma.

> Are you a chief [Maqoma asked Sandile] and led by black men? Who are Tyala, Xokwana, Umnxamisa and Umqhati that they should cultivate against the order of [Sarhili] and Umhlakaza, and induce you to do the same? What other chief has been likewise led? Show your authority and put these men to death, and discontinue your cultivation.[61]

When Sandile's resistance to the Cattle-Killing finally collapsed on 29 January, the position of the *amagogotya* became completely untenable. Namba's messengers demanded that Sandile chase the unbelievers from his Great Place and kill them if they continued to argue with him. Sandile formally expelled all unbelievers in early February, and compelled the steadfastly unbelieving brothers, Xokwana and Norhwana, to kill their cattle. They were married to his sisters and, he said, 'though they had no regard for their own safety and welfare, he did not see why they should lead his sisters to destruction'.[62]

Commissioner Brownlee urged Maclean to allow the estimated 150-200 unbelievers (out of nearly 7,000 men in Sandile's chiefdom) to settle temporarily in the Crown Reserve. But Maclean was having none of it. If he helped Brownlee's unbelievers, he would have to help others elsewhere as well. They should join Chief Anta. On 12 February, the fourth of the last eight days, the desperate unbelievers came to Brownlee for the government response. Deeply ashamed of his superior's reaction, Brownlee was forced by the rules of the service to put the best face on his instructions that he possibly could. He told the unbelievers that they still had a duty to Sandile, even though he had cast them off. They should stay in his district so that he could join them if he changed his mind. The unbelievers had no choice but to agree under protest. They asked if the government could not clear a space for them somewhere, but Brownlee could promise them nothing.[63]

For a brief moment after the Great Disappointment, it seemed as if Sandile might rally to the unbelievers, but his resolve soon crumbled in the face of continued pressure from Maqoma and Mhala. The unbelievers begged for permission to establish an armed camp in a natural stronghold protected on three sides by the winding Kubusi River. Unfortunately, this was situated in the Crown Reserve. Brownlee supported them to the best of his ability. 'In their present position they cannot [hold their ground]. We weaken our own cause by refusing support and assistance to those who have so manfully resisted the delusion.' Governor Grey, now returned to King William's Town, gave the decided negative himself.[64]

The long-awaited storm broke on 12 March. A large party of believers headed by the Gcaleka chief Gunuza attacked the isolated homesteads of Pityi and Sam, two relatively powerless unbelievers. One of Pityi's men was killed and all their cattle taken. A believer sent by Pityi to intercede on his behalf was told that the *amathamba* would return to kill the remainder of his men, and their cattle were but a provision on the road to attack the unbelievers Neku and Soga. Two days later, a large party of mounted horsemen attacked Neku's place and Wartburg mission. Soga's younger brother Ngcuka was killed defending the family herds. Neku and Soga fled by night to the rear of Dohne post in the Crown Reserve. There they were joined by other unbelievers who had suffered similar attacks. Backed once again by Commissioner Brownlee, they addressed an urgent appeal to the Governor:

> Regardless of the orders of our chiefs and in opposition to the taunts and threats of our countrymen, we cultivated our fields and retained our cattle. . . . Sandile and his believing councillors maintain that in pursuing the course we have, and from our constant intercourse with Brownlee, we are seeking their ruin and our promotion. . . . We have already been called 'traitors to our country'. . . . If the Governor refuses us, we will have to join Kama where we will at once lose our cattle by lungsickness, and having no crops to live on we and our families will be reduced to poverty and starvation. . . .
>
> Before taking a step which will involve us and our families in misery, we would again lay our earnest appeal before the Governor for a temporary asylum in the rear of the Post; we do not ask for land, and will quit this place as soon as the circumstances of the country admit. . . . We are unable to return to our kraals to be plundered, and to become a derision to those whom we have opposed, and who have brought ruin upon the Tribe and who are now our bitter enemies.[65]

Chief Commissioner Maclean remained unmoved. He made the alleged crime of one unbeliever the excuse for the condemnation of all:

> Is the man Soga now in the Reserve — one of those upon whose co-operation and support I am expected to rely — the same man who treacherously assisted in the massacre of the people in the military village of Woburn? I will not allow [Xhosa] to remain in the Crown Reserve. If the people alluded to will not take my advice by forming in front of the post — they can go to Kama's location if that chief will admit them.

Greatly shamed, Brownlee was forced to evict them.

A similar scene was played out near the coast, where Magistrate Gawler was receiving messages from various minor chiefs declaring themselves *amagogotya* and begging the government to take care of them and tell them what to do. Chief Smith Mhala, Ndayi and other unbelievers came in a body to see him and to say that if the government was to help anybody, it should help them first. Mhala had called his council together to decide on a course of action and they were sure it would be war. Gawler urged them to concentrate their forces on the Qinira River, where he was trying to organize a police force for their protection. The unbelievers agreed although, as they pointed out, the believers were on the watch and would attack them as soon as they attempted to move their cattle. 'Here's an end to us non-believers,' said Ndayi as the first news of fighting came in, 'unless the government who gave us encouragement to hold out will help us.'[66]

For one brief and awful moment after the Great Disappointment, the believers had stared into the black hole of the future, and that was enough to show them that any hope was better than none. The latest excuse from the Gxarha and from the secondary oracle at the Mpongo River, that the new people had been delayed by their failure to decide which among their ranks had the seniority to rise first,[67] was flimsy indeed but it was sufficient for a movement now fuelled by despair rather than hope. The helpless state of the unbelievers — demoralized, disorganized and abandoned to their fate by the colonial government — laid them wide open to attack. Hungry Xhosaland teetered on the brink of a bloody civil war.

On 3 March 1857, Sir George Grey issued a proclamation declaring 'that all persons caught attempting to commit, or having committed, robberies with arms in their hands, will when convicted with such offence, be punished with DEATH'.[68] But so long as the Governor was unwilling to commit any troops to the defence of the unbelievers, so long was his proclamation a threat without teeth. It was Major John Cox Gawler, the magistrate with Mhala, who supplied the deficiency.

4. The Hard and the Soft

We have referred so often to the existence of two parties in Xhosaland, the believers and the unbelievers, that we have begun to take them for granted. And yet there was more to the formation of the two groups — termed by the Xhosa, the *amathamba* ('soft ones' or believers) and the *amagogotya* ('hard ones' or unbelievers) — than the simple decision of an individual whether or not to believe in Nongqawuse's prophecies. Most Xhosa did not personally visit the prophetess but depended on rumour and report from others. The information they received was ambiguous and contradictory. The individual had to weigh the accounts of those who had seen miracles against those which dismissed the prophecies as fraudulent. Even though the Xhosa King sided with the believers, the unbelievers included some of the most influential and far-sighted men in the kingdom. Given the conflicting nature of the information received, it seems fair enough to suggest that most people would have decided whether or not to slaughter on the basis of pre-existing attitudes. It is the purpose of this section to identify and assess what such predispositions might have been.

The effects of lungsickness

Wherever lungsickness travelled in Xhosaland, cattle-killing almost always followed. From Mossel Bay, where it landed, it travelled to Uitenhage (March 1854), Fort Beaufort (April 1854), King William's Town (March 1855) and Butterworth in Sarhili's country (January 1856). The Ngqika Xhosa, living far to the north of the waggon road, were the last to be affected.[69]

It was in the areas first attacked by lungsickness that the earliest prophecies exhorting cattle-killing were heard. By October 1855, there were five prophets operating in the districts of Chiefs Kama and Phatho, ordering the people not to cultivate and to slaughter their cattle. Across the Kei, the spread of lungsickness was directly linked to visions of Mlanjeni and prophecies of resurrection.[70]

Sarhili put more than twenty people to death for witchcraft or for breaking the quarantines established on the movement of cattle, but he could not check the spread of the disease. By 1856, it was reported that many cattle had died of lungsickness in the lower part of Sarhili's country where Nongqawuse lived, and in April 1856 she began to prophesy. In that very month, lungsickness broke out among the homesteads bordering Sarhili's own Great Place.[71] It is small wonder, therefore, that the King was receptive to a prophecy which predicted that 'a fresh stock of cattle free from lungsickness' would arise.

Chief Sandile's Ngqika Xhosa took strenuous precautions against lungsickness, burning the pasturage on their perimeter and forbidding the introduction of strange cattle to their district.[72] Sandile received Sarhili's orders to kill without enthusiasm, and Chief Commissioner Maclean reported that the Ngqika Xhosa generally remained indifferent to the prophecies, 'the excitement being confined to those districts in which from the prevalence of the lungsickness the people have lost their wealth and chief means of subsistence'.[73] Very few Ngqika killed their cattle during the early phase of the movement prior to the first

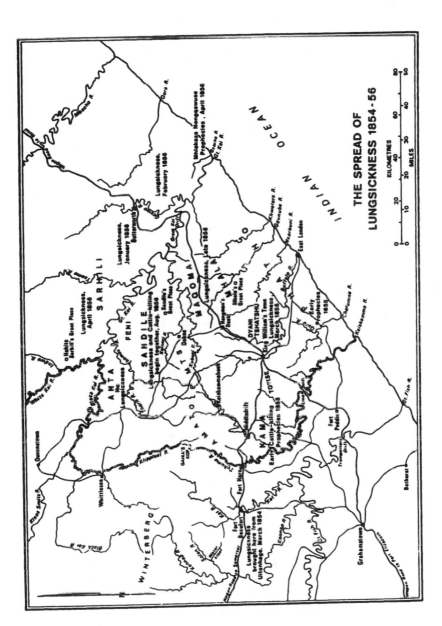

Map 4: The Spread of Lungsickness (1854-56)

failure of the prophecies on 15 August 1856. Unfortunately, we have no evidence on the crucial question of when lungsickness became general in the Ngqika district, but it is tempting to ascribe the increasing tempo of Ngqika cattle-killing after the second wave of prophecies (September 1856) to the slow spread of the disease. Important support for this hypothesis comes from the case of Chief Feni, who opposed the movement from its inception in May 1856 and right through the Great Disappointment of February 1857 until April 1857, when lungsickness broke out among his own cattle and he too began to slaughter despite the palpable failure of the prophecies.[74] Conversely, lungsickness never reached the herds of Chief Anta high up in the Windvogelberg in the far north of the Ngqika location, and this probably explains why, alone of all the Xhosa chiefdoms, Anta's entirely refused to participate in the Cattle-Killing.

Lungsickness was thus a necessary cause of the Xhosa Cattle-Killing. Where there was no lungsickness, the words of Nongqawuse fell on deaf ears. On the other hand, lungsickness is not a sufficient cause which completely explains the entire Cattle-Killing movement. The Cape Colony's Mfengu allies suffered extensively from lung-sickness with reported cattle losses of 90 per cent and more. Yet virtually all Mfengu, even those resident in Xhosaland under the orders of Xhosa chiefs, refused to kill their cattle.[75] The Christian chief Kama opposed the movement, even though their district had suffered heavily from the epidemic. Chief Toyise, resident near the centre of infection at King William's Town, refused to kill and carried the majority of his people along with him, even though in their district 'the lungsickness had made such ravages that but comparatively few [cattle] were left'.[76] Clearly, lungsickness alone cannot account for the pattern of division between believer and unbeliever.

Attitudes to the Cape Colony

At first glance, it might seem that the Cattle-Killing was mainly supported by those hostile to the Cape Colony and mainly opposed by those well disposed towards it. Certainly, many of the leading believers had been in the forefront of the War of Mlanjeni, which had ended a mere three years previously. Sarhili, Sandile, Maqoma and other lesser chiefs had been strong fighters and now turned strong believers. Chief Mhala, another strong believer though outwardly neutral, had secretly aided the belligerents with supplies and refuge. Conversely, the unbelieving Mfengu and the majority of chiefs on the unbelieving side — Kama, Toyise, Siwani, Jali — were either allies or clients of the colonial government. But any attempt to equate attitudes

Chief	Cattle-Killing	Land*	Religion	Lungsick
Sarhili	Strong believer	Unchanged	Strong precolonial	Heavy
Mhala	Strong believer	Unchanged	Strong precolonial	Heavy
Phatho	Strong believer	Unchanged	Strong precolonial	Heavy
Maqoma	Strong believer	Severe losses	Strong precolonial	Heavy
Bhotomane	Strong believer	Severe losses	Precolonial	Heavy
Sandile	Waverer	Severe losses	Precolonial	Delayed arrival
Feni	Waverer	Severe losses	Precolonial	Delayed arrival
Kama	Strong unbeliever	Gainer	Christian	Heavy
Dyani Tshatshu	Strong unbeliever	Unchanged	Christian	Heavy
Toyise	Strong unbeliever	Gainer	Strong precolonial	Heavy
Anta	Strong unbeliever	Severe losses	Precolonial	Light
Mfengu chiefs	Strong unbelievers	Large gains	Christian leanings	Heavy

Table 1: Known Dispositions of Xhosa Chiefs

* Refers to effect of Frontier Wars on land holdings.

towards the Cattle-Killing with attitudes towards the colonial government breaks down in a rash of exceptions. Chief Anta had shot one of his brothers to prevent him surrendering during the War of Mlanjeni and he had been deprived of his ancestral lands, yet he remained on the unbelieving side. Chief Sigidi, the leader of the Gcaleka Xhosa unbelievers in British Kaffraria, had openly defied his newly appointed magistrate just before the Cattle-Killing, and remained under threat of arrest throughout. On the other hand, Chief Phatho had protected colonial supply routes during the War of Mlanjeni to the great detriment of the Xhosa war effort. Yet he was a great believer in Nongqawuse.

Although land loss in war led to material deprivation and thereby contributed to the tensions which exploded in the Cattle-Killing, it is impossible to make a direct correlation between land loss and participation in the movement. If land loss had been an immediate cause, we would expect those chiefdoms which lost most land to have slaughtered most cattle. Instead, it was Sarhili, Mhala and Phatho, who had lost no land whatever in the 1850-3 War, who took the lead in killing cattle, while the Ngqika, who lost most, lagged behind and Anta, a Ngqika chief, slaughtered not at all.

The lack of congruence between political attitudes towards the Colony and belief in Nongqawuse's prophecies is even more marked in the case of commoners. Soga, a leading unbeliever in Sandile's chiefdom, played a leading part in the 'Tyhume valley massacres' of military settlers in 1850. Mjuza, the son of the wardoctor Nxele, led the attack on Butterworth mission in 1851 and was later shot in the stomach by British troops. When he heard that the Russians were coming, he prepared to place himself at their head. Yet he became one of Nongqawuse's most determined opponents.[78] Political commitments may, of course, have influenced the decisions of many individuals during the Cattle-Killing, but they clearly cannot fully explain the division between believers and unbelievers.

Religious faith

Perhaps, it may be argued, we are mistaken in looking for material causes when the decisions must have been taken on the basis of personal faith. Most Xhosa remained orientated towards the precolonial religious tradition, while a few leaned towards Christianity. Some Xhosa were credulous of diviners and prophecies, while others were frankly sceptical. Should one not, perhaps, see the decision to slaughter as an individual act of conscience explicable only in religious terms?

Once more, this is an approach which seems reasonable enough at first sight but fails to stand up to detailed analysis. Certainly, Kama and Dyani Tshatshu, the only professedly Christian chiefs, vigorously opposed the Cattle-Killing and the mission stations seem to have retained almost all their adherents. But it would be a grave mistake to perceive a sharp dichotomy between the precolonial tradition and Christian religion. The Cattle-Killing incorporated many Christian elements which the believers themselves recognized and used as arguments in favour of the truth of the prophecies. 'All that was done [in the Cattle-Killing],' wrote one missionary, 'was in the name of God, or that His Word says so. It was as profusely as it was vainly used.' Sarhili himself was much taken by a picture of Christ walking on the sea, and startled the local missionary by his knowledge of the story of the raising of Lazarus.

On the other hand, many of the chiefs on the unbelieving side displayed little affinity with Christianity. Toyise was the last chief in British Kaffraria to execute a man for witchcraft, and at his trial he and his councillors 'declared to the last their firm belief both in the power of those who used bewitching matter and in the power of "smelling out" the offender'. Mjuza, the son of wardoctor Nxele, believed that his father was the leader of the Russians who had returned from the dead, and he was prepared to believe the prophecies of Nongqawuse until he visited her in person and concluded she was a fake. Chief Ngubo, another strong unbeliever, burned a woman to death for witchcraft several years after the Cattle-Killing. Soga, who refused to believe Nongqawuse, had trusted in the powers of the wardoctor, Mlanjeni.[79] If, indeed, most Xhosa made their choice according to their existing predispositions, it is clear that neither Christianity nor precolonial religion *per se* was a determining factor.

Kin, age and gender

The bonds of kinship were not lightly set aside in Xhosa society, and during the Cattle-Killing they were stretched to the limit to rally the waverers. Many Xhosa killed their cattle unwillingly, according to W.W. Gqoba, 'but they were threatened by the stabbing-spears of their relatives'. On the other side, Moto Kantolo remembers that his unbelieving great-grandfather was supported by all his brothers. Ngcuka, Soga's younger brother, was killed defending the family herds.[80] Nevertheless, the Ngqika Commissioner seems not to have exaggerated when he wrote that 'the differences arising in this matter caused estrangement betwen parents and children, between husbands and wives, and for the time severed all the ties of kinship and friendship'.[81]

Cleavages were most pronounced in chiefly families where the quest for political power was added to the other stakes involved. Makinana, Chief Mhala's Great Son, stood by his believing father although he personally doubted the truth of the prophecies. Smith, Mhala's second-ranking son, used his unbelief to ingratiate himself with the magistate and was consequently recognized as chief of the Ndlambe Xhosa. Chief Maqoma's sons split along similar lines. Chief Sandile wavered throughout the movement with his two full brothers taking strong stands on opposite sides.[82] Similar divisions appeared in commoner families, although documentation is lacking. Nkonki, an unbeliever, begged cattle from his believing elder brother to prevent them being slaughtered. Ndayi, the leader of the Ndlambe Xhosa unbelievers, was unable to convince his cousin Tshisela, who killed all his cattle. The Quluba family was likewise split: the father and some sons were believers, but another son and his cousins preserved their cattle.[83]

It is not possible to trace any consistent pattern in these family divisions. It might seem probable that the older generation, with their greater herds of cattle accumulated over a lifetime, might be more resistant to the movement than younger men, whose expectations of wealth and inheritance were frustrated or had perished in the lungsickness epidemic. Certainly, there was no shortage of 'old councillors' among the small number of unbelievers, and Magistrate Gawler observed that since his old councillors had abandoned the believing chief Mhala, he had surrounded himself with 'a number of young second rate counsellors ambitious of distinction and ready to take their chance in forwarding any of the current nonsense'. On the other hand, advancing age may also bring with it increased fear of death, and many believers, including Mhala himself, were certainly motivated by the hope that they would be 'made young again'. Sometimes it was the young heirs who resisted their fathers' desires to slaughter their inheritance. Futshane, one of Mhala's old councillors, resisted belief for over a year but something snapped at the very end, and he began killing furiously to the alarm of his son, who fled with his own herds as fast as he could. Similarly, Feni, a councillor of Chief Xhoxho's, violently persecuted his son for the latter's unbelief, and Qongo, a councillor of Sandile's, attempted to kill his son for the same reason. William Mtoba of the Ndlambe district is remembered as opposing the Cattle-Killing while still a *rwala*, that is, a young man recently circumcised and not yet married.[84]

The idea that women's oppression in male dominated societies such as that of the Xhosa predisposes women to participation in ecstatic religious movements has become a dubious cliché, but one that will not go away.[85] Certainly, there is plenty of evidence that Xhosa women overwhelmingly supported a movement which promised that 'nobody would ever live a troubled life' and that people would get 'whatever they wanted'.[86] Nongqawuse herself, her cousin Nombande, and Nonkosi, a Cattle-Killing prophetess in British Kaffraria, were all young girls. The view that there was something peculiarly feminine and adolescent in Nongqawuse's behaviour was one shared by many Xhosa men, as this story from oral tradition indicates:

> [The unbelieving Chief Anta] had a councillor named Nombhaca, who
> . . . said to Anta when they were in the court, when the other chiefs had
> agreed [to kill their cattle] and he said 'Take a bite of *qaqaqa* grass, and
> see if you can swallow it nicely.' Anta listened to these words. . . .
> [Then] Nombhaca said they must bring that girl for him to lie with, and
> then she would stop telling such lies.[87]

The implication, quite clearly, is that Nongqawuse's visions were the result of the unconscious sexual frustrations of an adolescent girl. Many Xhosa men, asked to explain Nongqawuse's visions, simply assert that she was a *binqa*, a female, and that was the sort of behaviour one expected from a *binqa*. According to a regrettably brief report, the unbelieving Chief Ngubo visited Nongqawuse, 'beat her and called her an impostor'. The image is one of an indignant father chastising his daughter for causing trouble. One cannot imagine Ngubo confronting an adult male in this manner.[88]

Because of their own inferior position in Xhosa society women were probably more inclined to welcome change than men. Widows, in particular, fallen from their high social position, might be expected to hope for the resurrection of their late husbands. Chief Sandile's mother urged him to kill his cattle, saying, 'It is all very well for you, Sandile. You have your wives and children, but I am solitary.' Chief Mqhayi's widows 'cried and howled' in their attempts to get his young heir Jali to kill his cattle. The widow of Sandile's brother Tyhali was likewise incessant in demanding that her son, Feni, should kill.[89] Another of Tyhali's widows, the mother of Chief Oba, fled to her paternal home (as did all her son's wives) to force Oba to kill. The mother of Kona Maqoma was so angry with him for working in his gardens that she left him — until hunger forced her back. The wives of the unbeliever Ndayi fled out of terror at his unbelief. Clearly, women had everything to hope for from a future in which widows might recover their lost status and wives become free at last of the burden of wearisome and oppressive labour for their husbands. The economic element behind female belief was clearly perceived by Tiyo Soga, the Xhosa missionary, who wrote:

> The women, the cultivators of the soil in Africa, were the warmest supporters of the prophet, as they rejoiced in the anticipation of getting crops without labour.[90]

Even so, there seem to have been many women who were sceptical of Nongqawuse's prophecies. Noposi, the Great Wife of Sandile, worked her gardens with Sandile's permission until she was stopped by the pressure of her co-wives. A Mfengu woman was murdered when she attempted to turn her Thembu husband against killing his cattle. At least one young woman was critical of her father's cattle-killing beliefs:

> I used to laugh at my father, and he would call me a mad English girl and say he could not call me his child if I was so foolish a girl. . . .

> My father scolded me and said: . . .'Can you not see the things on the side of that hill?' 'No: I can see nothing but thorn bushes.' He said that it was not bushes but I thought that the men had eaten too much corn and

meat, and drunk too much of the [Xhosa] beer to know what they saw. . . . So my father got very angry with me: he told me if I dared to say it was bushes again he would kill me. But I saw nothing else.[91]

In this case, quite obviously, the full patriarchal authority of the male homestead head was engaged on the side of the believers, and it was the 'foolish young girl' who resisted wishful thinking. Clearly, the believer/unbeliever divide followed no set pattern of kinship, age or even gender.

The amathamba *and the* amagogotya

We have yet to consider the effects of social class, which seems to deserve special attention in as much as it lies at the root of the names which the Xhosa themselves gave to the two contending parties. To understand this fully, however, we must pause for a closer look at the structure of Xhosa society in the 1850s.

The effects of fifty years of colonial pressure had fatally wounded but not yet killed the old structure of precolonial Xhosa society. This had revolved around the relationship between chiefs and commoners, in which the chief as guarantor and nominal owner of the land and cattle of the commoners had exacted tribute from them and collected judicial fines in his court. The scale of exactions had been minimal, however, since there was rivalry between the chiefs and infinite land available for exploitation. In order to maintain their authority, the chiefs were forced to win the favour of influential commoners ('councillors') by redistributing most of the tribute and judicial fines they received. Nevertheless, the chiefs retained the right, which they exercised as often as they dared, to bring their subjects to court and to confiscate their possessions for real or imaginary offences.[92]

The colonial presence afforded wealthy councillors new opportunities to escape the restrictive powers of the chiefs. Ironically enough, old forms of sociability broke down less because of the impoverishment of the many than because of the enrichment of a few. Before the advent of an open market for food, rich men had invited their neighbours around when they slaughtered a beast or opened a grainpit. But now meat could be sold by the portion (*thengisa isimausi* − to sell like a trader)[93] and corn could be sold by the bucket in exchange for colonial money, a form of wealth which the chiefs could neither provide nor control. At the same time, the chiefs' capacity to regulate the wealth of their councillors was limited by the decisive action of the colonial authorities against witchcraft accusations, accurately described at the time as the '[Xhosa] state engine for the removal of the obnoxious'.[94] Prosperous commoners were thus partially liberated from the rapacity of their chiefs, and, shortly before the Cattle-Killing, Governor Grey held forth the prospect of total liberation in the form of magistrates who would take over the chiefs' judicial duties and employ the councillors directly and independently of the chiefs.[95]

A new disposition of social forces was thus emerging on the very eve of the Cattle-Killing. On the one hand, the chiefs, formerly the rulers and economic exploiters of their subjects, now stood forth bravely as the champions and defenders of the old order, which, with all its faults, had guaranteed land and cattle to all. On the other side stood the 'many well-disposed persons' described by one missionary, 'who would be glad . . . to be relieved of feudal servitude and be subject to British authority'.[96]

It is only fair to the unbelievers to point out that many of them were courageous and patriotic individuals who had fought hard for their country and people in the earlier frontier wars. Only with the crisis of the Cattle-Killing did they come to realize that their interests lay unambiguously on the British side.

The literal meaning of the word *amathamba*, used by the believers to describe themselves, is 'the soft ones'.[97] Alternatively, it might be translated, 'those who drill like soldiers'. The two translations are not as incompatible as they might seem. 'Soft' does not have the same connotation of weakness in Xhosa as it does in English. Rather 'soft' indicates the abnegation of self and willing submission to a greater duty than self-interest. One of A-I. Berglund's Zulu informants gave him an excellent description of the concept, which is equally valid in Xhosa:

> [A successful diviner] must never think of himself. He must learn to kill his thoughts and desires and just think of the shades [ancestral spirits]. He must do what they tell him. That is to have a soft head.[98]

Similarly, when the historian S.E.K. Mqhayi refers to Chief Maqoma as being 'soft' (*ethambele*) to the orders of King Sarhili, he means this as a compliment.[99] This renunciation of self lay at the heart of the old Xhosa ethic of mutual aid and communal solidarity, now under threat.

> [Xhosa] are hospitable by custom more than by nature. It is considered disgracefully mean to eat in the presence of any one not provided with food, without offering them some . . . . Should a person be found dead from the effects of hunger near a kraal the headman or master thereof is held responsible, and has to pay the '*isizi*' [death dues]. Children are taught habits of generosity as far as food is concerned from their infancy; and little creatures of two or three years of age may be seen handing their morsel from one to another, so that each may have a taste.[100]

It was precisely such behaviour, itself a manifestation of the deeper dependence springing out of the communal division of labour, which was under threat from the new market-orientated behaviour which chose to sell cattle and corn rather than share them out in community feasts. From the historical perspective, therefore, it is entirely appropriate that cattle and corn were the battlefield on which the struggle between the old and the new was finally played out.

The strength of the Cattle-Killing movement undoubtedly lay in its appeal to the ordinary homestead heads, reeling as they were from the blows of blight and lungsickness on top of the social pressures generated by military defeat and increasing landlessness. Commissioner Brownlee wrote at an early stage that 'the movement seems peculiarly to have been one of the common people'. The missionary Bryce Ross reported that 'when the people are reminded that their chiefs disapprove of this work, their answer is that they don't care for their chiefs'.[101] Chiefs who took a strong stand against the Cattle-Killing found that the majority of their subjects effectively deserted them in favour of pro-Nongqawuse members of the royal lineage. Thus Chief Kama lost most of his followers to his nephew Mate, Chief Siwani lost his to his nephew Bangayi, and the young chief Jali was challenged by his genealogically junior brother, Tabayi. Fadana, the disgruntled ex-Regent of the Thembu, recovered a prominence lost for over twenty years, as hundreds of Thembu abandoned their unbelieving chiefs and rallied to his leadership.[102]

The chiefs were more divided than the people because of their greater exposure to the pressures and temptations of the colonial government, but with the exceptions of Anta and Sigidi, every strong-willed, intelligent chief who perceived the threat which British Kaffraria and Governor Grey posed to the old order in Xhosaland finally backed the Cattle-Killing. Reliable figures from the seven most affected chiefdoms in British Kaffraria show that at least 85 per cent of Xhosa males adhered to the *thamba* party.[103] It is thus no exaggeration to describe the Cattle-Killing as a popular mass movement of a truly national character, uniting both chiefs and commoners, the major social classes of the precolonial social order, in a communal defence of their way of life.

There was a sharp contrast between the *thamba* ethos, one of receptive submission to the common good, and the unyielding self-interest of the unbelieving *gogotya* party. *Gogogotya* means 'hard', just as its opposite *thamba* means 'soft', but, significantly, *gogotya* is usually translated as 'stingy' or even 'disloyal'.[104] The *amathamba* regarded the *amagogotya* as selfish, greedy men, whose miserly determination to risk their own cattle prevented the entire nation from enjoying the fruits of the resurrection. Even those Xhosa who recognized that the *amagogotya* were correct to dismiss the prophecies had little positive to say about them. The historian W. W. Gqoba, himself a Christian and an eyewitness of the Cattle-Killing, defined the verb *ukugogotya* as 'to sit still, not doing anything [for anyone else], to stand on one's own side'.[105]

We may take two leading *amagogotya*, Soga and Ndayi, as exemplars of their party. Soga, the son of Jotelo, was a man of about sixty at the time of the Cattle-Killing. He was a convert to the form of Christianity preached by the early Xhosa prophet, Ntsikana (d. 1822), but he did not see this as incompatible with the magic of the wardoctor, Mlanjeni. Soga was a spearmaker and a smelter of iron, one of the few crafts practised in precolonial Xhosa society, and this may have paved the way for his enthusiastic adoption of mercantile principles of exchange as soon as contact with the colonial economy made this possible. The traveller, James Backhouse, provides us with this description of Soga fourteen years before the Cattle-Killing:

> The common custom among the [Xhosa] was to share their provisions with those who were not supplied; and by thus allowing the idle to live upon the industrious, exertion was paralyzed; but Soga had had moral courage enough to break through this bad custom as well as some others; he would not allow the other [Xhosa] to work for him without wages, and when they came to beg of him, he told them, that he paid them for his work, and they must pay him for his corn. In case he slaughtered an ox, he also sold its flesh, and refused to give it away, according to the common custom of his nation.[106]

It is here, perhaps, that we see the origins of selling meat, *isimausi*, that antithesis of communal slaughtering and feasting. Soga had eight wives, a sure sign of wealth during a period when only about 20 per cent of Xhosa men had more than one.[107]

We know comparatively little about Ndayi, except that he was a wealthy man, married to several wives. His praises, fortunately preserved, provide us with a vivid insight into his character.

> Here is the great one of Tsora.
> The wearer of the armband, the ox of Ziya.
> The one who struggles for his home.
> Here is the forest of the cowards who fear hunger.
> The bird of prey which carries water in its wing.
> The thing as large as the plough of Simpkins,
> The great plough which cultivates potatoes.
> Great pot, which cooks with salt water,
> Why do you cause confusion among the people of your chief?
> You are aiming to scold them.

You are aiming with a rough blanket.
He is like a snake of the river,
The thing of the old village with *imituma* bushes.
He wants to see the place where the sun rises,
Where it shines its rays and disappears.
He smokes from a pipe made of ox's horn.
He does not eat the cattle of another's homestead.
He eats the beast of his own home.
They are striped, those oxen like springboks.
The horns of the harrow are pointing upwards.
The rhinoceroses are following one another.
The one who does not flinch crosses even through rock.
The great one of Tsora.[108]

If we except a few local references and conventional praises, it is apparent that the poem revolves around three themes: Ndayi's independent and self-sufficient spirit, his relationship with the commercial world, and his relationship with his fellow Xhosa. Ndayi is presented as a strong man in a dubious cause. He is a great provider, but he provides for the *amagogotya*, the 'cowards who fear hunger'. He does not demand food from others, but — a very double-edged compliment this — he eats by himself. He is thirsty for knowledge, but he wants to know everything, even what the sun is doing, more than he has any right to know. References to trade goods and agricultural implements recur constantly: ploughs, harrows, blankets, potatoes (not an indigenous crop) and salt (not used by the Xhosa before traders commercialized it).[109] Ndayi's actions sow discord among those who adhere to the old ways, namely 'the people of the chief'. He stands accused of wanting to exalt himself above his fellows, and order them around.

Ndayi's character stands out in even sharper relief if we digress briefly to consider the praises of Tobi, Chief Sandile's father-in-law, one of the highest ranking believers in the Ngqika district.

The great pot of Zimela.
The child of a chief who is truly a great loafer. He never milks the beasts of his home at Zimela's.
The son of Qelo, who sews the rough blanket.
The child of a chief, who avoids meetings at the chief's place.
The one who never carries anything difficult to grasp.[110]

Like Ndayi, Tobi is a 'rough blanket' (abrasive personality), but there the resemblance ends. Whereas Ndayi is ambitious of power and prestige, Tobi tries to avoid public gatherings. Whereas Ndayi will press on even through rock, Tobi will not undertake anything risky or unusual. Whereas Ndayi is a great provider, Tobi cannot even make the most of his inherited cattle. Although it would be unfair to suggest that the indolent Tobi is typical of all believers, yet the contrast between the driving activity of Ndayi and the unenterprising passivity of Tobi probably does reflect the real difference in outlook between the *amathamba*, hoping for the regeneration of an old world, and the *amagogotya*, grasping eagerly at the new.

Not all of the rich and prominent councillors were to be found on the unbelieving side. Much of the wealth in pre-capitalist Xhosa society was distributed by chiefly patronage, and its recipients quite naturally attached themselves strongly to the fortunes of their chief. In the case of Sandile's chiefdom, it would seem that the younger Great Council-lors, such as Vena (who was circumcised with Sandile), were strong supporters of the Cattle-Killing, while Soga, Tyhala, Neku and Nxokwana, the leading members of the *gogotya* faction, were all sons of the councillors of Sandile's father and hence inheritors of wealth accumulated independently of the chief. Commissioner Brownlee informs us that 'in many cases, the indigent adherents of heads of kraals have been either compelled to destroy their little stock or quit'.[111] The point is not, however, that all wealthy councillors were *amagogotya*; but only that wealthy councillors made up the backbone of the *amagogotya* faction. Of this there can be little doubt. Tyhala and Soga, the two leading unbelievers in Sandile's chiefdom, had thirteen and eight wives respectively.[112] At least six out of the twenty-eight second-ranking councillors were unbelievers, a high percentage (21 per cent) when one considers that only 5-10 per cent of the Xhosa in Sandile's chiefdom opposed the movement.[113]

In Mhala's chiefdom, Magistrate Gawler predicted that 'all large cattle owners will be of opinion that a bird in the hand is worth two in the bush', and, initially at least, he seems to have been right. The 'old counsellors' and the 'big swells' opposed Mhala's orders to kill, and the chief was forced to turn to 'young, second-rate counsellors'. Later, however, the enormous pressures brought to bear by the believers caused seven out of ten great councillors to slaughter, though one of these only succumbed in the final months of the movement. Another strong unbeliever in Mhala's chiefdom, Bulungwa, is described as 'a great beggar, and over-ambitious'.[114] Makaphela, the leading un-believer in Feni's chiefdom, was a wealthy man with eight wives. Koka, an unbelieving councillor of Chief Oba, had six. Gxabagxaba, one of the old unbelievers among Sarhili's councillors, was possessed of 'large flocks'. Mgwagwa, the old councillor who kept young chief Jali out of the Cattle-Killing, owned fourteen cattle and ten calves. 'A considerable number' of Chief Siwani's old councillors ended the Cattle-Killing period 'well-off'. Like Sandile's unbelieving councillors, they invested their capital in ploughs, waggons and oxen.[115]

Conclusion

It was the great lungsickness epidemic which initially suggested cattle-killing, and the first chiefdoms to be affected by lungsickness were also the first chiefdoms to kill. But lungsickness alone was not enough to drive people into the movement as the examples of the Mfengu and of Chief Toyise demonstrate. Political commitments played their part, but while these were enough to ensure that heavily implicated colonial clients such as Chiefs Siwani, Toyise and Kama adopted the colonial line against cattle-killing, they were not enough to carry the vast middle ground, and men like Anta, Mjuza and Soga, who fought on the same side as the believers during the War of Mlanjeni, fought against them over Nongqawuse.

The Cattle-Killing split every chiefdom and, indeed, many home-steads from within. Religious attitudes are difficult to disentangle, as the believers clearly accepted significant elements of Christianity while the vast majority of unbelievers remained fully convinced of the validity of divination, prophecy and magic. Inter-generational conflicts between fathers and sons pulled sometimes one way and sometimes the other, and produced a thorough mix of young and old on both sides. Women, however, seem overwhelmingly to have supported the believers.

This leaves the factor of social and class attitudes, which the Xhosa themselves used to characterize the two parties as 'soft' and 'hard'. The 'soft' party of believers saw themselves as properly loyal and submissive adherents of the old order, who put their nation first in giving up their cattle for the good of all. They viewed the *amagogotya* as selfish and even despicable 'cowards who fear hunger'. The unbelievers probably thought of themselves as sensible men, who realized that one could not eat grass, but their unbelief was probably sustained by a deep unwillingness to slaughter their cattle.[116] Their sense of priorities was aptly expressed by Mhala's unbelieving son, Smith, when he said, 'They say I am killing my father [by refusing to slaughter] — so I would kill him before I would kill my cattle.'[117]

The little evidence we have strongly suggests that the *amathamba* were a party of the common people, whose material subsistence was largely eroded by conquest, drought and lungsickness, and for whom Nongqawuse's prophecies were probably the last chance to avoid migrant labour and the final disintegration of the old way of life. The *amagogotya* were largely a party of men who had benefited from the new opportunities offered by the colonial presence, and whose anti-social behaviour stemmed from the fact that they had broken free from the trammels of the precolonial order. Certainly, the division between *amathamba* and *amagogotya* ran much deeper than the division between belief and unbelief, and the Xhosa, in conferring these names, seem to have recognized the fact.

Notes

1. BK 70 C. Brownlee-J. Maclean, 19 Oct. 1856; GH8/49 J. Maclean-G. Grey, 3 Nov. 1856; BK 81 J. Gawler-J. Maclean, 14 Oct. 1856; BK 89 Communication from Lieut. Lamont, 2 Jan. 1857; GH 8/30 C. Brownlee-J. Maclean, 7 Dec. 1856.
2. GH 8/49 C. Brownlee-J. Maclean, 10 Dec. 1856.
3. GH 8/49 J. Gawler-J. Maclean, 11 Oct. 1856; GH 8/49 H. Lucas-J. Maclean, 10 Dec. 1856; BK 371 J. Maclean-G. Mackinnon, 4 Jan. 1856.
4. BK 71 C. Brownlee-J. Maclean, 21 Jan. 1857.
5. BK 70 C. Brownlee-J. Maclean, 11 Dec. 1856.
6. GH 8/30 C. Brownlee-J. Maclean, 7 Dec. 1856; BK 86 F. Reeve-J. Maclean, 27 Nov. 1856; GH 20/2/1 C. Brownlee-J. Maclean, 25 Aug. 1856; ZP 1/1/217 (Microfilm) R. Birt-G. Grey, 3 Oct. 1856; *Anglo-African*, 1 Jan. 1857; GH 8/49 J. Maclean-G. Grey, 17 Nov., 22 Dec. 1856; BK 89 Communication from Lieut. Lamont, 2 Jan. 1857; GH 8/29 H. Lucas-J. Maclean, 27 Sept. 1856.
7. GH 8/30 C. Brownlee-J. Maclean, 7 Dec. 1856; BK 81 J. Gawler-J. Maclean, 26 Jan. 1856; GH 8/30 C. Brownlee-J. Maclean, 7 Dec. 1856. For role of sacrificial cattle, see J.H. Soga (n.d.), p.322; Alberti (1810), pp.95-6.
8. BK 70 C. Brownlee-J. Maclean, 19 Oct. 1856; BK 70 C. Brownlee-J. Maclean, 19 Dec. 1856.
9. GH 8/30 C. Brownlee-J. Maclean, 11, 19 Dec. 1856; BK 89 John Ayliff jnr.-J. Maclean, 22 Dec. 1856; *Grahamstown Journal*, 15 Nov. 1856.
10. The fullest account of the story of Nxito is in GH 8/31 C. Brownlee-J. Maclean, 4 Jan. 1857. See also GH 8/29 C. Brownlee-J. Maclean, 22 Oct. 1856; GH 8/30 C. Brownlee-J. Maclean, 19, 25 Dec. 1856; BK 14 Examination of Nombanda, 28 Feb. 1858; BK 14 Statement by Umjuza, 24 Feb. 1856. For Nxito's rank among the Gcaleka chiefs, see Peires (1981), p.61. Nxito's age is calculated from the fact that he was older than Sarhili's father Hintsa, that is, born before 1785.
11. BK 81 J. Gawler-J. Maclean, 21 Dec. 1856; GH 8/49 J. Maclean-G. Grey, 4 Dec. 1856; BK 89 Secret Information, 8 Dec. 1856; BK 70 C. Brownlee-J. Maclean, 19 Dec. 1856; GH 8/49 J. Maclean-G. Grey, 11 Dec. 1856.
12. CO 2935 W.G.B. Shepstone-R. Southey, 17 Dec. 1856; GH 8/30 Information from a person beyond the Kei, 25 Dec. 1856; GH 8/30 C. Brownlee-J. Maclean, 25 Dec. 1856. It should be noted that the exact sequence of events related in the following paragraphs is somewhat obscure. It is certain that Sarhili made two distinct visits to Butterworth in December, returning from the first on 17 December, and departing for the second

about a week later. It is uncertain, however, when it was that Nxito made his ill-starred attempt to spy on Mhlakaza. Some of the sources also mention two unnamed messengers whom Mhlakaza threatened with death. It is not clear whether this is a garbled version of the mission of Ndima and Bhotomane, or whether it is a reference to a separate event.

13. GH 8/30 Information from a person beyond the Kei, 25 Dec. 1856.

14. GH 8/31 C. Brownlee-J. Maclean, 4 Jan. 1856; BK 70 C. Brownlee-J. Maclean, 25 Dec. 1856.

15. BK 89 Communication from Lieut. Lamont, 2 Jan. 1857; GH 8/31 C. Brownlee-J. Maclean, 4 Jan. 1856.

16. LG 410 J. Warner-R. Southey, 30 Dec. 1856; GH 8/31 C. Brownlee-J. Maclean, 4 Jan. 1856.

17. BK 89 Secret Information, 7 Jan. 1856; *Grahamstown Journal*, 17 Jan. 1857; *Berlin Missionberichte* (1858), p.38.

18. BK 89 Secret Information, 8 Jan. 1857; GH 8/31 C. Brownlee-J. Maclean, 11 Jan. 1856. Various colonial newspapers and certain colonial informants subsequently claimed that the story of Sarhili's attempted suicide was false, but it was formally conveyed by Sandile to Brownlee, and fits in well with our other information, especially with Sarhili's visit to Waters.

19. GH 8/31 C. Brownlee-J. Maclean, 31 Dec. 1856.

20. GH 8/30 C. Brownlee-J. Maclean, 19 Dec. 1856.

21. Bk 71 C. Brownlee-J. Maclean, 21 Jan. 1856; Bk 82 H. Lucas-J. Maclean, 4 Feb. 1856; BK 81 J. Gawler-J. Maclean, 26 Jan. 1857; GH 8/50 J. Maclean-G. Grey, 2 Feb. 1856; GH 8/31 C. Brownlee-J. Maclean, 5 Feb. 1857.

22. Brownlee (1916), pp.148-9; Acc. 793 J. Gawler-J. Maclean, 24 Oct. 1856. Descendants of Hlanganise and Tyhala remember their forefathers hiding Sandile's cattle in Bomvanaland during the period of the Cattle-Killing. Interviews with N. Mona and N. Somana, Kentani District, 23 and 24 Aug. 1983; C. Brownlee-J. Maclean, 7 Dec. 1856; *Grahamstown Journal*, 27 Dec. 1856.

23. Bovine victims, of course. 8/30 J. Gawler-J. Maclean, 25 Dec. 1856.

24. 8/31 C. Brownlee-J. Maclean, 4 Jan. 1856; Mic 172/2, Reel 8, Cory Library, H. Waters-H. Cotterill, 10 Jan. 1857. It should not be thought that the reference to the odour is an exaggeration. The Thembu chieftainness Yeliswa attempted to conceal her participation in the Cattle-Killing, but was given away by the smell.

25. GH 8/31 Information communicated, 18 Jan. 1857.

26. MIC 172/2, Reel 8, Cory Library, H. Waters-H. Cotterill, 10 Jan. 1856.

27. GH 8/50 J. Maclean-G. Grey, 15 Jan. 1856; BK 71 C. Brownlee-J. Maclean, 21 Jan. 1857.

28. GH 8/31 Information communicated, 18 Jan. 1857; BK 71 C. Brownlee-J. Maclean, 20 Jan. 1857.

29. BK 81 J. Gawler-J. Maclean, 6 Feb. 1856; BK 82 H. Lucas-J. Maclean, 4 Feb. 1857; LG 410 J. Warner-R. Southey, 6 Feb. 1857; *Berlin Missionberichte* (1858), p.39.

30. BK 89 J. Crouch-J. Maclean, 3 Feb. 1856; BK 89 Substance of statements made to the Chief Commissioner, 5 Feb. 1856; BK 89 Memorandum of Information communicated to the Chief Commissioner, 25 April 1857.

31. BK 83 Memorandum by H. Vigne, 11 Feb. 1856; GH 8/31 H. Lucas-J. Maclean, 14 Feb. 1856.
32. *Berlin Missionberichte* (1858), p.39.
33. GH 8/50 J. Maclean-G. Grey, 9 Feb. 1857; BK 89 J. Crouch-J. Maclean, 9 Feb. 1857.
34. GH 8/31 Information communicated from the Transkei, 24 Feb. 1857.
35. BK 71 C. Brownlee-J. Maclean, 25, 31 Jan. 1856; Interview with Chief Nqwiliso Tyhali, Gqumahashe Location, Victoria East, Aug. 1975.
36. GH 8/31 C. Brownlee-J. Maclean, 31 Jan. 1857; BK 71 C. Brownlee-J. Maclean, 4 Feb. 1857; Brownlee (1916), p.153.
37. Brownlee (1916), pp.149-51.
38. Chalmers (1878), p.121; R. Mullins Diary, Cory Library, 5 Feb. 1857; BK 71 C. Brownlee-J. Maclean, 2 Feb. 1857.
39. *Grahamstown Journal,* 7 Feb. 1857; *Graaff-Reinet Herald,* 14 Feb. 1857; R. Mullins Diary, Cory Library, 7 Feb. 1857; MS 8172, Cory Library, J. Ross-J. Laing, 14 March 1857.
40. Gqoba (1888), Part I; GH 8/31 Information communicated by a person from the Transkei, 24 Feb. 1857.
41. *Berlin Missionberichte* (1858), p.40; Cory Interviews, Cory Library, Interview with Sijako, Jan. 1910.
42. GH 8/31 Information communicated from across the Kei, 24 Feb. 1857.
43. CO 2949 J. Warner-R. Southey, 28 Feb. 1857; GH 8/31 Information communicated by a person from the Transkei, 24 Feb. 1857.
44. BK 71 C. Brownlee-J. Maclean, 21, 24 Feb. 1857.
45. BK 83 H. Vigne-J. Maclean, 17 Feb. 1857.
46. BK 71 C. Brownlee-J. Maclean, 11 March 1857. See also BK 89 Secret Information, 28 Feb. 1857.
47. CO 2949 J. Warner-R. Southey, 18 Feb. 1857; BK 71 C. Brownlee-J. Maclean, 21 Jan., 21 March 1856; Memorandum by H. Vigne, n.d. [22 Feb.].
48. BK 70 C. Brownlee-J. Maclean, 2 Oct. 1856; GH 8/30 R.E. Robertson-J. Maclean, 23 Nov. 1856; BK 81 J. Gawler-J. Maclean, 14 Jan. 1857; GH 8/30 C. Brownlee-J. Maclean, 25 Dec. 1856.
49. BK 81 J. Gawler-J. Maclean, 14 Jan. 1857.
50. Bk 89 J. Crouch-J. Maclean, 3 Feb. 1857; BK 89 Memorandum by H. Vigne, 25 Jan. 1857; GH 8/31 Information communicated, 8 Feb. 1857; BK 70 C. Brownlee-J. Maclean, 25 Dec. 1856; BK 71 C. Brownlee-J. Maclean, 4 Feb. 1857.
51. GH 8/31 C. Brownlee-J. Maclean, 4 Jan. 1857.
52. 8/31 C. Brownlee-J. Maclean, 4 Jan. 1856; GH 8/32 C. Brownlee-J. Maclean, 23 May 1857; BK 81 J. Gawler-J. Maclean, 20 June 1857; CO 3122 C. Brownlee-J. Warner, 24 Jan. 1867.
53. Brownlee (1916), p.134; BK 81 J. Gawler-J. Maclean, 17 Nov. 1856; GH 8/30 C. Brownlee-J. Maclean, 7 Dec. 1856; BK 82 H. Vigne-J. Maclean, 1 Feb. 1856.
54. MIC 172/2, Reel 8, Cory Library, Journal of W. Greenstock, 30 May 1859.
55. The Bulungwa incident will be fully covered in Ch. VI/3.
56. BK 81 J. Gawler-J. Maclean, 7, 10, 21 Dec. 1856; 14 Jan. 1857.
57. GH 8/31 C. Brownlee-J. Maclean, 4 Jan. 1857.
58. GH 8/30 Schedule 372, 29 Dec. 1856; GH 8/31 Schedule 389, 2 Feb. 1857.
59. GH 8/49 Marginal note on R. Tainton-J. Maclean, 29 Dec. 1856.

60. GH 8/49 F. Reeve-J. Maclean, 9 Nov. 1856; GH 8/49 H. Lucas-J. Maclean, 8 Dec. 1856; GH 8/49 J. Fitzgerald-J. Maclean, n.d.; GH 8/49 D. Davies-J. Maclean, 26 Nov. 1856; GH 8/30 H. Lucas-J. Maclean, 22 Dec. 1856; GH 8/30 Schedule 370, 25 Dec. 1856.
61. GH 8/31 C. Brownlee-J. Maclean, 15 Jan. 1857.
62. BK 71 C. Brownlee-J. Maclean, 4, 8 Feb. 1857.
63. GH 8/31 C. Brownlee-J. Maclean, 5, 12 Feb. 1857; Marginal note by Maclean, 6 Feb. 1857.
64. GH 8/31 C. Brownlee-J. Maclean, 1 March 1857; Brownlee (1916), p.152.
65. BK 71 C. Brownlee-J. Maclean 15, 21 March 1857, annotated by Maclean.
66. BK 81 J. Gawler-J. Maclean, 21, 24, 28 Feb., 1 March 1857; GH 8/50 J. Gawler-J. Maclean, 25 Feb. 1850; GH 8/31 J. Gawler-J. Maclean, 21 Feb. 1850; GH 8/31 Memorandum by H. Vigne n.d. [22 Feb. 1857].
67. BK 89 Secret Information, 28 Feb. 1857.
68. *King William's Town Gazette*, 17 March 1857.
69. On the spread of lungsickness, GH28/70 J. Jackson-G. Grey, 5 Feb. 1856; GH8/28 C. Brownlee-J. Maclean, 6 Feb. 1856; E. Robertson-J. Maclean, 30 July 1856; Acc 793 J. Gawler-F. Reeve, 7 July 1856; *Grahamstown Journal*, 24 March 1855; MS 7639, Cory Library, Grahamstown, B. Ross-J. Ross, 8 May 1854; N.J. Merriman (1957), p.215.
70. GH 8/27 C. Canham-B. Nicholson, 30 Sept. 1855, enclosed in J. Maclean-J. Jackson, 16 Oct. 1855.
71. Merriman (1957), p.216; *Grahamstown Journal*, 4 Aug., 8 Sept. 1855; GH 8/49 J. Maclean-G. Grey, 31 July 1856; GH 8/28 C. Brownlee-J. Maclean, 5 April, 1856; GH 28/70 J. Jackson-G. Grey, 5 Feb. 1856.
72. BK 70 C. Brownlee-J. Maclean, 18 Aug. 1856.
73. BK 373 J. Maclean-W. Liddle, 4 Aug. 1856.
74. BK 71 C. Brownlee-J. Maclean, 1 May 1857.
75. *Grahamstown Journal*, 29 Sept. 1856; BK 24 J. Douglas-J. Maclean, 21 Oct. 1856.
76. GH 8/34 J. Ayliff-J. Maclean, 23 Jan. 1858.
77. Acc.793 J. Gawler-J. Maclean, 28 July 1857; H. Smith-Earl Grey, 10 May 1851, Imperial Blue Book 1380 of 1851, p.19; CO 4386 Information received from Toise, 18 March 1852.
78. CO 4386 Statement by Manquidi, 17 Dec. 1851; interview with M. Soga, Kobonqaba Location, Kentani District, 25 Aug. 1983. Sarhili's unbelieving councillor, Gxabagxaba, was also a leading hostile during the war. BK 431 J. Maclean-G. Mackinnon, 21 March 1851.
79. Merriman (1957), p.218; BK 14 Statement of Umjuza, 24 Feb. 1857; 1/KWT W. Fynn-Colonial Secretary, 15 March 1873; Interview with M. Soga (note 78 above).
80. Interview with M.Soga (note 78); Interview with M.Kantolo, Kantolo Location, Kentani District, 22 Aug. 1983; W.W. Gqoba,'Isizatu sokuxelwa kwe nkomo ngo Nongqause,' Part 2, *Isigidimi samaXosa*, 2 April 1888. Gqoba's actual word for 'relatives', *imizalwana*, means 'people of the same descent.'
81. C. Brownlee (1916), pp.170-1.
82. BK 81 J. Gawler-J. Maclean, 23 Nov. 1856; BK 71 C. Brownlee-J. Maclean, 4 May 1857; GH 8/49 J. Fitzgerald-J. Maclean, n.d. (Dec. 1856); Brownlee (1916), p.134.

83. CO 3122 C. Brownlee-J. Warner, 24 Jan. 1867; Interview with R. Tshisela, Mncotsho Location, Berlin District, 23 Aug. 1982; Interview with A. Nkonki, Ngcizele Location, Kentani District, 7 Jan. 1976.

84. GH 8/29 J. Gawler-J. Maclean, 14 Aug. 1856; BK 81 J. Gawler-J. Maclean, 20 June 1857; GH 8/32 C. Brownlee-J. Maclean, 23 May 1857; 'Nzulu Lwazi' (S.E.K. Mqhayi), 'Umfi Wm. C. Mtoba,' *Umteteli waBantu*, 28 Jan 1928.

85. See, for example, I.M. Lewis, *Ecstatic Religion* (Harmondsworth, 1971), esp. Ch. 3 and 4.

86. Interview with Masiphula Ngovane, Mahlahlane Location, Willowvale District, Oct. 1975.

87. Interview with with Bomvane Fikile Anta, Teko Location, Kentani District, 8 Jan. 1976.

88. GH 8/49 J. Maclean-J. Jackson, 30 Oct. 1856.

89. Bk 71 C. Brownlee-J. Maclean, 1 May 1857; BK 82 H. Vigne-J. Maclean, 1 Feb. 1857; Brownlee (1916), p.134; GH 8/49 F. Reeve-J. Maclean, 9 Nov. 1856; BK 71 C. Brownlee-J. Maclean, 25 Jan. 1857; BK 81 J. Gawler-J. Maclean, 17 Nov. 1856.

90. T. Soga-R. Bogue, 10 Aug. 1857, *U.P.C. Mission Record*, Dec. 1857. See also, GH 8/30 C. Brownlee-J. Maclean, 7 Dec. 1856; GH 8/30 J. Maclean-G. Grey, 3 Nov. 1856.

91. GH 8/30 C. Brownlee-J. Maclean, 7 Dec. 1856; CO 2949 J. Warner-R. Southey, 7 April 1857; J. Goldswain (1946-9), 2, pp.192-3.

92. See Peires (1981) Ch.3, where this view of precolonial Xhosa society is argued at length.

93. A. Kropf and R. Godfrey (1915), p.230. Gqoba, 'Isizathu', Part 2, refers to the phrase as having been used by Nongqawuse herself.

94. H.H. Dugmore, 'Rev. H.H. Dugmore's Papers', in J. Maclean (1858) p.38.

95. Rutherford (1961), pp.330-4.

96. GH 8/25 R. Niven-J. Maclean, 17 Jan. 1854.

97. Kropf and Godfrey (1915), pp.402-3.

98. A-I. Berglund (1976), p.162.

99. S.E.K. Mqhayi, *Ityala lamaWele*, (Lovedale: Mission Press, n.d.), p.113. Another example of 'softness' in this sense is supplied by the unbeliever Gxabagxaba, who eventually agreed to kill his cattle saying, 'that the wealth and cattle which he possessed were obtained from [Sarhili] and his father, Hintsa, but as they were now determined to deprive him of all he had, he could do nothing but yield. He would kill his cattle in compliance with the orders of his chief, and not because he believed in the announcement made by the prophets.' This 'softness' cost Gxabagxaba his reason, and he died insane shortly thereafter. Brownlee (1916), pp.157-8.

100. South African Library, Cape Town, Uncatalogued Manuscripts, Rough Notes on Kafir habits, customs etc., presented to Sir George Grey by J.C. Warner, 1859.

101. GH 20/2/1 C. Brownlee-J. Maclean, 25 Aug. 1856; GH 8/49 J. Maclean-G. Grey, 10 July 1856; MS 7666, Cory Library, B. Ross-J. Ross, 9 Aug. 1856.

102. BK 83 H. Vigne-J. Maclean, 27 Feb. 1857; BK 86 F. Reeve-J. Maclean, 27 Nov. 1856; GH 8/31 R. Hawkes-J. Maclean, 17 March 1857; CO 2949 J. Warner-R. Southey, 2 June 1857.

103. This figure is calculated from the 'Population Returns for British Kaffraria,' enclosed in Maclean, (1858). It is derived from the difference in male population between January 1857 (the height of the cattle-killing) and December 1857 (by which time most of the believers had left their homes in search of food.) The seven chiefdoms in question are those of Sandile, Mhala, Phatho, Maqoma, Botomane, Xhoxho and Feni. Figures from the other chiefdoms, which experienced an influx of refugees from the core believer districts, were not considered. The precise figure for those who remained is 16,6%, but this would include the believing chiefs and their close associates, as well as believers who found refuge on mission stations.
104. Kropf and Godfrey, (1915), pp.122-3.
105. Gqoba, 'Isizatu,' Part 2, 2 April, 1888.
106. J. Backhouse, (1844), p.211. For more on Soga, see Peires (1981), p.108.
107. J. Lewis, 'The Rise and Fall of the South African Peasantry: a Critique and Reassessment,' *Journal of South African Studies*, 11 (Oct. 1984), p.4.
108. Merriman (1957), pp.98-9. The praises are printed in W.B. Rubusana (1906), pp.270-1. Translated with the help of D.L.P. Yali-Manisi.
109. J.T. Van der Kemp, *Transactions of the London Missionary Society*, 1, (1804), p.438.
110. Rubusana (1906), p.275. Translated with the help of D.L.P. Yali-Manisi.
111. 'Nzulu Lwazi,' 'UTyala Nteyi,' *Umteteli waBantu*, 22 Nov. 1930; GH 8/31 C. Brownlee-J. Maclean, 4 Jan. 1857. The 'indigent adherents' mentioned by Brownlee had possessed four head of cattle, and were not therefore as indigent as all that.
112. Interview with M. Torha, Ngede Location, Kentani District, 24 Aug. 1983; Interview with M. Soga (note 78 above).
113. There is a list of Sandile's headmen ranked according to status in BK 70 C. Brownlee-J. Maclean, 4 Sept. 1856. Of the 28 second-class headmen, six can be firmly identified as unbelievers, and only three as believers.The figure of 5-10% is calculated as follows: According to the 1857 returns, there were 14,000 adults in Sandile's chiefdom in January 1857. If we assume that 47.7% of these were males (this figure is calculated from the eleven chiefdoms in which male:female ratios are known), this would give us a figure of 6681 adult males. There were only 798 adult males left by December 1857 (11.95% of the January total), including Chiefs Sandile and Dondashe and other believers. Elsewhere, (BK 71 C. Brownlee-J. Maclean, 11 Aug. 1857) Brownlee refers to 250 (3.7% of 6,681) unbelievers in his district.
114. GH 8/29 J. Gawler-J. Maclean, 14 Aug. 1856; GH 18/6 J. Gawler-J. Maclean, 15 Aug. 1856; Acc.793 J. Gawler-J. Maclean, 14 July, 29 Oct 1856.
115. T.Soga (1983), pp.48-9; GH 8/41 J.C. Kayser-J. Maclean, 20 June 1860; GH 8/49 R. Tainton-J. Maclean, 29 Dec. 1856; Brownlee (1916), p. 158; Personal communication from Mr M.V.S. Balfour of Idutywa, a descendant of Makaphela.
117. This was the usual argument of the unbelievers according to oral tradition. Interviews with Tshisela (note 83) and Anta (note 87).
118. BK 81 J. Gawler-J. Maclean, 4 Dec. 1856.

CHAPTER 6

The Apotheosis of Major Gawler

1. A Disciple of Colonel Eyre

If it is true, as some maintain, that action is a combination of theory and practice, then in British Kaffraria in 1857 the theory was Governor Grey's but the practice was Major Gawler's. Alternatively, one might say that the ends were conceptualized by Grey but the means were devised by Gawler. Grey's theory was born of abstract reflection in his quiet, book-lined study, while Gawler's practice was forged in the gritty tension of his magistrate's offices at Waterloo Huts, near the Great Place of Chief Mhala. If we wish to understand the astonishingly brutal reaction of the colonial authorities to the Cattle-Killing, we have to retrace our steps to January 1856 and the arrival of a young officer at the lair of an old chief.

The young officer was Major John Cox Gawler, born in 1830 to an old and honourable military family.[1] His great-grandfather, also John Gawler, stormed the Heights of Abraham with General Wolfe in 1759 and features in West's famous portrait of the dying hero. His grandfather, Samuel Gawler, was killed at Mysore during the British conquest of India. His father, George Gawler, was wounded in the Peninsular War and led a company at the battle of Waterloo. In 1838 George Gawler was appointed Governor of South Australia, the chaotic finances of which were further confused by his massive and unauthorized expenditures. His term of office, however, was brought prematurely to an end by the secret denunciations of a military officer whom he had once hospitably entertained. This was none other than the young George Grey.

John Cox Gawler was born at Derby and educated at Rugby and Kings College, London. When a youth of seventeen, he volunteered as a special constable to police the Chartist demonstration in the City of London and spent several happy weeks of anticipation, making bullets with the help of his sisters. In 1849, he was commissioned an ensign in his grandfather's regiment, the 73rd, which was stationed at the Cape when the War of Mlanjeni broke out. The 73rd soon developed the reputation of the toughest regiment on the Eastern Frontier, and its commander, Lieutenant-Colonel Eyre, has already been singled out as the man whose energetic and merciless tactics won the war for Britain. We do not know too much about Gawler's part in these events, but he must have witnessed the ruthless and callous acts — the whippings, the burnings, the lootings, the casual executions, the bodies hung in the trees — which were Eyre's hallmark as a soldier. He almost certainly participated in the massacre of Sotho civilians which the 73rd perpetrated north of the Orange River in 1852, and he played a leading part in saving the British forces from humiliation at the battle of Berea when he led the company which stormed a virtually inaccessible mountain and caught the victorious Sotho by surprise. Gawler ever paid tribute to the memory of Colonel Eyre and, as we shall see, he proved himself a worthy disciple: brave, energetic, tough to the point of brutality, and supremely convinced of the innate superiority of the British officer to his 'barbarian' opponent.[2]

When the War of Mlanjeni was over, Gawler was appointed Field Adjutant in Natal, but he did not stay there long. He had married the daughter of Canon Judge of Simonstown, and through this Anglican connection he was offered the position of resident magistrate in British Kaffraria. It is not certain whether Grey realized that he was appointing the son of his old acquaintance, but Gawler made it quite clear that he had no intention of being beholden in any way. He refused to thank the Governor for his appointment, as custom required, and he passed through Cape Town on his way to the frontier without so much as sending Grey his card. He stirred up an immense amount of trouble in the gossipy atmosphere of the King William's Town officers' mess by reporting the private conversations of Reverend Allen and Captain Espinasse to Chief Commissioner Maclean. Few can have lamented his departure for his small and isolated station near the Great Place of Mhala, son of Ndlambe, the second-ranking chief in British Kaffraria.[3]

Mhala was often called by his praise name, A! Mbodla! — Wildcat! — and rarely was a salutation more appropriate, for his was a solitary nature which preferred the shadows to the open spaces, hard to pin down and ferocious when cornered. Chief Commissioner Maclean described him as 'a shrewd man, and very crafty', and Archdeacon Merriman called him 'the craftiest and most hardened chief in [Xhosaland]'. His intellectual abilities were widely renowned among the Xhosa and the expression '*Hayi! Ubulumko bukaMbodla! Asinokuba bukhulu*' ('Ah, the wisdom of Mbodla! There is nothing else so great') achieved a literally proverbial status.[4]

In fact, Mhala's deservedly great reputation was based not so much on breadth of knowledge or depth of insight as on his ability to anticipate and outwit opponents whose resources and natural advantages were far greater than his own. He was not born a great chief, being the son of a lesser wife, but had intrigued his way into it partly through discrediting the most qualified heir on a charge of witchcraft and partly through getting his father's councillors to recognize that he had been 'given gifts of chieftainship, which were not given to the other sons of his father'.[5] The Mhala style of wheedling and flattery, of promises and evasions, of never refusing to obey a command but never obeying it either, bamboozled and frustrated a long succession of colonial officials, notably Sir Harry Smith, who wrote of him:

> He never quailed in the slightest as all the others did, under my most violent animadversions. He gave me more trouble to render obedient than all the other chiefs. Still he respected me and I him. . . .[6]

Never the best judge of character, Sir Harry was perhaps influenced by Mhala's decision to rename his Right-Hand Son 'Smith' in the Governor's honour. He renamed his Great Son 'Makinana' after Mackinnon, the first Chief Commissioner of British Kaffraria.

Mhala's political style extended also to the field of military operations. He was an inveterate enemy of the Colony and the settlers, having grown up west of Grahamstown in the days when the lands of his father Ndlambe stretched almost to Port Elizabeth. He was old enough to remember the catastrophic defeat of the Fourth Frontier War (1811-2) and the death of three brothers in the battle of Grahamstown during the Fifth (1818-9). Mhala's hostility did not abate when he assumed the Ndlambe chieftainship in 1828, but his relatively flat and open territory did not permit the sort of sustained guerilla warfare which Maqoma and his brother Ngqika chiefs waged in the forested and inaccessible Amathole mountain ranges. Mhala's strategy in the Sixth (1834-5) and Seventh (1846-7) Frontier Wars was one of pretended neutrality, remaining technically at peace but sending out raiding parties, supplying the Xhosa fighters in the mountains and sheltering their women, children and cattle. Once and only once did Mhala come out into the open, an exception to his normal behaviour which he was greatly to regret. He was asked to join in an attack on Fort Peddie, which would have necessitated his marching during daylight hours. 'I am the wildcat,' Mhala protested, 'a thing which walks by night.' Accused of cowardice, he eventually gave way against his better judgement.[7] The British cavalry caught the Ndlambe army on the plains of the Gwangqa and 500 Xhosa perished in the biggest Xhosa military disaster for nearly thirty years. Mhala lost two brothers killed virtually before his eyes in the very bush where he, too, was hiding. In the War of Mlanjeni, therefore, he resumed his old method of malevolent neutrality, aiding and abetting the Ngqika Xhosa every way he could short of open warfare. Although his duplicity was recognized by Maclean and Governor Cathcart, they had enough on their hands without a shooting war near the strategic port of East London and so, despite the ranting of the settler press, Mhala ended the war in full possession of his territory and his cattle.

Mhala did not, of course, enjoy living under the colonial government, but up until the initiation of Grey's new policies, he had managed fairly well. His immediate superior was Maclean, resident at Fort Murray forty kilometres away. As we have seen, in the days before Grey's governorship Maclean had been most reluctant to interfere with the prerogatives of chieftainship, believing as he did that Smith's deposition of Sandile was the main cause of the War of Mlanjeni. William Greenstock, the Anglican missionary at St Luke's in Mhala's territory, was sympathetic to the Xhosa and inclined to support the chief's authority.

Mhala rightly feared that the introduction of a resident magistrate would interfere with his freedom of action but after some procrastination he agreed to receive one on the understanding that he would get a cash income in compensation for the loss of criminal fines and court fees.[8] He expected to pick his own magistrate, from among the Tainton family, simple Christians of humble origins who had lived among the Xhosa for many years and were unlikely to adopt a high-handed tone or manner. Moreover, by naming his own magistrate Mhala was emphasizing the conditional nature of his acceptance: if he asked for a magistrate, then by implication he could have him removed.

One can only imagine Mhala's displeasure when Maclean arrived in November 1855 with Gawler in tow, and announced that this was the chief's new magistrate. The Chief Commissioner lost no time in disabusing Mhala of the idea that this was a voluntary agreement between equals. Mhala had 'accepted the whole of the Governor's terms', said Maclean, and he had lost the right to pick and choose. If

Mhala insisted, he would submit Mhala's request for another magistrate to Grey, but Gawler would remain at nearby St Luke's until the matter was finally decided. Mhala raised objections to this, too, but when Maclean asked him pointedly whether he was ordering them out, Mhala decided that he dared not venture so direct an insult. 'I agree to the magistrate sitting at the [mission] station until the reply is received from the Governor,' he said, adding in a more conciliatory fashion, 'I have no personal dislike to the Gentleman, the only thing is he is new to me.'

Predictably enough, Grey refused to consider Mhala's request and, in January 1856, Gawler was formally installed as Mhala's magistrate.[9] For three months outward peace prevailed in Mhala's district as chief and magistrate felt their way towards a better understanding of the politics of the new situation. Then, in April 1856, the tension finally exploded over the issue of the councillors' salaries.

The only attraction of Grey's system, as far as the chiefs were concerned, was the payment of cash salaries. In Mhala's case, this amounted to £96 per annum. The value of such a guaranteed income lay less in the number of consumer goods it could purchase than in its function as a means of patronage for the chief. But the whole purpose of the new system was to undermine the control of the chief over the more enterprising of his commoner councillors. The colonial adminis- tration could not prevent the chiefs from doing what they liked with their own personal stipends but it could force the more important councillors to look to the government rather than the chiefs for their incomes. This point was so central to Grey's strategy and so repugnant to the chiefs that it had been glossed over during the initial discussions. Even Brownlee did not fully understand it, and he continued to give Sandile the councillors' salaries to allocate as he pleased. On the first occasion that payments were made in the Ndlambe chiefdom, Mhala too was permitted to name the councillors he wanted paid.[10]

By April 1856, Gawler was sufficiently established to challenge Mhala on this point. Acting on Maclean's specific instructions, Gawler informed Mhala that he need not assemble his councillors for their monthly payment. He, Gawler, would pay councillors of his own selection privately and in his own time.[11] It is not clear whether Mhala misunderstood this instruction or whether he simply chose to misunderstand it, but when payday came around the chief had assembled 120 or so junior chiefs and councillors at Gawler's office.

'We have come for the money,' Mhala said, naming ten men whom he wanted paid. 'I am glad to see all your faces,' responded Gawler, 'but am sorry you have come to be disappointed. I told [Mhala] the last time that I should send for those I wish to pay.' 'Pay these men,' Mhala insisted, 'because they are here and it is far for them to come again.' Gawler refused. 'I have paid the only two that I intend to pay,' he said. 'It is your fault bringing them so far. I told you last time that I had my orders and if I want any of these I will send for them.'

Mhala then accused Gawler of planning to pay his favourites twice over. 'Pay these men,' he demanded for the second time, indicating his nominees. 'I shall pay whom I please,' retorted Gawler, flourishing an official paper at the chief. 'Here are ten names. Read, Umhala, if you can! No! No one but myself, the Government, and the [councillor] that receives the money shall know about it. The money belongs to the Government and they may give it to whom they please.'

Gawler had won the first round. The next day, he followed up his victory by attempting to subvert two leading councillors.

> I then told them the Government did not wish them to be entirely at Umhala's mercy and had therefore sent the instructions. Umhala had insulted me while carrying out these, but I did not care, I shall stick to them. As long as Umhala received his own money that was all he had to trouble himself about. They were very cordial, and they were very glad and hoped they should be sent for sometime [to get a salary]. I replied if I send for one I shall not tell another of it and I will make no promises. I have seldom seen men so perfectly satisfied.[12]

Mhala came to call the next morning. Gawler refused to shake his hand and reprimanded him severely. It must have been galling for Mhala to be thus put down in his country by a young man rather less than half his age, a man who was not even born when he started to reign.[13] But circumstances soon turned the tables on Gawler. Very shortly after the salary incident, a man named Gabinyana stole a gun from a Mfengu living in Mhala's district.[14] Gabinyana was a follower of Sigidi, a Gcaleka Xhosa chief in no way genealogically junior to Mhala but resident within the district in which the colonial authorities recognized Mhala as the sole responsible chief. Gawler made out a clear case for theft against Gabinyana, but neither the thief nor Sigidi his chief would appear in the magistrate's court. Gawler then approached Mhala who said that 'he did not see what he had to do with it', but eventually gave his consent for a punitive expedition to be organized by the magistrate.

Gawler assembled some eighty men, including three of Mhala's sons, a large but somewhat half-hearted party. What incentive might a Xhosa have to raid a fellow-Xhosa at the behest of a colonial magistrate? Major Gawler was soon to get his first lesson in practical

Xhosa politics. At dawn on 18 April, Gawler's party surprised Gabinyana's homestead. Two of his men ran away but Gabinyana planted himself boldly in the doorway of his dwelling holding the stolen carbine in his hand and daring all eighty opponents to take him if they could. Gawler ordered his men to fire the dwelling but by this time his unwilling followers were completely beyond his control. Gawler's personal servant tried to set the thatch alight, but it was too damp and would not burn. Finally, giving up on Gabinyana, Gawler ordered his party to seize the cattle. This was done, though in a state of complete confusion, the posse all milling around uncertain what to do and getting increasingly worried as the war cry resounded among Gabinyana's neighbours.

Not without difficulty Gawler sent some of the men ahead with the cattle, while he struggled to get the rest of them into line. At this point, Gabinyana pulled the trigger, and the mere sound of the shot sent the rearguard fleeing in all directions. Another blast panicked the cattleguard, and the rout was completed by the whistling of Gabinyana's followers, which stampeded the cattle so that Gawler's party scattered in all directions pursued by the very beasts they were supposedly trying to capture. They ran for more than two kilometres without stopping, Mhala's sons jumping off their horses to avoid recognition. The shots they fired in return only served to frighten the cattle into returning back to Gabinyana's homestead. Gawler tried his best, swearing at his men in English and beating them with his cane, but his first attempt to enforce British justice had been comprehensively smashed by no more than one determined Xhosa.

Unwilling to risk another defeat, Gawler ordered Sigidi, Gabinyana's chief, to pay a fine of fifty cattle and deliver up the thieves and their guns within six days 'or take the consequences'. After Gawler's debacle, Sigidi was not afraid to take the consequences and six days passed, twelve days, eighteen days without any fine.[15] The old British Kaffraria hands were openly critical of Gawler's judgement. A fine of fifty cattle was too heavy, they said: Sigidi would gladly have paid a smaller fine to be rid of the incident. Gawler was told not to impose a fine unless he was certain either that it would be paid or that he was in a position to enforce it. As the Cattle-Killing approached, Gawler's standing in Mhala's country could hardly have been lower.

2. Mhala Gets a Message

Mhala's people were initially cool to the news of Nongqawuse's prophecies. 'Oh go to the Bashee [River] they are killing plenty,' Smith

Mhala told Gawler in June 1856, 'but this news is not quite strong enough for us to kill ours.' 'My father and mother are dead,' said another, 'and I shall wait until I see them among the Russians before I kill my cattle.' Far from rushing off to slaughter their cattle, most of the ordinary Ndlambe Xhosa hastened to buy the cattle and goats that their believing Gcaleka neighbours were bringing for sale at rock bottom prices.[17]

But there was at least one man among them whose heart yearned after a better world, and who grasped eagerly at every hope that Nongqawuse held out to him: Mhala, the chief. How great was the change which time had wrought in the bright young man of thirty years ago, whose outstanding qualities had led the councillors to nominate him old Ndlambe's successor despite the lowliness of his birth! How great the change in that much-vaunted wisdom which had led Governor Smith to call Mhala 'a man of superior intellect, and the only [Xhosa] who could judge cause and effect and future results'.[18] Although no more than sixty years old, Mhala was feeling his age and the pains of lumbago. His increasingly uncertain grip on political affairs was visibly undermined by the growing vigour and self-confidence of Makinana and Smith, his capable and ambitious sons. Now, in the twilight of his long reign, Mhala found his liberty of action and his rights of patronage subject to the whim of his young British magistrate. For all his shrewdness and all his cunning, Mhala was a man whose vision of the future was blocked by a host of threatening and insuperable obstacles, and his mind naturally preferred to dwell on the past, when he was still in the prime of life, and his power and his freedom were quite unfettered. He was moreover, in S.E.K. Mqhayi's words, 'a man who was humble to authority. There was nothing done at the Great Place, home of Sarhili which he did not follow after.'[19]

When, therefore, Mhala heard officially of the prophecies through Sarhili's messenger Kinco (late June 1856), he sent a delegation headed by his favourite son Mtshatsheni to the Gxarha, where they saw Nongqawuse 'talking' to the new people in the magic bush. Even though they themselves saw nothing at all, the delegates were very impressed and Mtshatsheni slaughtered one of his cattle as soon as he reached home.[20]

But no matter how much Mhala may have wanted to believe in the Cattle-Killing, he had to proceed carefully. Makinana, his Great Son, said that he 'would believe the reports when he saw his grandfather H'lambie and not till then; and that he would cut the throat of any fool in his kraal that commenced killing his cattle'. Smith, his Right-Hand

Son, who openly referred to Xhosa diviners as frauds and who had himself survived a witchcraft accusation the previous year, likewise opposed the movement.[21] Even more important to Mhala was the opposition of leading councillors such as old Gqirana, who had milked for him when he was a boy, and Ndayi, son of Tsora, whose praises have already been discussed.[22] 'They are men without whom Umhala cannot stir a finger,' exulted Gawler. Several of them were already on his secret payroll. 'There is no danger,' they told the magistrate, 'as the great ones are not with [Mhala].'[23]

Faced by this opposition, Mhala adopted a public position of apparent neutrality, 'saying it [the Cattle-Killing] was a foolish thing that he should not trouble his head about'. Warned by his fellow believer Maqoma to act with discretion lest the government find out, Mhala opened his campaign in favour of the Cattle-Killing by attempting to promote believers — 'a number of young second-rate counsellors, ambitious of distinction and ready to take their chance in forwarding any of the current nonsense' — at the expense of the established, mostly unbelieving councillors.[24] He brought five of these to Gawler, asking quietly yet decidedly that these should be paid since they were his councillors. Gawler told him to take them away and walked off, leaving the chief speechless with anger and frustration. Mhala sent the magistrate a message, saying he did not like him and would ask for his removal, but Gawler remained unmoved, retorting that far from learning his lesson, Mhala was getting worse. The chief had no option but to back down once again.

Gawler's little victories did nothing to increase his influence. Unable to challenge their magistrate openly, the Xhosa responded to his arbitrary behaviour by killing their cattle against his wishes. When Gawler and his interpreter approached a homestead where the believers were feasting on slaughtered cattle, the Xhosa deliberately slaughtered more cattle in their presence, defiantly rejecting their arguments to the contrary. There was nothing that either Gawler or the leading councillors could do to curb the mounting enthusiasm for cattle-killing which spread like wildfire among the Ndlambe. 'Within the last few days,' wrote Gawler towards the end of August, 'the lower orders have taken to cattle-killing. . . . I am not yet aware of any influential person having yet commenced.'[25]

After a great deal of hesitation, Mhala appears to have concluded that since the Cattle-Killing could not be hidden indefinitely from the colonial authorities, it would be best to have it out in the open as soon as possible. For this reason, he officially notified Governor Grey of the message he received from Sarhili towards the end of September, and he even invited Gawler to be present at the public reception of Sarhili's messenger, Sixaxa. Gawler's lengthy account leaves no doubt that the meeting was staged especially for his benefit. Sixaxa, 'an old man with cross eyes', said very little, simply restating the orders to kill, and none of the assembled crowd said very much, either. Gawler, backed by Ndayi, urged them not to kill their cattle, but his speech was received in silence. Mhala had gained his point: the government could not accuse him of hiding anything, neither could it prevent the people from killing cattle which were, after all, their own private property. Sixaxa stayed on at Mhala's Great Place long after the public meeting and doubtless communicated all of Sarhili's wishes in a suitably private manner.[26]

Mhala now recovered something of his old zest and energy. He was prepared to admit out of deference to the sceptics that the prophecies should not be acted upon without some kind of tangible proof, and a delegation headed by three of his sons, Smith, Mtshatsheni and Gemptu, was despatched to the Gxarha. Mhala did not conceal his hope that they would return with a positive report. He was sufficiently confident, even before they returned, to send official messages to the unbelieving Ndlambe chiefs, Siwani, Toyise and Dyani Tshatshu, informing them of Sarhili's orders and instructing them to kill their cattle. Finally, and most significantly, he secretly ordered his people not to cultivate their fields in the coming season and threatened to confiscate the property of any who disobeyed. Aside, he said to a councillor that if there was any objection from the government, they could just go and pick away at the hills, pretending to cultivate but not putting any seed into the ground.[27]

All Mhala's old lassitude had vanished. 'He has brightened up wonderfully lately,' wrote the missionary, Greenstock. Even Magistrate Gawler reported that Mhala's 'former dull and frequently sullen and uncivil demeanour towards me has lately changed — he is now very civil, high-spirited and witty'. So certain was Mhala of the truth of the prophecies that he sent Chief Commissioner Maclean himself a message, urging him not to prejudge the Cattle-Killing, but 'to listen to me and not to be too hasty in telling the people to plough or to stop them killing their cattle'.[28]

3. Bulungwa Ploughs

Only one man had the courage to cultivate in spite of Mhala's interdict. This was his nephew Bulungwa, described by Gawler as 'courageous and straightforward though a great beggar and over-ambitious'.[29] His

Xhosa neighbours also thought Bulungwa over-ambitious, and they rightly suspected him of acting as a colonial informer. As a member of the royal clan, he was fully a chief in his own right, and he had allowed many Mfengu to settle on his lands around the Gxulu river. On 11 October, about a week after Mhala had issued the ban, Bulungwa gave his people the word to cultivate.[30]

It was whispered among the people that Bulungwa should be killed because 'he was always with the English and thought to make himself great by not killing his cattle and continuing ploughing in spite of Umhala'. Towards the end of October, Mhala sent for a Xhosa doctor to discover who had made himself and Makinana sick. As Bulungwa was sitting in the dwelling of a fellow unbeliever, the doctor looked in on them meaningfully. The other unbeliever killed an ox that very day and stopped digging up his garden, but Bulungwa refused to take the hint.[31]

In the early afternoon of 28 October, Magistrate Gawler was disturbed by a shout and, looking out of his makeshift office, saw a posse of men rushing from Mhala's Great Place towards Bulungwa's homestead. He scrambled out and joined the runners, asking innocently where they were going and what they wanted, although he knew very well that they were off to seize Bulungwa as a witch. Mhala's son Ghoghoshe, who led the party, looked sourly at Gawler, but nobody interfered with him, nor did they slacken their pace.

> The Doctor, stark naked, ran in front occasionally smelling round a bush or in the grass, or stopping and looking wildly round and sniffing the breeze. With the exception of a few such lulls we kept up a pretty smart pace, and when he stopped to smell we chanted loud to encourage him in his laudable search but while at full speed, an occasional yell or whistle sufficed to keep his spirits up.[32]

After about six kilometres, they reached Bulungwa's residence. The doctor demanded that he give up his *ubuthi*, the secret substance which he was using to bewitch Mhala and his son. Bulungwa denied that he had any *ubuthi*. The people then rushed in and searched the dwelling but to no avail. When the great doctor himself entered, however, he returned in triumph with a piece of fat 'half the size of a thimble' on the point of a needle. From another dwelling he drew forth another piece of fat, to the infinite satisfaction of the crowd. Gawler did nothing except warn the doctor not to destroy property, but his mere presence probably saved the unbeliever's life. Nobody raised a hand against Bulungwa and the whole party returned to Mhala's Great Place. When the doctor secluded himself, as was the custom before announcing his findings, Gawler took Mhala aside and extracted assurances from the chief that neither Bulungwa nor his property would be touched.

Despite these assurances, Bulungwa's life hung by a very slender thread and early the next day the unbeliever arrived at Gawler's place in a state of utter terror. Sure enough, the doctor followed close behind him, accompanied by a group of leading believers who publicly accused Bulungwa of witchcraft and asked him to make a statement in his own defence. A large party of armed men appeared over the brow of the hill and another sealed off the drift over the river. Bulungwa pleaded his innocence and threw himself on the mercy of the court. More and more Xhosa pressed in behind those already confronting Bulungwa and Gawler in the magistrate's little hut. A party of twenty men armed with spears and guns patrolled to and fro in front of the doorway. The believers hoped that the mounting threat of violence would frighten Gawler into surrendering their enemy, but they were disappointed. Mhala, of course, was absent to avoid being implicated and the magistrate took full advantage of this. He told the councillors that their chief had promised to spare Bulungwa, and he sent Mhala a message: 'What are these armed men about my place?' he demanded. 'Are you going to eat [Bulungwa] up? By your agreement with Government all fines go to Government, therefore you must send his cattle to me.' Mhala weighed his answer for nearly an hour. He must have considered an all-out attack, but he decided to give Gawler another chance to deliver Bulungwa up. 'Bulungwa is a bad man,' he replied eventually. 'You yourself saw the [medicine] taken out of his hut — he was killing me. Why should I not kill him — what business had he to come talking to you about what I was doing to him?'[33] Gawler saw that the old chief had drawn back from the brink, and pressed home his advantage. 'What sort of chief do you call yourself? What confidence can I have in you. . . . Let me go.' Mhala considered his answer for two more hours and then he caved in. 'My heart was very sore,' he complained, 'when rolled in two pieces of fat are bits of my own and my father's [Ndlambe's] hair, shown to me — both found in Bulungwa's kraal. I had assembled men and had given orders to kill him but this time I hear your word. Bulungwa may go in peace but let him take care how he plays tricks again.'

It was a great victory and a great precedent. Bulungwa had disobeyed his chief by cultivating, he had been charged with witchcraft and, with the help of the magistrate, he had survived. In making this concession to Gawler, Mhala had surrendered his power to put his subjects to death, even when Xhosa law and Xhosa judicial processes warranted it. The way was open for all unbelievers to shake off the chiefly yoke and to cultivate and preserve their cattle under the protection of the colonial government. Gawler had no illusions that it was going to be easy. He realized that Bulungwa was a marked man and wanted him resettled in the Crown Reserve. He heard that the councillor Xayimpi was likewise suspected of witchcraft on account of his unbelief, and he helped him to flee.[34] There were too many opportunities for killing a man on the quiet for their lives to be truly secure. Gawler wanted Maclean to send troops to his headquarters. He had threatened Mhala with troops, which was one reason why Mhala had given in.

But the magistrate's victory was not followed up and government support for the unbelievers nowhere equalled that which Gawler, personally and at the risk of his own life, had given to Bulungwa. It has already been pointed out that Grey and Maclean had taken a very clear-cut decision to encourage the unbelievers to hold their ground, but not to support them with any colonial military force. Maclean did come to Mhala's Great Place in person, affirming his support for Gawler and the unbelievers and temporarily suspending the pay of Mhala, who was careful to be absent. He offered Bulungwa a refuge, though not in the Crown Reserve. But he did not make any promises of concrete military support, and departed leaving Gawler and the unbelievers to face the wounded and enraged Mhala as best they could. Two days later the chief reiterated his order not to cultivate, and once again none of the Ndlambe Xhosa, apart from Bulungwa, dared to disobey him.[35]

Mhala's decision to spare Bulungwa was probably influenced by the thought that it was not worth risking a confrontation with the colonial government when ultimate salvation lay just around the corner. Thus, although much of the chief's energy was absorbed by his need to dodge the authorities, the main focus of his attention remained fixed on the Gxarha River. These hopes were not in the least diminished by the disappointing report of the delegation he had sent to Mhlakaza in early October. The delegates had been informed that the new people were away for the time being, although one or two of them might still be seen at the river mouth. Three members of the delegation kept watch for three days but saw nothing. Mhlakaza then told them that the new people were sure to be back soon and that they should return the following month. Some of the delegates were noticeably disillusioned by this reception, most significantly Mhala's son, Smith, who sent his oxen to St Luke's mission for safe-keeping shortly after he returned.[36]

Early in November, the delegation left for its second visit to the Gxarha. Mhala was 'sanguine' about their prospects and slaughtered an ox 'to clear their eyes'. He had heard once that he was to be made young again, and he did not want to hear anything different. The delegates, by contrast, were considerably less hopeful, and Smith and some of the others expressed the hope that they might get back quickly so as to be in time to plough. It took them longer than expected to return — they were delayed for nine days at the Kei drift — and the waverers began once more to swing towards the side of unbelief.[37] Then the great news arrived that the British warship, the *Geyser*, had been destroyed by the new people, and unbelief was suddenly at an end. Mhala began to kill his cattle in earnest. The word was spread about that the new people were getting tired of all this endless talk and querying, and had said that the people should waste no more time, but go immediately and kill all their cattle. This enthusiasm was not tempered by the second delegation's somewhat unsatisfactory report.[38]

The delegates reported that Nongqawuse kept them waiting for two days, and on the third day took them to a vantage point from which they could see some figures in the mist. They were not allowed to address these figures or go near enough to see them distinctly. It was not much to go on, but it was enough. As Gawler put it, Mhala had been promised 'youth, beauty, cattle and no end of things and he does not like giving up the idea'.[39]

A formal meeting was held on the day after the delegation's return. All the delgates except Smith announced their belief in the prophecies. Almost every homestead in Mhala's district slaughtered cattle that night. More meetings were held on the following days. Support for the Cattle-Killing was overwhelming, and Gawler could do nothing about it. Mhala told him that the government should have sent its own man to the Gxarha and then it would have seen the truth. Makinana, Mhala's Great Son, spoke out strongly against the Cattle-Killing but loyally elected to stand by his father and his people, despite their error. Smith, on the other hand, quarrelled violently with Mhala and told a large crowd that 'They say I am killing my father — so I would kill him before I would kill my cattle.' 'Show now whom you are for,' demanded Mhala of Ndayi, his Great Councillor, 'the English or me?' 'What river do you now intend crossing?' responded Ndayi, reminding Mhala of his past mistakes and defeats. 'You were once [living] near Grahamstown.' But all argument was in vain. Mhala committed himself irrevocably to the course he had long desired. 'I believe,' he informed Sarhili, his King, 'I am killing.' And he did.[40]

4. Nonkosi Speaks

Mhala spent most of December 1856 killing his cattle, pressurizing the unbelievers and distracting Gawler by repeated promises to cultivate.[41] Two great believers, his nephew Yosi and a councillor named Nkwintsha, were sent to Mhlakaza to ask if Mhala should also kill the funeral cattle of his father Ndlambe, something never before contemplated. They returned with an affirmative answer, but they saw nothing at the Gxarha. Killing continued apace and by the middle of the month most of Mhala's loyal subordinates had killed all their bulls and all their oxen, and started on the calves and the milk-cows. Disappointed by the recent news from the Gxarha, Mhala sent Nkwintsha yet again, hoping to get 'a report in accordance with his wishes'. On 28 December Nkwintsha returned, having once more seen nothing.

By this time, the excitement surrounding Nxito's return was at its highest. Mhala sent his brother Nowawe to the meeting held in Butterworth at the beginning of 1857. There was general consternation among the believers when he returned without news.[42] But Mhala was not easily discouraged and, besides, he now had no further need to look to the Gxarha. A prophetess had arisen at the Mpongo River in his own country.

In the valley of the Mpongo, there lived a lame old Xhosa doctor named Kulwana. He believed in the prophecies as did his neighbours, including a woman named Nonkazana, who began to prophesy in support of Nongqawuse. Kulwana's little daughter Nonkosi, a girl of about eleven years, was naturally affected by the prevailing excitement. She used to play near a pool in the Mpongo River and, early in January, she too began to see strange people. Her first recorded statement is strongly reminiscent of normal childhood fantasies concerning imaginary friends.

> I was going down to water one day with a lot of little girls, near my father's kraal on the Umpongo. A man suddenly showed himself out of the water. I ran home, and went down next day and saw him again, and he spoke to me, but when he found I was afraid of him he spoke to another girl. A few days after, he found that she lived at a distance, so he took to me again.
>
> And the second time, after I had got confidence, he told me that I was to let 'Umhala' and the other chiefs know about it. He showed me a lot of cattle in the water, and some milking outside; also several other men in the water, and he dived about himself. He told me everything was to be said through me, and no one was to speak to him but me, and he did not always promise to speak when spoken to, or to show any wonders.
>
> As I often went to the river, I and my companions built some huts on

the bank of the river, and he used often to sleep in them. He said he had come to put the country right, that he had already been to 'Moshesh' and taken him some corn; and half 'Moshesh's' people were destroyed because they were not quick in believing. That everything the [Xhosa] possessed now was to be done away with, and that the Fingoes would be destroyed, and the English would all run to King Williams Town, and be destroyed there. . . .[43]

In most respects, the message of the new people through Nonkosi was the same as that of Nongqawuse, 'that cattle-killing is to be carried on and that until the present cattle are all destroyed, the new cattle will not be provided'. All the Xhosa territories invaded and settled by whites would be restored to them as far as Grahamstown, and the fallen heroes who had formerly lived there would rise and reoccupy their old homes. Nonkosi was quite definite that ornaments should be disposed of rather than worn, and that fires should be made of sneezewood rather than mimosa. Believers should shave off their eyebrows to distinguish them clearly from unbelievers.[44]

It was a simple fantasy and not, perhaps, remarkable under the circumstances, but its effect in Mhala's country was electric. For the many believers who had committed their all to the prophecies and who yet lacked any concrete reward for their sacrifice, it was a welcome confirmation of the rightness of their actions.

[Nonkosi] used to lead the people to a pond there at the Mpongo, and there used to see *abakweta* [newly-circumcised youths] dancing on the surface of the water, and they thought that they heard the thudding of the oxhide, accompanied by a song, to which the *abakweta* danced. Truly the people were so deluded that they went so far as to claim that they had seen the horns of cattle, heard the lowing of milk-cows, the barking of dogs, and the songs of milkmen at milking-time.[45]

Old Kulwana supported the prophecies of his daughter, saying that he himself could hear the cattle bellowing underground.

Mhala came often to Nonkosi, seeking comfort and reassurance as his entire world crumbled about him. There is something unbearably pathetic in this picture of the venerable old chief — in his day, perhaps the shrewdest, richest and most powerful man in British Kaffraria — begging advice and guidance from an imaginative eleven-year-old. Phatho, Qasana, Namba and other chiefs brought low by their own errors and misjudgements came likewise.[46]

Nkwintsha, the head councillor of the Mpongo district, was sometimes present at these interviews. Many months later he was to confess — under circumstances we shall discuss in detail later on — that he had given Nonkosi money, that he had told her the names of her distinguished visitors, that he had described to her the physical attributes of the dead chiefs she said she saw, even that he had helped her to simulate new stock, new corn, and the voices of the dead from the pool. He may have done some or all of these things. So much of his confession was clearly fabricated under pressure from his captors, that there is no reason to believe any of his statements. But even if Nkwintsha did help Nonkosi with some parts of her performance, his assistance only elaborated and confirmed her prophecies: it did not create them. Nonkosi's prophecies, like those of Nongqawuse, arose out of the spiritual and material anguish of the Xhosa nation, and the chiefs and people believed them for the same reason.

Under Nonkosi's influence, Mhala rapidly ran through the last of his cattle, slaughtering at the rate of four or five a day. By the end of January, he was killing those set aside at Ndlambe's death. They were his last. In the final days before the Great Disappointment, he roamed the country exhorting, threatening and demanding cattle from those who still retained a few, and then killing them in furious abandon.[47]

5. The Battle is Joined

After the rescue of Bulungwa, Magistrate Gawler asked Chief Commissioner Maclean for troops to defend the unbelievers in his district. Towards the end of November he asked him again, with no better success. Gawler was sure that many of the waverers wanted to preserve their cattle and cultivate their gardens, but he was unable to promise them military protection against the wrath of Mhala. Ndayi, Bulungwa and Smith Mhala appealed repeatedly for troops and Gawler repeatedly assured them that troops were on the way, even though he knew very well that Grey and Maclean had already refused to consider such assistance.[48]

Gawler did his best to boost the confidence of the unbelievers, taking a select group to East London to show them the ships in which the German Legion had recently arrived. The unbelievers returned greatly impressed by British technology and their own courage in ignoring the warnings of the believers that they would be kidnapped and sent to England.[49] While the believers were wasting their last resources, the unbelievers were slowly mustering their strength as isolated *amagogotya* from as far away as Sarhili's country fled their homesteads and joined up with the more powerful members of their party.[50]

After the Great Disappointment the believers pressed Mhala for action, telling him that they were starving through following his orders. The chief sent to the Gxarha and the Mpongo for advice, but it was now clear, even to Mhala, that the period of waiting was over. He and his believing councillors met to plot revenge against the unbelievers, whom they held responsible for the failure of the prophecies.[51] The unbelievers visited Gawler in a great panic, begging him to establish a military post in the district. Cattle raids were becoming increasingly frequent, and they dared not move their cattle from where they were located since the believers were on the watch for just such a move.[52]

The first attacks were led by the believing chief Qasana, nephew to Mhala and brother to the collaborating Siwani. Qasana was a great militant who had led a contingent of Ndlambe volunteers to help the Ngqika fighting in the Amathole Mountains during the War of Mlanjeni. On the morning of 28 February he sent a scout patrol against Bulungwa, who personified unbelief to many of the *amathamba*. Gawler informed Mhala who remarked sourly that Bulungwa was a hasty man and had probably attacked some innocent people walking on a footpath near his place. Gawler then rode to Bulungwa and suggested that he send his cattle away. Bulungwa refused, knowing that it was more dangerous to move his cattle than to stand and fight for them. At least you could post a lookout, Gawler suggested. 'Why?' asked Bulungwa, laconically. 'There will be enough time to look at the attackers when they come to my place.'[53] Bulungwa did not need Gawler's advice. He needed men and arms, and the magistrate could supply neither.

Just before sunset the war cry sounded and Qasana swept down on Bulungwa's homestead at the head of a large party of mounted men. Bulungwa stood at the gate of his cattle kraal and blazed away with a gun, but his oxen were trained for racing and leaped over the fences when the believers called out to them. Bulungwa lost sixty cattle altogether, and one of his men was killed. There was very little that Gawler could do about it. He could spare none of the few men at his disposal, and he was forced to request Chief Mhala, the arch-believer, to discipline his comrade Qasana for the sake of the arch-unbeliever, Bulungwa.

Mhala probably enjoyed hearing Gawler's demand for action. In any event, he hammed it up, pretending to be very angry at Qasana. 'Go on and kill him [Qasana],' he ordered his followers, tongue firmly in cheek. 'You are hungry my children but do your best.' Many of Mhala's men had actually joined in the attack on Bulungwa themselves, and they travelled no more than three kilometres in Qasana's general direction before turning back, claiming that they were tired.[54] The unbelievers were appalled. It was absurd that they, who had stubbornly thwarted Mhala's dearest wishes, should be dependent on that very chief for their protection. 'Here's an end to us non-believers,' said Ndayi, 'unless the Government who gave us encouragement to hold out will help us. Let Gawler take Smith to Government as our chief, and ask for a word.'[55]

The troubles of the unbelievers were only just beginning. Between 3 and 5 March, organized parties of believers smashed into the more isolated of the *amagogotya*, carrying all before them. Councillor Wuwu with two junior headmen raided the Mfengu population on the Kwelera River. Four other councillors attacked and wounded Tamo, a second-class headman, and carried off all his cattle. On the borders of Ndlambe territory, Phatho's Great Son Dilima mustered an armed force of believers to root out the adherents of his father's unbelieving cousin, Montawuli. Take their cattle, ordered Dilima, but don't throw your spears unless they attack you. Montawuli fled in the face of overwhelming numbers, leaving 170 cattle behind him. The believers robbed the dwellings, plundered the cornpits, killed the chickens and then fired some of the homesteads.

In this crisis, the unbelievers were rallied by a new hero. This was none other than Mjuza, the son of the prophet Nxele, who had predicted the resurrection of the dead in 1818. Mjuza was brought up in Mhala's country, but had left it in the early 1840s after falling out with the chief. Like his father Nxele, Mjuza was a great anti-colonial militant. He fought vigorously in three Frontier Wars, burning down Butterworth mission in 1851, and nearly perishing from a bullet in the stomach. When the first prophecies of cattle-killing were heard in the land, Mjuza, who had carefully preserved his father's weapons, announced that his father was returning at the head of the army of black Russians to liberate the country. But when he visited Nongqawuse, he perceived to his horror and dismay that her prophecies were false and became a convinced unbeliever. In November 1856, he returned to Mhala's country where he immediately took a strong stand against the orders of the chief. Attacked in March by the desperate believers, Mjuza rallied Montawuli and the other isolated *amagogotya* of his district, and led them forward in military order, skirmishing all night until they reached the main body of unbelievers under Gawler and Ndayi. Mjuza was to prove of inestimable value to Gawler, for not only was he a battle-hardened veteran but he hated Mhala with all the furious intensity of an ancient grudge.[56]

Meanwhile Gawler had managed to persuade Governor Grey to allow him to raise an irregular 'native police'. Towards the end of February he jotted down his ideas in an official dispatch. The unbelievers should all concentrate in a single place. He would raise from them a police force of 120 to 150 men at the cost of 7s 6d per man per month, plus rations. One ox every two days should be enough to feed them all.[57]

In the aftermath of the raids, Gawler held a meeting of the unbelievers to explain the self-defence plan to them. For the unbelievers, already watching all night and tracking stolen cattle all day, the most significant aspect of the proposal was the refusal of the government to commit troops to their defence. They strongly suspected that Gawler was only temporizing and that the government, which had already rejected their earlier requests for aid, was planning to desert them. Gawler duly put in a request for 200 troops, but his mind was already running on beyond the immediate needs of self-defence. The title of one of his notes to Maclean, 'Proposal for creating a revolution in Umhala's country' did not in the slightest degree overstate the magnitude of the change he had in mind. His vision of a native police commanded by paid headmen directly appointed by the magistrate realized perfectly if brutally Grey's original dream of a British Kaffraria free of Xhosa chiefs, Xhosa law and, indeed, any indigenous Xhosa traditions at all.[58]

But Mhala was not finished yet. He perceived accurately enough that many of his troubles were directly due to Gawler's obstinate determination. A Magistrate Lucas or a Magistrate Vigne he could have twisted around his little finger as Maqoma and Phatho had done. Mhala had long been considering a means of killing Gawler, but had not been able to hit on anything practical.[59] He was thoroughly alarmed by the magistrate's talk of arming the unbelievers and establishing a new military post in the district, and he tried a last direct appeal behind Gawler's back, sending a secret message to Governor Grey through his missionary.

> Umhala says the police[man] who [fires] the guns is Gawler — Whose permission did he ask? That his people, the unbelievers who did not kill, are coming to Gawler — they did not acquaint him of it — the [military] post is coming to Gawler without Umhala's knowledge.
>
> Umhala says he never enters Gawler's house — Gawler drives him away, although petty chiefs and common people are permitted to enter. He does not know this white man Gawler, he said this to Maclean at the commencement — he won't have him. Another white man must come who is good.
>
> Gawler treats Umhala wrongly — he knows not how to treat the country right. He is passionate [quick-tempered]. Umhala says — Government said he was to have money given him — now his money is small — it was said counsellors must have money given to them — now then he does not know who pays the money. . . . Gawler acts wrongly. Another white man must come who is good.[60]

On 14 March there was a great public show of strength in front of the magistracy. Four or five hundred of the *amathamba* demonstrated and gesticulated at Gawler and his unbelievers for about fifteen minutes before marching off in military order.[61]

Mhala himself was clearly nervous and tried to be friendly to Gawler, as if knowing that his letter to Grey would misfire. On 16 March, Gawler summoned the chief to hear the Governor's reply, which was mild enough, all things considered. Grey informed Mhala that he should have sent his complaints through Gawler to afford the magistrate the chance of a reply; that Mhala was at fault for urging on the Cattle-Killing; and that he should now do his best to suppress thieving and to save his people from starvation by encouraging them to take up colonial employment. Grey's letter contained no comfort for Mhala, though it did not question or threaten his existing privileges and authority.

But for Mhala, it was too much to take. He was buoyed up by righteous anger, by the presence of his strongest supporters, and, it would seem, by a little too much in the way of brandy. In any event, he displayed none of the shrewdness or restraint which had hitherto marked his dealings with the colonial authorities. From the depths of his frustration, he denounced the magistrate who had done so much to block his designs and break his power.

> When you were sent here, you were told by Maclean to be my friend, but our blood runs differently; We have had many quarrels — how is it your blood will not run with mine?

Inevitably, the chief raised the question of the salaries. 'You see my friends,' he exclaimed, turning to his supporters, 'he acknowledges that when I got it straight from Maclean, I got it all-all-all!' Mhala wanted to be able to name the councillors to receive the government salaries. He wanted money to give to his friends like the magistrate gave money to his own friends. Gawler objected that it would be very odd if he did not pay his friends. Mhala interrupted with terrible anger, shouting furiously at his hated enemy:

> That's all I want, no more, no more! He's said it — did you hear? he pays his own friends — he takes my money — Run my children, tell the Government he pays his own friends.
>
> Where's the kraal of Ndlambe [Mhala's father]? Nowhere. Here's his child — that's all. True, I was not born the Great Son, but I made myself great. Where's Ndlambe? Gone. Where's his house? Gone.
>
> You've destroyed it [vehemently] killed it. It's nowhere. Gone. Be off, you. Tell the Governor, Gawler has ruined the house of Ndlambe.[62]

With that, Mhala sank back, his eyes bright and staring, his breath coming in short gasps. It was the funeral oration of a great chiefdom.

The veneer of mutual respect and cooperation carefully preserved by both Mhala and his magistrate through all the long months of the Cattle-Killing was finally shattered. Gawler turned on his heel and walked out. Behind him, Mhala was shouting furiously, 'Come back, I've not done with you yet!' The believing councillors followed, thoroughly alarmed at their chief's rashness, calling, 'Don't listen to Umhala, he's drunk now.' Other councillors were reproving the chief, saying, 'You've done yourself for once. . . . You're in a pretty mess now.'[63]

Over the next few days, Mhala tried desperately hard to retrieve the situation. He called a meeting of unbelievers and promised that they would not be molested again, but Smith and Mjuza were intransigent:

> What are we to do? We disobeyed his orders and were to be driven into the sea — now he wants to make friends. We *don't* want — he threw us away and Government picked us up.[64]

Mhala even approached Gawler, saying he hoped that the magistrate had informed the government that he wanted peace and a trading station. Gawler, however, was no longer interested in trying to work with Mhala and had already concluded his official dispatch describing the chief's outburst with the words, 'There never was a better opportunity of breaking Umhala's influence and bringing forward young [Xhosaland].'

Grey and Maclean were at last ready to grasp the opportunity that Gawler had created. They authorized the establishment of a new post on the Tshabo river, where Gawler might headquarter his police and gather in the unbelievers.[65] Mhala protested. He said he did not thank the messenger for this news, and that the post would 'spoil the country'. Gawler should write immediately to the Governor and say that he, Mhala, had not been consulted and that he refused to have the post. It seems as if the old chief was still under the impression that his opinion counted for something, but he was speedily disillusioned. Gawler replied sarcastically that Mhala had many warriors and if he wanted the post removed, he should do it himself. At the end of March, Gawler escorted Mjuza and 500 cattle to the new camp on the Tshabo.

On 1 April, Mhala made one last attempt to prevent the disintegration of his chiefdom.[66] He called a meeting of the unbelievers and tried to persuade them to stay with him. He apologized for his people, saying they were very hungry and that he had already forbidden any further raiding and stealing. The chief seemed at a loss for words, and indeed there was very little that he could say. In the plenitude of his power he had fought the unbelievers and they had beaten him, and now nothing he could do would stop them going. They walked out on Mhala before he had finished speaking.

From April onwards, a steady stream of unbelievers left Mhala's country to join Gawler and his police. Smith Mhala and Ndayi came in the middle of May, and Montawuli, the leader of the unbelievers in Phatho's country, arrived in early June. The most unexpected recruit was the Gcaleka chief Sigidi, who had sheltered the gun thief Gabinyana at the very commencement of Gawler's career, and still had not paid the fifty cattle fine that the magistrate had imposed on him. Gawler got his revenge by brushing Sigidi aside the first time he asked for help; but when Sigidi renewed his appeal, saying that he was 'alone against the wolves' and would gladly pay double the fine, Gawler agreed to receive him. Since he was senior by birth to all, even Smith Mhala, he soon acquired a position of leadership in the unbelievers' camp.[67]

Saddest of all was the Great Councillor Gqirana, who was so old and infirm that it took him five days to cover the twenty kilometres between his homestead and the Tshabo. In his youth, old Ndlambe had given him to Mhala to act as his councillor. He had milked Mhala's cattle while Mhala was yet a boy. 'He was always well disposed,' wrote Gawler, 'and did not kill his cattle, but did not take the decided course that Ndayi did. He was much attached to [Ndlambe] and therefore considered it as his duty to stick to Umhala, but he says he has now become too much for him.'[68]

6. Gawler Triumphant

The terrible disappointment of 16-17 February nearly extinguished the hope of the believers, but that hope flickered on because now it was the only alternative to starvation or exile. Muddled explanations began to emerge from the Gxarha and the Mpongo. The new people had been unable to decide who among them should have the honour of rising first.[69] Or, it was the fault of Nxito and his spies who had insulted the new people. Or, it was the fault of all the unbelievers collectively for not killing their cattle. Maqoma's son Namba and Sandile's nephew Oba visited Mhlakaza towards the end of March and returned with hope renewed.[70] The new people would make their appearance before the moon of June 1857 was out, provided that the Xhosa returned to their country, which they were now leaving in such numbers, and killed the remainder of their cattle.[71]

The effect on the believers was remarkable, considering the number of disappointments they had already suffered, and is indicative of the extent of their desperation. Many who had found employment or a safe refuge returned to the destitution and starvation of their deserted homesteads. They busied themselves building huge new kraals to receive the cattle that were to rise, burning patches for gardens that would automatically fill with maize and pumpkins, digging pits for corn and cleaning threshing floors.[72] Confirmed believers like Mhala, Maqoma and Sandile plunged with renewed frenzy into cattle-killing, slaughtering in many cases the very cattle which they had with difficulty extorted from their subjects. The cattle of Sandile's nephew Feni, which he had carefully preserved in spite of the prophecies, fell victim to lungsickness, and the young chief began to slaughter the survivors with all the zeal of a recent convert.[73] Mhala insisted that he did not wish 'to see a head of cattle in the country' and forced many former faithful and believing councillors, including his brother Nowawe, to flee to Gawler's police camp. His Great Son Makinana, always an unbeliever but nevertheless devotedly loyal to his father, fled to a mission station with his remaining five cattle. I never killed of my own free will, he told Mhala, I had hoped your eyes were open.[74]

Mhala's eyes, so long and so tightly closed, opened at last after the June disappointment, but there was little left in the country to gladden his sight. The cattle were all slaughtered. The believers were either dead or gone. The unbelievers had rejected their old chief with contempt, and had joined forces with his mortal foe, Gawler, at the police camp on the Tshabo. Deprived now even of his hopes, Mhala threw himself on the mercy of his enemies.

> [Mhala told the Bishop of Grahamstown] that they had been deceived by the false words of a female; that she had told them that they were soon to see again their ancestors, their fathers and mothers, their wives and friends, who had died, that their desire to see them was so strong that this had caused them to fall into error. . . .
>
> Tell [the Governor] that you have seen me, that Umhala was a great chief, but now he is fallen, from having been deceived, through a desire of seeing those that were dead, and he begs the Government to help him.[75]

Unfortunately for Mhala and all the other devoted believers, this final renunciation came much too late, not only for their crops and their cattle, but for the colonial government as well. In the last stages of the Cattle-Killing, many of the starving believers had committed thefts and petty crimes, and these had the effect of setting them up for Governor Grey's final solution.

Believing chiefs attempted to stop unbelievers taking their cattle out of their districts. Hungry believers raided the gardens of the missions and the unbelievers in order to keep themselves alive. Believers turned highwaymen stalked the convoys of goods on the main thoroughfares, especially the road from King William's Town to East London, and their regretful chiefs had neither the will nor the ability to stop them.[76] Minor chiefs not under the immediate surveillance of the colonial government — Tola, Gunuza and the turbulent Qasana — organized large-scale raiding parties of mounted men which openly attacked the herds of unbelievers in Anta's country and the neighbourhood of Hangman's Bush. Qasana's men murdered Captain Ohlssen of the German Legion, sparking off full-scale riots between Xhosa and Germans in the port of East London.[77]

Of all the thieves then active the most energetic was Nqono, a follower of Qasana. Then in his early fifties, Nqono stood all of six foot seven inches tall and had escaped from colonial convict gangs on three separate occasions. Late in June 1857, Nqono stole three cattle from some Mfengu in the Crown Reserve and, according to his custom, retired to his hiding place in Mhala's district to eat them. Fusani, a neighbouring councillor in the pay of Gawler, informed the magistrate and late that night a patrol of Gawler's police surrounded Nqono and called on him to surrender. The thief seized his weapons and attempted to charge his way through the encirclement, but they shot him dead. Less than a week later, a party of men from Maqoma's chiefdom surprised Fusani's homestead and killed the informer in revenge for the part he had played in Nqono's death. Gawler's police were anxious to retaliate against Maqoma, and Gawler was right behind them. 'I do not think I shall interfere,' he wrote, and he himself advocated a night attack on Maqoma and on those who had killed Fusani. The political implications of such a raid induced Maclean to forbid it.[78]

But that was the last time that the muzzle was applied to Gawler and his police. Gawler was a tough man, and so were his top lieutenants, Tawa the son of Xayimpi and Jan Bushman, a former Kat River rebel who committed such unspeakable acts in Gawler's service that he dared not remain in Xhosaland after his master had left it. Other policeman were turncoats, such as Mhala's son Mtshatsheni, who played as violent a part in putting down the believers as they had formerly played in persuading them to kill their cattle. Gawler was a great believer in the sjambok, and 'he flogged so freely that [his police] were known by their backs'.[79] Across the bleak landscape of Mhala's devastated and largely abandoned country, and far beyond it, galloped the brutalized police of Major Gawler, leaving in their wake the smoke of smashed, looted and burning homesteads. Triumphant and unrestrained, Gawler's police emulated the scorched earth policies which

Gawler's hero, Colonel Eyre, had pioneered during the War of Mlanjeni. This time, however, the enemy were not bands of armed warriors openly in the field, but the few wretched and starving believers who still attempted to cling to life in a country which Governor Grey had earmarked for white settlement.

Writing of the period some ten years later, Commissioner Brownlee said:

> I freely admit that during the disorders and excitement attending the cattle killing we did many things which would not be justifiable under ordinary circumstances and which if judged by the standard of peacable times would be proved faulty and antagonistic to law. In 1857 I have done things which I could not do now. . . . I do not now ask you to judge of the acts of 1857 by the law of 1867.[80]

Brownlee was writing in support of an unbeliever named Mbilini, whose cattle were confiscated by Gawler's police. Brownlee's correspondent, the Thembu Agent J.C.Warner, opposed giving compensation to Mbilini for being 'eaten up by Gawler during the time when the law of "might" was considered "right" '. There were 'scores' of such cases, said Warner,

> And if Umbilini gets compensation you may prepare a *long purse*; for all sorts of unjust and outrageous things were perpetrated in those days of disorganization. . . . I am of opinion that Umbilini deserved to be eaten up as much as any that were eaten up in those days of necessary severity and drum-head court martial.

'Antagonistic to law', 'the law of might was considered right', 'all sorts of unjust and outrageous things', 'necessary severity and drum-head court martial': the reader is startled by such phrases from the pens of high-ranking colonial officials. What was the secret history of those terrible days of 1857, blandly described in the colonial records as a period of relief and reconstruction? Was it starvation alone which drove tens of thousands of hungry believers forever from their homes and their livelihoods? The records draw a discreet veil of silence over Gawler's six-month rule of fear, broken only occasionally by the terse official protests of neighbouring magistrates. Magistrate Hawkes, another tough soldier, complained about Gawler's police operating in his district without his authorization. Magistrate Lucas passed on the complaints of Maqoma's family that his Great Place had been looted by the police when they came to arrest one of the residents, and stated further that 'frequent complaints have been made to me by [Ngqika Xhosa] that they have been plundered by Major Gawler's police'. Magistrate Vigne enclosed a list of eight homesteads in his district 'robbed and burnt by the police of Major Gawler', and gave details of one old man of known good character robbed 'even of his blanket'. Six weeks later, Vigne protested again to Maclean concerning Gawler's police and threatened to resign.

> If you approve of all these acts which are in my opinion defeating justice and degrading the office of magistrate into one I have no wish to fulfil the duties of, I trust you will inform me. Things are daily happening that I neither have conscience nor inclination for − and as I have no control over them and little chance of redress, I must beg you to allow me to confine my duties to Jali's tribe.[81]

The most complete description we have of Gawler's method comes from a case which had nothing whatsoever to do with the Cattle-Killing.[82] The statement of a nine-year-old Mfengu boy persuaded Gawler that a certain woman had been murdered by Sibunu, a resident of Peelton mission station. Acting on this suspicion, a party of forty armed police invaded Peelton towards the end of December 1857 and dragged Sibunu from his dwelling, without allowing him time to dress. They slapped him repeatedly on the face, and Mhala's son Mtshatsheni, formerly the great believer, hit him four times with a stick. They put a thong around his neck and dragged him violently about, then took his cattle off, saying, 'What kind of school people are you to murder so many people, you will be transported!' His wife was beaten and trampled on, so much so that the next day she vomited blood. In all this time, Sibunu was not charged nor asked to make a statement.

The next day a potential witness named Kese was taken off to Gawler's headquarters.

> Major Gawler then said, the Missionary has bribed you to deny any knowledge of the case, say what has he given you. I denied the charge when Major Gawler jumped up and struck me thrice with his hand on my face and called for a stick. He ordered a *riem* [thong] to be put round my neck, and taken away a prisoner and tied to a pillar of a hut.
> Some days after I was taken down to the river and met some police there who stated they were ordered to take me aside and interrogate me. They then added, 'What did the missionary do at your place. He must have gone to warn you what to say.' I held to my former statement. I was then taken to the kraal. . . . All the police surrounded me saying 'Why will you die by hiding what the Missionary said to you, you will be transported with Sibunu. Say did he give you a cow or money?'

When the missionary, Kayser, approached Gawler about the case, the magistrate 'left his office in a rage, charging me with incivility and adding he was not responsible to me', after which 'a head policeman shamefully abused me, shaking his sambok at me'. The matter was only resolved when Kayser found the alleged victim still alive, and took her to Gawler to prove to him that she had not been murdered.

Gawler's methods were approved, if not actually encouraged, by Maclean for the simple reason that they worked. The other magistrates likewise put in for police forces of their own, partly to suppress robbery and partly, one suspects, to keep Gawler's police out of their districts. Brownlee, Vigne and Lucas all established police forces paid for from the salaries of believing councillors struck off the payroll, though the solidly pro-government chiefs Kama, Toyise and Siwani were not affected.[83] British soldiers were not suited to the kind of policing Maclean had in mind; Xhosa police were 'much cheaper and more efficient for the work here'. 'With such a police,' Maclean wrote, 'Mr Brownlee might keep order and accustom the people to the idea of European rule in earnest.'[84]

Late in September 1857, Gawler's police, 'in a playful humour', visited Nonkosi's homestead on the Mpongo river. They found the bodies of a woman and three children dead from starvation. They found the crippled old doctor, Nonkosi's father, half-dead 'and he died of fright when they brought him outside the hut'. Or so they said. Then they found Nonkosi herself and they brought her back with them to Major Gawler.[85]

Notes

1. For the Gawler family and John Cox Gawler's early life, see C.W.N. (1900).
2. For Gawler's admiration of Eyre, see Gawler (1873), p.5. For his role in the battle of Berea, H. Pearse, 'The Kaffir and Basuto Campaigns of 1852 and 1853', *United Services Magazine*, 17 (1898), pp.530-4. For looting by the 73rd Regiment, see Acc. 8402-5, National Army Museum, Diary of L. Graham, 23 June 1852. For massacre and rape on Sotho, Acc. 8108-5, Diary of W.J. St John, 23 Dec. 1852. For hanging corpses in trees, see Ch. 1, Note 76.
3. GH 8/27 Schedule 225 of 24 Nov. 1855; Witwatersrand University Library, Journal of R. Wilmot, pp.207-8.
4. On the Ndlambe succession, see Peires (1981), pp.82-4; on Mhala, see also 'Nzulu Lwazi,' 'Umhala A, Mbodla!', *Umteteli waBantu*, 26 Sept. 1931; Appleyard (1971), p.52; Maclean, (1858), p.132.
5. 'Nzulu Lwazi', *Umteteli*, 26 Sept. 1931.
6. H. Smith (1901), Vol. 2, p.73.
7. Peires (1981), p.139.
8. GH 8/27 J. Maclean-W.F. Liddle, 23 Nov. 1855.
9. Uncatalogued MS, Cory Library, Diary of Clerk to Colonel Maclean at Fort Murray, 19 Jan. 1856.
10. BK 81 J. Gawler-J. Maclean, 16 March 1857.

11. The entire account of Gawler's confrontation with Mhala over pay is taken from Gawler's extremely detailed letter to Maclean, in BK 81, 24 April 1856.
12. BK 81 J. Gawler-J. Maclean, 24 April 1856.
13. Mhala was born about 1800 and became chief of the Ndlambe in 1829. Gawler was born on 7 April 1830.
14. The Gabinyana affair is described in detail in BK 81 J. Gawler-J. Maclean, 19 April 1856. This occurred after the quarrel over pay, though the despatch is of an earlier date.
15. GH 8/28 J. Gawler-Chief Commissioner, 13, 23 May 1856.
16. GH 8/28 Schedule 267, April 1856, marginal note by J. Ayliff.
17. Acc 793, J. Gawler-J. Maclean, 30 June 1856; BK 1 J. Gawler-J. Maclean, 28 July 1856.
18. H. Smith (1901), Vol. 2, p.83.
19. 'Nzulu Lwazi' in *Umteteli*, 26 Sept. 1931; Acc 793 J. Gawler-R. Graham, 11 April 1865.
20. GH 8/29 Information communicated to the Chief Commissioner, 1 July 1856; BK 81 J. Gawler-J. Maclean, 7 Oct. 1856; Acc 793 J. Gawler-J. Maclean, 25 July 1856. For a fuller description of what the delegation saw, see Chapter 3/3 above.
21. Acc 793 J. Gawler-J. Maclean, 2 Aug. 1856; Cory Library, R.J. Mullins diary, 21 June 1855; GH 8/49 J. Gawler-J. Maclean, 5 Nov. 1856.
22. BK 140 J. Maclean-C.J. Boyle, 20 Jan. 1856; for full Ndayi praise poem, see above, Chapter 5/4, pp.177-8.
23. GH 18/6 J. Gawler-J. Maclean, 15 Aug. 1856.
24. BK 70 C.Brownlee-J. Maclean, 9 Aug. 1856; GH 8/29 J. Gawler-J. Maclean, 14 Aug. 1856.
25. BK 81 J. Gawler-J. Maclean, 30 Aug. 1856; Cory Interviews, Cory Library, Interview with W.R.D. Fynn, 16 April 1913.
26. BK 81 J. Gawler-J. Maclean, 1 Oct. 1856.
27. BK 70 C. Brownlee-J. Maclean, 19 Oct. 1856; BK 81 J. Gawler-J. Maclean, 7, 14 Oct. 1856; BK 89 R. Fielding-J. Maclean, 14 Oct. 1856; BK 140 Information communicated 8 Oct. 1856; GH 20/2/1 John Ayliff jnr-J. Maclean, 11 Oct. 1856.
28. Microfilm 172/2, Reel 8, Cory Library, W. Greenstock-USPG, Nov. 1856; BK 81 J. Gawler-J. Maclean, 14 Oct. 1856; Acc 793 J. Gawler-J. Maclean, 29 Oct. 1856.
29. GH 8/49 J. Gawler-J. Maclean, 11 Oct. 1856.
30. For Bulungwa's spying, see BK 373 J. Maclean-W. Liddle, 20 Sept. 1854; for Xhosa knowing about it, see Rubusana (1906), p.529.
31. Acc 793 J. Gawler-J. Maclean, 29 Oct. 1856; BK 373 J. Maclean-G. Grey, 3 Nov. 1856.
32. Acc 793 J. Gawler-J. Maclean, 29 Oct. 1856.
33. Acc 793 J. Gawler-J. Maclean, 31 Oct. 1856.
34. *Ibid.*
35. For Maclean's own account, see BK 373 J. Maclean-G. Grey, 3 Nov. 1856. Mhala retracted his ban on cultivation under pressure from Gawler but said 'it would not be necessary' to send a special messenger to inform his people of the change. Needless to say, none of Mhala's subjects were in any doubt concerning his real wishes. See Acc 793 J. Gawler-J. Maclean, 31

Oct., 2 Nov. 1856; BK 81 J. Gawler-J. Maclean, 17 Nov. 1856.

36. GH 8/49 J. Gawler-J. Maclean, 5 Nov. 1856; GH 8/49 J. Maclean-G. Grey, 6 Nov. 1856. Smith paid a private visit to the Gxarha relatively early on, and returned 'infected' with the idea of the Cattle-Killing. BK 81 J. Gawler-J. Maclean, 7 Sept. 1856. But this did not last.

37. BK 81 J. Gawler-J. Maclean, 7, 17 Nov. 1856.

38. BK 81 J. Gawler-J. Maclean, 20 Nov. 1856.

39. For the detailed description of the visit of the delegation contained in BK 81 J. Gawler-J. Maclean, 22 Nov. 1856, see Chapter 3/3. See also, GH 8/49 J. Gawler-J. Maclean, 22 Nov. 1856.

40. I have slightly rephrased part of this extract from BK 81 J. Gawler-J. Maclean, 30 Nov. 1856. Mhala is reported as having said that the prophets 'could not deceive a white man', implying thereby that no deception was involved. See also BK 81 J. Gawler-J. Maclean, 30 Nov., 7 Dec. 1856.

41. BK 81 J. Gawler-J. Maclean, 7, 10, 18, 30 Dec. 1856; GH 8/30 C. Brownlee-J. Maclean, 25 Dec. 1856.

42. BK 81 J. Gawler-J. Maclean, 14 Jan. 1856.

43. GH 8/33 Schedule 519, 29 Oct. 1857.

44. GH 8/31 Information communicated, 16 Jan., 8 Feb. 1857.

45. MIC 172/2, Cory Library, USPG Archives, Reel 1, W. Greenstock Journal, 22 Sept. 1857. Jordan (1971), p.73. Usually I have preferred my own translations of Gqoba (1888), but here I quote Jordan's very free translation simply because it is so much more evocative than a more literal translation would be.

46. GH 8/33 Schedule 519, 29 Oct. 1856. For more on the evidence of Nonkosi's activities, see Chapter 4.

47. BK 81 J. Gawler-J. Maclean, 26 Jan., 7 Feb. 1857.

48. BK 81 J. Gawler-J. Maclean, 30 Nov., 10 Dec. 1856, 26 Jan. 1857.

49. BK 81 J. Gawler-J. Maclean, 26 Jan. 1856.

50. BK 81 J. Gawler-J. Maclean, 10 Dec. 1856.

51. GH 8/31 Memorandum by H. Vigne, n.d. [22 Feb. 1857].

52. BK 81 J. Gawler-J. Maclean, 24 Feb. 1857.

53. GH 8/31 J. Gawler-J. Maclean, 1 March 1857.

54. BK 81 J. Gawler-J. Maclean, 1 March 1857; GH 8/31 J. Gawler-J. Maclean, 1 March 1857.

55. BK 81 J. Gawler-J. Maclean, 1 March 1857.

56. BK 89 Statement by Umjuza, 12 Nov. 1856; GH 8/31 Schedule 417, 20 March 1857, statement by Toise; BK 14 Statement by Umjuza, 24 Feb. 1858; MS 566, Cory Library, C. Brownlee-n.a., 17 Dec. 1851. BK 81 J. Gawler-J. Maclean, 5 March 1857; BK 140 Trial of Dilima, 21 April 1858; Acc 793 J. Gawler-J. Maclean, 7, 9 March 1857.

57. BK 81 J. Gawler-J. Maclean, 28 Feb. 1857. For the eventual pay scales and more details concerning conditions of service, see GH 8/31 J. Maclean-G. Grey, 16 April 1857.

58. BK 81 J. Gawler-J. Maclean, 12 March 1857.

59. BK 81 J. Gawler-J. Maclean, 18 Dec. 1856.

60. BK 86 The words of Umhala to the Great Chief of the Government, 13 March 1857.

61. BK 81 J. Gawler-J. Maclean, 14 March 1857.

62. I have changed the spelling 'Hlambie' to the more familiar 'Ndlambe'.

63. For all of the above, see BK 81 J. Gawler-J. Maclean, 16 March 1857.
64. *Ibid.*
65. BK 81 J. Gawler-J. Maclean, 21 March 1857. Gawler also mentions a post on the 'Diggedo' River, but this was not established as far as I am aware.
66. BK 81 J. Gawler-J. Maclean, 1 April 1857.
67. Bk 81 J. Gawler-J. Maclean, 3 June, 15 July 1857; GH 8/50 J. Maclean-G. Grey, 14 May 1857.
68. BK 81 J. Gawler-J. Maclean, 20 June 1857.
69. BK 71 C. Brownlee-J. Maclean, 4 May 1857; GH 8/32 Schedule 455, 1 June 1857; *King William's Town Gazette*, 7 March 1857.
70. BK 89 C. Brownlee-J. Maclean, 1 April 1857.
71. GH 8/32 Anon-J. Maclean, 27 May 1857.
72. BK 71 C. Brownlee-J. Maclean, 28 May 1857; BK 80 R. Hawkes-J. Maclean, 17 June 1857; Acc 793 J. Gawler-J. Maclean, 10 June 1857.
73. BK 71 C. Brownlee-J. Maclean, 1, 18 May 1857.
74. BK 81 J. Gawler-J. Maclean, 5 June 1857.
75. *Church Chronicle*, 4 (Grahamstown: 1883), p.68.
76. BK 81 J. Gawler-J. Maclean, 20 June 1857; BK 82 H. Lucas-J. Maclean, 21 April 1857; Acc 793 J. Gawler-J. Maclean, 21 April 1857; BK 83 H. Vigne-J. Maclean, 24 Aug. 1857; GH 8/32 H. Vigne-J. Maclean, 30 July 1857; GH 8/50 J. Maclean-G. Grey, 4 May, 21 June 1857.
77. BK 71 C. Brownlee-J. Maclean, 3 July 1857; BK 81 J. Gawler-J. Maclean, 15 July 1857; Cory Library, Diary of Clerk to Chief Commissioner, Fort Murray, 9, 11 April 1857; GH 8/32 L. Traherne-J. Maclean, 4 May 1857; GH 8/50, 4 May 1857.
78. GH 8/32 Memo enclosed in Schedule 474, 23 July 1857; GH 8/32 J. Gawler-J. Maclean, 10 July 1857.
79. D.B. Hook, *With Sword and Statute*, 2nd edition (Cape Town: Juta, 1907), p.139. BK 96 J. Gawler-Lieut. Governor, 22 April 1863; GH 8/34 Schedule 9, 26 Jan. 1858.
80. CO 3122 C. Brownlee-J. Maclean, 24 Jan. 1867; CO 3122 J. Warner-R. Southey, 1 Feb. 1867.
81. BK 81 J. Gawler-J. Maclean, 10 Dec. 1856; BK 81 J. Gawler-R. Hawkes, 18 Dec. 1856; BK 83 H. Vigne-J. Maclean, 1 Dec. 1857, 21 Jan. 1858.
82. GH 8/34 Schedule 9, 26 Jan. 1858.
83. BK 83 H. Vigne-J. Maclean, 3 Oct. 1857; GH 8/32 Schedule 467, 3 Sept. 1857; BK 71 C. Brownlee-J. Maclean, 17 Oct. 1857; BK 82 H. Lucas-J. Maclean, 3 Oct. 1857.
84. GH 8/32 J. Maclean-G. Grey, 3 Sept. 1857.
85. Acc 793 J. Gawler-J. Maclean, 22 Sept. 1857. Rev. Greenstock noted that Kulwana was pulled at the last minute from his blazing hut. He did not die immediately, but perished of starvation 'gnawing at grass' with no one to dig roots for him. MIC 172/2, Cory Library, Reel 1, W. Greenstock Journal, 22 Sept. 1857. I have preferred Gawler's version to Greenstock's because I can see no reason why Gawler should have invented it. The story about Kulwana trying to eat grass seems to have been hearsay.

CHAPTER 7

The Chiefs' Plot

1. 'The Late Great Plot'

It is time to return to Governor Sir George Grey. As we have seen, the role of the colonial authorities throughout the Cattle-Killing was one of reacting to crises rather than setting the pace, of waiting on events rather than dictating their course. The only two initiatives taken by Grey, the introduction of paid headmen and the cruise of the *Geyser*, had succeeded only in strengthening the believers' cause. Grey, moreover, had signally failed to support the unbelievers in the hour of their greatest need, at a time when strong support might well have brought the waverers round to unbelief and thus minimized the impact of the delusion. Any successes the colonial administration had thus far achieved were due to the personal qualities of magistrates such as Gawler and Brownlee, and owed little to the central direction of Grey or Maclean. It is possible that Grey had even begun to feel ineffectual, and that this prompted a recurrence of his mysterious illness during his visit to the frontier in October 1856.[1]

Yet Grey's hour was to come. His great strength as a colonial governor lay not in the immediate details, which he ignored and frequently bungled, but in the breadth of his vision and the fixity of his purpose. The tumult in British Kaffraria between May 1856 and June 1857 deflected him not one whit from the original prescription for the future of the province which he had laid before the Cape Parliament in 1855. It was still his intention to destroy the stubborn independence of the Xhosa nation by breaking the political and judicial powers of its chiefs, by encouraging its commoners to abandon their communal and pastoral ethos in favour of wage labour, and by disrupting its territorial integrity through the settlement of whites in British Kaffraria and of Xhosa in the Cape Colony. None of these aims had changed on account of the Cattle-Killing. The only change was that starvation and disorder made it possible to pursue these aims further and faster than anyone, including Grey himself, had yet contemplated.

It was an important part of Grey's style that every one of his meanest, most underhand and most ruthless actions was subsumed under the name of some high ideal. His initial onslaught on the Xhosa way of life was justified in the name of 'civilizing' the Xhosa. His brutal persecution of the wretched and helpless survivors of the Cattle-Killing was justified in the name of the 'chiefs' plot'.

The nub of the 'chiefs' plot' hypothesis, as expounded by Grey himself, was that 'the conduct of the [Xhosa] nation resulted [not from a 'superstitious delusion' but] from a deep laid political scheme to involve the Government in war, and to bring . . . a host of desperate enemies upon us'. Moshoeshoe, the king of Lesotho, and Sarhili had cold-bloodedly combined to drive the credulous but peaceable Xhosa into a war they did not want. Mhlakaza was 'merely a secondary instrument in the hands of the Great Chiefs working on the superstition and ignorance of the people'. Sarhili was alleged to have given the true reasons for the Cattle-Killing as follows:

> That it was his intention to make war with the English, and that he killed his cattle so as to have none to guard, and more men available to fight, that he did not see the use of cultivating as the crops would only be cut down by the troops, and that the cattle of the white people and [Thembu] would furnish them with food when fighting.[2]

By now the reader will know enough about the Xhosa and the Cattle-Killing to dismiss this explanation. It should be clear enough that cattle-killing was the logical response, in Xhosa terms, to lungsickness, military defeat and other signs of witchcraft, and that starvation, far from rendering the Xhosa desperate to fight, weakened and divided them as never before. It would be a waste of effort to refute the 'chiefs' plot' theory item by item — I have set out the argument in full elsewhere[3] — but it is necessary to say something about it because all the brutal and heartless policies of Grey and Maclean were justified and explained in terms of it. The question we need to answer is not whether the 'chiefs' plot' actually existed, but how and why Grey and Maclean came to propagate it.

The notion that the Cattle-Killing originated in a plot by the Xhosa chiefs to bring about war was not an unreasonable one for a colonial official to hold during the early days of the movement. All were aware that the prophecies of Mlanjeni barely six years previously had triggered the Eighth Frontier War, that Sarhili was sending messages to Sandile, Mhala and the other chiefs, and that a frenzy of religious excitement was sweeping through Xhosaland. It was known that Nongqawuse had predicted the imminent destruction of the white man, and that there was some talk of recouping cattle from the settlers if the prophecies failed. It seemed logical that starving people would rob and even kill to get food. Small wonder that every colonial administrator from the authoritarian Maclean to the sympathetic Brownlee initially suspected that the prophecies were put about by the chiefs to foment war. Grey was informed accordingly, and he made every effort from promises to threats to stop the people going ahead with the destruction of their cattle and corn.

From the beginning, however, there were clear signals that the Cattle-Killing was the result of a sincere belief, and, as the movement progressed, these signals grew louder and louder. It became increasingly obvious, for instance, that many of the initial reports of warlike behaviour were exaggerated, that the ordinary believers were not especially hostile towards the whites, and, above all, that starvation and destruction were wreaking such havoc among the Xhosa that they were incapable of fighting or doing anything at all. As late as September 1856, Grey could still write:

> The most vigilant exertions on the part of the authorities in British Kaffraria have failed to elicit any proofs of combination for evil purposes amongst the chiefs, whilst conclusive proof has been obtained of the entire erroneousness of several reports of an unfavourable nature.[4]

Even later, in December 1856, Chief Commissioner Maclean was still writing that the Cattle-Killing was 'too suicidal for a mere political move'.[5] It was only after the Great Disappointment that Grey asked Maclean to write up the proofs of the 'chiefs' plot'.[6] By that time, the failure of the movement had become apparent and all disturbances had been put down. Whatever the truth of the 'chiefs' plot' theory, whatever the chiefs may or may not have intended, it was incontestably true that the crisis was over and that not one chief had actually done anything that could be interpreted as an attack on the settlers or the Colony. As Sarhili said, 'He has offended in destroying his own. He has not thrown an assegaai at the Governor.'[7]

But Grey was unable to leave it at that. It may well be that he was genuinely paranoid. It may well be that he had good cause to be suspicious of Sarhili, who had rejected his official warning, and of Moshoeshoe, who had sent him a lying message.[8] But throughout

Grey's career, conspiracy theory had always served to advance his measures and cut down resistance to his goals. We have already seen how he scapegoated Te Rauparaha in New Zealand to put an end to the Maori war, and how he used the rumoured 'Fingo alliance' of 1854 to extort £40,000 a year from the British government. Sarhili's Xhosaland was the key to the annexation of the transKei. Moshoeshoe's Lesotho was the key to the annexation of the Orange Free State. The exile of tens of thousands of Xhosa would make space for the white settlers whom Grey had always wanted to place in British Kaffraria. Grey was not interested in saving the starving Xhosa from the consequences of their actions, or in helping them to rebuild their shattered lives and homesteads. Rather, he intended to strike them when they were down, annihilate their nationhood and their way of life, and disperse them in the Colony as labourers while he gave away their land to white farmers. The Cattle-Killing presented the Governor with a unique opportunity to advance on all these fronts, and Grey was not about to let it slip away. His pursuit of the 'chiefs' plot' was not, therefore, an act of retributive justice — it was an integral part of his future policy.

Evidence was the least of Grey's problems. There were so many rumours and reports chasing each other around the Eastern Frontier, so many Xhosa and Mfengu ready to furnish satisfactory information at the hint of a bribe, so many statements forthcoming from the victims of Gawler's police, that it was easy for an experienced author of misleading dispatches like Grey to pick what he wanted and leave the rest. Later in this chapter and again in Chapter 8, the reader will be given detailed instances of deliberate and cynical falsification of evidence by Grey and his subordinates. Here one brief illustration will suffice. On 8 December 1856, Maclean took a statement from a 'trustworthy native' to the effect that Sarhili had privately informed him that the purpose of the Cattle-Killing was to bring about a war. Even Maclean dismissed this statement at the time, because the informant was a Thembu Christian, who habitually wore European clothes, and he knew that Sarhili would never trust such a man. And yet, later on, when they needed the 'evidence', both Maclean and Grey laid considerable emphasis on this information without ever mentioning the reservations which had led them to reject it in the first place.[9]

2. Transportation

The instrument which Grey employed to carry his plans for British Kaffraria into effect was his proclamation of 3 March 1857, issued shortly after his arrival on the Frontier to take charge of the crisis which had developed in the wake of the Great Disappointment.

> His Excellency the High Commissioner hereby acquaints the [Xhosa] chiefs that acts of robbery by armed men have been recently committed. . . . His Excellency feels that it is necessary at once to check proceedings which . . . are unpardonable, as labour is provided for all industrious, well-disposed persons, who may be in a state of destitution.
>
> He has therefore directed that four [Xhosa], who were caught this morning in the Crown Reserve, in circumstances which leave no room for doubt that they were thieves, shall be forthwith transported; and he notifies generally, that all persons caught attempting to commit or having committed, robberies with arms in their hands, will, when convicted with such offence, be punished with DEATH.
>
> He also warns the chiefs that all [Xhosa] found robbing in the Colony or elsewhere will be fired upon, if it is found impossible to capture them. His Excellency therefore urges upon the chiefs the necessity of warning those people of the danger they will incur if they become marauders.[10]

Such a proclamation was not unreasonable given the disorder of the times, and even its harshest provisions — transportation for petty theft, and the right of the private individual to kill in defence of property — might be regarded as justifiable in the circumstances, if the proclamation had been accompanied by a vigorous attempt to protect the endangered unbelievers and if it had been superseded at the earliest opportunity by a law defining in greater detail the degree of gravity of specific offences. The phrase 'attempting to commit robberies . . . with arms in their hands' was broad enough to embrace almost anyone carrying a stick outside of his normal residential area.

But far from relaxing the harsher provisions when the crisis was over, and far from introducing amendments to protect the innocent or to mitigate the responsibility of the starving, the colonial government applied the proclamation more severely and on a broader front as time went on. Its ulterior purpose was not to protect property and to punish theft but to force as many Xhosa as possible to leave British Kaffraria. Of the 32 Xhosa transported in the first four weeks after the proclamation, 18 were not actually accused of anything worse than travelling without passes 'under suspicious circumstances'.[11] And yet, at the very same time that the colonial government was so busily employed rooting unauthorized Xhosa out of the frontier districts, it was deliberately failing to come to the assistance of the embattled unbelievers within British Kaffraria whose very lives were in constant danger.

The news of the proclamation spread rapidly among those Xhosa contemplating entering the Colony without a pass. The sea voyage, even more than the punishment at the other end of it, was looked upon 'with almost as much dread as death itself'. Magistrate Reeve reported with satisfaction 'that a feeling of FEAR and RESPECT towards the Government is evidently obtaining' in Kama's district, while the *King William's Town Gazette*, equally pleased, remarked that transportion was 'the order of the day'.[12]

Implementation was not, however, without its problems. Transportation was unknown in southern Africa, and it had recently (1852) been abolished in Australia. Grey had received no permission from London, and the Cape Parliament had already voiced disquiet over the 'possibility of the undue exercise of arbitrary power'. Maclean was most anxious to guard against 'any objection which may check or interfere with what is really necessary' by giving his measures a veneer of legal responsibility.[13] He therefore commissioned Henry Barrington, the Attorney General of British Kaffraria, to devise judicial procedures which would do 'what is really necessary' without compromising his government in the eyes of the outside world. Barrington's response shows just how well he understood his brief.

> As to the [Xhosa] prisoners it is my opinion that a return will be called for by and bye showing all sorts of things.
>
> And you and the Governor will have to defend the sentences and explain the whys and wherefores to the English Parliament which I think can only be done by showing that each case was fully considered and sentence justified by being in accordance with the spirit of English criminal law or of some special law made by His Excellency to meet the difficulty of the position here.[14]

The 'special law' which Barrington had in mind was one designed to cope with the alleged untruthfulness of the Xhosa nation.

> No one who has studied the wild [Xhosa] properly can persuade himself that there is any form of oath or anything else that will bind the conscience of such a one.[15]

Under such circumstances, the magistrate was forced to assume the role of a policeman and 'pump out' (Barrington's phrase) the truth from the Xhosa before the trial even began. The purpose of the court was not therefore to discover whether the accused was guilty or not, but simply to demonstrate the fact of his guilt. The problem, Barrington realized, was that if standard English procedures were observed, it would prove next to impossible to obtain enough sworn evidence to secure a conviction. A regular court following regular procedures might well be forced to acquit the accused, a possibility which Barrington was determined to forestall.

> I do not see that the Chief Commissioner ought to let off a rogue upon a technicality except where life is concerned and not always then perhaps, things are not settled enough for that — If I were sitting in a regular court I should be obliged to do so [acquit on a technicality].

Barrington's task was to create some form of judicial procedure which would dispose of Xhosa trespassers in the shortest possible time with the least possible danger of acquittal. His official response to Maclean rationalizes but does not disguise the arbitrary nature of the courts he is proposing.

> Considering the circumstances of British Kaffraria, a country peopled as yet by uncivilized heathen tribes who therefore are unable to comprehend our laws and usages. Also the dangerous state the country is now in and the necessity of putting down crime quickly and effectively. . . . It seems expedient and not unjust to omit the forms usual among the civilized people of Europe in criminal cases and trials and to proceed in the simplest and most natural manner. The supreme power should be satisfied of the guilt of the prisoners and the punishment ordained should be sharp and severe.

The 'simplest and most natural manner', 'expedient and not unjust' of administering law and order was to establish special courts composed exclusively of special magistrates and military officers. Prisoners were allowed in theory to call and cross-examine witnesses and to make statements, but they were denied any legal representation or legal advice from anyone familiar with 'civilized' notions of justice. Wives could be called on to give evidence against their husbands because, according to Barrington, 'Marriage is a Christian or a legal institution. Amongst the [Xhosa] it does not exist.'[16] The court passed judgement, but sentencing was left in the hands of the Governor and the Chief Commissioner. One result of this was that many prisoners were transported without ever hearing their sentences, or being told how many years' hard labour they were expected to serve.[17]

The range of offences dealt with by these summary courts was even broader than that indicated in Grey's proclamation, which had only referred to thieves 'with arms in their hands'. Maclean acknowledged this but maintained that the 'spirit and intention' of the proclamation justified him in sentencing even unarmed potential thieves to transportation. English law did not define the plucking of standing corn as 'larceny', but Maclean thought it 'should be considered, even when committed by unarmed men, as a crime of some magnitude'.[18] Finally, Maclean thought it necessary to bring robberies and trespasses committed outside British Kaffraria under the jurisdiction of its special courts. He was quite open about the reason for this. 'By the ordinary law of the Colony,' he wrote, '[such offences as the theft of corn from unfenced gardens] cannot be punished in the summary or severe manner which the general safety of the country demands.'[19] He invoked one of Governor Cathcart's old proclamations from the War of Mlanjeni which placed the frontier districts under martial law. All

Xhosa found without passes in the Colony, whether residents of British Kaffraria or not, were to be sent into British Kaffraria to face the special courts. Even Barrington was a little disturbed about the legal aspects of this — Cathcart's proclamation had referred specifically to 'rebels' and said nothing about thieves — but he acquiesced like a good subordinate.[20]

Despite the severity of the penalties involved, many Xhosa were prepared to risk defying the law. There was no work for them inside British Kaffraria. Indeed, two of the four men mentioned in the initial proclamation had applied unsuccessfully for employment on the public works a few days before they were caught in the Crown Reserve.[21] A full discussion of the sort of employment on offer must be deferred to Chapter 8, but it is sufficient to mention here that the conditions under which 'industrious and well-disposed persons' were expected to sign labour contracts were such that they amounted to transportation in any case. Only by foraging in secret for food could most Xhosa hope to maintain a foothold in their home areas.

A few cases from the early days of the special court will illustrate the sort of 'crimes' being punished and the sort of sentences these 'criminals' received.[22] Tiligana, for instance, was one of a party of Xhosa who tried to steal maize from the gardens at Peelton mission. The Peelton people fired on them and they all ran away, offering no resistance. Tiligana was unarmed when he was captured but he admitted — presumably after the examining magistrate had 'pumped' the 'truth' out of him — that he had been carrying a spear. He was found guilty of armed robbery and transported for seven years. Yobogana and Lumka borrowed a horse in order to search for some cattle they had sent to Thembuland. On their way back, they were accused of riding a stolen horse, and they were transported for three years. No one ever claimed the 'stolen' horse and it was eventually sold off by public auction. Vuso was arrested when a party of police passing his homestead noticed a newly dug hole marked with blood. Vuso admitted that he had shared in a meal of stolen cattle though he had not stolen anything himself. He was transported for three years. Nojihle and four companions were arrested after six or seven maize cobs were found at his homestead. Nojihle was sentenced to ten years, though his companions got off because they were only visitors. Maclean described the feasting group as a 'large armed and organised marauding party' and regretted the acquittals.

Other cases could be quoted, but enough have already been cited to show the way in which Grey's proclamation was used, not against aggressive mounted marauders but against hungry and pitiful individuals attempting only to keep themselves alive until the next harvest. By mid-January 1858, 359 Xhosa men and women had been transported in this manner.[23] The Frontier Armed and Mounted Police drove back 200 hungry Xhosa, attempting to cross the Keiskamma to get at the prickly pears on the other side. Other Xhosa were forcibly ejected from Mfengu locations where they had been hospitably received and fed in exchange for rendering domestic services. Police staged regular raids on Xhosa living among the Mfengu in the Crown Reserve, often extorting bribes under threat of transportation. After transportation was brought to an end, starving Xhosa caught in the Crown Reserve without a pass were put to work on the East London harbour, chained together in heavy irons to prevent any possible escape. Those who infringed prison discipline were flogged on their shoulders, faces and stomachs by white convicts 'who appear[ed] to take a savage delight in it'.[24]

That part of Grey's proclamation permitting farmers and un-believers to shoot in defence of property deterred but did not entirely stop Xhosa raiders desperate with hunger. Some starving Xhosa caught stealing pumpkins and green maize wearily invited the farmers to go ahead and shoot. Certain farmers were quite willing to do so, and one transport contractor actually boasted that he had shot nine Xhosa in three trips through British Kaffraria. The number of Xhosa dead through Grey's licence to kill is hard to calculate, though one hopes it was not very large. The proclamation of 3 March 1857 was finally withdrawn early in September the following year. Even the *King William's Town Gazette* acknowledged that it had rendered life in British Kaffraria very cheap.[25]

3. The Clear Sweep

In contrast to the harshness with which they treated the ordinary commoner believers, Grey and Maclean still held back from a frontal assault on the chiefs. But, once again, events played into their hands, and the chiefs themselves provided the openings which led to their eventual destruction. The catalyst was the Ngqika chief, Maqoma.

It will be remembered that the old warrior and his Great Son, Namba, had been foremost in spreading the message of the Cattle-Killing in the Ngqika district. They actively promoted the movement long after the Great Disappointment in February 1857, and Namba paid a personal visit to the Gxarha in April.[26] But though the chiefs still continued hopeful, many of their followers had abandoned belief in the prophecies, and were pouring out of the district to save their lives and what was left of their property. Maqoma's neighbour Bhotomane, who had killed every head of cattle he possessed, watched them leave with sad tolerance. 'Look,' he said, 'the people are dying before our eyes. We have nothing to give them. Let them go where they can get meat.'[27]

But this was not Maqoma's way. Early in March he confiscated the property of one of his men who was trying to take three cows and three goats out of his district. 'I know the fines I promised to give [the government],' he told his magistrate. 'This is not one of them.' Maclean forced him to retract by suspending his salary which was all he had to live on. This did not stop Maqoma dunning his remaining subjects or restrain him from urging on the Cattle-Killing during the movement's last flicker in May-June 1857, but when that too failed Maqoma was desolate. Drink had always been his foe, and he now spent all the money he could get at the taverns opened for the German Legion in Stutterheim. He came home so drunk from his binges that he could hardly move for several days after, and eventually Maclean ordered the tavern keepers to stop selling the chief liquor.[28]

Meanwhile, in early July, a party of men from Maqoma's district surprised and killed the informer Fusani, who had betrayed a number of people to Gawler's police, including the daring thief Nqono and a man named Qoqola, who had died shortly after being released from custody. Fusani had long been unpopular in Maqoma's country.[29] He was, in fact, a Ngqika Xhosa who had been fined by Maqoma and Sandile about six months prior to the Cattle-Killing for incest with his widowed cousin. Nongqawuse had specifically denounced 'fornications' as a type of witchcraft and declared that widows, being wives of the dead, should not be touched by other men. Unbeliever, fornicator, informer and murderer — Fusani virtually stank of evil. Maqoma must have approved the raid, but there is no evidence that he ordered the premeditated murder of Fusani, as even Maclean recognized. 'In all Gawler's charges against Macomo,' he informed Grey, 'no proof could be produced of his participation in Fusani's murder.'[30] Maclean was, however, convinced that the chief's erratic behaviour would soon present the government with a clearer case for disciplining him.

The Chief Commissioner was right. One of Maqoma's wives, after repeated efforts to get away from him, fled into the Crown Reserve. Maqoma asked Lucas, his magistrate, for a pass to go and look for her, but he was refused. The chief was furious. 'I am an aged chief and a great man,' he said, 'not inferior to Sandile and much abler to manage the [Xhosa] nation. Mr Lucas is a boy, and the Queen's commission does not always bring with it knowledge and experience.' On 8 August, returning drunk from one of the German villages, Maqoma slashed at Lucas with a sjambok. Maclean called him in, but found to his surprise that it was the chief who was delivering the reprimand. Maqoma declared that he had supposed Maclean had forgotten him, 'considering that he was almost dead from hunger, his money having been stopped by the government, how could he have strength to visit Maclean, he was nobody, what could Maclean wish to see him about?' Maqoma criticized Lucas and defended his seizure of unbelievers' cattle. 'He did not see what right the Government had to interfere in any of these cases, as none of them were connected with white people.' He knew that the Queen and the government over the sea were still well disposed towards him. All the injustices he had suffered were the fault of the local officials in British Kaffraria.[31]

Still defiant and still without a pass, Maqoma rode into the Colony to look for his wife. He was arrested and thrown into jail in Alice to await Grey's pleasure. Maclean was still unwilling to press ahead with charges connected to Fusani's murder. There was too little evidence, it was too long after the event, it looked underhand to arrest a man thus far from home. It would upset the chiefs, he informed Grey, thus showing how far he still was from conceiving the scenario, long advocated by Gawler, of a British Kaffraria entirely without chiefs. But by now Grey was fully alert to the unique opportunity with which chance had presented him. On 17 September, he unambiguously ordered Maclean to try Maqoma for the Fusani murder. Ever the loyal servant, Maclean complied. He had been impressed by the lack of Xhosa reaction to Maqoma's arrest. The other chiefs all recognized the recklessness of Maqoma's conduct, and many must have blamed him for involving them in the disaster of the Cattle-Killing. The only talking point seemed to concern the fate of his salary.[32]

Gawler started picking up the men involved in the raid on Fusani, and Barrington started to prepare the evidence. The prosecution strategy was simple: get one or two of the raiders to be Crown witnesses and implicate Maqoma in return for immunity from prosecution. Of the four witnesses they had in mind, two escaped and one, Zazini, joined Maqoma in the dock rather than betray his chief. But in the end it did not matter. The trial was held at Fort Hare in front of a military court presided over by Colonel Pinckney, the magistrate of the Crown Reserve. The extent of Pinckney's impartiality may be gauged from a letter he wrote to Maclean *before* the trial.

> I shall be at Fort Hare as directed for the trial of that savage villain Macomo and his gang. Not as I go prejudiced against the man in this

particular instance but the numerous charges you have sent against him, cunningly devised, he will be a fortunate fellow to clear away the whole. I am glad Mr Barrington will be there, and my friend Gawler will prove no doubt a terrible prosecutor on the part of Government.[33]

Maqoma never had a chance. Of the nine witnesses he called in his defence, only one appeared.[34] There was no defence lawyer and the charges, as Pinckney had said, were 'cunningly devised'. None of the government evidence remotely connected Maqoma with Fusani's death, and one important Crown witness stated explicitly that both Maqoma and Zazini, the leader of the raiders, had categorically forbidden the killing of the informer.[35] Even Colonel Pinckney was reluctantly forced to state that Maqoma was 'quite innocent of Fusani's death. The whole of the evidence acquits him of that crime.' Nevertheless, Pinckney managed to find Maqoma guilty on three capital charges relating to the receipt of stolen goods which, he advised Maclean, 'will enable you to keep him in durance vile for as long as you like'. Grey agreed:

The High Commissioner thinks that although Macomo has been acquitted of the murder of Fusani, he is morally responsible for that murder, committed by persons acting under his orders.[36]

Maqoma and the nine members of the raiding party were all sentenced to death, which Grey, in his infinite mercy, commuted to twenty years' imprisonment. But that was only the beginning.

One of those to applaud Maqoma's arrest was the Gqunukhwebe chief Phatho, who called Maqoma 'one of the greatest rascals in [Xhosaland]', hoping perhaps to imply that he, Phatho, was very different.[37] But Phatho's days were numbered. With the insignificant exception of his cousin Montawuli, all his people had gone whole-heartedly into the Cattle-Killing. Phatho, his brother Kobe, and his brother-in-law Stokwe had all been fervent believers. His Great Son Dilima had been a frequent visitor to the Gxarha, and had led the armed attacks on the unbelievers in March. His son Mate had raised the standard of the Cattle-Killing in Kama's country, and had roused the majority of Kama's nominal subjects to open defiance of their Christian chief. The Gqunukhwebe Xhosa had united under Phatho's leadership to obstruct all the measures of Magistrate Vigne, who had been unable to make any headway against their policy of passive non-cooperation. The strategic significance of Phatho's territory athwart British Kaffraria's main highway between King William's Town and East London was highlighted by the chief's unwillingness to protect passing colonial travellers. Clearly, if any major changes were to be achieved in the state of British Kaffraria, Phatho, his close associates and all his people would have to go.

Phatho seems to have had little apprehension of the danger threatening him from the colonial state. In April 1857, he undertook a personal pilgrimage to Sarhili, who treated him with some coolness, killing only two goats for his sustenance and insisting on addressing him impersonally through a spokesman. He spent some time begging cattle in the district of his brother Kama, and clung hopefully to the final illusions of May-June 1857.[38] Even after this disappointment, Phatho remained unwilling or unable to court the goodwill of the government, on which any hope of his future survival necessarily depended. The major sticking point was once again the security of goods passing along the highway, which provided too easy and tempting a target for the starving Xhosa. After several months of attempting to work with Phatho, Magistrate Vigne finally gave up. In early October, he sent the following letter to Maclean:

> Of the dishonesty, duplicity and utter uselessness of Pato's councillors or headmen . . . I have already written. They have been dismissed one by one for misconduct and although I know most of the people of the tribe I am at a loss to replace them. — Every one of the people told me plainly that they were glad to be dismissed. . . .
>
> They only used, I always found, their temporary authority as a means of beguiling me to believe any long plausible rigmarole story exculpatory of themselves and friends which they were too well aware I was unable to disprove — the police at my place only acted the part of spies and invariably backed the councillors in their lies. . . . The almost total dearth of all information regarding the true state of things was well known to you, sir: Everything was either hid from me or so altered and added to that all hope of tracing out the perpetrators of any act was lost.[39]

When eventually Vigne was given permission to form his own police force on the Gawler model, this proved so effective that any help Phatho and Dilima might have been prepared to lend the colonial authorities was rendered entirely redundant. Phatho's country was becoming increasingly attractive as a target area for white settlement. The Gqunukhwebe Xhosa had started killing their cattle a full year before the advent of Nongqawuse, they had been blasted by drought and lungsickness, and they had not planted for two seasons. As emigration and starvation took their toll, the country became increasingly denuded of population until only the chiefs and a few hangers-on remained to stake the Gqunukhwebe claim to their formerly extensive territory.

Ever since the decision had been taken to prosecute Maqoma, the colonial authorities had been looking round for evidence against the other chiefs.[40] They had been looking for Qasana ever since his attack on Bulungwa in March, and Brownlee had Sandile's brother Xhoxho tried for horse theft in mid-October. By November, Maclean was sure that he had cases against Phatho, Dilima and Stokwe. 'Your Excellency may be satisfied I will not allow myself to be hurried into any adventure,' he reassured the Governor. 'In the present state of the country a few police may do anything without resistance.' And so they could. On 25 December, in a letter to Maclean beginning 'a Merry Christmas to you and yours', Major Gawler suggested a 'clear sweep' of all the guilty chiefs. Maclean was cautious, but by the end of January 1858, Phatho and his sons Dilima, Mate and Mpafa, together with Chiefs Qasana, Tola and Xhoxho, were all in prison.[41]

No one anticipated that one of Grey's courts might find the chiefs innocent, but an unexpected hitch occurred when Phatho and Mpafa went on trial for possessing stolen horses. The trial was initially delayed when Phatho's brother Kama inconveniently arrested the thieves who had actually committed the theft. Since Grey's entire plan for the settlement of whites in British Kaffraria depended on getting Phatho out of the way, the chief was accordingly charged with being an accessory after the fact. But another unexpected obstacle then raised its head in the form of Magistrate Vigne. No one had suffered more at Phatho's hands than Vigne, who had been systematically blocked, tricked, deceived and made to appear a fool in the eyes of his brother magistrates. But, for all that, Vigne could not swallow the worst excesses of drumhead law. He had objected to some of the practices of Gawler's police, and on one occasion he had even declined to issue a sufficiently strong statement against four Xhosa whom Maclean badly wanted to transport on suspicion alone.[42] At Phatho's trial, he let slip some information in evidence which showed quite clearly that Phatho and Mpafa had not realized that the horses in question were stolen. Even the special court was left with no option but to acquit the two chiefs. Maclean was furious and ordered an immediate retrial at which Vigne was asked some slightly different questions and the prisoners were duly found guilty. In the teeth of strong objections from the Cape Attorney General, Grey insisted on the guilty verdict. The 'technical informality' of the second 'guilty' trial did not invalidate it, the Governor wrote. After all, the 'natives' could not very well be allowed to 'claim every technical advantage which would be awarded to a British subject'. Phatho and Mpafa were transported for five years.[43]

Of the chiefs who had strongly promoted the Cattle-Killing, only four still remained at liberty: Chief Bhotomane, who was over eighty years old; Stokwe, who hid out a full fifteen months in the Fish River bush with the police on his tail the whole time;[44] Maqoma's son Namba; and the greatest prize of all, Chief Mhala, the Wildcat.

4. The End of Mhala

After the departure of the unbelievers to Gawler's camp on the Tshabo and the failure of the June prophecies, the silence of desolation descended on Mhala's district. The country was virtually empty outside of Mhala's Great Place and St Luke's Anglican mission. Greenstock described the scene as it existed in September 1857.

> The country is almost deserted. The greater part of the natives have gone to seek employment in the Colony. A person may travel miles in [Xhosaland] through parts once densely populated, without meeting a single human being or seeing a single head of cattle. Umhala still holds on in his old place — he gets a little help from the Government, but he is becoming very thin, and both he and his son Mackinnon evidently suffer much from anxiety about the sad condition into which they have brought themselves by their blind obedience to Nongaule. . . .
>
> Umhala's power is but the shadow of what it was — his followers are a few infirm old men. He says he obeyed the prophetess and killed his cattle, and neglected to plant, because he believed that he should be restored to youth and see the resurrection of his father and all his dead relatives.[45]

Even this little that Mhala retained was soon to be taken from him. Those few of his remaining followers who had planted in the early spring found they could not hold out until harvest time, and abandoned their homesteads to look for work. All but one of his wives ran away. Two of them came to his arch-enemy, Gawler, saying they were starving. He sent them into the Colony for service.[46] But Mhala's greatest grief was reserved for his son Makinana, loyal despite his unbelief, who had lost the rich patrimony of the house of Ndlambe, while his junior brother Smith raised himself to greatness on his father's ruin. Mhala hoped that Makinana would be 'picked up' by the Anglican mission, and he himself came to church for the first time in two years, while Makinana was assiduous in attendance. But Maclean and Gawler disliked Greenstock, whom they regarded as far too liberal — an opinion shared by his Bishop, who wrote of Greenstock that 'he is respected by the [Xhosa] for his simple Christian character, but has not rigour of mind enough to deal with them'. St Luke's was closed down and Greenstock packed off to East London, where it was hoped that his overly Christian and unrigorous approach would no longer interfere with the good government of British Kaffraria. His mission was relocated on a new site, out of the way of the white colonists whom Grey wished to settle in Mhala's country.[47]

Mhala was left alone to face the coming storm. 'I have yielded,' he told Gawler. 'I am dying of hunger. I have fallen — I fell because it was said that my forefather Rarabe would appear, and my father would appear, and my mother would appear, and that I should not be old.' But Gawler was no longer interested in reconciliation. He told the old chief that if he was hungry, he could go to Lesotho or Mpondoland, where there was plenty of food. He warned Mhala to stay away from 'his' people, the unbelievers, and reprimanded Smith in public for talking to his father.[48] As the danger of civil war receded, the heads of the colonial authorities were increasingly filled with notions of the 'chiefs' plot', and Mhala was a prime suspect. If Mhala rode around too much, if he talked to the unbelievers, if he was even 'in better spirits than he ought to be', then it was very obvious that he was up to something. If Mhala's followers managed to find food and shelter among hospitable Mfengu within the colonial border, then Maclean maintained that the chief was planning an invasion. And indeed there were signs that all but the strongest of the unbelievers were taking pity on their old chief in his misery, sympathizing with him, even wanting him back. But Grey was determined to get rid of him:

> It is quite clear . . . that Umhala was the very chief leader in the late great plot. If evidence can be obtained that will convict him of the intention to levy war against the Queen or implicate him in recent murders and robberies, he should be apprehended and brought to trial.[49]

Such evidence was indeed at hand. It will be remembered that in September 1857 the police had arrested the Mpongo prophetess, Nonkosi. When they arrived at Gawler's place, Nonkosi had frustrated all of his questions by obsessively repeating that the dead cattle would certainly rise. Maclean wrote to Grey that he would examine Nonkosi, and 'if nothing could be made of her', she would be kept under surveillance at the Native Hospital in King William's Town.[50]

Two weeks later, Maclean wrote to the hospital and asked Dr Fitzgerald to take permanent charge of the prophetess 'as she is reported to be of weak intellect'.[51] But Gawler was not quite ready to quit, and, by 15 October, he had extracted a coherent statement from Nonkosi, in which she described her interviews with Mlanjeni, in the occasional presence of six spirits of departed chiefs who sat silently on the water 'as we sit on the ground'.[52] This was not very promising material for the 'chiefs' plot' and so Gawler was forced to conclude that the young girl had been 'imposed upon by . . . half-dozen fellows chosen for their general resemblance to the old chiefs they represented'.

Suspicion for these 'tricks' (still only a hypothesis of Gawler's) naturally fell on Nonkosi's uncle Nkwintsha, a leading believer who was Mhala's councillor in charge of the Mpongo River area. Nonkosi's interrogators decided to push this line of questioning, and when the prophetess was handed over to Maclean, she suddenly and mysteriously broke down and confessed that she had acted under Nkwintsha's instructions. In his dispatch on the subject, Maclean remarked piously that he had discontinued his questions at an early stage, lest these should influence the child's testimony.[53] This is misleading to say the least, since, by Maclean's own statement, Nonkosi had 'persisted in her misrepresentations' for more than a month before her sudden, amazing, 'spontaneous' confession.[54]

Gawler, who had got nothing out of Nonkosi, made amends by successfully interrogating Nkwintsha. Nkwintsha was made to confess that:

> Nonkosi said nothing of herself; all that she said was from Umhala through me . . . the object was a war . . . . The cattle-killing was got up to deprive the people of property that required so many to look after, the people would go more free to fight, and the English would have nothing to take. It failed because it was not done quick enough; half were starved before the other had killed.[55]

In Maclean's capable hands, Nkwintsha's story became even further embellished. He described how he had impersonated cattle bellowing in the water, and (this gem is an interpolation in the original script):

> Whenever I was alone, I could not refrain from laughing when I thought of the deceptions I practiced at the *vley*, and I often roared out 'Are [Xhosas] fools to be thus deceived?'[56]

Grey was delighted with Nkwintsha's statements and urged that Mhala be brought to trial for levying war against the Queen. Gawler persuaded Mhala to visit the Chief Commissioner to beg forgiveness, thus giving Maclean a chance to arrest him without any trouble.[57] But Attorney General Barrington spoiled the party by warning that the evidence was still inadequate, and Mhala was allowed to depart in peace, ignorant of his narrow escape. Barrington finally solved the evidence problem by threatening Nkwintsha with twenty years' transportation for robbery.[58] Nkwintsha suddenly remembered several warlike conversations between various chiefs and councillors. He also made two attempts to break out of prison (presumably he had stopped roaring with laughter), but there was to be no escape for him.

At long last, Gawler got the go-ahead to arrest his old enemy. But it was not to prove easy. Smith Mhala, possibly remorseful and possibly disillusioned by challenges to his leadership within the unbelievers' camp, tipped off his father that they were coming to get him. Mhala took to the bush. As he pointed out at his trial, he could easily have fled to Sarhili, or Faku, or Moshoeshoe. But he could not bear to leave the country over which he had once been chief. Gawler's police followed hot on his trail, and he and Makinana were forced to split up. Mhala was old and he was hungry; of his followers only one or two remained. At times he was close to surrendering, but his councillors told him he would be better off dying of starvation. He was sustained by news of the Indian Mutiny, and he managed to send Sandile a message saying he should not sleep at home for the government was trying to arrest all the chiefs before the Indians arrived.[59]

Two brothers named Nduna and Mbilini, unbelievers who had joined Gawler's police, remained loyal to their old chief. They kept him supplied with food and secretly informed him of the movements of the patrols. The police surprised Mhala's hideout in May 1857, but the councillors fended them off while Mhala escaped down a kloof.[60] After five months in hiding, Bulungwa caught one of Mhala's servants and forced him to talk. Another implacable enemy, Mjuza the son of Nxele, armed sixteen police and found the wildcat's last lair in a secret place on the Kubusi River, surrounded by immense rocks and thick bush. As Mjuza approached the hut in which he was hiding, the chief appeared armed in the doorway and dared the policeman to come on at him. But Mjuza, younger and more athletic, sprang on Mhala and forced him to the ground. In the hut they found the chief's last and most treasured possession — a bundle of spears belonging to Ndlambe, the dead father whom Mhala had so much wished to see.[61]

As might be expected, Nkwintsha was the star witness for the prosecution. But even under the expert tuition of Major Gawler, his confession left much to be desired. To begin with, it conflicted with Nonkosi's statement in respect of the all-important issue of Mhala's role. In his initial statements of October and November 1857, and again in January 1858, Nkwintsha repeatedly said that he had instructed Nonkosi on Mhala's orders, and he never alleged that Mhala had instructed Nonkosi himself. But in his statement at the trial, he maintained that Mhala had personally described the appearance of his dead forefathers to the young prophetess, and that Mhala had told her that he approved of Nkwintsha's actions.[62] Nonkosi, however, did not implicate Mhala at any point. He often came to see her, he gave her presents, but his part was entirely that of the innocent dupe. Indeed, in one (unpublished) examination, Nonkosi specifically remarked that Nkwintsha deliberately misled Mhala into thinking that he had gone away so that the chief would not notice him manipulating the prophetess from behind the bushes.[63]

Unsurprisingly, these discrepancies were not picked up by Mhala's judges, who were all officers and officials. There was no jury and no defence counsel. Of the six witnesses Mhala had wanted, only two — Gawler and Smith, his renegade son — actually appeared. Although he was not familiar with British legal procedures, Mhala was able to make one telling point in cross-examining Nonkosi — that the alleged deceptions were instigated not by himself but by Nkwintsha.

William Porter, the Cape Attorney General, commented that the verdict was a foregone conclusion:

> I cannot, however, say that the evidence appears to me to be such as would satisfy a Jury composed of strangers to the country. I mean no disrespect to Members of the court when I say that, in all probability, they were perfectly satisfied before the trial began that plots had been hatching, and that, where plots were hatching, the old Kaffrarian Fox was sure to be at work. They had no need of witnesses. But had they brought sceptical doubts, instead of formed convictions, to the trial of the case, I lean to the conclusion that much more evidence would have been obtained, and that the evidence actually given, would scarcely have been deemed conclusive.

Porter attacked the court for failing to ask Nonkosi whether she had ever been personally instructed by Mhala, and added that, in the event of any discrepancy, the evidence of the child Nonkosi should have been preferred to that of the adult Nkwintsha. On the broader legal front, Porter pointed out that Mhala was being tried under British laws inapplicable to Kaffraria. There was considerable doubt that Mhala was 'a subject of our lady the Queen' in the legal sense, which meant that he could not be charged with treason. Porter concluded his comment by pointing out that if Mhala were indeed a threat to the peace of the country, then it would be far better for the integrity of British justice that he be openly detained under martial law than convicted 'under a defective statute, supported by what strikes me as a somewhat defective evidence'.

Grey could have ruled it a mistrial and started all over again, as he had done when his kangaroo court foolishly found Chief Phatho innocent of the charges against him.[64] Instead, Grey sentenced Mhala to a mere five years' imprisonment, with provision for remission of sentence 'if it should subsequently be thought that the Attorney-General is right and I am wrong'. It is hard to overstate the significance of this concession. Whereas the other chiefs had been convicted for common crimes such as theft, Mhala alone was charged with treason. Not only he, but the entire Cattle-Killing movement, was in the dock for levying war against the Queen. Had the trial been a success, Mhala would have been transported for life and the Cattle-Killing exposed as a treacherous plot. By retreating in the face of Porter's carefully reasoned arguments, Grey tacitly admitted that he was wrong, that Mhala was innocent, and that the 'chiefs' plot' remained, at most, an unproven assumption. As Mhala told his judges, he had slaughtered on account of Nongqawuse, not on account of a war. They would have done well to heed his final appeal.

> I have nothing further to say but I wish this recorded and await what is in the heart of the court and beg them to remember that words do not perish, that though I may die [you had better judge me truly] that nothing hereafter may arise to disturb you. People die of sickness, and are killed in war; my words seem few but they are long enough.

Long enough indeed! Grey had intended the trial of Mhala to be the final proof that the Cattle-Killing was a plot of the chiefs. But it proved instead that, if any plots were afoot, they had been hatched not by the chiefs but by Sir George Grey himself.

Mhala's agony was not, however, quite over yet.

> When the soldiers brought him [Mhala] down to the beach, they put him under a crane, and told him they were going to hang him. They actually put the rope round him to frighten him, but an officer stopped them.
>   When they got on board ship . . . Umhala suddenly gave three most dreadful yells which startled them a good deal at first. But they found out the deposed chief was terrified at the appearance of the waves as they broke outside, and he fancied the sea was coming in upon him. This made him cry out for fear . . . Umhala was very low-spirited, and sat on deck looking wistfully at the land that was once his own.[65]

Notes

1. GH 8/49 J. Maclean-G. Grey, 30 Oct. 1856; GH 23/27 G. Grey-H. Labouchere, 6 June 1857.
2. GH 8/30 Information communicated to the Chief Commissioner, 8 Dec. 1856; R. Rawson — Lieut. Governor, 25 Aug. 1857, quoted in *Grahamstown Journal*, 8 Sept. 1857; BK 373 J. Maclean-W. Liddle, 18 Aug. 1856.
3. Peires (1985).
4. GH 23/26 G. Grey-H. Labouchere, 20 Sept. 1856.
5. GH 8/30 Information communicated to the Chief Commissioner, 8 Dec. 1856, minute by Maclean.
6. Maclean wrote two very lengthy dispatches (bristling with enclosures), dated 20 and 27 March 1857, to be found in BK 373. The former, which dealt with Moshoeshoe's alleged involvement, was published in Imperial Blue Book 2352 of 1857, pp.72-84.
7. GH 20/2/1 H. Waters-G. Grey, 5 Nov. 1857.
8. Imperial Blue Book 2352 of 1857, J. Maclean-G. Grey, 20 March 1857. It is

unlikely that Moshoeshoe had any motive in lying to Grey about his knowledge of the Cattle-Killing beyond the understandable if misguided object of not wanting to antagonize so powerful an enemy. For further discussion on the role of Moshoeshoe, see Chapter 4/1 and Peires (1985), pp.257-8.

9. GH 8/30 Information communicated to the Chief Commissioner, 8 Dec. 1856; BK 373 J. Maclean — G.Grey, 27 March 1857; GH 20/2/1 'Kreli's conduct', undated MS in Grey's handwriting.
10. *King William's Town Gazette*, 7 March 1857.
11. *King William's Town Gazette*, 28 March 1857.
12. *King William's Town Gazette*, 21 March 1857.
13. GH 8/31 J. Maclean-J. Jackson, 27 April 1857.
14. BK 14 H. Barrington-J. Maclean, 24 April 1857.
15. BK 14 H. Barrington-J. Maclean, 11 Jan. 1859, 14, 25, 30 April 1858.
16. BK 14 H. Barrington-J. Maclean, 30 April 1857; GH 8/31 Schedule 441 Circular to Magistrates, 28 April 1857.
17. CO 715 Statement of Holo.
18. GH 8/31 Schedule 436, 23 April 1857.
19. GH 8/32 J. Maclean-H. Barrington, 2 June 1857.
20. BK 14 H. Barrington-J. Maclean, 6 June 1857.
21. *King William's Town Gazette*, 14 March 1857.
22. GH 8/31 Schedule 436, 23 April 1857.
23. *Grahamstown Journal*, 23 Jan. 1858.
24. GH 8/50 F. Pinckney-J. Maclean, 8 Nov. 1857; MIC 172/2, Reel 8, Cory Library, USPG Archives, Journal of W. Greenstock, 6 April 1857; 2 Sept., 23 Oct. 1858; *Cape Argus*, 14 March 1857.
25. *Cape Argus*, 13 March 1858; *King William's Town Gazette*, 11 Sept. 1858.
26. BK 89 Secret Information, 4 May 1857.
27. MS 8172 J. Ross-J. Laing, 17 March 1857.
28. GH 8/31 H. Lucas-J. Maclean, 7 March 1857; BK 82 H. Lucas-J. Maclean, 21 April, 30 May 1857; GH 8/32 H. Lucas-J. Maclean, 12 July 1857.
29. BK 82 H. Lucas-J. Maclean, 14 July 1856.
30. GH 8/50 J. Maclean-G. Grey, 31 Aug. 1857; GH 8/32 Schedule 474, 23 July 1857.
31. *Cape Argus*, 16 Sept. 1857; BK 82 H. Lucas-J. Maclean, 8, 25 Aug. 1857; BK 82 Minutes of a conversation, 12 Aug. 1857.
32. BK 82 J. Maclean-G. Grey, 31 Aug. 1857; GH 8/32 J. Maclean-F. Pinckney, 24 Aug. 1857; GH 30/4 G. Grey-J. Maclean, 17 Sept. 1857; GH 20/2/1 J. Maclean-G. Grey, 7 Sept. 1857; GH 8/50 J. Maclean-G. Grey, 17, 24 Sept. 1857.
33. GH 8/50 F. Pinckney-J. Maclean, 8 Nov. 1857.
34. BK 82 Certificate by R. Southey, 4 Nov. 1857.
35. Cape Parliamentary Paper, G 4 of 1858, 'Proceedings and findings of the court . . . and sentence . . . upon Macomo and other Kafirs'.
36. *Ibid.*, p.2; GH 20/2/1 F. Pinckney-J. Maclean, 20 Nov. 1857.
37. GH 20/2/1 J. Maclean-G. Grey, 7 Sept. 1856.
38. BK 89 Secret Information, 26 April 1857; Uncatalogued MSS, Cory Library, Diary of Clerk to Colonel Maclean, 14 May 1857; GH 8/36 Schedule 129, 5 Oct. 1858.
39. BK 83 H. Vigne-J. Maclean, 3 Oct. 1857.

40. GH 8/50 J. Maclean-G. Grey, 14 May 1857; BK 71 C. Brownlee-J. Maclean, 17 Oct. 1857.
41. GH 20/2/1 J. Maclean-G. Grey, 5 Nov. 1857; GH 8/50 J. Gawler-J. Maclean, 25 Dec. 1857; GH 8/50 J. Maclean-G. Grey, 31 Dec. 1857.
42. BK 23 H. Barrington-J. Maclean, 17 May 1858.
43. GH 8/34 Enclosures to Schedule 34, 8 March 1858; BK 14 H. Barrington-J. Maclean, 27 Feb. 1858; BK 2 G. Grey, enclosed in F. Travers-J. Maclean, 25 July 1858. Grey's fury at the acquittal of Phatho is clearly seen by his vindictive refusal to give Captain Fielding, one of the special magistrates involved in the acquittal, a full-time position later on. The Phatho case is specifically cited as a reason for this. See GH 8/34 Schedule 40, 15 March 1858.
44. BK 140 J. Maclean-R. Taylor, 20 April 1859. The duel between Stokwe and his pursuers is a minor epic which I am sorry to be unable to deal with fully here. See, for example, BK 83 H. Vigne-J. Maclean, 31 March 1858.
45. MIC 172/2, Reel 1, Cory Library, USPG Archives, W. Greenstock-USPG, 2 Oct. 1856.
46. Acc 793 J. Gawler-J. Maclean, 17 Oct. 1856.
47. MIC 172/2, Cory Library, USPG Archives. Reel 1, Journal of W. Greenstock, 24 Sept., 19 Oct. 1857, 9 Jan. 1858; Reel (?), H. Cotterill-H. Bullock, 7 Aug. 1857. Greenstock did not last long in East London, from which town he was removed for being too attentive to the prisoners in the local jail.
48. BK 81 Memorandum, enclosed in J. Gawler-J. Maclean, 12 Dec. 1857; GH 8/36 Schedule 129, 5 Oct. 1858.
49. Acc 793 J. Gawler-J. Maclean, 11 Jan. 1857; GH 8/50 J. Maclean-G. Grey, 30 Nov. 1857; GH 30/4 G. Grey-J. Maclean, 6 Dec. 1856; GH 8/50 J. Maclean-G. Grey, 10 Sept. 1857. Gawler and Maclean were especially worried about the jealousies that had arisen within the ranks of the unbelievers, and they were afraid that Mhala might take advantage of them. Even so, the accusations they levelled against the chief were quite absurd.
50. GH 8/50 J. Maclean-G. Grey, 24 Sept. 1857; MIC 172/2, Cory Library, USPG Archives, W. Greenstock Journal, 22 Sept. 1857.
51. GH 8/33 J. Maclean-J. Fitzgerald, 10 Oct. 1857.
52. BK 81 J. Gawler-J. Maclean, 15 Oct. 1857.
53. This is the examination which was printed in Cape Parliamentary Paper G 5 of 1858. Maclean's success astonished Gawler, who wrote to Maclean congratulating him. BK 81 J. Gawler-J. Maclean, 24 Oct. 1857.
54. GH 8/50 J. Maclean-G. Grey, 26 Oct. 1857.
55. Cape Parliamentary Paper G 5 of 1858, p.4.
56. BK 81 Examination of Kwitshi [Nkwintsha], enclosed in J. Gawler-J. Maclean, 24 Oct. 1857.
57. BK 81 J. Gawler-J. Maclean, 12 Dec. 1857; GH 8/50 J. Maclean-G. Grey, 14 Dec. 1857.
58. GH 8/50 H. Barrington-J. Maclean, 19 Jan. 1858; BK 14 Examination of Kwitshi, 14 Jan. 1858.
59. Uncatalogued MSS, Cory Library, Diary of Clerk to Colonel Maclean, 19 Jan. 1856; GH 20/2/1 C. Lange-J. Maclean, 9 March 1858; BK 78 Information received, 1 April 1858; GH 20/2/1 J. Maclean-G. Grey, 29 March 1858; BK 71 C. Brownlee-J. Maclean, 16 Feb. 1858.

60. CO 3122 W. Fynn-C. Mills, 17 Jan. 1866; BK 81 Trial of Umhala, 23 Sept. 1858.
61. GH 8/35 Schedule 93, 24 June 1858, Statement of Mjuza, 24 June 1858.
62. All references to the trial of Mhala are from the very full details in GH 8/36 Schedule 129, 5 Oct. 1858. Porter's memorandum and Grey's response to it, both of a later date, have been filed with this schedule.
63. BK 14 Examination of Nonkosi the Umpongo Prophetess, before the Honourable Henry Barrington. Gawler was present throughout.
64. BK 2 F. Travers-J. Maclean, 25 July 1858.
65. MIC 172/2, Reel 8, Cory Library, USPG Archive, Journal of W. Greenstock, 15 Oct. 1858.

CHAPTER 8

Kaffir Relief

1. The Poor Calves of the Road

The continuous eating, drinking and dancing which characterized the Cattle-Killing at its height made it all the more difficult for the believers to conceptualize the famine which would follow the feast. Because they were allowed to partake only of freshly slaughtered cattle, there was more meat lying around than anyone could eat, and visiting believers were welcomed at every believing homestead. In those parts of Phatho's and Kama's districts which had been severely affected by drought, lungsickness and the prophecies of Nongqawuse's predecessors, there were many people depending on such visits for subsistence as early as August 1856.[1] As time passed and feasts became less frequent and less plentiful, the believers attempted to slow the rate of slaughter, killing more reluctantly and attempting to preserve their milk-cows to the end.[2] But they were trapped by the evil logic of the Cattle-Killing, that they could not fairly expect the fulfilment of the prophecies until they had wholly fulfilled the orders of the prophets to slaughter every last head of cattle.

For a time, the believers staved off hunger by using the proceeds of the sale of their hides and ornaments to puchase food from the traders and the Mfengu. Even though these had laid in good stocks of corn in anticipation of the expected demand, the desperate hunger of the believers soon pushed the price of maize and sorghum to five and even eight times its normal level.[3] In addition to grain the believers were able to survive — up to a point — on the edible roots and berries which they often ate to bridge the hungry months between sowing and harvest. As early as November 1856, there were several homesteads which were completely dependent on what they could gather from the veld. By April 1857, 'large numbers of people — the whole population of kraals — [could] be seen in the open country, digging for roots, others gather in the inside bark from the mimosa thorn, and all presenting an abject appearance'.[4] The believers tightened their *lambiles* (belts worn during times of famine to still the pains of hunger) and waited hopefully for the day of fulfilment.

It did not come. Early in October 1856 the child of a diviner, who had destroyed all his cattle and corn in 1855, died in Phatho's country, the first of some 40,000 victims of the prophecies.[5] Other children in the district fainted from hunger. By January 1857, deaths of children and old people were regular occurrences in all the strongholds of the Cattle-Killing. The believers, secure in the belief of their own coming resurrection, simply said that they had gone to call the other dead home.[6] Nevertheless they sold their horses, their guns, their spades, their hoes, their jack-chains and everything else they had.[7] They stole from the unbelievers and they stole from each other. They boiled up old bones that had been bleaching in the sun for years, and ate the broth as soup. They broke into the stables around East London and ate the meal meant for the horses.[8] Desperate to keep alive, they ate food that they would not normally have contemplated, such as horses, pigs and shellfish. They stole and ate the well-fed dogs of the white settlers in King William's Town. They even tried to eat grass.[9] In a very few cases, believers maddened with hunger attempted to kill and eat little children.[10]

The majority of believers, though starving themselves, were horrified by this last excess and hunted down and killed any who were suspected of cannibalism. Indeed, cannibalism or attempted cannibalism was a sign of insanity rather than hunger. In Gcalekaland, a man driven mad by guilt killed his wife and children because he could not bear to hear their reproaches, and at least two others committed suicide. Parents snatched the bread their children had begged, and deserted children they could no longer feed. Mothers whose breasts had long dried up were forced to choose between their children, usually taking the food from those liable to die and giving it to the older and stronger children who might still conceivably survive. On other occasions whole families sat down to die as one, and for years afterwards pathetic little clusters of skeletons might be found under the shadow of a single tree, the parents and their children dead together.[11]

Some, perhaps, were hoping to cling to life until the next harvest came around. Most, however, simply sat, waiting for death or resurrection, which ever came first. Many feared to apply for work in the Colony, believing that if they did so they would be transported overseas. Commissioner Brownlee found 'many wretched objects' sitting motionless in their homesteads, saying that they did not know how to work, or saying 'in the most apathetic manner that there was no help for them and if they died, they died'. Dying wives watched helplessly while the family dogs ate the corpses of their husbands. There are reports of children falling down from hunger and unable to rise again, and one missionary referred to starvation victims receiving relief 'cast[ing] a wistful glance at the food and [falling] down dead at our feet'. Other believers perished by fire when the grass dwellings in which they had been abandoned caught alight.[12]

Many believers never quite stopped hoping till the last moment, and stayed at home in the expectation of the imminent fulfilment of the prophecies.

> One poor old man was found dead with his head over-hanging his corn pit. He had gone with his last breath to look if it had not yet been filled, and falling, never rose again.[13]

Some had dug such great pits to ensure a massive bounty of the new corn that when they got down into them to see if any corn had appeared, they were unable to get up again and died just so. In other cases, the empty pits were used as graves for the mass burial of the dead. But most bodies were left unburied in the places where death had overtaken them, there to be picked at by vultures and gnawed at by dogs.

Death was not always the result of starvation, pure and simple. Cold, for example, was a great killer, and on especially cold days the believers simply 'lay down and died like rotten sheep among the houses'. The efforts of the hungry to eat strange roots and berries in the absence of more usual foods often resulted in dysentry or diarrhoea, and the starving often died helplessly immobilized in pools of their own vomit and faeces. Even worse was the bloating of the body which accompanied malnutrition, where the skin burst into sores and swelled out like a balloon before sloughing off in sheets, as in this case, described by Dr Fitzgerald:

> [A boy] about sixteen years of age was very much emaciated and covered with large bloody blisters from head to foot. On enquiring the cause I was informed that they had been living for some time on nothing but roots and gum, that as soon as they arrived at this [homestead] they eat Kaffir corn, that this boy immediately after eating was seized with vomiting and purging, followed by large bloody blisters all over the body.

The vitality of the body appeared so reduced that wherever the slightest pressure was made, decomposition and destruction of the skin immediately took place. Of this body it might be truly said that before life was extinct the exterior was fast running into decomposition. I sent out a mattress to be filled with grass and a blanket as this poor lad had only a hard cows hide to cover his raw and blistered body with. I also sent everything necessary for his case in the shape of suitable food and medicine, but I am sorry to add without any further effect than to mitigate his sufferings as he has since died.[14]

Another case, related by an inhabitant of King William's Town, was that of a 'skeleton child, endeavouring vainly to suck milk from a starved mother . . . so reduced in vitality that the pressure of the mother's arms produced sloughing of the body which was covered over in putrid sores'. Fitzgerald and his small team did their best, and the putrid smell of mimosa and diarrhoea, which infected his consulting chambers and frightened away even the army from the neighbourhood of the hospital, afflicted the good doctor all his life. Even so, the hard core of believers preferred to die rather than trust a white man, and they deliberately hid the sick from their only possible means of salvation.

The Xhosa historian W.W. Gqoba recounts the story of a group of old women, who had gone to a place called Ngxwangu where the new people were expected to appear, and were deserted by their younger, less feeble companions.

It is said that on the morrow of the eighth day, when nothing had occurred, then the young people said, 'Let us go and investigate. . . . Stay here, and we will tell you what has happened.' Then all the people who still had strength departed.

Those old women of Ngxwangu stayed until one morning they picked up their walking sticks and headed for Peelton mission. Some left with speed, others walked and fell, others had difficulty getting up, those arriving from behind simply walked past without helping those who had already collapsed. Those were sad and evil days. . . .

It is said that when they came to that high spot [along their route] those who were leading were heard to say, 'Today, we are the poor calves of the road, the eighth day has passed, we are left behind by those who have the power to walk.' [15]

Very many never made it. The dead and dying lay about the roads and the dongas, lost to all sense of feeling. Their skins were cracked and their eyes were sunk, and their swollen joints contrasted pathetically with tiny waists made even narrower by tightened hunger belts.

Those who survived were so emaciated that they 'resembled apes rather than human beings', while the children looked more like monkeys or bats. Many had lost their voices, and could make only indistinct sounds in their throats like the chirping of birds. Mentally and emotionally, they seemed 'stupid from want and indifferent as to their fate', moving more by instinct than by conscious will. And as this ghastly procession of skeletons converged on the capital of British Kaffraria in the desperate hope of some assistance, it seemed to one observer that the prophecies had indeed come true, that the dead had risen from their graves at last, and were walking towards King William's Town.[16]

2. No Bread for the Idle

On 2 May 1857, the following advertisement appeared in the *King William's Town Gazette* :

> DESTITUTE KAFFIR CHILDREN
> The Missionary with Umhala is constrained to appeal earnestly to the Benevolent throughout the Colony for assistance, to enable him to feed the STARVING CHILDREN of the T'Slambie Tribe. Great numbers are reduced (by no fault of their own, but the errors of their parents) to a wretched existence on GUM and ROOTS, and even these resources are now failing them.
> This appeal is made in the confident hope that good Christians will help these poor children in the time of their need.

It is difficult to believe that anyone could object to this simple request, yet such indeed was the case. The *Gazette* responded in its editorial of 13 June:

> Is the [Xhosa] a fit and proper subject for the receipt of charity? The question having a reference to the generality — not individuals — we answer No. . . . Were all [Xhosa]land to be maintained in charity for six months, the effect upon the natives would probably be to unman them and leave them in a worse position than they are now. Instead of stirring themselves up and endeavouring to gain a livelihood, they would remain listless, as at present. . . . Work is to be had in plenty if the trouble of application be not too great. Notwithstanding that thousands of hungry [Xhosa] have already entered the Colony in search of employment, there is still labour open to thousands more. . . .
> They [cannot] appreciate a generous action. They would consequently attribute, as they always have done, our charity either to some unexpected weakness or fear. Sir George Grey has distinctly given them to understand that there is plenty of work for all those who would be industrious but that there is no bread for the idle. . . . It would consequently be a direct interference in the policy of His Excellency. It would be a premium on idleness, and prevent the [Xhosa] from becoming what we would find it so much to our and their interest for them to be — labourers.

Clearly, humanity and compassion could not be allowed free rein in relieving the mass starvation that followed the Great Disappointment. When they arrived in King William's Town, the hungry Xhosa found themselves in a world whose idea of charitable aid was dictated by values which differed greatly from the simple concept of *ubuntu* (the quality of being human) which had perished along with their ruined homesteads. 'The [Xhosa] would have helped the English if they had killed their cattle,' said Sarhili, and there is no reason to disbelieve him.[17] But the Victorian concepts of charity operative in the Colony, even as applied to Europeans, were based on the British *Poor Law Report of 1834*, which made a careful distinction between 'indigence', that is 'the state of a person unable to labour', and 'poverty', that is, 'the state of one who, in order to obtain a mere subsistence is forced to have recourse to labour'.[18] By this definition, the Xhosa were poverty-stricken rather than indigent. The Victorians considered poverty to be 'the natural, the primitive, the general and the *unchangeable* lot of man', and it was not, therefore, to be pitied. Some writers even thought that poverty was good for the indolent lower classes, since 'it is only hunger which can spur and goad them on to labour'.[19] Labour was good for children too, and the childless philosopher Jeremy Bentham did not scruple to exalt the benefits of apprenticeship above the sanctity of family life.[20] The central tenet of the New Poor Law was that 'no relief [be] allowed to be given to the able-bodied or their families, except in return for adequate labour'.[21]

These attitudes were naturally most congenial to the industrializing middle classes of England, and, after the Whig (Liberal) election victory of 1830, they completely ousted notions of charity based on Tory paternalism, Christian humanity or Radical convictions of the natural rights of man. Bentham's disciples readily equated the principle of the 'greatest happiness of the greatest number' with that of the 'greatest national profit', and condemned 'reckless private charity' for increasing the misery of the poor by violating the 'laws' of economics. Such charity was not 'real benevolence', but was benevolent in name only.[22]

Concepts of charity rooted in the labour needs of industrial Britain were not inapplicable at the Cape, which had suffered a chronic shortage of agricultural labour ever since the emancipation of the slaves in 1834. Twenty of twenty-one Cape districts responding to a questionnaire in 1848 reported a scarcity of unskilled labour; ten of these spoke of a 'great dearth' or worse. The labour shortage in Malmesbury district was such that 'in many places the oats and rye are still uncut, consequently the damage caused through want of labour is estimated at some thousand muids of corn'. Not only were 'millions of acres of fertile land . . . lying waste . . . from a scarcity of suitable available labour', but the effects were felt throughout the remainder of the Cape economy in the form of higher wages and prices.[23] Sir Harry Smith's attempts to remedy the situation by introducing a vagrancy law and indenturing Xhosa apprentices did much to provoke the War of Mlanjeni and the Kat River Rebellion. The aftermath of the war brought no alteration. 'I come from a wool-producing district and I can state that the farmers cannot get their sheep washed,' complained the representative for Beaufort West in 1854, and the *Graaff-Reinet Herald* declared that there was 'no evil so detrimental and of such magnitude as the want of labour'.[24] Some pressed for white immigration, while others pinned their hopes on Chinese labour. More hard-headedly, the tough farmers on the Cape Select Committee for Frontier Defence called for:

> The removal or dispersion of all tribes, chieftaincies, or congregations of natives; such individuals amongst them who may have claims, or who may appear eligible or willing, to be located in the same manner as Europeans; all others to be placed in apprenticeship, or to take service, or to go beyond the colonial boundary.[25]

This was the solution adopted by Sir George Grey.

Commissioner Brownlee was the first official to consider the possible consequences of the unchecked destruction of food supplies, and it was at his suggestion that the colonial authorities began to buy up the unwanted corn of the believers. Magistrate Reeve of Middledrift, a district afflicted by cattle-killing prophecies for a full year before Nongqawuse, was the first official to think of sending the hungry believers to fill the huge gaps in the Cape labour market.[26] But it was Governor Grey who thought of making labour the essential exchange for famine relief, and it was Grey who first perceived in their gross magnitude the enormous potential advantages which the Colony might gain from the Cattle-Killing.

> Instead of nothing but dangers resulting from the [Xhosa] having during the excitement killed their cattle and made away with their food, we can draw very great permanent advantages from the circumstance, which may be made a stepping stone for the future settlement of the country.[27]

The Cattle-Killing did not change Grey's objectives, which were first stated as early as 1855. He still wanted to break the power of the chiefs and end the political threat on the Eastern Frontier. He still wanted the Xhosa to become 'useful servants, consumers of our goods, contributors to our revenue'. He still wanted Xhosaland settled by a substantial white population. But the Cattle-Killing enabled him to bring about these changes immediately, totally, and without hope of a resurrection.

The Xhosa nation was to be broken up entirely. It was to lose its home and its culture, it was to be scattered to the furthest reaches of the Colony, and it was never to go back again.

> They must be widely dispersed over the Colony and . . . thus brought under the charitable influence of individual employers [so that] they will become a settled and valuable rural population attached to their employers and homes, and . . . trained to habits of industry and imbued with Christian principles.[28]

The essential instrument for bringing about this desired end was already available in a circular issued by Maclean in November 1856, which instructed the magistrates to inform the chiefs that they were ready to find work in the Colony for any Xhosa who wanted it.[29] Magistrates were empowered to issue rations to Xhosa contracting for labour in the Colony, but nothing was said of giving food to anyone else. Maclean subsequently claimed that his instructions provided for a more general relief of the destitute, but at the time magistrates were clearly given to understand that they were entitled to ration only those Xhosa who registered as labourers.[30] 'Unless they apply for work or aid, we cannot help them,' wrote Brownlee.[31] On 9 June, Maclean instructed the magistrates to issue food to children 'for a limited period . . . on condition of their being willing to take employment', but as if afraid of the consequences of his own generosity, he qualified this concession the very next day.

> It is not intended that *all the young* are to be supplied with food, as this would only bring for Government support the *whole* of the children of [Xhosa]land to whom it would be impossible to furnish relief, and whose relief in this way would only prevent the grown up members from supporting their families by labour. . . . While relief is given to the really destitute, it is not afforded in such a way as will bring unnecesary burden on the Government, or tend to increase the idleness of the able-bodied, or check the immigration for service in the Colony.[32]

Maclean used the term 'really destitute' in the particular sense acquired in the workhouses of England; not destitute of all possessions, but destitute through bodily weakness even of the ability to travel and work. As soon as a man's health had recovered, he was no longer destitute, and could therefore be sent off to work in the Colony. For willingness to work *per se* was not good enough — the Xhosa must be willing to work in the Colony. For this reason, Maclean declined to provide Chief Sandile with seedcorn.

> Those who have money must purchase, those who have not must work. I cannot authorize the issue of seed unless in exceptional cases — Everything is being done by Government in meeting the wants of the

people, the destitute are fed, and labour is provided for all who are able or willing to work. . . . I will find employment for all who wish it in the Colony.[33]

In August 1857, the Attorney General of British Kaffraria devised a form of agreement to be entered into by Xhosa agreeing to be sent into the Colony for service. It is worth quoting in full:

I the undersigned a [Xhosa] of .... of the kraal .... hereby of my own free will undertake to proceed to any part of the Colony of the Cape of Good Hope, and in such fashion and in such manner and mode as I shall be ordered by the Chief Commissioner, and I further undertake faithfully and truly to perform such contract of service as the Resident Magistrate of .... [the district to which sent] shall enter into on my behalf, it being understood that such contract shall not exceed the term of three or five years from the day of agreement entered into on my behalf and that he will fix at his discretion the wages and food to be allowed me during the continuance of the said contract to which I willingly consent.[34]

Here was a remarkable redefinition of 'free will' and 'willing consent'. The willing volunteers in question were literally starving to death. The only way they could get food was to give themselves bodily into the hands of the Chief Commissioner, who could send them wherever he liked to do any sort of work at any wage for any length of time not exceeding five years. Only the five year limit distinguished this from actual slavery, and, as Grey's private secretary pointed out to Maclean, the five year limit did not apply to juveniles.[35]

With the martial law apparatus in British Kaffraria hard at work pumping Xhosa into the Colony, Grey introduced a battery of laws into the Cape Parliament to ensure their smooth disposal. The Kaffir Pass Act effectively prevented any Xhosa from seeking work in the Colony on their own initiative, and forced them to submit to the slave-like contracts imposed in British Kaffraria.[36] The Kaffir Employment Act provided for the registration of contracts between employer and Xhosa. Once the contract expired, the Xhosa had fourteen days to find a new contract or leave the Colony. A further Act 'for preventing Colonial Fingoes . . . being mistaken for Kaffirs and thereby harassed' forced the loyal Mfengu to carry 'certificates of citizenship', which were, in effect, nothing but a perpetual pass. Another act forbade settlers to abduct children from Xhosaland, which must have pleased the Colonial Office in London but did nothing to hinder Grey's campaign to 'apprentice' Xhosa children to the Western Cape far from homes and parents.[37]

By the end of June 1857, 13,137 Xhosa had been sent into the Colony as labourers under these regulations.[38] This might seem like a large number, but it had barely begun to relieve the desire of the colonists for cheap labour. These first refugees were eagerly snapped up for the Eastern Province by farmers who arrived at the magistracies, asking for servants by the thousand and taking them away in waggonloads.[39] As late as the end of July, Commissioner Maclean in King William's Town informed the Central Road Board that he could send them no labourers as there were too many farmers clamouring on the spot. No labourers whatsoever had yet reached the western districts.[40] In November 1857, the Colonial Secretary in Cape Town was still complaining that the Western Province had received only the 'refuse' — the 'aged and infirm' of Xhosaland, and 'it is time we should come in for our share of the cream'.[41]

The continuing colonial demand for labour encouraged independent agents such as Piet Loots, the representative of the 'distressed farmers of Murraysburg', to set up as dealers in human flesh, collecting starving Xhosa from their homes and selling them to farmers at £1 to £5 a head.[42] The most successful of these agents was James Hart, junior, who placed the following standing order with Maclean.

> I require *as many* as can be procured without limit to number — all of them in the first plan to be registered to me. One thing is much required and that is some thirty (30) young boys and girls for the residents in the town of Graaff Reinet. . . . I should be glad to get the boys and girls separately registered to avoid further disputes; I mean separate from their parents.[43]

Grey instructed Maclean to refrain from interfering in Hart's activities 'as they tended to disperse the [Xhosa] in the interior of the Colony', drawing the line only when Hart staged auctions of his recruits at Graaff-Reinet and Beaufort West. By that time 711 Xhosa had passed through his hands.

Grey's attempts to recruit Xhosa soldiers for service during the Indian Mutiny were not as successful. Although the Governor originally hoped to enlist several detachments of 500 or 600 men each, and although he offered recruiters 7/6 per head, the Xhosa refused in horror to cross the sea, and many ran away if the topic was even mentioned. Hundreds of starving men deserted their jobs on the public works in June 1858 for fear that they might be entrapped into the British regiments, and even Major Gawler's loyal police declined to follow him to the transKei for fear that his secret intention was to convey them to India.[44]

3. Enter the Kaffir Relief Committee

The Kaffir Relief Committee was founded on the initiative of Henry Cotterill, the newly arrived Bishop of Grahamstown. In May 1857, he wrote to Grey offering the assistance of his diocese in providing relief in whatever manner the Governor might suggest. Grey gave the Bishop a polite brush-off, informing him that he would ask his magistrates to ensure that 'none who cannot seek employment shall be allowed to perish from want'.[45] Maclean declared that although 'great distress and destitution' did prevail, this was due to Xhosa laziness and the Xhosa chiefs.[46] Nothing was done. When the Bishop toured Kaffraria late in June, he found conditions even worse than he had expected. This time, he did not make the mistake of asking the Governor's permission first. The Kaffir Relief Committee was founded in King William's Town on 17 July 1857 with all the publicity it could muster.

It was a highly respectable body, comprising most of what passed for high society in King William's Town. Its president was the Bishop of Grahamstown. The vice-president was Richard Taylor, the resident magistrate. The 23 members included 5 merchants, 4 ministers of religion, 2 army officers, 2 lawyers, a hotelier and the master of the local grammar school. Six members were on the Provisional Committee of the Bank of British Kaffraria. Four were members of the Kaffrarian Agricultural Society. Three were stewards at a race meeting held the day the Committee was formed. Other members included Dr Fitzgerald, the superintendant of the Native Hospital, and Stair Douglas, a Mauritius official on sick leave, who acted as secretary. So fashionable was the Kaffir Relief Society when first it started that it had to have a special meeting to enroll new members anxious to join.[47]

Civilians, doctors and missionaries in British Kaffraria could not help noticing the starvation which local magistrates found so difficult to detect. Among Bhotomane's people, where Magistrate Lucas could find 'not one' case of real want, the local missionary reported that 'distress . . . is already great, and becoming daily more so. I have had many cases of parents wishing to give their children away so that they may be supported but owing to limited means cannot accept them.' At Tshatshu's location, where Magistrate Fielding likewise reported 'not one case', the missionary John Brownlee found 'a number of children suffering want of food, and some cases of dysentery which must soon prove fatal'. Magistrate Ayliff noticed 'no cases of great destitution' in Toyise's country, but Dr Wilmans found too many to report fully. He contented himself with mentioning 'one whole family consisting of sons, father, grandfather and great-grandfather . . . all meagred to skeletons, unable to work for support, having before their eyes a dreadful death'.[48] Catarrh, diarrhoea, headache and burning pains in the stomach were all common. Nor was it necessary to travel to the remote rural areas to witness the devastation.

> Every day King Williams Town was thronged and its inhabitants
> distressed at the sight of emaciated living skeletons passing from house
> to house. Dead bodies were picked up in different parts within and
> around the limits of the town, and scarcely a day passed over that
> [Xhosa] — men, women or children were not found in a dying state from
> starvation. My consulting room was every day surrounded with
> emaciated creatures craving food, having nothing to subsist on but roots
> and the bark of the mimosa, the smell of which appeared to issue from
> every part of the body, and to whom it would be a mockery to say, you
> must seek employment, or proceed on to the Colony.[49]

In July and August 1857, 99 persons died of starvation in the hospital
itself.

Although the Kaffir Relief Committee did not share the government
view of distress as mostly native exaggerations, and although it was
founded expressly without the permission of Governor Grey and
Commissioner Maclean (most opportunely out of town when the first
meeting was held),[50] it nevertheless exerted itself to the utmost to win
the approval of the colonial authorities. Its opening statement made
that clear.

> Care is being taken that the succour be so directed as in no wise to
> interfere with that system of support of which the Government has
> assumed the responsibility. . . . The primary object of the Committee
> will be to supplement the action of Government, by placing within the
> sphere of Government influence and assistance a class of people who
> might otherwise never live to come within its reach. . . . The Committee
> will strengthen the hands of the Government in the wise endeavour it is
> making so to use the existing crisis as to secure the permanent
> advantage not only of the needy objects of its sympathy, but also of the
> whole of South Africa.[51]

The Kaffir Relief Committee defined its field of operations very
narrowly in order to avoid obstructing government plans. Its main task
was to accommodate the overflow from the Native Hospital, persons
who, while not actually afflicted by any specific disease, were
nevertheless dying of starvation. Since such people were unable to eat
the usual government ration of bread and meat, they were fed more
digestible foods and sheltered until they were strong enough to be sent
into labour service. The Committee also originally intended to search
the neighbouring roads and bushes for the dying, but dropped this
plan when they found that they could not even care for all those Xhosa
already in King William's Town.

The Kaffir Relief House consisted of five pensioners' cottages,
accommodating about 100 people. Consideration was given to building
Xhosa huts as well, but this was rejected for fear that it would
encourage 'vagabondage'. 'Inmates', as the Committee called them,

were admitted only after referral by the Native Hospital. Lady volunteers came down twice a day to feed the children sago and arrowroot. Gentlemen supervised the preparation of meat-flavoured soup, thickened with rice and barley in a huge outdoor boiler. The menu was modelled on the charitable kitchens of the Crimean War, but most of the grains and vegetables required were unavailable or too expensive. At eleven o'clock, Dr Wilmans came down from the hospital with new applicants, and inspected the inmates. At twelve o'clock, the police arrived to take those certified fit off to the magistrate to sign their labour contracts. Some mothers of sick children were allowed to remain, but were fully utilized cutting wood, cleaning pots, fetching water or smearing floors 'so that no able-bodied are idle'.[52] There can be no doubt that the Kaffir Relief Committee lived up to its promise to Commissioner Maclean:

> In no instance will an able-bodied person be permitted to receive relief, or one who had been restored to a state which enables him to earn a livelihood be continued as a recipient of charity.[53]

Town begging was put down by the distribution of 'mendicity tickets' to the charitably disposed. A 'mendicity ticket' entitled the recipient to one free meal at the Kaffir Relief House — and brought him or her within the ambit of the relief/rations/labour contract circuit operating in King William's Town.

4. Private Benevolence Is not Requisite

Despite the frantic efforts of the Kaffir Relief Committee to secure the good graces of the authorities, Governor Grey and Commissioner Maclean were disturbed by this new development. By acting first and asking permission later, the Committee had caught them unawares. They were unable to frame a response which would instantly squash the Committee's relief measures. Maclean informed the Committee that its proposals 'were not in my opinion calculated to interfere with the plans of the Government'. He permitted the use of the pensioners' cottages, reminded the Committee that the demand for labour was greater than the supply, and warned it to relieve only those Xhosa about to proceed to labour service.[54]

Grey, however, was not prepared to leave it at that. He opened his attack on the Kaffir Relief Committee by refusing to print its appeal in the Government Gazette,[55] and then set out to subvert the two most important local committees established outside King William's Town to raise funds for the Relief House. In Grahamstown, local officials obstructed the Committee's appeal by making it known 'that

Government is prepared to render to the natives all the assistance they require, and as a consequence of course, that private benevolence is not requisite'. Such unofficial hints were enough to deter the charity of the Grahamstown branch, which stalled on transferring the relief funds collected, informing Stair Douglas in King William's Town that it required further information.[56]

In Cape Town, the Bishop and the Attorney General informed the local philanthropists that it would be better to entrust their charitable money to Chief Commissioner Maclean. They stressed that the government was itself perfectly capable of relieving all the truly destitute. The problem was that the Xhosa were 'a very difficult people to deal with'. They wanted to be supported in idleness and they had no desire for work. Profitable employment was readily available for hundreds of Xhosa but they were not coming forward. The Attorney General rattled off a great deal more of this humbug, but at least one of his statements was sincere. 'It is impossible in British Kaffraria to separate private charity from public policy,' he said. Grey and his executive council were worried that the activities of the Kaffir Relief Committee threatened their plans. Clearly, it had to be eliminated.[57]

The first intimation the Committee had of this intention was the letter from its Grahamstown branch asking for more details of its activities. In his reply, Stair Douglas expressed his surprise at the Grahamstown officials' contention that private benevolence was not required. The government, he wrote, undertook no relief work as such beyond the issue of rations to those departing for labour in the Colony. The magistrate had no shelter but the jail, and the rations he issued would kill the majority of the starving. Anticipating the objection that his committee abetted the idlers and the won't-works, Douglas proudly pointed out that 'Our Relief House is in fact an Immigration Depot which keeps people together till the Magistrate be ready to send them on.'[58]

At the same time the members of the Relief Committee wrote to Maclean in the hope that he would reiterate, perhaps publicly, his earlier statement that the measures of the Committee did not interfere with those of the government.[59] They were disappointed. Not only did Maclean make no such statement, but he bitterly attacked the was not an appeal for funds but a request for government approval — Maclean concluded by stating in the bluntest possible manner that the Committee would get no assistance whatsoever from the public funds.[60]

The most influential newspaper in the Eastern Province, the *Grahamstown Journal*, turned against the Committee the very next day. Up to this point it had maintained a mildly favourable attitude, but now, making up for lost time, it drew a distinction between 'feelings and sympathies' on the one hand, and 'sense and reason' on the other. The trouble was that the Colony's 'reason and calculation had been utterly overborne in the presence of the deep distress and starving misery of the human sufferers'. The schemes of the Kaffir Relief Committee would lead to an increase in the price of food, and to a falling off of white immigration. Even worse, 'every [Xhosa] then that is saved from starvation . . . is just one more enemy fattened and rendered effective at our expense. We cannot hope that gratitude will quench a single spark of that enmity.' The temptations of relief would draw large masses of starving wretches into the Colony. Even if 'prudential motives' could not eliminate the impulses of those hell-bent on charity, the *Journal* hoped that they might guide the flow. Charitable funds should all be placed under government control.[61]

The Kaffir Relief Committee stood its ground as well as it could. Surrounded as they were by the horror all around them, its members could not understand why they were being attacked so vehemently.

> The dead were around the Town, and the dying were in the streets. It was a fact to which no eye here was blind, that whatever preparation had been made, and whatever exertions were in progress, they had not sufficed to meet these cases, men, women and children were dying notwithstanding them — It was a sad thing to live in the presence of so much misery, to have witnessed it idly would have been wicked.[62]

The Committee proved without any difficulty that the number of Xhosa in the streets of King William's Town had declined since the commencement of its work, and that the notion of thousands streaming into town on account of the Relief House was nonsense. Dr Fitzgerald vouched for the fact that all those treated in the Relief House were truly destitute and urgently in need of care.[63]

But Grey was implacable. On 25 August 1857, he wrote a deliberately insulting dispatch on Kaffir Relief, addressed to the Lieutenant-Governor.[64] The document is a superb example of Grey's distinctive style of invective: vicious, exaggerated and recklessly untruthful. It began with the usual government claims that its relief measures were being misrepresented. The starving Xhosa had not forsaken their original intention of destroying the Colony, and should be treated with caution. Then followed the well-worn argument about indiscriminate charity attracting destitute masses to King William's Town, the imagined invasion now reaching epic proportions.

> It should be remembered that large numbers of Zulu's from Panda's country are at the present moment pressing into Natal, through which country they filter into Kaffraria, whence, if care be not taken, we shall draw them down upon our own border, and again bring streams of new coloured races into that very territory which His Excellency was hoping to have filled up with a European population.

Who but the sagacious Governor Grey could have appreciated the powerful attraction of Kaffir Relief House soup? It would have been a great marvel, as one observer put it, 'if the Zulu will come through the rich corn lands of Natal to the vast graveyard of King Williams Town'.[65]

With pitiful optimism, the Kaffir Relief Committee attempted to persuade the Governor that he had misunderstood their intentions. Stair Douglas responded to the published attack by writing directly to the Governor, enclosing the Committee's correspondence with Maclean.[66] Dr Fitzgerald wrote another long letter to Maclean demonstrating the extent of the starvation and the usefulness of the Relief Committee.[67] A correspondent signing himself 'A.B.C.' wrote to the *Grahamstown Journal*, exposing the inadequacy of the relief afforded by Magistrate Reeve at Middledrift and showing that a starving Xhosa on the King William's Town/Fort Beaufort road could expect only one meal in eight days.[68] A public meeting of the Grahamstown Relief Committee rejected the Catholic Bishop's suggestion that they turn over their subscriptions to the Governor, and supported instead Bishop Cotterill's motion to carry on regardless.[69]

This resistance only increased Grey's resolve to destroy the Kaffir Relief Committee. His exalted position as Governor enabled him to slap down the individual members of the Committee without ever bothering to respond to their honest representations. The Bishop of Grahamstown was curtly informed that Grey was 'too busy' to add to his published letter on Kaffir Relief.[70] The magistrate of King William's Town was denounced by Maclean as a 'complete tool' of the Committee and reprimanded for showing an official document to one of its members.[71] Dr Fitzgerald was reproached for giving his old patron the Governor 'considerable pain' by his misrepresentations, and he humbly begged forgiveness, asking Grey to remember 'that I am human and subject to all defects'.[72]

Stair Douglas was the only Committee member to go down with all guns still firing. Maclean was sure that Douglas was trying to blacken his name in order to succeed him as Chief Commissioner. 'Mr Stair Douglas is a candidate for civil employment in this Colony,' he confided privately to Grey.[73] He further believed that Douglas was the mysterious 'A.B.C.' who had exposed the deficiencies of the government relief operation at Middledrift.[74] Douglas's response to Grey's published letter on Kaffir Relief further infuriated the authorities by asserting that the Committee's duty to God was higher than their duty to the government. But it also gave Grey the opportunity of crushing the Committee.

Since Grey had criticized the Kaffir Relief Committee in public, Douglas probably assumed that he was entitled to respond directly. But in terms of the formal etiquette of the day, all letters written in British Kaffraria were required to pass through the hands of Chief Commissioner Maclean. Douglas wrote directly to Grey, a breach of official procedure which gave the Governor the opening he required. He returned Douglas's letter without comment, leaving it to Maclean to deliver the *coup de grâce.*

> As an officer in Her Majesty's Colonial Service at Mauritius, you must have well known that this was the line of proceeding which the rules of the Public Service required you to follow — and that it is His Excellency's intention to make your breach of that rule, that ground of complaint against you to Her Majesty's Government, and at the same time to complain to them of the misrepresentations regarding the proceedings of the Government which you have made in the public prints, and which have had a mischievous and embarrassing effect.[75]

The Kaffir Relief Committee, in whose name Douglas had written the offending letter, was stunned. With ruin and official disgrace staring them in the face, Stair Douglas and the other 'official' members of the Committee, mostly army officers, resigned. The shocked rump of the Committee voted to dissolve itself.[76] There were a few kicks of protest. The Methodist minister refused to participate in the government's relief programme until it withdrew its 'slurs' on the Committee.[77] There was some thought of publishing the Kaffir Relief correspondence in full, but Grey stopped this by drawing up yet another vicious memorandum accusing the Committee of various further crimes, most notably Anglican domination.[78] Stair Douglas sailed for England to defend himself in person. Grey refused his request for details of the accusations to be brought against him, saying that he was too busy dealing with the Indian Mutiny crisis, but that he would attend to the matter 'when I have the time'.[79] He never did, and Stair Douglas must have greatly puzzled the Colonial Office in his attempts to defend himself against charges which had never been brought. In any case, it hardly mattered. The Kaffir Relief Committee was dead.

Grey and Maclean adhered closely to the principles of 'true charity' as generally understood in Victorian Britain. They distinguished between 'real distress' on the one hand, and mere 'want' which did not deserve 'gratuitous relief' or 'indiscriminate benevolence'. The acid test of candidates for relief was whether or not they were 'unable to work'. At a stretch this might include those who were unable to travel long distances on foot, but, by and large, only the 'young and infirm already found deserted by their friends' qualified for the category of 'real distress', and even these were to be sent on their way as soon as possible.[80] 'Everything is being done by Government in meeting the wants of the people,' Maclean assured Sandile, 'the destitute are fed, and labour is provided for all who are able or willing to work.'[81]

Maclean acknowledged that great destitution and distress prevailed and that 'many pitiable sights' were to be seen. But that was the Xhosa's own fault, for refusing the government's generous offers of labour contracts. Many gullible observers were misled by Xhosa exaggerations, and were too easily fooled by the mere appearance of starvation. Magistrate Reeve of Middledrift, whose relief operation had been severely criticized in the *Grahamstown Journal*, exposed these welfare scroungers in a dispatch which drew Grey's particular approval.[82] Some of these ungrateful people had deceived Captain Reeve into accommodating them in the prisoners' hut and feeding them at government expense! Alerted by such deceptions, Reeve's police had begun searching relief applicants, and had found that many of them had 'considerable sums of money' concealed about them. One 'very miserable looking [Xhosa] . . . from the man's appearance I should have said he was a starving man' was in fact possessed of a tin box containing nine golden sovereigns. The moral was clear: the emaciated Xhosa on your doorstep was in all probability a rather wealthy man — he was starving to death only in order to elicit sympathy and avoid an honest day's work! Many of the deaths had occurred only because the government ration was too generous.[83] Many Xhosa had died out of sheer stubbornness, Maclean insisted. 'The vast majority of cases [of dead Xhosa] would not accept the relief so freely proferred to them.'[84]

The colonial press and public enthusiastically supported the government's version of true charity. The *King William's Town Gazette* continued to urge that 'the healthy and strong — whether men, women and children — should obtain a living by the sweat of their brow and not from the resources of pseudo-philanthropy'. The notorious laziness of the Xhosa 'would induce him to walk twenty miles for the mere chance of a laborless living', and relief was certain to attract 'the whole of Kaffirland' to King William's Town. The *Grahamstown Journal* followed up its earlier exhortations to 'guide the flow' of charity by bravely declaring that it was its public duty 'however unthankful the task' to support the Governor.

> All will admit, considering that the lives of our children, and our own, that the property and civilization of the country are all at stake, as well as the lives of the [Xhosa], that this Government plan .. should meet with no obstacle in the opinions and feelings of individuals. Here alone can we hope for the exercise of the largest benvolence; a benevolence which will include the Colonist as well as the [Xhosa].

Mr J.J. Meintjes, speaking at a Kaffir Relief meeting in Graaff-Reinet, felt obliged to assure his charitable audience 'that there could be no intention to feed [Xhosa] in idleness. He believed that they would be fed no longer than was absolutely required to bring them to the Colony and employ them for their benefit.' Newspapers further westward were more concerned with the utilization of Xhosa labourers once they arrived than with the means employed to get them there. The *Zuid Afrikaan*, most notably, reminded its readership that female labour in the fields was a 'national institution' among the Xhosa, and urged that Xhosa women be employed as agricultural labourers as well as domestic servants. Even the liberal *South African Commercial Advertiser* expressed fear of the 'barbarous and savage millions of the interior' and urged that 'of benevolence, as of courage, the best part is discretion'.[85]

The other sort of charity, the sort so blasted and condemned by worthy citizens and officials, was defended only very occasionally, mainly in the form of letters to the press. One of the few to assert unequivocally that humane charity should take priority over political considerations was John Richards, a Methodist minister from Grahamstown.

> We have nothing to do with the policy of emptying [Xhosaland] into the Colony, be it right or wrong. We have a right to be charitable, and it is our duty to be so when helpless destitution is before us, and no man has a right to interfere with the exercise of that charity in a way such as best commends itself to our judgement. I neither advocate nor oppose any political schemes with reference to [Xhosaland]. I simply let them alone, and say that as a Committee for relieving [Xhosa] destitution we have nothing to do with them.[86]

The great weakness of the Kaffir Relief Committee was that it never dared to assert the primacy of humane and moral action over the political decisions of government. On the contrary, it emphasized from the first 'that the succour be so directed as in no wise to interfere with that system of support of which government has assumed the responsibility'.[87] It devised a relief scheme which served, in its own words, as 'an Immigration Depot which keeps people together till the Magistrate be ready to send them on'.[88] Even after Grey had launched his merciless and unprovoked public attack, the Relief Committee persisted in interpreting the Governor's attitude as one of mis-understanding.[89] In a final attempt to assuage Grey's anger, it pledged itself to 'a line of conduct which shall be supplementary to the Government Scheme for inducing [Xhosa] to migrate to the Colony for service'.[90] Having thus failed to assert the right of private individuals to give whatever charity their consciences demanded, the Kaffir Relief Committee could not withstand repudiation by the very authorities whose approval it so ardently sought.

The most puzzling aspect of the affair is why exactly Grey and Maclean were so determined to break the Committee, a naturally obedient body 'responsive to the slightest hint from headquarters'.[91] The reason most often publicly urged, that it was drawing thousands of starving Xhosa to King William's Town, was as patently false as it was ridiculous. Even if this had been the case, it would have accorded perfectly with Grey's declared policies. At the same time that Grey was condemning Stair Douglas for bringing a 'ruthless and pitiless flood' on the Colony, he was sending John Crouch to the transKei to recruit even more.[92] The 302 Xhosa relieved by the Committee hardly posed a threat to his master plan. Of these, 116 were handed over to the magistrate and another 52 died, thus demonstrating beyond all shadow of a doubt that they were fit candidates for relief.[93] It was true, as Grey did not fail to point out, that 40 inmates escaped from the Relief House, but desertions of up to 60 per cent of travelling parties were not uncommon at the time.[94]

The theme that emerges most strongly from both the official and the private correspondence of Grey and Maclean is the fear that the efforts of the Committee were bringing discredit on the government. Some advocates of relief were indeed outspoken in their criticisms — J. Williams of Grahamstown, for example, who informed a meeting that 'the government or the officials had been very remiss in the performance of their duty', or A.B.C., who exposed conditions at Middledrift.[95] But even the mild comments ('imputing blame to the Government is far from my thoughts')[96] of Stair Douglas were an implicit criticism of official relief.

Of course, Grey could have come out into the open and frankly admitted that his relief scheme necessarily entailed death and starvation. Maclean came quite close to it, when he wrote, 'however painful the sight of such distress . . . any general relief would be neither politic nor true charity'.[97] But that was not Grey's style. In all his forty years of colonial service he never admitted to a worse fault than misplaced trust in treacherous colleagues. His whole reputation as a great administrator rested on his ability to hide his indifference towards the sufferings of individuals behind an extravagant display of concern for the Maori or the Xhosa as a people.[98] Far easier to blame the Kaffir Relief Committee.

Whatever personal reasons Grey and Maclean may have had for acting against the Relief Committee, the Cape press and public had none. Their objections to the Kaffir Relief Committee were in fact objections to the 'indiscriminate benevolence' which they mistakenly thought the Committee represented. Less inhibited than Governor Grey in their public expressions, they were forthright in asserting the priority of settler interest.

> We have no right whatever to neglect our duty to the Colony in endeavouring to perform what we think is our duty to the [Xhosa], on the contrary, we humbly deem that our first duty is to our country and our race.[99]

5. The True Charity of Governor Grey

The starving believers had few alternatives to the 'true charity' of Governor Grey. Some hundreds of the fit and the strong reached the comfort and safety of Mpondoland and Lesotho.[100] Many more headed for neighbouring Thembuland, where several of the waverers had hidden their cattle during the height of the movement.[101] The Thembu Regent, Joyi, was initially inclined to be sympathetic, but his sympathy declined as he found his own authority undermined by Fadana, the leader of the Thembu believers. Fierce fighting broke out in June 1857, and from that time on it was no longer safe for Xhosa to take refuge in Thembuland.

The Mfengu allies of the Cape Colony had ignored the prophecies of Nongqawuse and grown rich on cattle bought cheap from Xhosa believers. They had planted extensively when the believers had refused to cultivate, and had sold the produce of their labour to needy Xhosa at exorbitant prices.[102] But they also provided homes and shelter in exchange for labour and guard duties. They slaughtered cattle for the *amafaca* ('emaciated ones'), feeding them with the contents of the stomach until they were strong enough to eat the meat.[103] The colonial authorities were not, however, prepared to tolerate such humanity in their allies and forced the Mfengu to expel the Xhosa who had found refuge among them. Three hundred Xhosa who had taken shelter among the Oxkraal Mfengu were compelled to leave their hosts, and, in the Crown Reserve, two Xhosa committed suicide after repeated hounding by the 'native police'. In Kama's district, no fewer than 2,000 refugees were handed over to the colonial labour machine on the direct orders of Magistrate Reeve.[104]

Those who entered the Colony did not lose hope. Many of them carried large milk sacks in readiness for the great day which they still awaited.[105] It took only the smallest hint to re-ignite the millenarian expectations for which they had already suffered so much. A Methodist missionary, who somewhat tactlessly chose to preach on the topic of the Flood, inspired the remaining believers in Kama's country to collect huge piles of wood in preparation for the building of an ark.[106] The Indian Mutiny of 1857 sustained Mhala's last desperate efforts to evade his enemies and convinced many believers that the Indians, who were known to be black men like themselves, were the 'new people' predicted by Nongqawuse.[107] As late as 1859, many of the believers labouring on the farms around Cradock were still exchanging tales of the wonders and miracles which were coming to pass. The army of the uHlanga had destroyed the Governor in Cape Town, they said, and freed the Xhosa chiefs on Robben Island. Maqoma was gone to London to plead the Xhosa case directly to the Queen. Mlanjeni himself had appeared in Cradock, complete with a long beard of green slime. When the terrified whites had tried to bribe him, he had contemptuously thrown their money into the air where it had vanished. Twenty years after the Great Disappointment, there were still true believers who maintained that the fault was not with the prophecies but with the failure of the Xhosa to obey Nongqawuse's orders.[108]

Alas for the believers! The Brave New World was the fruit, not of their imagination, but of Governor Grey's. With the Kaffir Relief Committee safely out of the way, Grey and Maclean could proceed unchecked with their own system of relief. Dr Fitzgerald and the Native Hospital took over the Relief House and the soup kitchen, but steps were taken to ensure that benevolence did not get out of hand.[109] Maclean keenly scrutinized the relief lists submitted by the magistrates, and made many helpful suggestions for cutting these down.[110] Gawler, for example, was still feeding the family of Fusani, the man murdered for passing on information to the police. 'Is it necessary?' asked the Chief Commissioner, 'might not the men be taken in the police, or sent to the works or service?' Vigne was reprimanded for his indulgence towards females. 'Too much seems to be afforded to women,' he was told. 'The women ought to be sent for service in the Western districts if deserted.' As for Brownlee, he was much too generous to children under eight. 'Why not indenture deserted children at mission stations, or into respectable families?' Maclean suggested. The select few deemed worthy of relief were to be located in huts at the magistrate's own place in order to stop them secretly feeding their idle neighbours and relations.[111] A circular reminded the magistrates 'to lose no opportunity of sending into the Western Districts of the Colony the destitute wives and families of any men who have been transported'.[112] The government's relief plan was a great success. By the end of February 1858, a total of 25,362 Xhosa had been relieved. Of these, 87 per cent (22,150) were sent into the Colony as homeless labourers.[113]

The missions in Xhosaland, which Grey had initially conceived as the vanguard of the 'civilizing' process, played no part whatsoever in his schemes for reconstructing British Kaffraria after the Cattle-Killing. Most of the mission residents had relatives and friends among the believers, whom they helped to find food and accommodation on the mission stations. Hundreds of parents, unable to support their children, gave them up to the missionaries rather than expose them to a horrible death.[114] Even those chiefs who had formerly resisted the establishment of missions in their territories now looked to them as a valuable resource. 'Look after my country,' Sarhili asked the missionary Waters, 'Keep as many men as you can — drive away all strangers.'[115]

The colonial authorities, on the other hand, now came to distrust the missions which they viewed as Trojan horses through which the exiled Xhosa might re-enter the districts set aside for white occupation. Maclean was particularly hostile to missions, which he accused of 'indiscriminate benevolence', and he fretted over the possibility that they might serve as potential rallying points for the scattered Xhosa.[116] Even Grey, who softened some of Maclean's harsher decisions, opposed the blanket relief for children which the missions were striving to provide.

> I am not satisfied of the prudence of taking all their children into schools at certain localities thus almost necessitating the return of the parents to these parts, and certainly giving them great inducements to remain there instead of betaking themselves to an honest mode of livelihood.[117]

The easiest way to put down the missions was to deny them financial aid. Mission resources were genuinely unequal to the expense of relief, and from June 1857 they began turning away starving children whom they were unable to feed.[118] In refusing government funds to the Anglican Church, Grey made it clear that he disapproved of some of their missionaries, particularly William Greenstock who had carried messages for Mhala behind Gawler's back. Greenstock's mission of St Luke's was, moreover, an obstacle to the settlement of whites in Mhala's country. St Luke's was closed down, and its converts packed off to a new site under the care of a former convict chaplain, who embezzled its money and oppressed its converts but did not mind informing on Mhala.[119]

Missionaries like H.T. Waters, who distinguished himself by his 'somewhat severe discipline and very active employment',[120] were able to continue on their stations, but were soon confronted with difficulties relating to their newly acquired non-Christian residents. Before the Cattle-Killing, all the residents had been more or less inclined towards Christianity and willingly obedient to the discipline of the station. But those who came out of necessity were not nearly as obedient, and they were moreover determined to observe traditional rituals which the missionaries regarded as immoral. Many of these were expelled from the stations, among them the noted Gcaleka unbeliever Ngubo, who had thrashed Nongqawuse and called her a fake. From 1860 onwards, the missions launched an offensive against 'heathenish practices and customs' such as polygamy, circumcision and female initiation. This backfired badly on the Church as the Bishop of Grahamstown later admitted. 'Injudicious meddling in family matters, and the turning off of whole families . . . from Mission lands . . . is among the many causes why the progress of Christianity has been retarded in this country.'[121] Indeed it was. The net result of a decade's mission was to inspire the Gcaleka Xhosa with 'an inveterate hatred to the Gospel'. One of the former refugees told Tiyo Soga ten years later that 'of all sounds, that which grates most upon my ears is a church bell; I have been sickened with it in the past and I care not although I never hear it again'.[122]

The Cattle-Killing also enabled Grey to revive his pet project of a 'Kaffir College' in Cape Town. He had proposed just such a school to the Xhosa chiefs in 1855, but none of them were prepared to consider parting with their children. On the eve of the Great Disappointment, Sarhili had declined to send away one of his favourite daughters. 'No! No!' the King had cried, 'She is the child of my bosom. I cannot part with her.' Grey's interest in the scheme was unwittingly rekindled by Sandile in April 1857, when he asked Commissioner Brownlee to take care of three of his children. Maclean reacted sharply to the prospect of feeding Sandile's children at government expense, and issued

Brownlee with the following specific orders:

> I have forwarded your letter to His Excellency and until I hear his reply,
> I have to request you will not receive any more [of Sandile's]
> children. . . . I request to be informed whether Sandilli is prepared to
> hand over his children to Government to be educated and of course
> removed, for I see no other condition open for them.[123]

Grey was fascinated by this correspondence, and minuted, 'I am
anxious to have these children sent to me to take care of.'

From that moment, the pressure was on Sandile to give up his
children to the government. But the chief refused to send them away,
though he was quite willing to have them educated in Brownlee's
house. Grey continued to press for Xhosa children, and in October
1857, he was rewarded with a couple brought in by Mjuza, the son of
Nxele. Mjuza was hopeful that the Governor would appoint him in
Mhala's place, and, besides, he was under the impression that the
children would be sent to England. 'Tell Victoria that these are my
bones,' he said, indicating his own son, 'and she must take care of
them and look after me too.'[124]

Still Sandile refused his consent. He told Tiyo Soga, the Xhosa
missionary, that he had spent five days at the Anglican mission
watching the school there and that he did not approve of it at all. He
wanted his children educated at the Presbyterian mission which Soga
was about to establish near his Great Place.[125] But in the fury of
February 1858, with most of his brother chiefs arrested and an
expedition fitting out to attack Sarhili, Sandile felt that he could no
longer resist. His Great Son Gonya, his eldest daughter Emma, and
seventeen of his councillors' children were dispatched to Cape Town in
May. Several more Xhosa children followed in the succeeding months,
including the sons of Mhala, Phatho, Anta, and Kama, and several
grandchildren of Maqoma.[126]

The purpose of Grey's Kaffir College in Cape Town (later renamed
Zonnebloem) was to transform its pupils into black Englishmen.[127] The
boys were dressed in flannel shirts and moleskin trousers, and the girls
wore dresses and aprons. But although their education in English,
reading and arithmetic was not neglected, they were subjected to
Grey's emphasis on the 'discipline of honest industry'. The children
spent half the day working at trades such as carpentry and
dressmaking, though they drew the line at agricultural labour. They
were kept in almost total isolation, having little contact with the
outside world beyond their regular attendance at church on Sundays.
As the years passed by and Zonnebloem lost its novelty value, its
buildings decayed and its sanitary facilities deteriorated to an

'appalling' extent. The pupils contracted tuberculosis at an alarming rate (20 per cent actually died of it in 1868), and the flow of volunteers dried up.

Sandile was so affected by a seeing a photograph of his absent children that he conquered his fear of the sea and, in 1861, asked to be allowed to visit them in Cape Town.[128] Grey agreed, 'to give Sandilli confidence in himself, and in the kindness of the English people' and to witness for himself 'the greatness and the power of Great Britain'.[129] Far from being convinced that civilization was in any way desirable, Sandile returned even more determined to uphold Xhosa customs. He attempted to withdraw his daughter Emma from Zonnebloem for the purpose of arranging her marriage, but the Bishop of Cape Town refused to let her go.[130] Eventually, a compromise was arranged whereby Emma would marry Qeya, the heir-apparent to the Thembu throne, by Christian rites. This marriage, too, fell through because the Thembu people were not prepared to allow their future King to marry a convert. To prevent his second daughter, Victoria, from falling into the same trap as her sister, Sandile removed her from Tiyo Soga's church at Mgwali.[131] On the colonial side, Grey's successor barred any further enrolment of girls from Zonnebloem. As for Emma, she seemed bound for the eminently Christian life of a spinster mission teacher, but saved herself from this respectable fate by commencing an affair with a married man. Expelled from the mission, she lived happily ever afterwards, bearing her heathen husband five happily illiterate and non-Christian children.

Grey's dream of a self-reproducing black upper-class elite was thus frustrated. Not only that, but those Xhosa who did graduate from Zonnebloem or its sister institution in Grahamstown found it very difficult to make a place for themselves in nineteenth-century South Africa. Gonya, Sandile's Great Son and prospective successor, was rejected by most of his people because he had not been circumcised. On the other hand, white prejudice would not tolerate the employment of 'educated natives' in white areas. Far from taking a lead in the making of a new South Africa, as Grey had hoped, the unhappy graduates settled down in an uncomfortable and anomalous niche as 'native teachers' or court interpreters.[132]

Nor did they become British patriots. Far from recoiling in disgust at their heathen forebears, the students at Zonnebloem regarded Maqoma as quite the equal of the Duke of Wellington and repeatedly petitioned for the release of their imprisoned parents and grandparents. When the last of the Xhosa chiefs were released from Robben Island in 1869, their offspring followed them home. In 1880, College graduates Gonya Sandile and Kondile Mhala returned to the Western Province to complete their education, but not at Zonnebloem. On the Island.

Though Sir George Grey failed to win the hearts and minds of the Xhosa people, he was completely successful with their bodies. A total of 29,142 Xhosa registered for service in the Colony by the end of 1857, and an equal number must have passed through unregistered.[133] By the end of 1858, such labour-hungry districts as Graaff-Reinet and Beaufort West were completely saturated, and the employers of the Western Province were beginning to weigh up the social costs of a continuing Xhosa immigration ('they will murder us and drive us into the sea').[134] By the time the first labourers returned to Xhosaland, they found their old homesteads crammed into tiny villages or expropriated for white farms. Grey boasted that he had brought peace to Xhosaland. It was the same peace which Rome brought to Carthage.

Notes

1. GH 20/2/1 C. Brownlee-J. Maclean, 25 Aug. 1856.
2. *Grahamstown Journal*, 27 Dec. 1856.
3. London Missionary Society papers, Box 30, H. Kayser-L.M.S., 23 Jan. 1858; J. Brownlee-L.M.S., 5 Jan. 1858.
4. MIC 172/2, Reel 1, Cory Library, H. Waters Journal, 31 July, 9 Sept. 1856; *King William's Town Gazette*, 3 Jan. 1857; GH 8/30 C. Brownlee-J. Maclean, 7 Dec. 1856.
5. Microfilm ZP 1/1/217, Cape Archives, R. Birt-G. Grey, 3 Oct. 1856. For calculations of approximate mortality in the Cattle-Killing, see Chapter 10, Note 4.
6. J. Goldswain (1949), Vol. 2, p.191.
7. *Cape Argus*, 21 Feb. 1857; *King William's Town Gazette*, 28 March 1857.
8. *King William's Town Gazette*, 13 June 1857; MS 15413, Cory Library, R.F. Hornabrook, 'Cattle killing mania'.
9. *King William's Town Gazette*, 21 March 1857; Goldswain (1949), Vol. 2, p.194; GH 8/50 J. Crouch-J. Maclean, 29 Oct. 1857; MIC 172/2, Reel 1, Cory Library, W. Greenstock Journal, 22 Sept. 1857.
10. One is tempted to dismiss these reports as fantasy, but there seem to be a few well-attested cases. See Goldswain (1949), Vol. 2, pp.193-4; *Cape Argus*, 3 March 1858; GH 8/32 J. Crouch-J. Maclean, 2 July 1857; *King William's Town Gazette*, 31 Oct. 1857.
11. *King William's Town Gazette*, 26 Sept. 1857; MS 15413, Cory Library, Hornabrook, 'Cattle killing mania'; MS 3329, Cory Library, J. Ross-n.a. 30 Oct. 1856; Theal (1876), p.55.
12. BK 71 C. Brownlee-J. Maclean, 20 July, 1 Oct. 1857; MIC 172/2, Reel 1,

Cory Library, H. Waters Journal, 30 July 1857; GH 8/32 J. Maclean-F. Travers, 5 July 1857.

13. C. Brownlee (1916), p.137; Cory Interviews, Cory Library, No. 109, Somana, 24 Jan. 1910, No. 112, Maseti, Jan. 1910.

14. *Cape Argus*, 3 March 1858; *King William's Town Gazette*, 1 Aug. 1857; PR 3624, Cory Library, Letterbook of Dr J. Fitzgerald, Report on the state of the gaol in King William's Town, 15 March 1858; GH 8/32 Dr Wilmans-J. Fitzgerald, 2 July 1857; Burton (1950), p.73.x

15. Gqoba (1888), Part II.

16. GH 8/50 F. Reeve-J. Maclean, 23 Aug. 1857; Cory Interviews, Cory Library, No. 119, J. Crouch, 16 April 1913; *King William's Town Gazette*, 8 Aug., 31 Oct. 1857; Berlin Mission Archives, Abt.III, A. Kropf-B.M.S., Report for second half-year, 1857.

17. *Church Chronicle* (Grahamstown), Vol. 4 (1883), p.61.

18. Crowther (1981), pp.18, 25. It has not been possible for me to obtain all the relevant literature on English Poor Relief. I have found the following useful, though stronger on exposition than analysis: Finer (1952), Poynter (1969), Crowther (1981).

19. Poynter (1969), pp.42, 119.

20. Poynter (1969), p.136; Crowther (1981), p.43.

21. Finer (1952), p.47.

22. Finer (1952), p.25; Crowther (1981), p.21; J. Bronowski and B. Mazlish, *The Western Intellectual Tradition* (Harmondsworth, 1963), p.496.

23. *Minutes and Proceedings of Cape of Good Hope Legislative Council on Law of Master and Servant* (Cape Town, 1848), p.22; R. Godlonton, quoted in Kirk (1980), p.233.

24. House of Assembly Debates, 18 July 1854; *Graaff-Reinet Herald*, 14 June 1854; *Grahamstown Journal*, 5 Aug. 1854.

25. Cape of Good Hope, *Votes and Proceedings, Select Committee on Frontier Defence* (1855), p.v.

26. BK 70 C. Brownlee-J. Maclean, 2 Aug. 1856; F. Reeve-J. Maclean, 15 Oct. 1856.

27. Quoted in Rutherford (1961), p.355.

28. Government notice published in the *Grahamstown Journal*, 5 Sept. 1857.

29. GH 8/30 J. Maclean-Magistrates, 7 Nov. 1856.

30. GH 8/30 J. Maclean-Magistrates, 7 Nov. 1856. A similar circular was issued in March 1857, BK 406 J. Maclean-Magistrates, 10 March 1857. Maclean referred in subsequent correspondence to an order of his, dated 20 Sept. 1856, authorizing the issue of rations. I have not been able to find a copy of this order, either in Maclean's dispatch book (BK 406), or in the volume of his circulars to magistrates (BK 114), or enclosed in his dispatches to Grey. Whatever instructions Maclean may have issued on that date, he did not do much by way of disseminating them.

31. GH 8/32 C. Brownlee-J. Maclean, 17 June 1857.

32. BK 114 J. Maclean-Magistrates, 9, 10 June 1857.

33. GH 8/32 Memo of conversation between the Chief Commissioner and Sandile, 11 Sept. 1857, enclosed in Schedule 493, 14 Sept. 1857.

34. GH 8/32 Enclosed in Schedule 47, 3 Aug. 1857.

35. GH 30/4 F. Travers-J. Maclean, 29 July 1857.

36. The Kaffir Pass Act was largely motivated by the large number of Xhosa

who deserted the official parties and wandered off to find work on their own as soon as they were inside the Colony. In one case, only 17 out of an original 122 Xhosa arrived at their appointed destination (CO 2950 W. Surmon-W. Currie, 27 July 1857). Over-enthusiastic application of this law — for example, to children travelling with their parents — led to at least two cases of babies sentenced to imprisonment with hard labour (Marginal note by R. Rawson on R. Southey-Col. Secretary, 29 Aug. 1857).

37. Acts 23, 27, 24 and 22 of 1857; *Grahamstown Journal*, 13 June 1857.
38. GH 8/32 Schedule 483, August 1857.
39. BK 65 R. Taylor-J. Maclean, 9 June 1857, gives one application for 1,000 servants.
40. *Grahamstown Journal*, 11 July 1857; *Cape Argus*, 25 July 1857.
41. Acc 611/7 R. Rawson-R. Southey, 20 Nov. 1857.
42. *Cape Argus*, 1 April 1858.
43. *Graaff-Reinet Herald*, 28 Nov. 1857, 27 March 1858; *Cape Argus*, 1 April, 11 May 1858; GH 8/35 J. Maclean-F. Travers, 29 April 1858. Hart, naturally enough, denied that he was staging an auction — just arranging his commission.
44. BK 71 C. Brownlee-J. Maclean, 12 June 1858; BK 78 Information received from a native, 4 April 1858; *Anglo-Germania*, 1 Feb. 1858; *King William's Town Gazette*, 27 Feb. 1858.
45. GH 30/12 G. Grey-H. Cotterill, 4 June 1857; GH 22/9 H. Cotterill-G. Grey, 1 Sept. 1857.
46. GH 8/32 J. Maclean-F. Travers, 5 July 1857.
47. *King William's Town Gazette*, 18, 25 July 1857.
48. GH 8/32 H. Lucas-J. Maclean, 13 June 1857; GH 8/32 H. Kayser-H. Lucas, 18 June 1857; GH 8/32 J. Ayliff-J. Maclean, 15, 25 June 1857; J. Brownlee-J. Maclean, 26 June 1857; GH 8/32 Dr Wilmans-J. Fitzgerald, 2 July 1857.
49. GH 8/32 J. Fitzgerald-J. Maclean, 30 Aug. 1857.
50. The Kaffir Relief Committee later claimed that they had been unable to contact Maclean at his coastal cottage. Maclean responded that it would have been easy for them to get in touch with him if they had tried. This time it is probably Maclean who was telling the truth. The Kaffir Relief Committee were rightly nervous of Maclean, and quite conceivably used his temporary absence as an excuse for failing to consult him.
51. Kaffir Relief Committee advertisement, *King William's Town Gazette*, 18 July 1857.
52. There is a detailed description of the Relief Houses in S. Douglas-R. Roberts, 12 Aug. 1857, published in the *Grahamstown Journal*, 22 Aug. 1857.
53. GH 8/32 Kaffir Relief Committee-J. Maclean, 3 Aug. 1857.
54. GH 8/32 J. Maclean-S. Douglas, 6 Aug. 1857. A more detailed account of the proceedings summarized in this section may be found in Peires (1984).
55. CO 694 H. Cotterill-G. Grey, 17 Aug. 1857; CO 694 G. Grey-H. Cotterill, 22 Aug. 1857; GH 22/9 H. Cotterill-G. Grey, 1 Sept. 1857.
56. GH 8/32 R. Roberts-S. Douglas, 17 Aug. 1857.
57. *South African Commercial Advertiser*, 18 Aug. 1857.
58. S. Douglas-R. Roberts, 14 [sic] Aug. 1857, *Grahamstown Journal*, 1 Sept. 1857.
59. GH 8/32 Kaffir Relief Committee-J. Maclean, 21 Aug. 1857.

60. GH 8/32 J. Maclean-J. Douglas, 24 Aug. 1857.
61. *Grahamstown Journal*, 25 Aug. 1857.
62. GH 8/32 J. Douglas-J. Maclean, 31 Aug. 1857.
63. GH 8/32 J. Fitzgerald-J. Maclean, 30 Aug. 1857.
64. *Grahamstown Journal*, 8 Sept. 1857.
65. *Grahamstown Journal*, 12 Sept. 1857.
66. GH 8/32 Schedule 499, 28 Sept. 1857, contained the original of this letter. It was returned to Stair Douglas for reasons to be explained below. I have not been able to find a copy of it.
67. GH 8/32 J. Fitzgerald-J. Maclean, 15 Sept. 1857.
68. *Grahamstown Journal*, 19 Sept. 1857.
69. *South African Commercial Advertiser*, 12 Sept. 1857.
70. Cotterill saw a copy of Grey's letter to the Lieutenant-Governor before it was published. He wrote to Grey asking Grey to refrain from casting such aspersions on himself and the rest of the Committee. Not only did Grey go ahead regardless, but — in typical Grey fashion — lifted a phrase in Cotterill's letter out of its context and twisted it to suit his own purposes. By way of rebutting Grey's charge that the Committee was drawing a flood of unwanted black immigrants into the Colony, Cotterill pointed out that the government itself had encouraged immigration by opening the drifts across the rivers. Grey caused a reply to be published saying that the river drifts were planned a long time before the Cattle-Killing, and that the opening of them had nothing to do with the relief question. Anyone who had not read Cotterill's original letter (which Grey did not publish) would have concluded that the Bishop was a complete fool. GH 22/9 H. Cotterill-G. Grey, 1 Sept. 1857; CO 694 H. Cotterill-G. Grey, 3 Sept. 1857; CO 5106 R. Rawson-H. Cotterill, 9 Sept. 1857.
71. GH 8/32 Schedule 495, 21 Sept. 1857, note by Maclean; GH 8/50 J. Maclean-G. Grey, 21 Sept. 1857.
72. GH 8/32 Schedule 488, 3 Sept. 1857; GH 8/50 J. Maclean-G. Grey, 21 Sept. 1857; GH 8/32 Schedule 499, 28 Sept. 1857, marginal note by Grey; GH 8/32 GH 8/32 Schedule 511, 15 Oct. 1857, note from Maclean enclosing letter from Fitzgerald, 12 Oct. 1857.
73. GH 8/50 J. Maclean-G. Grey, 27 Aug. 1857. See also GH 8/50 J. Maclean-G. Grey, 21 Sept. 1857, in which Maclean complains that 'Their [the Committee's] appeals to you [Grey] look rather like an attempt to prove me the culprit.'
74. GH 20/2/1 J. Maclean-G. Grey, 24 Sept. 1857.
75. GH 8/32 J. Maclean-S. Douglas, 26 Sept. 1857.
76. *Grahamstown Journal*, 3 Oct. 1857; *King William's Town Gazette*, 3 Oct. 1857.
77. GH 8/33 Schedule 512, 15 Oct. 1857.
78. GH 8/50 J. Maclean-G. Grey, 29 Oct. 1857; GH 20/2/1 Memo by Grey, 21 Sept. 1857.
79. GH 8/33 S. Douglas-R. Taylor, 15 Oct. 1857; GH 8/33 Schedule 513, 19 Oct. 1857.
80. BK 114 J. Maclean-Magistrates, 9, 10 June 1857.
81. GH 8/32 Schedule 493, 14 Sept. 1857.
82. BK 85 F. Reeve-J. Maclean, 30 Sept. 1857.
83. GH 8/32 H. Lucas-J. Maclean, 13 June 1857.

84. GH 8/32 J. Maclean-J. Douglas, 10 Sept. 1857.
85. *King William's Town Gazette*, 4, 18 July 1857; *Grahamstown Journal*, 1 Sept. 1857; *Graaff-Reinet Herald*, 5 Sept. 1857; *South African Commercial Advertiser*, 12 Sept. 1857.
86. *Grahamstown Journal*, 19 Sept. 1857. See also letter by 'Fair Play' in *Grahamstown Journal*, 25 July 1857.
87. *King William's Town Gazette*, 18 July 1857; GH 8/32 Kaffir Relief Committee-J. Maclean, 3 Aug. 1857.
88. *Grahamstown Journal*, 1 Sept. 1857.
89. *South African Commercial Advertiser*, 12 Sept. 1857.
90. GH 8/32 S. Douglas-J. Maclean, 13 Sept. 1857.
91. *King William's Town Gazette*, 12 Sept. 1857.
92. GH 8/32 Authority and instructions given by the Chief Commissioner, 7 Sept. 1857.
93. *King William's Town Gazette*, 3 Oct. 1857.
94. On one occasion, only 50 out of 150 Xhosa who left Elands Post arrived at Fort Beaufort, less than 50 kilometres away, *South African Commercial Advertiser*, 3 Oct. 1857. Another party lost 222 out of 255 over a similar distance, and a third lost 105 out of 122. CO 1950 R. Southey-R. Rawson, 13 Aug. 1857; CO 1950 W. Surmon-W. Currie, 27 July 1857.
95. *Grahamstown Journal*, 15 Aug., 19 Sept. 1857.
96. *Ibid.*, 1 Sept. 1857.
97. GH 8/32 J. Maclean-F. Travers, 5 July 1857.
98. Consider, for example, Grey's reproach to R. Taylor, the magistrate of King William's Town, who had told the Relief Committee that his instructions did not permit him to issue appropriate food to starvation victims: 'With my known desire for the welfare of the [Xhosa], after the expenses I had incurred, and after the efforts I had made for the relief of even ordinary cases of sickness amongst them, [how could any government officer believe that] he would have been justified in letting them die in the streets from want of the proper articles of food?' GH 20/2/1 Memo by G. Grey, 21 Sept. 1857.
99. *Grahamstown Journal*, 1 Sept. 1857.
100. *King William's Town Gazette*, 16 May 1857, 2 Jan. 1858; CO 2949 J. Warner-R. Southey, 18 Feb. 1857.
101. BK 89 Memorandum of information communicated, 25 April 1857; GH 8/50 H. Waters-J. Maclean, 7 July 1857.
102. *King William's Town Gazette* 17 Jan., 4 April 1857; *Cape Argus*, 21 Jan. 1857.
103. Interview with M. Ngovane, Majonga Location, Willowvale District, 15 Nov. 1975; Kropf-Godfrey (1915), p.100.
104. MIC 172/2, Cory Library, USPG Archive, Journal of W. Greenstock, 6 April 1859; CO 2951 R. Southey-R. Rawson, 31 Dec. 1857; BK 24 (?)-J. Maclean, 30 March 1857; BK 86 F. Reeve-J. Maclean, 5 Sept. 1857.
105. BK 71 C. Brownlee-J. Maclean, 18 May 1857.
106. BK 2 J. Miller-J. Maclean, 2 Sept. 1858; BK 2 Information received from a trustworthy native, 24 Aug. 1858.
107. BK 2 Report of a spy, 16 Oct. 1858; BK 89 Secret information, 2 Feb. 185[8].
108. BK 3 J.C. Warner-Capt. Smyth, 12 April 1859; Theal (1877), p.288.
109. *King William's Town Gazette*, 17 Oct. 1857.

110. See Maclean's comments on GH 8/32 Schedule 494, 17 Sept. 1857.
111. BK 114 Circular to special magistrates, 1 Oct. 1857.
112. BK 114 Circular, 16 Oct. 1857.
113. GH 8/34 Schedule 25, 22 Feb. 1858.
114. Goedhals (1979), p.46.
115. MIC 172/2, Cory Library, USPG Archives, Journal of H.T. Waters, Reel 8, 9 Jan. 1858. See also the case of Mhala [Ch. VII/4].
116. GH 8/32 J. Maclean-F. Travers, 5 July 1857; Goedhals (1979), p.82; BK 2 G. Grey-H. Cotterill, 8 Feb. 1858; GH 8/50 J. Maclean-G. Grey, 17 Sept. 1857.
117. GH 30/12 G. Grey-H. Cotterill, 7 July 1857.
118. GH 8/32 H. Kayser-H. Lucas, 18 June 1857; Goedhals (1979), p.44; GH 8/32 W. Greenstock-J. Gawler, 26 June 1857.
119. MIC 172/2, Cory Library, USPG Archives, Reel 2, H. Cotterill-Bullock, 9 June, 7 Aug. 1857; MS 16713/3 H. Cotterill-H. Kitton, 18 Jan. 1859; Goedhals (1979), p.32; GH 20/2/1 C. Lange-J. Maclean, 9 March 1858.
120. MIC 172/2, Cory Library, USPG Archives, Reel 2, H. Cotterill-USPG, 21 Jan. 1858.
121. BK 382 Schedule 52, 29 Aug. 1861; Goedhals (1979), p.108; Chalmers (1878), pp.263-8.
122. Chalmers (1878), pp.373, 392, 395.
123. GH 8/31 C. Brownlee-J. Maclean, 11 April 1857; GH 8/50 J. Maclean-C. Brownlee, 13 April 1857.
124. GH 8/50 J. Gawler-J. Maclean, 27 Oct. 1857.
125. MSB 139, South African Library, Cumming Papers, Item 17, Diary, 14 Sept. 1857.
126. For a list of the chief's children who went with the main party in February 1858, see GH 8/39 J. Maclean-G. Grey, 15 Aug. 1859. For an indication that some chiefs gave their consent voluntarily, see BK 82 M. Kayser-J. Maclean, 2 March 1858.
127. This section is based on J. Hodgson (1979). I am aware that there are other dimensions to the Kaffir/Zonnebloem College story, especially with regard to the role of Bishop R. Gray, but constraints of space and structure prevent me from entering more fully into the matter.
128. GH 8/35 C. Brownlee-J. Maclean, 9 Aug. 1858. It is clear from this letter that the idea of visiting Cape Town originated with Sandile himself and not with Grey or Brownlee.
129. Soga (1983), p.85. There is an account of Sandile's visit to Cape Town in Hodgson (1980).
130. For Emma Sandile, Hodgson (1987).
131. Brownlee (1916), pp.252-4.
132. Theal (1876), Vol. 2, p.59; Goedhals (1979), p.142.
133. GH 8/30 Schedule 372, 29 Dec. 1856; GH 8/31 Schedule 378, 10 Jan. 1857; GH 8/34 Schedule 6, 18 Jan. 1858; LG 410 J. Warner-R. Southey, 11 Sept. 1857.
134. Comment of Mr Blanckenburg, one of Cape Town's city commissioners, *South African Commercial Advertiser*, 1 Oct. 1857. The Xhosa immigration to the Western Province and the colonial reaction to it is a vast subject which cannot be dealt with here.

CHAPTER 9

Under Our Thumb

1. The Fadana Patrol

In the open plains between the Drakensberg and the northern border of Sarhili's territory lay the Thembu kingdom. The Cattle-Killing movement in Thembuland has not featured prominently in these pages, partly because of lack of information and partly because the circumstances there were somewhat different: Thembuland was outside British Kaffraria and hence beyond the immediate purview of Grey and Maclean. Since Thembuland lay north and east of Xhosa-land, it was shielded from the full impact of colonialism by the Xhosa kingdom, which provided it with a sort of protective barrier. The Thembu King and most of his subordinate chiefs regarded the colonial government as valuable allies in their historical rivalry with the more powerful Xhosa, and had consistently if passively supported the colonial side during the many frontier wars of the nineteenth century.

But the Tshatshu and the Ndungwana Thembu, who bore the brunt of settler expansionism from the northeastern Cape, shared most of the attitudes of the Xhosa to their south. The Tshatshu had lost both their lands and their chief, Maphasa, during the War of Mlanjeni, and Qwesha, chief of the Ndungwana, was deprived of his chieftainship by his son Darhala and the pro-colonial faction of his chiefdom. Their country was given out to settlers as the new district of Queenstown and they themselves were resettled in the so-called 'Tambookie Location' under the supervision of Agent J.C. Warner. It was among these dispossessed and relocated Thembu that the Cattle-Killing took deepest root. Despite all the efforts of the chiefs, the missionaries and the colonial authorities, about one third of the Thembu living in the Tambookie Location' killed their cattle and over half failed to plant.[1]

The leader of the Thembu believers was Chief Fadana, who had been Regent of the Thembu kingdom betwen 1830 and 1844, but whose political star had long since waned. Fadana had been chased into the 'Tambookie Location' along with all his neighbours after the War of Mlanjeni. He was living the quiet life of a minor chief, head of about twenty homesteads, when Nongqawuse's prophecies were heard in Thembuland.[2] Fadana was a relation by marriage of the strongly believing Maqoma, and he was moreover a diviner and magician of some repute. He was joined by Qwesha and some of his sons, who wished to recover the power they had lost to Darhala after 1853. Yeliswa, the widow of Maphasa, wavered but ultimately obeyed the order to kill. 'Umhlakaza spoke with God,' she said, 'therefore we must believe him.'[3] All the other Thembu chiefs came down firmly against the movement, most crucially the Regent Joyi, who visited the 'Tambookie Location' at Agent Warner's suggestion to lend his weight to the struggle against the prophecies. He was still there after the Great Disappointment, when the repentant Thembu believers cast themselves on his mercy:

> Your children have fallen; the cattle are dead; but now we see your [Joyi's] face we shall live and not die. We have been listening to a lie; we have been led astray by falsehood, and have got bewildered in a black mist. . . .
>
> Mercy! Mercy! Mercy! Your children have not so far gone astray that they may not be recovered; they have not all fallen; many have been wise enough not to listen to these lies; and many who have listened have only done so with one ear; the cattle are not all dead, and there is still a little corn left for our children to eat. Mercy! Mercy! Mercy! We are your children. Finish us, but remember that we are your children![4]

Fadana did not attend the meeting, nor was he ready to ask anyone for mercy or forgiveness. 'I will not die like a dog from starvation,' he declared, 'but will take cattle from whomever I can.'[5] The pace of the Cattle-Killing actually accelerated in parts of Thembuland as lung-sickness spread. One former unbeliever, suddenly seized by a conviction of the truth of the prophecies, caught his calves and slit their throats, then drove his fifty cattle into their kraal and stabbed them all in a single frenzy.[6] Fadana's men travelled the country in armed bands, attacking unbelieving Thembu who were trying to get their cattle out of the danger zone. They killed a poor Mfengu woman for trying to stop her husband killing his cattle. They plundered the cornpits of unbelievers 'for the children of Fadana' but they refused to eat the new maize just harvested.[7]

Even before the final extinction of all hope after June, Fadana was attacking unbelieving chiefs, wealthy commoners and Thembu police in a style more appropriate to a warrior chief than to a simple robber or a starving thief. He invited the Xhosa believers to join him, and even though Sarhili reluctantly declined, his close associate Bhotomane participated in the raids. In the midst of starvation and death, Fadana's followers briefly relived the heady feasting and celebration of the height of the Cattle-Killing. They slaughtered every beast they stole as soon as they got it home, and huge hunks of meat lay about their dwellings, some recently killed and some putrefying uneaten. Heads and hides of slaughtered cattle carelessly littered the courtyards and, in Fadana's own place, burnt cattle bones lay in heaps 12 metres round and 1 metre high.[8] Success bred success, and Fadana's fighting strength snowballed at the rate of fifty or so believers a week. At first they consciously restricted themselves to the cattle of fellow Thembu, but by the middle of July they had gained sufficient confidence to attack the convoys supplying provisions to the colonial troops and even to challenge patrols of the Frontier Armed and Mounted Police. As Fadana's power soared, the morale of the unbelievers collapsed, for what, they said, was the use of fighting one so blessed by the uHlanga? In early August, Fadana attacked Darhala, the collaborating son of his ally Qwesha, and got off with 200 cattle.[9]

By this time, it was clear to the colonial authorities that they had a genuine military threat on their hands: not a make-believe crisis brought about by an imaginary chiefs' plot, but a real crisis brought about by their refusal to send troops to support the unbelievers in the heart of the threatened areas. The Thembu unbelievers had been asking for military assistance ever since December 1856, just as the Xhosa unbelievers had done, and their pleas, like those of the Xhosa unbelievers, had been ignored. As late as July 1857, the colonial administration was trying to shuffle off its responsibility, refusing to commit white soldiers to the help of black unbelievers. Warner, the agent in charge of the 'Tambookie Location', strongly urged the government to abandon its scruples.

> If we are to be shackled and hampered by the quibbles of colonial law in managing a barbarous people like these . . . then all hope of restoring the country to a state of tranquility and security is at end. . . . If Colonial law is an insuperable obstacle, then declare martial law.[10]

The scruples restraining the colonial government were probably more political and financial than moral — they had to sell the Fadana campaign to the Cape Parliament, which paid for the Frontier Armed and Mounted Police — but there was a very real sense in which the commando eventually sent against Fadana breached a moral barrier when they crossed into the 'Tambookie Location'. They left behind them, as it were, a world in which behaviour was ordered by rules and regulations, and entered a new universe where norms and ethical standards no longer applied.

Commandant Walter Currie — 'half measures are no use, and leniency not understood by savages' — mustered a force of about 1,500 men against Fadana's 300 or 400 believers.[11] The 'friendly' unbelievers were evacuated in advance 'to prevent accidents', and they even agreed to burning the homesteads of their own people so that the expedition might 'have a clear field to work in'. Moving slowly over difficult terrain in wet weather, the patrol arrived at Fadana's place to find the chief and the main body of his followers gone. They found a number of women and children in the last stages of death by starvation, 'children often being unable to walk from the attenuation of the limbs'. Dogs were seen, half-starved, eating the corpses of other dogs. A few men were hiding in inaccessible rocks and caves from where some of the followers of the Thembu chief Maneli dragged and butchered them. 'We hunted this tribe . . . for three days,' reported Currie. 'Hunt' seems to have been a most appropriate word for what was happening. Fadana himself managed to get away to Sarhili's country, but the Xhosa King, under pressure himself, was persuaded by the missionary Waters to ask him to leave.

Meanwhile Currie's men rounded up Chief Qwesha and burned out all suspected believers and all Gcaleka — termed 'squatters' — resident in the 'Tambookie Location'.[12] There was no resistance. Finally, Inspector Griffiths tracked Fadana to a hut in Chief Fubu's country, and threatened to burn all its occupants alive unless they surrendered. Fadana was marched on foot back to Queenstown with a noose around his neck, arriving so lame and injured that he had to be carried further in a waggon. When they eventually stood trial, fortunately for them under colonial law, Fadana got seven years and Qwesha one. Currie got a knighthood.[13]

The Fadana patrol was, perhaps, nothing more than a minor incident on the periphery of the Cattle-Killing. Its historical significance lies less in what it did than in what it foreshadowed. A mixed colonial force had crossed the frontier and attacked a group of believers outside colonial territory. At least fifty unresisting and starving people had been shot and killed, many in a callous fashion. The rest of the people, equally unresisting, had been cleared out of their lands and Currie was suggesting that 144 square miles of the 'Tambookie Location' — mostly the land of the friendly unbelievers —

be given out to white settlers. And that was not all. The easy pickings in the Thembu location had given the bold commandant further ideas:

> The only thing that is worth staying here for now is to pitch into Krelie [Sarhili], which I think I could undertake without putting the Government to any expense. Krelie avoids us on all occasions and will not come into action, although twice I fired upon his people whilst passing through his country finding them mixed up with Fadana's. . . .
>
> Now I hope if the Governor finds fault with me for going too far, you must soften it down, but I agree with you that silence gives consent, and now that all is over as far as regards the Tambookies, why it does not much matter, but *I am itching to go in at Krelie.* We never had the [Xhosa] as a nation under our Thumb before, and it is our policy to keep them there.[14]

2. Eating Thorns

In the eight days preceding the Great Disappointment of 16-17 February 1857, popular support for the Cattle-Killing movement reached its height. That terrible failure split the believers into two factions. The less committed, those who had slaughtered some of their cattle but hidden the rest, now abandoned the prophecies and were only too glad to beg milk and pumpkins from their former enemies, the unbelievers.[15] But the hard core of believers, those who had ruined themselves beyond any possibility of recovery, continued to hope for the fulfilment of the prophecies on which they had staked their all. They heeded the confused excuses from the Gxarha and Mpongo rivers, and refused to seek work or eat new corn.[16] Chief among these inveterate believers was King Sarhili himself.

We last saw Sarhili just after the Great Disappointment, which left him 'very much disconcerted and does not know what to do with himself'. His feelings of guilt were not long sustained, however, and within a very short time he was once again blaming the unbelievers for the catastrophe and blocking their attempts to escape with their cattle. Nongqawuse had begun to speak again, and now she was joined by a new prophet named Tsimbi, who lived near Sarhili's capital of Hohita. Tsimbi told Sarhili that the new people, though disappointed by his failure to carry out Nongqawuse's orders, were merciful. More, they were poised to rise again from under the ground below the King's own Great Place (9 April 1857).[17] Once again the prophecy failed, and once again Sarhili sent a trusted messenger down to the Gxarha to investigate.

Bhotomane, the messenger, returned unimpressed. 'What is the use of sending me?' he asked. 'There is nothing there. The prophet is no one.'[18] With a heavy heart, Sarhili informed his followers that the prophecies should be abandoned, and that the people should gather all their breeding cattle to rebuild the national herds. The venerable chief Bhurhu, the King's uncle, took the lead in denouncing Sarhili's mismanagement to the assembled crowd. '[Sarhili] was sullen and gloomy, [Bhurhu] was savage, and the common people were furious.'[19] Despite the criticism, or perhaps because of it, the stubborn King refused to give up hope. A message from Mhlakaza, that the first of the new cattle had arrived, filled him with renewed expectation and he departed once again for the Gxarha, assuring the chiefs that they should not despair: the sayings of Mhlakaza would yet be revealed.[20]

The reappearance of lungsickness did much to encourage this last wave of cattle-killing, but many of the true believers lacked the cattle to kill. The emphasis of the prophecies switched to promises of abundant maize, and the faithful busied themselves with cleaning their threshing floors and digging enormous storage pits. Messengers from Sarhili hastened into the Colony and Thembuland, summoning the Gcaleka Xhosa to return from food and refuge to a land of inevitable death.[21]

Tsimbi the prophet died of starvation in August 1857, and Mhlakaza followed him in November.[22] The hopes of the believers died forever with the uneventful passage of the so-called 'moon of wonders' in June 1857. In as much as Sarhili still had a dream and a hope, it was to start afresh and build a new life by his own endeavours. He wanted to leave Hohita, the Great Place where he had known such evil days, and begin anew at Butterworth, which had been his father Hintsa's capital. He begged some cattle from neighbouring chiefs and redistributed most of them among his followers. About 150 families gathered at Butterworth and ploughed up extensive new grounds for planting in the new season. They traded their horses and guns for horned cattle and corn to keep themselves alive until the coming harvest. Despite these efforts, Sarhili and his immediate circle were still very much reduced in circumstances. In October 1857, the trader Crouch reported that Sarhili, who had once possessed more than 6,000 oxen of his own, was sharing the milk of seven cows with his brothers and sixty women and children. It was all he had. 'You may guess he is hard up,' wrote Crouch in a typically cynical vein, 'for I know for certain that there have been *two horses* eaten at [Sarhili's] place'.[23]

The ordinary Gcaleka were even worse off.

> Large numbers of people — the whole population of kraals may be seen in the open country digging for roots, others gather in the inside bark from the mimosa thorn, and all presenting an abject appearance. Their

cattle are all gone excepting a few milk cows — say one cow to 500 souls. They have a few goats from which they get a little milk. . . . Mothers show me their breasts without milk and hundreds of other sad signs of want. Krili [Sarhili] the chief is hungry, and comes to beg of me. . . .[24]

Sarhili's country was rapidly denuded of its people through death and emigration. The land was littered with unburied bodies: vultures eating men, and vultures eating dogs, and dogs eating men. Chief Bhurhu, who had been forced into the Cattle-Killing by his sons, was one of these. He refused to flee, but sat down to await death in the empty ruins of his deserted homestead. 'In spite of this thing that has come over me,' he declared, 'I will not serve another man. I will die here on the site of my village.' Crouch found him a few days later.

I rode over to his place. I found him dead in his hut and one of his wives — the dogs were eating him — his wife must have died the day before I got there — the dogs had eaten a great part of Buru while his wife was alive — this you may rely on as I saw them myself. There is scarcely a hut in this part of the country but you can find dead [Xhosa] in.[25]

Another notable victim was the Great Councillor Gxabagxaba, who was brought by his sons to St Marks mission destitute even of the will to live. In his youth, Gxabagxaba had killed the Landdrost of Graaff-Reinet, and he had fought in every single one of the Frontier Wars since 1811. He had never believed in the prophecies but had slaughtered his herds out of obedience only, saying that he had obtained all his cattle through the goodness of Sarhili and his father Hintsa, and must yield them up again when asked to do so. He died later the same year, quite literally a 'raving maniac'.[26]

Nor was the mass starvation Sarhili's only worry. Although the Thembu Regent Joyi had begun by showing sympathy for the stricken Xhosa, his attitude had changed under the pressure of Fadana's revolt. He longed to recover the extensive territory between the Indwe and the Bolotwa, which Sarhili's father had seized from his father nearly thirty years previously. Fighting between the Thembu and the Xhosa broke out in June 1857, and September and October saw a number of pitched battles. Though starving to death and much reduced in numbers, the frenzied Gcaleka more than held their own. On one memorable occasion, Joyi narrowly escaped with his life, leaving 38 Thembu dead on the field and several drowned trying to flee across a flooded river. But Joyi had time and numbers on his side and hit back repeatedly, killing Sarhili's Right-Hand brother Ncaphayi in January 1858.[27]

Sarhili was anxious for a showdown with the Thembu, but he held back for fear of antagonizing Joyi's colonial allies. Ever since the final disappointment in June, he had been striving to open communications with Governor Grey. When the Bishop of Grahamstown visited him in early July, he asked for food to help his people. 'There would be no help for the idle who would not work,' retorted the Bishop. Sarhili laughed — it was the sort of reply he had come to expect — and held up his hands, saying, 'These are not hard. I cannot work.' He admitted that it had been a great mistake to listen to the prophecies, but again and again he tried to divert the Bishop's inordinate curiosity concerning the past to a more meaningful discussion of the measures to be taken in the present. What should Sarhili and his people do now?

The Bishop's reply when it came was not very satisfactory.

> The Missionary comes here to preach the word of God not to give food; it is your duty to provide food for yourselves. . . . We are Christians, and love you, and wish to do you good; but when you bring God's judgement upon you for your sins, we do not know what is best to do for you.[28]

Such tortuous reasoning was completely alien to the Xhosa. What it meant was that the Bishop was refusing to assist them. 'The amaXosa would have helped the English if they had killed their oxen,' said Sarhili simply. He was very anxious to hear something from the government and, when the Bishop suggested that he seek an interview with Grey, responded that, although nervous, he would meet the Governor if asked to do so.

The Bishop of Grahamstown had done little enough by way of helping Sarhili, but even this was too much for Chief Commissioner Maclean. 'Your Excellency must not think of asking Krieli to come and see you,' he urged Grey. 'He must ask of his own accord.'[29] And ask Sarhili did, to little avail. After the failure of indirect messages through the Bishop, the missionary Waters and the trader Crouch, Sarhili summoned Crouch to a formal meeting and, in the presence of a large crowd, entrusted him with the following message to Grey:

> I, this day, in the presence of my brothers and counsellors, ask the forgiveness of the Governor for what I have done. I have fallen. I and my family are starving. I ask help from the Governor to save me from dying. I this day place myself in the hands of the Governor. I am willing to come to any terms the Governor may think fit to dictate to me — I wish to be subject to the Governor — I ask the Governor to help me with a plough, oxen and seed; I also ask the Governor to assist me with food for my family, and those of my brothers. If he does not assist us, we must all die of starvation. I this day place myself entirely in his hands.[30]

To emphasize the formality of the proposal and the sincerity of his words, Sarhili insisted on signing the paper himself, and all his brothers and Great Councillors did the same. Crouch himself added,

'My opinion is that Kreli is so entirely subdued, that His Excellency may exact any terms he pleases, and Kreli will submit to them.'

But Grey did not reply, and when Sarhili sent another message the same month, again with Crouch, Grey did not reply to that message either. In January 1858, alarmed by news of the arrests of his brother chiefs, Sarhili sent an official messenger named Possi to King William's Town to beg forgiveness from Maclean personally, and to find out whether the government intended to arrest him too.[31] Sarhili's state of mind during those troubled months is well expressed in one of his unanswered messages to the Governor, sent through Waters:

> The chief Krili has been here today and with tears begged me to write to your Excellency for assistance in his present great need. He remembers your letter to him advising him not to kill his cattle and not to throw away his corn — he is sorrowful for having neglected that advice and for having followed that of Umhlakaza. He hopes Your Excellency will deal kindly by him . . . that you will make him your friend again, and not leave him to perish on the mountains. He has offended you in destroying his own, he has not thrown an assegai at the the Governor. He looks to Your Excellency for a few milch cows, and seed for his gardens, so that he may keep life in his children: for himself, he wishes the dead to call for him, for he has sinned greatly.[32]

Such words might have moved a heart of stone. But Grey's heart was made of stronger stuff.

Far from extending the hand of friendship and forgiveness, Grey made up his mind to 'punish' Sarhili by invading his country. No crime that the Governor and his administration committed against the starving Xhosa people — not the raiding and plundering of believers by Gawler's police, not the kangaroo courts and the transportations by sea, not even the closing of the Kaffir Relief House and the hounding of thousands of famished people into slave-like forced labour — was quite as black as the ruthless and brutal expulsion of Sarhili and his people from their homes and lands, for no other reason than to turn their beautiful country into a Colony of white settlement. Sarhili and his people did not live in British territory as the Xhosa of British Kaffraria did. They had not, as Fadana had, raised an open standard of revolt. They had not harmed anyone but themselves in their vain strivings after an impossible dream.

Grey justified his attack on Sarhili by claiming that the Xhosa King was planning an attack on the Cape Colony.[33] He informed the Cape Parliament that in the light of information just received 'the matter now became one of life and death to the Colony'.[34] Yet the information in question stated, in part, that Sarhili was starving and had only one hundred men with him. Even more misleading was Grey's statement to the Colonial Secretary in London.

> No sooner does he [Sarhili] find out we are pressed for troops in India than he again begins the same system [of plotting]. . . . I cannot send enough troops to India with such a thorn in my flesh.[35]

The truth of the matter, was that, far from meditating an attack on the Colony, Sarhili was desperately seeking peace and reconciliation. Grey's trusted spy and agent, John Crouch, had already advised him that the Xhosa King would submit to any terms Grey proposed, and, in November 1857, Crouch sent in the following unequivocal estimate of Sarhili's military strength.

> My opinion is that Kreli cannot recover his power, and although he is reconciled with unbelievers, not able to do mischief. . . . You have him in your power to do as you like with him. . . . You could take his whole country with a force of 100 men — for the whole of his country is nearly desolate. 100 cows would buy all their guns — they even offer powder for corn. You can dictate any terms to him. . . . He will be beat if he crosses the Bashee, for I am quite sure he can't muster more than 500 men. They can't mount more than 200.[36]

Chief Commissioner Maclean concurred entirely with this estimate and stated, 'I doubt whether Kreli can, in the present deserted state of his country, do more than make the occasional foray.'

And yet, despite being in possession of such precise information concerning Sarhili's actual military strength, Grey did not scruple to make the quite unsubstantiated assertion that the Xhosa King could bring 24,000 warriors into the field. In the letter just quoted, Crouch went on to make some helpful suggestions concerning where and when Sarhili might be made a prisoner. Clearly, it was the colonial Governor who was plotting against the Xhosa King and not the other way around. As clearly, it was the temptation presented by Sarhili's weakness rather than the threat posed by his strength which led the Governor to invade the Xhosa King's territory.

Ever since the Fadana commando, Commandant Currie and Agent Warner had been pressing the government to attack Sarhili, although in truth Grey needed no urging.[37] He was an ardent imperialist and colonialist, who had stripped the Maoris of their land in New Zealand to make way for white settlers and had long desired to do the same in southern Africa. Although he never expressed the idea in so many words, he believed it was the right and the duty of white European civilization to swallow up the rest of the world and remould it in the white European image. His vision of a united and integrated South Africa was one in which the political independence and social structure of the black nations were shattered and the majority of their people relocated as labourers in the Cape Colony, while white settlers moved in and occupied the lands thus vacated. 'You cannot maintain your frontier in a state of prosperity and advancement if that frontier abuts upon a barbarous race,' he wrote in 1860, looking forward to the time when Thembuland, Mpondoland and all the other independent black states along the Cape coast were annexed. 'Natal must thus become our real frontier.'[38] This was written three years after the Cattle-Killing, but it is worth noting that as early as April 1857 — before the Indian Mutiny, before Fadana's raids, long before the so-called 'revelations' of Nonkosi and Nkwintsha, Grey was telling the Cape Parliament of his plans to establish a white settlement in 'Kaffraria Proper', Sarhili's country:

> I hope . . . I may be able to devise means which will not only enable the Government to fill up the vacant portions of British Kaffraria with a European population sufficiently large to maintain itself . . . but which will also enable it to establish a European settlement in Kaffraria Proper, sufficiently strong to control and keep in check those tribes beyond the Kei.[39]

A second reason for Grey's attack on Sarhili lay in the increasing criticism which he was receiving from his superiors in London. In his determination to remodel British Kaffraria, the Governor had brazenly disregarded Colonial Office and War Office instructions, and even told the occasional outright lie. He had failed to promulgate letters patent which would have granted British Kaffraria a constitution, preferring to keep the territory under his own unfettered control through the exercise of martial law. He had failed to render accounts showing what he had done with the £40,000 year subsidy which he had extorted from the British Parliament. He had refused to send the regiments required by the War Office to quell the Indian Mutiny. He had kept the German Legion on full pay, instead of retiring them on half pay as he had been commanded to do. And he had placed an order for 500 more German immigrants from a private commercial establishment in Hamburg several days after receiving a letter from the Colonial Secretary expressly forbidding him to do any such thing. Any one of these offences was sufficient in itself to warrant his recall.[40] In order to justify his extravagant behaviour — in particular his refusal to cut the pay of the German Legion or to send the required regiments to India — he required a crisis. Grey had, as usual, many excuses for his strange behaviour, but the central theme of all of these was that his various actions had been motivated by the need to prevent another Frontier War. Only Governor Grey's wise foresight had saved the

Cape from the monstrous conspiracy hatched by Sarhili and his cohorts.

Grey needed Sarhili as an enemy more than he wanted him as a friend. How could Grey seize Sarhili's country and justify his own self-willed disobedience to the Secretaries of State if he admitted the truth, that the Xhosa power was broken and that all the Xhosa King wanted was submission, reconciliation and a little help? How else could Grey rationalize the trials, the expulsions, the shootings, the transportations, the labour contracts and all the other unnecessary acts which amounted to the persecution of a starving and helpless people? How could he defend all this, even to his own conscience, if not in terms of the wickedness of Sarhili?

The decision to invade Sarhili's territory bears all the hallmarks of a Grey initiative. He arrived in King William's Town towards the end of January, and less than a week later, without any preliminaries, he sent Sarhili a note through the Thembu agent informing him that 'I [Grey] do not choose to have him for a neighbour and shall certainly punish him if I can.' A combined force of Frontier Armed and Mounted Police and citizen volunteers under Commandant Currie, fresh from their triumph over Fadana, entered Sarhili's country from its northeastern corner near the Hohita. Currie's troops swept the country as far as the Ebb and Flow Drift on the Mbashe River, where they met 300 of Gawler's police coming from Mhala's country via Butterworth. Meanwhile Joyi's Thembu, at Grey's invitation, launched a fresh attack on the remnants of the Gcaleka army which they had been engaging for several months. Their orders were to capture Sarhili 'or drive him so far away that he would never be heard of again'.[41]

'Never was there such an easy conquest,' wrote Gawler. 'Caesar's are a joke to it.'[42] He was proud of the way his police did their duty, inspired by 'good feeling and a judicious application of the sjambok'. The only problem Currie experienced besides the rain was the difficulty of keeping pace with the fleeing Xhosa. 'So precipitate was their retreat that with forced night and day marches, it was as much as my best horses could do to come up with [Sarhili's] rear, in order to capture as many cattle as would serve for immediate use. . . . No determined opposition was anywhere offered.' By 25 February, almost all the surviving Xhosa had crossed the Mbashe into the territory of Moni, chief of the Bomvana people. Despite their difficulties, Currie's men succeeded in shooting at least 83 Xhosa and capturing 500 head of cattle — 'a great number considering the impoverished state of the country', bragged Currie, seemingly unaware of how his own pen condemned him. Gawler bagged 70 cattle, not counting calves, and all but four of Sarhili's horses.

None of the volunteers who participated in that infamous commando have left a detailed account of the crimes that were committed against a starving and defenceless population. Even Maclean was disturbed by the 'several cruelties' that were committed, and he never enumerated them on paper.[43] With a little imagination, however, the reader may try and fill in the blanks. First, the scene: the abandoned dwellings, the empty cattle kraals, the untilled fields, and scattered, burned-out heaps of cattle bones. Next, the survivors: small knots of pathetic believers, living on roots and berries, all the grand expectations of the past reduced to the simple hope that they might hang on to life until the harvest in two months' time. Now imagine, if you can, the sound of horses and the sight of the Frontier Armed and Mounted Police advancing over the horizon. . . .

Those unwilling to use their imaginations will have to settle for the two accounts of the expedition that we do have. The first is from one of the volunteers, who related with obvious relish the summary execution of two alleged 'spies' who were caught 'hiding' in the road.[44] His detachment then captured some 90 cattle, mainly cows and calves, and, not content with stealing these, tracked down their owners too. 'In we dashed,' the anonymous volunteer recalled nostalgically. 'It was tremendous hard work, the bush being so thick and in about half an hour 22 out of 26 fat Kaffirs were killed and stretched out at our feet.' It is the language of the chase, and the author seems to have forgotten that he was hunting not deer but human beings. That the volunteers viewed the entire enterprise as a spot of fun is evident from our only other source of information, a liberal land surveyor then based in Queenstown:

> I have seen several of the Queens Town Burghers who were on this expedition — and the accounts they give, and, I am sorry to say, gloat over, are enough to make one's blood run cold. If a man with a black skin was seen he was immediately '*bowled over*'. On one occasion two unfortunate friendly [Xhosa] were sent to examine a bush. Five or six of the hunted sprang out and tried to escape — they were unarmed — the commando fired and by mistake shot their two allies — one was killed, the other severely wounded.
>
> If a [Xhosa] was seen running away — although alone and unarmed, a party of five or six were sent after him on horseback and he was generally shot. The [Xhosa] were always unprepared and in almost every single instance unarmed. The commando on horseback could hardly come up to them they fled so fast and still some scores were killed. Commandant Currie has not given the whole history of this second Glencoe. His men are the terror of the Eastern districts. They are deserters — discharged soldiers and scamps of all descriptions — a

daring but unprincipled lot. The young farmers who were called out to join this expedition gloat over the massacres they have taken part in. They acknowledge that the [Xhosa] never fought but were picked off as they ran — they shot men as they would bucks — and boast how one who was a great distance off, or in difficult ground was knocked over by a good shot.

Sir George Grey has cleared the country and added to the prestige of our name. How? By attacking men unarmed and unprepared and shooting them down whether they resisted or not. . . .[45]

By comparison with the human dimension, the other details of the expedition fade into insignificance. Gawler's detachment stopped off at the Gxarha, which was abandoned except for seventeen human skulls, one of them presumably Mhlakaza's. He then linked up with Currie at the Mbashe, where they halted according to their instructions, though Currie was strongly tempted to go further 'as we could still see plenty of cattle in Moni's country'. Gawler sent Moni, the chief of the Bomvana, a message telling him that the government had nothing against him 'but wished to see what sort of neighbour he would make'. He also demanded the prophetess Nongqawuse, whom Nxito had brought into Bomvanaland. Moni was only too pleased to comply, saying, 'he would be glad to get rid of her as they were afraid of her'. There was now 'little or nothing for us to do but destroy gardens', wrote Currie, and he and Gawler began to squabble over who had the right to command the expedition. By the end of March, Gawler was ready to leave. 'Times are very dull,' he informed Maclean. He would make one final sweep below Butterworth and then, as a last hurrah, 'pass through Umhala's country with fire and sword' on his way home.[46]

From the Kei to the Mbashe and from the Hohita to the sea, Sarhili's country was now virtually deserted, apart from the new colonial head-quarters at Idutywa. The few remaining cattle of the Gcaleka Xhosa had been captured by their merciless enemies, and their dwellings and carefully tended gardens wantonly destroyed. Sarhili himself, with a strong bodyguard, took refuge in the dense forests of Cwebe, just east of the Mbashe River mouth. He did not care what the government did, he said, for he would never be found alive. To his suffering people, he addressed the following message which has since passed into oral tradition.

Learn to satisfy your hunger on the acacia thorn tree. For you are the people of a chief who is hated.[47]

3. The Reward of Virtue

Ever since his arrival in southern Africa, Grey had wanted a vast increase in the white population of British Kaffraria. 'We should fill it up with a considerable number of Europeans of a class fitted to increase our strength in that country,' he told the Cape Parliament in March 1855.[48] He realized that most of the Xhosa who had left under duress of transportation or forced labour would wish to come home as soon as they had completed their prison sentences and their labour contracts, and he therefore pressed ahead with his plans to revolutionize the face of British Kaffraria before they returned. Finding settlers quickly was of paramount importance.

> It becomes of the utmost consequence for the final settlement of the [Xhosa] question, and of the difficulties which have so long harassed this Frontier, to increase as speedily as possible, the number of Europeans in this Country.

Grey's first experiment with white settlers had hardly been encouraging. The 2,300 men of the disbanded German Legion who had arrived in Kaffraria shortly before the Great Disappointment were not exactly the sort of immigrants calculated to spread European civilization among the Xhosa. Most of the Germans were decent enough fellows, perfectly willing to employ the odd servant, buy a Xhosa an occasional drink, or toss the intestines of a slaughtered beast to starving women and children. But there was a sizeable minority which 'accustomed to war from their youth [were] driven to the most horrific deeds by their warlike characters and their insatiable thirst for blood'.[49] Some of these were in the habit of wandering around blind drunk, weapons in hand, looking for a fight, and even their fellow Legionaries admitted that 'within all the German settlements, we have had several cases where unarmed [Xhosa] have been cruelly murdered by these evil-doers'.[50] The Belgians amongst them were referred to by the Xhosa as 'throat-slitters' on account of the long knives they habitually carried and their habit of biting each other like dogs while fighting.[51] The Xhosa accused the Germans of carrying long sticks to abduct Xhosa women, and sexual abuse by the Germans (2,000 of whom were unmarried) seems to have occurred.[52] Racial tensions in East London, where aggressive Germans confronted thieving Xhosa across the Buffalo River, exploded in at least two major riots within six months of the Germans' arrival.[53] Small wonder that the Ndlambe Xhosa appealed, 'If Gawler does have a post here for goodness' sake, don't let them be Germans.'[54] The situation eased only in September 1858, when Grey was able to ship off the unrulier elements of the Legion to fight in the Indian Mutiny.

Never one to learn from his mistakes, Grey continued to maintain that a European settlement in British Kaffraria would be of benefit to all. It was his intention, he informed Maclean in July 1858, that 'a

society of the most harmonious elements may be formed, in which the
two races live together in a state of happiness and contentment,
forming loyal subjects and a productive and well-organised society'.
But he added an important qualification to this praiseworthy objective.
Such a society, he wrote, could 'only be brought about by establishing
something like an approach to equality in numbers, or at least
influence between the two races'.[55]

In 1855, when the Xhosa of British Kaffraria outnumbered the white
inhabitants by close on a hundred to one, it would have been
ridiculous to talk about the black and white population 'approaching
equality'. But by the middle of 1858, this was no longer beyond the
bounds of possibility. Already the black population had dropped by
nearly two thirds, from 105,000 to 37,500, and it was Grey's priority to
reduce the residual Xhosa population even further while at the same
time giving out their lands to white settlers, 'for it is impossible to keep
such fertile lands bare of inhabitants', and if they were not given out
soon, they would soon become 'irregularly occupied . . . by a
population of dangerous inhabitants'.[56]

Apart from the Crown Reserve, from which Sandile's Ngqika Xhosa
had been driven after the War of Mlanjeni in 1853, there were three
districts of British Kaffraria virtually emptied of their starving
inhabitants by the Cattle-Killing: those of Phatho, Maqoma and
Mhala. A glance at Map 5 (p.320) will show that these three districts,
contiguous to each other, make up most of what is today the hinterland
of modern East London. Over 90 per cent of Phatho's people had left
by the beginning of 1858, and the few who still survived there were in a
very precarious position.

> Property in Pato's tribe is decreasing fast. Even those who had horses
> have sold or been dispossessed of them — no cattle or goats are seen.
> Most have planted but very little . . . there will be too little to support
> even the remnants of this tribe. People are stealing pumpkins etc from
> each other as soon as they become edible. There is a desire to possess
> goats, but no means except theft. . . .[57]

In March 1858, Maclean ordered these remnants out. 'Some have
moved, others will be made to move,' he informed Grey. Magistrate
Vigne was not without some misgivings concerning certain old men
who 'if removed from their homes will starve', but he nevertheless
patrolled the district registering for labour every 'squatter' he found
there.[58] It fell to Commissioner Brownlee to tell the 125 families under
old Chief Bhotomane and Maqoma's Great Son Namba to leave their
district. 'I informed the chiefs that I had been ordered to remove them
and not to consult their wishes and inclinations,' he wrote, but he

asked to be relieved of the job of actually forcing them out. Max Kayser, the rascally interpreter, was not so squeamish, and the people were harried out by the middle of July. 'There is not a single native left in either Namba's or Botman's locations,' he reported with satisfaction.[59] With all of Mhala's district already vacated, except for Gawler's unbelievers who were due to move to Sarhili's country, this gave Grey and Maclean something approaching 2,000 square miles to distribute to white settlers in British Kaffraria. But even this was not enough. For the full realization of Grey's Kaffrarian dreams, it was still necessary to humble the unbelievers.

For the unbelievers, and for those officials like Brownlee who wholeheartedly sympathized with them, the spring of 1857 was filled with hope and promise. All the old restraints which had hampered their desires to invest and accumulate and reap the rewards of their efforts had vanished. The believers who had tormented and threatened them were gone off to labour in distant places, and the chiefs who had extorted dues and tributes from anyone who seemed too rich were crushed and powerless. Sandile himself, mindful of the fate of his fellow chiefs, had meekly requested Brownlee to take him on as a 'policeman under Government'.[60] Now that the storm was over and the spring was nigh, the thoughts of unbelievers such as Tyhala and Soga turned to innovation and economic improvement. Brownlee saw these 300 or 400 energetic and self-confident men as the vanguard of a veritable agricultural revolution that would transform the face of Xhosaland.

> They are anxious to have their oxen trained, to obtain ploughs and to cultivate wheat and beans and potatos. We might even try woolled sheep. I would like to begin cutting a watercourse. . . .[61]

So enthusiastic were the unbelievers that they could not wait for the rains to plant maize, and eagerly experimented with winter crops such as the wheat, peas and lentils offered to them by Brownlee. 'We can have no better opportunity than the present for the introduction of any innovation,' wrote the Commissioner. He expected that he would soon be seeing three or four of his men ploughing with their own ploughs and their own oxen.

But there were not many officials in British Kaffraria who shared Brownlee's enthusiasm for the unbelievers. We have already seen how little support they had received from the administration when they needed it most, and many officials probably rejoiced in their hearts at the unbelievers' plight. As one young missionary put it, 'I wish their [the unbelievers'] cattle were done, so that they must all go into the Colony.'[62] Maclean, too, made no secret of his dislike of the number of unbelievers still clustered around Brownlee. 'The Gaikas have not yet availed themselves to the extent of other tribes of entering service,' he grumbled. 'Half of Sandile's tribe being still in his location.'[63]

Grey was by nature dismissive of the ideas and endeavours of others, claiming them as his own if they suited his purpose and denigrating and destroying them if they did not. The unbelievers who, by their own efforts and without Grey's aid, had clung stubbornly to their homesteads throughout the Cattle-Killing and now occupied their lands in their own right and not by any gift of the Governor, were not, in Grey's view, heroes to be rewarded, but untidy and inconvenient marks on the otherwise clean slate of British Kaffraria. Few as the remaining believers were, there were still too many of them for Grey's stated aim of equalizing the proportion of black and white in British Kaffraria. By 1858, it was already clear that the Governor's original plan of a relatively dense population of white smallholders was untenable, and that if whites were going to be persuaded to settle in British Kaffraria at all, they were going to require the large farms of over 1,500 acres apiece that the agricultural practices of the Cape Colony led them to expect. The large tracts of land already confiscated from the Xhosa did not amount to more than 200 such farms altogether.[64]

There was another, even more pressing reason for squeezing the unbelievers. The population of Sandile's country may have shrunk from 31,000 to 3,718, but its boundaries remained the same, and the principle of communal land tenure ensured that when the transportees and contract labourers returned, they would all get their land back. Clearly this could not be allowed to happen. Communal tenure had to give way to some form of individual tenure which would enable the authorities to monitor and control population influx and access to land. That such a scheme was in accordance with Grey's long-standing intention of promoting the individual at the expense of the chief was an added bonus rather than a substantive cause of the new policy, as can be seen from the fact that the system eventually adopted broke the chiefdoms without benefiting the unbelievers.

The solution to Grey's problem of administering the Xhosa areas of British Kaffraria was already to hand. It had long been argued by missionaries and others that the dispersed pattern of Xhosa settlement, that is of scattered, self-sufficient homesteads, obstructed the adoption of Christianity and civilization. In 1850 the whole of Xhosaland, according to Reverend Impey, superintendent of the Wesleyan missions, was 'one vast commonage where every man lives where he likes'. Impey was inspired by the example of Governor

Raffles in Malaysia to argue that the 'shortest and best way' of civilizing non-European peoples was by conquest. The 'strong arm of power' was necessary; the conquerors 'must think and act for them [the indigenous people] in matters concerning their welfare when too ignorant to come to right conclusions themselves'. In a noteworthy passage, Impey celebrated the virtues of centralization as an aid to physical and moral control.

> There are multitudes of localities where at present within a radius of 2 miles, or even less, there are numerous kraals consisting of from six to eight houses each; the whole of which could be collected to a central position from which the cattle might graze over the very same pasturage, the people obtain the same supply of water, and cultivate the same lands as they do at present, whilst they would be living in a village or Township of 100 families, get-atable for the purposes of instruction, and placed under the immediate government of a headman or local magistrate, who would be responsible to the Commissioner of the District.
>
> The hold which the Government would thus, from the concentration of persons and property, have over the population would be vastly increased; the way for the introduction of municipal and fiscal regulations would be opened up.[65]

Many liberals initially supported the village system because they associated it with the granting of title to land, and all that that implied in terms of security of tenure and the encouragement of economic individualism.[66] In the Cape context, however, individual title was very much the sugaring on the pill, and in any case it was never implemented in British Kaffraria outside the Crown Reserve.[67] What mattered most was that the Xhosa should be, in Impey's memorable phrase, 'get-atable' for the purposes of political management and the collection of taxes. This last factor became critical after June 1858 when the news came from London that Parliament had halved its subsidy to the government of British Kaffraria. It was now the urgent task of Grey and Maclean to make the surviving unbelievers pay the costs of their own oppression.[68]

Efforts had already been made to introduce villages among the Mfengu settlements in the Crown Reserve, where it was felt that the Mfengu were beginning to encroach on land set aside for white settlement.[69] When Grey visited the frontier early in 1858 to organize the expedition against Sarhili, he took the opportunity to order that all Xhosa remaining in British Kaffraria should be resettled in villages.[70] Magistrates were ordered to select sites suitable for villages of up to 200 'huts', and to move the people into them as soon as their crops were gathered. All their horses, cattle and small stock were to be registered and taxed, and they were to pay hut tax of 10s per 'hut' (that is, per family) per year. Grey hoped that this combination of villages and taxation would effectively discourage many Xhosa from returning to British Kaffraria after their labour contracts were completed. Those Xhosa who did return were required to register with the magistrate before receiving permission to occupy a village site, a regulation which enabled the authorities to restrict the movements of the returning labourers to their own satisfaction.[71]

It was Grey's intention that the village lots should eventually be surveyed and granted to their possessors on quitrent title, thereby completing the economic liberation of the individual from the communal authority of the chief. Each chief was to receive a private farm of 3,000 acres as compensation for the loss of his power to allocate land, just as he had previously received a salary in compensation for the loss of his power to levy judicial fines.[72]

But the bait of individual title was by no means a sufficient inducement to persuade the Xhosa to resettle themselves in villages. Even before the imposition of the village system, it had been colonial policy to settle blacks — even loyal blacks such as the Mfengu — on lands that were 'unsuitable for European occupation', that is, lands which were agriculturally inferior.[73] Most of the Xhosa areas were deficient in wood, soil or water, and sometimes in all three. In Commissioner Brownlee's district, for example, the arable land was located in narrow strips along the valley bottoms, so that the formation of villages would compel certain Xhosa to walk 12-15 kilometres to get from their village to their gardens. Even where this was not the case, moving into villages would necessitate breaking up new ground, which usually meant giving up all hope of crops in the first season.[74] Quite apart from these material objections, the Xhosa resented losing the freedom to change the locations of their dwellings and their gardens as and when they thought best, and they feared the social tensions that were bound to arise when formerly autonomous homesteads were closely concentrated together. 'We have lived together during wars,' they said, 'and have always experienced a great deal of evil; our corn is not safe; our wives and cattle are not safe.'[75]

Commissioner Brownlee moved his people into villages without much difficulty. It was not that the Ngqika Xhosa liked the idea of villages, but that they were 'broken down and reduced, consequently more easily managed'.[76] The collaborating chiefs, such as Siwani and Toyise, lacked the will to oppose the government in anything, and no villages were planned in the Cattle-Killing strongholds of Maqoma and Phatho, which were earmarked for white settlement. The strongest resistance to the village system came from the unbelieving chiefs Anta and Kama, whose alliance with government had hitherto been based on principle rather than expediency.

Anta, Sandile's brother, was 'a haughty man [with] a good mind and . . . [a] noble appearance'.[77] His influence was all the greater in as much as he was neither a Christian nor a collaborator, but one of the most prominent adherents of Mlanjeni. From the beginning, he had taken a strong stand against the Cattle-Killing and his steadfast opposition had greatly encouraged and sustained the unbelievers throughout the Ngqika Xhosa area. Hundreds of refugees had found shelter in his country with their cattle and, in consequence, Anta's chiefdom was better stocked, better populated and in every way better equipped to return to normality than any other chiefdom in Xhosaland.

Magistrate Robertson explained the village scheme to Anta and his councillors throughout most of February. A great meeting was called in early March to lay the scheme before the people, but Anta abruptly disappeared, and he continued to evade all Robertson's efforts to pin him down on the village issue. In the middle of May, the councillors addressed a protest to Maclean:

> We do not comprehend the object of these villages. . . . We are willing to serve the Government as far as it is in our power to do so, and do not think that forming ourselves into villages will enable us to do so better. Some of the English live in towns, others live on farms; we are like the farmers. We sow our lands and keep our cattle. The English farmers could not attend to their lands and cattle should they be formed into villages.[78]

Maclean was furious. He promptly disabused Anta and his people of any idea that their opinions were of the least importance, and threatened them all with transportation if they did not immediately move into villages.

> Acquaint Anta he must without further delay or evasion direct and superintend the formation of the several villages . . . that I will hear of no excuse . . . and that all pay to head men and others will cease if the slightest objection is offered, and to speak in plain terms they must and shall be at once concentrated in villages — that any person found squatting after due notice of removal will be liable to be apprehended and punished, and if necessary sent out of the country.
>
> Tell Anta not to oblige me to carry out the Governor's orders with any forced measure — but do it I will and if necessary will see it carried out myself. . . . Tell Anta that the Governor is the best judge of what is right; and it is for him [Anta] to obey or stand the consequences.[79]

Anta and his councillors heard this message in virtual silence. The chief indicated that the orders would be obeyed, but within the next few days he and his close neighbour, Chief Oba, disappeared beyond the borders of British Kaffraria. Magistrate Robertson passed the time by burning the dwelling of Siziba, the councillor Oba had left in charge of his people. The chiefs returned the following month, having had time to consider their alternatives. Having witnessed the arrests of their fellow chiefs and the expulsion of Sarhili, they realized that they had no choice but to submit.[80]

The fall of Chief Kama was harder still because Kama had further to fall. Regarded by the settlers as the only sincerely Christian Xhosa, he had long been thought of as someone special, the darling of the missionaries and the prized friend of the Colony. He had broken with his brother Phatho in the name of Christianity and civilization, and had established an independent chieftainship. He had played a heroic role in the defence of Whittlesea during the War of Mlanjeni, and had been rewarded with a prime slice of Ngqika territory. Finally, Kama had welcomed his magistrate, opposed the Cattle-Killing and acquiesced in all Grey's new administrative measures. He must have been waiting for another reward. But times had changed. Now that the power of the Xhosa was irrevocably broken, Kama was downgraded from a valuable ally to just another Kaffir. This was brought home to him sharply and in the most unpleasantly personal manner by that Hercules of the border, Commandant Walter Currie.[81]

Kama often played host to white farmers; and he was accustomed to make use of his privileged status to visit these farmers at their homes. After the drama of the Cattle-Killing was over, he decided to go on a month's holiday, visiting his white friends. He was enjoying the hospitality of a farmer on the Koonap River, when Currie arrived and demanded to know what right Kama had to travel in the Colony. Kama knew Currie and assumed he was joking, but the Commandant was not. He showed Currie his pass, but the Commandant found all sorts of fault with it. The pass did not name all the farmers Kama was visiting. It did not say that Kama was entitled to receive presents of goats. Currie told the chief that he would have thrown him into jail, except that he felt sorry for him. He confiscated Kama's goats and marched him to the waggon road, threatening him with prison if he ever returned. Kama was utterly humiliated. He had intended to be away for a full month.

In March 1858 Captain Reeve, Kama's magistrate, rejoined his regiment. Reeve was a tough man in the Gawler mould and he had pushed Kama hard, as well as starving thousands of Xhosa into taking labour contracts, but at least he had shown some appreciation for the Christian chief. His successor showed none. Maclean had asked for a strong replacement, who would deal with Kama's reprehensible 'sympathy' for his brother Phatho's people, and he got one in the person of a certain Joseph Miller.[82] Miller was, for a time, confused by Kama's apparent acceptance of the village system, but eventually he realized that the chief's attitude was only a front to cover up passive obstruction. He called on Maclean to support him in the use of outright force.

> Do give me more police (efficient) or don't hereafter blame me — it's quite out of the question to get on without 'Carte Blanche' to do as I find necessary in this respect. . . . Sans more troops and more police my own private opinion is that there will be great need of both.

The 'Carte Blanche' seems to have done the trick, for Miller was soon able to write:

> Old Kama and his people are in a nice funk. I am pitching into them nicely.[83]

So nicely did Miller pitch into Kama's people that in October 1858, the month that he implemented the village system, 1,446 registered for labour in the Colony.

These methods brought protests from Kama and his sons that Miller was burning dwellings indiscriminately, insulting Kama's authority and acting without any reference to the chief. Miller was quite unapologetic. He had simply told Kama that 'if he [Kama] did not carry out the views and orders of Government I [Miller] should'. Kama was playing 'a very deceitful game'. He was 'quite childish' and 'frequently drunk'. 'His influence for good with his people is nil.' By the end of 1858, Miller was speaking of 'destroying the power of the chief, which I think we can dispense with: at all events, in this location'.[84]

Grey hoped to diminish the black population of British Kaffraria still further by settling Smith Mhala, Ndayi, Mjuza and the other Ndlambe unbelievers on a portion of the lands seized from Sarhili. Most of these unbelievers had served in the transKei with Gawler's police and some had even picked out places for themselves, but none of them except Smith were prepared to settle there permanently.[85] They had no wish to commit themselves to a new life in a strange place as the pawns of the colonial government. Their adherence to Gawler had been, in a sense, coincidental, the product of the difficult position in which their unbelief had placed them. Now that the Cattle-Killing was over, they simply wanted to return as quickly as possible to their old way of life. They distrusted Smith Mhala as a drunkard and a sneak, and they were secretly committed to raising a young son of Mhala to be chief over them in the future. After the application of much pressure, Sigidi agreed to cross the Kei, and he soon became the leading chief of the new Idutywa settlement, outstripping Smith and recruiting his strength from expelled Gcaleka Xhosa whom he claimed as his own followers. The other unbelievers, led by Ndayi and Mjuza, refused to settle in Idutywa, and all Maclean's promises (no hut tax in the transKei) and all his threats (they were stripped of their salaries as headmen) could not induce them to change their minds.[86]

As a result, Maclean decided to bring the erstwhile Ndlambe unbelievers 'into discipline under the village system'. And so he did. Ndayi and the others had rid themselves of Mhala but in his place they found themselves exposed to the corrupt administration of Max Kayser, who extorted more cattle from them than Mhala had ever done and gave them nothing in return.[87]

Dunned for taxes, confined to villages and forced to break up new and infertile ground, the unbelievers may well have wondered how much they had gained by preserving their cattle. Nature herself turned against them during the summer of 1858, the first sowing season after the Cattle-Killing. The weather turned dry in January 1859, destroying the early crops and rendering further planting impossible. Anta's people, making the best of their villages, cultivated extensively, but frost was followed by drought and blight completed the wreckage of their hopes. Both Sandile's and Kama's chiefdoms suffered complete crop failures. The missionary at Newlands reported a similar situation among the Ndlambe Xhosa unbelievers in the following year.

> The heat and drought were very great, the hot winds dried up the gardens and the poor natives who had not yet recovered from the famine lost their little all. Our river dried up, the water became stagnant, the hot winds and dust brought on ophthalmia, low fever and dysentry. Within a very short time more than 50 of the station people died.[88]

The number of cattle in the Ngqika district actually decreased in the year after the Cattle-Killing. The unbelievers, having no other source of food to see them through the year, slaughtered the beasts they had fought so hard to preserve. In the Ndlambe district, many more were carried off through a renewed outbreak of lungsickness. Prospects for the coming season were further dimmed by a shortage of seed, and Commissioner Brownlee reported that far from being able to pay their taxes, the people were finding it difficult even to live.[89]

The government dropped its demand for a stock tax, but the hut tax was non-negotiable and so was the village system. The unbelievers were left with no alternatives. Between September and November 1858, 3,239 of them followed the footsteps of their erstwhile enemies, the Nongqawuse believers, and bound themselves to labour contracts deep within the Cape Colony. Nearly one third of the Xhosa who had survived the Cattle-Killing of 1857 failed to survive the new Kaffraria of 1858.[90]

4. Go to Jail

The prison at Alice where Maqoma was confined before his trial was described by an observer as nothing more than an unventilated 'den', directly comparable to the Black Hole of Calcutta. The verminous prison at Queenstown, originally a stables meant for five or six horses, held up to 90 Xhosa, male and female together, packed so closely that they slept at night in a crouching position with their knees cramped up to their chins. But the prison at King William's Town, where most of the convicts and transportees started their journey to the Western Province, was the worst of all. The cell where the majority of male prisoners were kept was dominated by a large tub serving as a toilet, 'half filled with urine and faeces, the smell from which was intolerable'. Within the narrow confines of this 8 by 5 metre cell, anything from 40 to 84 Xhosa prisoners were sometimes shackled together on the cold, damp flagstones. Because of the unnatural foods which they had been eating, many of the prisoners were afflicted by dysentery and diarrhoea, and they were constantly battling their way to and from the tub, necessarily accompanied by the other men to whom they were shackled. The British Kaffrarian doctors pronounced that in the hot and crowded conditions of the cell, the 'effluvia' from the large tub were actually poisonous. At least fifteen Xhosa died there within three months.[91]

Early in February 1858, while the Governor himself was in King William's Town, 21 prisoners led by the chiefs Tola, Qasana and Xhoxho escaped from this black hole.[92] About eight o'clock at night, the sentry heard the Xhosa prisoners laughing and a drunken white soldier named Hooper, imprisoned with them, shouting for help. When he went in to see what was happening, his candle was blown out and the prisoners, including Hooper, made a run for it across the yard and crashed through the rickety prison gate. One was shot dead and most of the others were soon recaptured, including Sandile's brother Xhoxho, who was caught by Commissioner Brownlee pathetically haunting the bushes around his old Great Place. Chiefs Tola and Qasana and their sons got away to Sarhili's deserted country which they roamed, in their own words, like 'wolves', preying on passers-by and killing anyone who looked like an informer.[93]

Qasana was never caught but after nearly a year of this hole-in-the-corner existence, Tola's hiding place was betrayed to Magistrate Colley at Idutywa, who assembled sixty men to apprehend him. Tola's men beat off the first party of police, who fled as soon as their ammunition was exhausted, but when reinforcements arrived most of the outlaws ran away. Tola and his sons, however, chose to stand and fight to the end. Wounded in three places, the chief nevertheless refused to surrender and, pulling a spear out of his body, he was killed in the very act of charging the police. Colley ordered his body hung up on a thorn bush near the waggon road. Tola only began to kill his cattle in the month before the Great Disappointment but he died still a firm believer. As W.W. Gqoba informs us, 'Tola fought so bravely with his sons, because he believed that he and his family would be rising from the dead in the near future.'[94]

The majority of Xhosa transported or contracted to labour in the Western Province travelled by ship. Their fear of the sea had a material as well as superstitious basis. Matthew Jennings, magistrate of the port of East London, was so pressed by 'natives flooding in daily' that he lost no opportunity to ship every Xhosa whom he considered strong enough to make the journey.[95] Many were put on board in a 'pitiable condition'. Five died on the *Phoenix*, and three on the *Pintado*, while 16 more died in Cape Town from the after-effects of their voyage. The master of the *Alice Smith* was fined £10 for unspecified 'cruelty' towards the unfortunate Xhosa on board his ship. Matters came to a head after the Superintendent of Convicts in Cape Town complained of the conditions on the *Munster Lass*. The Xhosa were fed 'rice unfit to eat' and 'salt junk not half-boiled'. They slept on the stone ballast that the ship was carrying and most of the children arrived in a 'shocking state of emaciation' and not expected to live. The owners of the *Munster Lass* professed themselves unable to understand how such conditions came about, though they did admit that the 'general character' of its captain was 'far from satisfactory'. Once again, the historian can only ask the reader to use the bare elements of the official record — the harsh living conditions, the dissolute captain, the starving and terrified people — to reconstruct in his or her own imagination the full story of that horrific voyage.

The Superintendent of Convicts and the other Cape officials who complained would deserve more credit if one did not suspect that their objections were grounded in reluctance to assume responsibility at the other end. The Superintendent complained of being forced to care for so many 'old worn-out men' and so many women with 'encumbrances', namely children. Employers did not want them. In fact, Xhosa above the age of twenty-five were not really 'in demand' in the Western Province.[96]

Most of the Xhosa transportees were held in the magazine of the old Amsterdam Battery, a large Dutch fortification which used to stand near the harbour at Table Bay.[97] They were kept under strict discipline and drilled for twenty minutes each morning and five minutes each night. They were compelled to wash, to make their beds and to wear European-style clothes, which many resisted at first. During the day, they worked on the harbour or digging in the new Botanical Gardens at Kirstenbosch. Their food was adequate, and the Superintendent enjoyed patronizing them with little gifts of tobacco and medicine. All in all, their living conditions were almost certainly better than those of the Xhosa auctioned off by James Hart in Graaff-Reinet. Nevertheless, they were not happy. Unlike the contract labourers who had 'volunteered' for service in the Western Province, they did not have their families with them and they did not get paid. Even worse, most of them had never been told how much longer they were bound to stay in Cape Town. 'We therefore thought it was the intention to keep us prisoners for ever,' said Holo, one of Sandile's councillors.[98]

Two days after Tola and Qasana broke out of King William's Town jail, the prisoners at the Amsterdam Battery made a bid for freedom.[99] They cut through the wooden gate which separated their cell from the yard, and, scrambling up the wall, dispersed along the ramparts of the old fort. One or two of them jumped the guard at the gate, and released the rest. But where were they to go? Twenty-two were captured next day, hiding under the overhanging rocks on the slopes of Devil's Peak. One of these was completely blind and had been escorted all the way by his friends. Eight were caught the following day, and three more by local farmers two days after that. Six of them were caught in Prince Albert, but they overpowered their captors and took their guns. Three — Pike, Nfamana and Ziki — actually made it back to Xhosaland, an epic journey which deserved a happier ending. They were all recaptured and sent back to Cape Town with increased sentences.[100]

This mass breakout was not the first escape from the Amsterdam Battery. Five men got away in November 1857, and one of them, through travelling along the coast and living on wild berries, got home to Xhosaland over two months later. But so sad and desolate was British Kaffraria that he no longer wished to stay there. He found his wife and they returned together to the Amsterdam Battery. For a Xhosa, there was no escape from Grey's new South Africa.[101]

5. The Island

'Esiqithini' is a Xhosa word meaning quite simply 'on the island'. No particular island is indicated but it would be difficult to find a Xhosa person who did not know exactly which island is meant. Even in English, the phrase 'the Island' has only one meaning for most South Africans. Robben Island, that pleasantly named home of seals, has burned itself into the collective conscience of us all. The author Mtutuzeli Matshoba recently called it 'the holy of holies', a place consecrated by the self-sacrifice of its victims. It was here that the Xhosa chiefs convicted by Grey's special courts were imprisoned.

Robben Island was known to Europeans for its valuable seal skins long before the arrival of Jan van Riebeeck in 1652.[102] When local Khoi drove off the cattle of the Dutch East India Company, Van Riebeeck fed his soldiers on Robben Island penguin eggs. The first colonial officials were sent to the Island merely to breed sheep and rock rabbits for meat. It was only in 1658 that Robben Island discovered its true destiny, when South Africa's first political prisoners — Khoi leaders known to us only as Harry, Boubo and Jan Cou — were transported there.

The Dutch valued Robben Island as a prison not only because the prisoners found it difficult to escape, but because it concealed the terrible conditions under which the convicts lived, and the dreadful punishments they suffered. Convicted prisoners were often sentenced to whippings with the cat-o-nine tails, to branding and pinching with red-hot irons and to the chopping off of hands. Hard labour could mean up to twenty-five years quarrying stone and burning lime, working and sleeping all the while in irons and chains.

The British conquest of the Cape (1806) eliminated most of these cruel punishments, but it did not change the essential function of Robben Island as a remote place where those who defied the colonial system could be dumped and forgotten. It was only in the 1840s, when an energetic official named John Montagu became Colonial Secretary, that the situation was altered. Montagu saw that hard labour convicts could serve the colonial economy more effectively by building roads, harbours and transport infrastructure than by toiling away unproductively on the Island. Thus, in 1844, the regular convicts left the Island for hard labour at 'convict stations' throughout the Colony.

Their place on the Island was taken by lepers, lunatics, destitute and chronic sick: social outcasts who had previously been accommodated on the Cape mainland at 'a very heavy annual expense'. Hundreds of physically and mentally crippled people were moved to the Island's old cells and jails. The male lunatics were set to work in the stone quarries — because hard work was thought to calm them down. Little attempt was made to rehabilitate these social discards. Lepers (a category which included syphilitics and skin cancer victims) and lunatics mingled with each other, the peaceful with the violent and the hopeful with the hopeless. They rarely saw friends or family, and they had very little chance of ever getting out again. When the Xhosa chiefs arrived in 1858, the Island was little better than a junkyard for the Colony's unwanted human beings.

They travelled in chains.[103] Fadana's were so heavy that they rubbed right through his skin. Maqoma's were 'heavy enough for a ship's cable', but he did not notice them. He was expecting to see Sir George Grey, hoping not only that the Governor would reverse his sentence, but that he would return the land Maqoma had lost in the War of Mlanjeni. Sadly for Maqoma's high hopes, Grey was not interested in meeting his victims. After some weeks in Cape Town jails, the Xhosa chiefs were moved to Robben Island.

Table Bay once swarmed with whales, and in 1806 a Mr John Murray was permitted to open a small whaling station at a sheltered inlet to the north of the main village of Robben Island, which became known as Murray's Bay. In 1820, the prophet Nxele and thirty comrades stole one of Murray's boats and, even though they were all drowned in their attempt to escape, the authorities were sufficiently alarmed to force Murray to close down his business. It was at Murray's Bay, described by a visitor as 'one of the bleakest and most wretched spots on the face of the earth', that the Xhosa chiefs were settled.

Dwellings in the usual Xhosa style, but covered with tarpaulins instead of reeds, were erected for them.[104] They received adequate food and tobacco but were denied the comfort of liquor. Siyolo and Maqoma were accompanied by their wives. Phatho's wife arrived in Cape Town, but the old chief was bedridden in Somerset Hospital and released shortly thereafter. The wives of Mhala and Xhoxho flatly refused to join their husbands. The letters of the exiles contain pathetic requests for news of distant homes and children. Clearly, the prisoners suffered most from a lack of human warmth. One of the young chiefs made love to a leper woman. They were detected in a field, and the young man was sentenced to solitary confinement on half rations.[105]

Boredom and meaninglessness were the main enemies of the Xhosa prisoners. They hunted after a fashion, catching hares and Cape pheasants. Siyolo, who had arrived earlier than the others, was allowed to herd a flock of goats. But then the nurses complained that he disturbed them by driving his goats along the main street, and he was forced to sell most of them. In 1863, Governor Wodehouse gave the prisoners four cows. But the pasturage on the Island was so poor that the cows gave no milk at all for the first six months and within two years all but one were dead.[106]

The prisoners made repeated but vain appeals to be released. One problem was that only Dilima spoke any English. When he was released in 1865, the isolation of the others was complete. They were forced to submit quietly to the abuse of white lunatics. A visitor described the encounter between Xhoxho and one of these:

> [The lunatic's] eye first fell on the unhappy Xoxo, who seemed to cower before him. . . . [Xhoxho], feeling that his presence was not further welcome, pointed to his brow, and whispered quietly that our friend was 'bayan malkop.'
>
> [Then Dilima entered the room.] The lunatic poured forth on him a pitiless pelting storm of insults. Ultimately he stood erect immediately in front of Delima, and raising his head, stuck out his lips. . . . Delima, no way frightened, simply imitated with exactness, the actions of the lunatic.[107]

Gradually, the chiefs found themselves joined by other Xhosa. Tyuli, transported for theft, contracted leprosy in Cape Town and was shipped over to the Island. Zidon served out his sentence, but was afflicted with an ulcer and could not return home. Signanda went blind. Nkohla lost an arm. All these helpless invalids joined the small Xhosa community at Murray's Bay.

No doubt the chiefs did what they could to resist. On one occasion, Siyolo beat a hospital attendant unconscious with a knobkierie, and there are further obscure references in the official papers to his repeated 'misconduct'. The wives of Siyolo and Maqoma smuggled messages back to Xhosaland. Hope often gave way to black despair. One of the invalids tried to slit his throat. Maqoma vented his rage on the Island officials whom he blamed for his continuing imprisonment. His wife, Katyi, falling sick refused medicine, telling the doctor, 'No, my heart is sore. I want to die.'[108]

One by one, the Xhosa chiefs served out their sentences. In 1869 the last prisoners, Maqoma, Siyolo and Xhoxho, were released. On their return home, they found their lands lost and their people scattered. They were forbidden to own land or to summon their followers. Maqoma, in extreme old age, refused to abide by the regulations imposed on him. Twice in 1871, with no aim in defiance but defiance itself, he left his appointed place of residence and returned to his old lands near Fort Beaufort and the Waterkloof. He was easily captured and, on the second occasion, he was summarily returned to the Island without a hearing or a trial.[102]   This time he was alone, utterly alone.

He never saw a visitor and there was no one else on the Island who spoke any Xhosa. Even the goats which he had formerly kept were dead. When in September 1873 he started sinking after eighteen months of solitude, the Island authorities sent for a companion and interpreter. But it was too late. This most brilliant of Xhosa warriors cried bitterly, according to the Anglican chaplain who witnessed his last moments, before he passed away 'of old age and dejection, at being here alone — no wife, or child, or attendant'.[110]

Four years later, the last Frontier War broke out. The sons of Maqoma, Mhala and Sandile were among the first of the next generation to take their places on Robben Island.

Notes

1. CO 2949 J. Warner-R. Southey, 24 Feb. 1857
2. CO 2951 J. Warner-R. Southey, 5 Oct. 1857; GH 28/72 J. Warner-G. Grey, 17 Nov. 1857.
3. Diary of R.J. Mullins, Cory Library, 25 May 1857.
4. CO 2949 J. Warner-R. Southey, 24 Feb. 1857.
5. BK 71 C. Brownlee-J. Maclean, 24 Aug. 1857.
6. GH 8/32 Anon-J. Maclean, 27 May 1857; CO 2949 J. Warner-R. Southey, 28 April 1857.
7. CO 2949 J. Warner-R. Southey, 28 April, 2, 9 June 1857; CO 2949 Deposition of Jonas, 11 May 1857.
8. LG 410 J. Warner-R. Southey, 14 July 1857; LG 152 W. Currie-R. Southey, 28 Aug. 1857; CO 1950 C. Griffith-W. Currie, 25 July 1857.
9. LG 410 J. Warner-R. Southey, 14 July 1857; CO 2950 J. Warner-R. Southey, 4, 6 Aug. 1857; CO 2950 J. Warner-W.G.B. Shepstone, 21 July 1857; CO 2950 W.G.B. Shepstone-R. Southey, 25 July 1857.
10. CO 2935 J. Warner-R. Southey, 23 Dec. 1856; CO 2950 R. Southey-R. Rawson, 1 Sept. 1856; CO 2950 J. Warner-R. Southey, 29 July 1856.
11. For some of Currie's arrangements, see CO 2951 J. Warner-R. Southey, 5 Oct. 1857. For Currie's own account, LG 152 W. Currie-R. Southey, 28 Aug. 1857. For an account by one of the volunteers, see *Cape Argus*, 19 Sept. 1857.
12. GH 20/2/1 H. Waters-J. Maclean, 5 Sept. 1857; GH 28/72 Government Notice 341, quoting W. Currie-R. Southey, 23 Sept. 1857. The term 'squatter' was used, of course, to imply that the Gcaleka in question had no right to be north of the Indwe in the 'Tambookie Location'. But the Gcaleka in question had always lived in this area, and were willy-nilly incorporated in it when the colonial government chose to accept the Thembu definition of the boundary.
13. GH 23/27 G. Grey-H. Labouchere 30 Nov. 1857; *King William's Town Gazette*, 26 Sept. 1857; *Cape Argus*, 5 Dec. 1857.

14. LG 152 W. Currie-R. Southey, 28 Aug. 1857; W. Currie-R. Southey, 23 Sept. 1857, quoted in Rutherford (1961), p.385. Note that the independent account in the *Cape Argus* gives a figure of 80 killed when the commando had still a month to run.
15. MS 3337, Cory Library, J. Ross-J. Laing, 9 March 1857.
16. MIC 172/2, Cory Libray, USPG Archives, Reel 1, H. Waters-R. Gray, 10 March 1857.
17. *Ibid.*, H. Waters-R. Gray, 10 April 1857; CO 2949 J. Warner-R. Southey, 18 Feb. 1857; GH 8/32 Anon (Thembuland)-J. Maclean, 27 May 1857.
18. BK 89 Memo of information communicated, 25 April 1857.
19. *King William's Town Gazette*, 2 May 1858.
20. GH 8/31 Memo of information, 26 April 1857.
21. GH 8/32 Anon (Thembuland)-J. Maclean, 27 May 1857; BK 71 C. Brownlee-J. Maclean, 18 May 1857.
22. GH 8/50 J. Maclean-G. Grey, 31 Aug. 1857. Tsimbi's attendant, Lingo, continued preaching cattle-killing, but without much success.
23. GH 8/32 Schedule 474, 23 July 1857; GH 8/50 Information received 28 Sept. 1850; GH 20/2/1 J. Crouch-J. Maclean 22 June 1857; GH 8/33 J. Crouch-J. Maclean, 16 Oct. 1857.
24. MIC 172/2, Cory Library, USPG Archives, H. Waters-R. Gray, 10 April 1857
25. T.B. Soga (n.d.), p.165; GH 8/33 J. Crouch-J. Maclean, 9 Nov. 1857.
26. MIC 172/2, Cory Library, USPG Archives, Reel 1, Journal of H. Waters, 5 Dec. 1857; C. Brownlee (1916), pp.140, 157-8.
27. GH 8/50 Information communicated by Nyila, 28 Sept. 1857; GH 8/33 J. Crouch-J. Maclean, 16 Oct. 1857; GH 20/2/1 J. Crouch-J. Maclean, 22 June 1857; GH 8/32 Information . . . by Mr Crouch, 21 July 1857; BK 89 Statement of Possi, 2 Feb. [1858]; GH 8/50 H. Waters-J. Maclean, 7 July 1857.
28. *Church Chronicle* (Grahamstown), Vol. 4 (1883), p.61.
29. GH 8/50 H. Waters-J. Maclean, 7 July 1857, and marginal notes.
30. GH 8/33 J. Crouch-J. Maclean, 19 Oct. 1857.
31. GH 8/34 Statement by Possi, a Gcaleka, before Commissioner Maclean, 2 Feb. 1858. Since Possi's statement was used by Grey in his dispatches and memorandum justifying his invasion of the transKei, it seems to warrant a little discussion. The precise statement to which Grey referred goes as follows: 'Kreli has not abandoned plans for war. In his house, he states that at present there can be no war on account of the destitution, but he still looks forward to a time when the people will have plenty and be in a position to renew hostilities against the English.' I shall restrict myself to three comments: (1) There is nothing in this to justify Grey writing to the Colonial Secretary that 'Kreili was openly proclaiming . . . that . . . he looked forward to a speedy time [of the renewal of hostilities]' or that, as Grey's memo to the Cape Parliament had it, the matter was one of 'life and death to the Colony'. Possi had allegedly said that the supposed statements were made in Sarhili's house, and that there could be no war at present. (2) Possi was supposed to be a formal ambassador from Sarhili. The main thrust of his message was that Sarhili would not attack the Thembu without Maclean's permission, even though they had killed his brother. The embassy was thus clearly intended to effect a reconciliation.

Any ambassador who allegedly makes statements so totally subversive of the main purpose of his embassy either has been misquoted or is totally untrustworthy. (3) The timing of the alleged statement (2 Feb. 1858) is suspiciously close to the time when Grey publicly launched the transKeian offensive. In any case, his official declaration of war (via Agent Warner, 1 Feb., see Note 41) actually precedes Possi's so-called information and cannot therefore be a reaction to it.

32. GH 20/2/1 H. Waters-G. Grey, 4 Sept. 1857.
33. See Peires (1985) for a full analysis of Grey's remarkable document in GH 20/2/1, 'Kreili's conduct', prepared for the Cape Parliament. To give but two examples, extensive use is made of the statement taken from a 'trustworthy native' on 8 Dec. 1856, which Maclean himself had dismissed when he first heard it (Chapter 7/1) and of Possi's alleged comments (Note 31 above).
34. GH 20/2/1 'Kreili's conduct'.
35. GH 23/27 G. Grey-H. Labouchere, 13 Feb. 1858.
36. GH 8/33 J. Crouch-J. Maclean, 9 Nov. 1856.
37. CO 2951 J. Warner-R. Southey, 29 Sept. 1857; W. Currie, quoted in Rutherford (1961), p.385.
38. Rutherford (1961), p.431.
39. Address to the Cape Parliament, April 1857, Imperial Blue Book 2352 of 1857-8, p.91.
40. Rutherford (1961), Chapters 26-28.
41. GH 30/12 G. Grey-J. Warner, 1 Feb. 1858; GH 30/12 G. Grey-Joyi, 12 Feb. 1858.
42. GH 8/50 J. Gawler-J. Maclean, 26 Feb., 17 March 1858; GH 20/2/1 W. Currie-G. Grey, 12 March 1858; BK 78 W. Currie-R. Southey, 1 March 1858.
43. GH 8/50 J. Maclean-G. Grey, 19 April 1858.
44. *Eastern Province Herald*, 19 March 1858. There is another account in the *Cradock News*, 30 March 1858, but the author seems to have seen only three occupied homesteads. He does not say what happened to the occupants of these.
45. Fairbairn Papers, University of the Witwatersrand, James Alexander Fairbairn-John Fairbairn, 15 May 1858.
46. GH 20/2/1 W. Currie-G. Grey, 12 March 1858; BK 78 J. Gawler-J. Maclean, 7 March 1858; GH 8/50 J. Gawler-J. Maclean, 26 March 1858; Cory Interviews, Cory Library, Interview 119, W.R.D. Fynn, 16 April 1913; CO 48/388, Public Record Office, London, J. Gawler-J. Maclean, 26 Feb. 1858.
47. BK 78 Statement received from a man who has come direct from Kreili, 1 April 1858; Anon [S.E.K. Mqhayi], 'USarhili' in W.G. Bennie (ed.), *Stewart Xhosa Readers*, Grade VI, (Lovedale: Lovedale Press, n.d.), p.102.
48. Rutherford (1961), p.315; MIC 172/2, Reel 2, Cory Library, H. Cotterill-H. Bullock, 15 Sept. 1857; Imperial Blue Book 2352 of 1857-8, Grey's address to the Cape Parliament, p.91.
49. Steinbart (1975), p.88. The standard work on the German settlers, Schnell (1954), is badly in need of revision.
50. Steinbart (1975), p.89; BK 14 Schedule 47, 10 July 1857.
51. A. Kropf-BMS, 12 July 1857, Berlin Missionary Archives, East Berlin.
52. GH 8/50 H. Vigne-J. Maclean, 1 Feb. 1857; GH 8/33 Schedule 509, 12 Oct. 1857; GH 28/73 Enclosure to Dispatch 47.

53. GH 8/32 L. Traherne-J. Maclean, 4, 8 May 1857; GH 8/32 N. Lamont-J. Maclean, 9 May 1857; GH 8/50 J. Maclean-G. Grey, 9 Feb. 1857.
54. BK 81 J. Gawler-J. Maclean, 16 March 1857.
55. BK 4 G. Grey-J. Maclean, 14 July 1858.
56. BK 2 G. Grey-J. Maclean, 14 July 1858; Bergh and Visagie (1985), p.56.
57. Population statistic obtained by comparing figures for 1 Jan. and 31 Dec. 1857 in British Kaffraria Census Returns. GH 8/34 H. Vigne-J. Maclean, 1 Jan. 1858.
58. GH 20/2/1 J. Maclean-G. Grey, 18 March 1858; BK 83 H. Vigne-J. Maclean, 24 March 1858.
59. BK 71 C. Brownlee-J. Maclean, 26 May 1858; GH 8/35 M. Kayser-J. Maclean, 20 July 1858. Namba and Bhotomane both wanted to go to Kama's country near the lands from which they were expelled after the War of Mlanjeni, but Maclean would not permit this. Bhotomane was sent to join Dyani Tshatshu while Namba was placed under Toyise. For Max Kayser, see Chapter 2, Note 50.
60. BK 71 C. Brownlee-J. Maclean, 24 Aug. 1858.
61. GH 8/32 C. Brownlee-J. Maclean, 11 June 1857; BK 71 C. Brownlee-J. Maclean, 20 July, 24 Aug. 1858.
62. Diary of R.J. Mullins, Cory Library, 3 June 1857.
63. GH 8/32 Schedule 476, 29 July 1857, marginal note by Maclean.
64. GH 8/36 Schedule 140, 4 Nov. 1858. For more on land distribution in British Kaffraria, see Chapter 11.
65. GH 19/8 W. Impey-H. Smith, 23 Oct. 1850. Impey renewed these proposals after the Cattle-Killing. GH 8/50 W. Impey-J. Maclean, 18 April 1857.
66. See, for example, R. Birt-J. Maclean, 6 July 1854; *Cape Argus*, 21 Nov. 1857.
67. *King William's Town Gazette*, 3 July 1865.
68. GH 23/27 G. Grey-H. Labouchere, 20 March 1858.
69. BK 24 J. Maclean-W. Liddle, 17 July 1856.
70. GH 30/4 G. Grey-J. Maclean, 5 Feb. 1858. This memorandum also made provision for taxes on stock, but these were never implemented.
71. BK 2 G. Grey-J. Maclean, 14 July 1856; BK 114 Circular to Special Magistrates, 9 Feb. 1859; BK 85 G. Thompson-J. Maclean, 25 March 1859; Brownlee Papers, Killie Campbell Library, J. Brownlee-[n.a.], 8 Jan. 1858. No Xhosa who had taken refuge in Thembuland or any other independent black state was allowed to return to British Kaffraria. See GH 8/41 J. Maclean-Magistrates, 1 May 1860.
72. GH 30/4 G. Grey-J. Maclean, 14 Feb. 1858. It should be pointed out that because of the expense and difficulty of finding surveyors, Grey's plans on this point were not fully executed.
73. Maclean's own memorandum entitled 'Occupation of the Crown Reserve' in BK 22 is a good example of this.
74. BK 71 C. Brownlee-J. Maclean, 8 March, 5 June 1858; GH 8/37 C. Brownlee-J. Maclean, 30 Aug. 1858; BK 85 C. Brownlee-J. Maclean, 6 June 1858.
75. BK 85 Memo by J. Kayser, enclosed in R.E. Robertson-J. Maclean, 14 May 1858.
76. BK 85 C. Brownlee-J. Maclean, 6 June 1858.
77. Maclean (1858), p.137. The full history of Anta's experiences during the

the Cattle-Killing is to be found in BK 85.

78. BK 85 R.E. Robertson-J. Maclean, 14, 19 May 1858.

79. BK 85 J. Maclean-R.E. Robertson, 16 May 1858.

80. BK 85 R.E. Robertson-J. Maclean, 28 May, 3 June 1858; GH 8/35 J. Maclean-F. Travers, 14 June 1858.

81. BK 86 F. Reeve-J. Maclean, 5 June 1857.

82. GH 8/35 Schedule 61, 12 April 1858.

83. BK 86 J. Miller-J. Maclean, 13, 14 Oct. 1858; GH 8/36, Schedule 143, 18 Nov. 1858.

84. BK 86 J. Miller-J. Maclean, 2 Dec. 1858; GH 8/36 J. Miller-J. Maclean, 1 Nov. 1858.

85. GH 23/27 G. Grey-E.B. Lytton, 17 July 1858.

86. BK 78 Interview of the Chief Commissioner with headmen of Umhala's location, 19 June 1858; BK 81 J. Gawler-J. Maclean, 29 May, 2 June 1858; GH 8/36 G. Colley-J. Maclean, 14 Dec. 1858. GH 8/35 Schedule 85, 3 June 1858. Mjuza, who had said from the beginning that he would not move, was allowed to keep his stipend. The others were deprived of their pay for breaking their word.

87. BK 81 M. Kayser-J. Maclean, 11 Feb., 4, 22 July, 31 Aug., 7 Oct. 1859.

88. GH 8/36 J. Miller-J. Maclean, 1 Nov. 1858; GH 8/36 G. Thompson-J. Maclean, 1 Nov. 1858; MIC 172/2, Cory Library, USPG Archives, Reel 8, C.R. Lange-USPG, March 1860.

89. BK 71 C. Brownlee-J. Maclean, 26 May, 7 July, 1 Sept. 1858; BK 81 M. Kayser-J. Maclean, 11 Feb. 1859.

90. GH 8/36 Schedule 134, 21 Oct. 1858; *ibid.*, Schedule 143, 18 Nov. 1858; *ibid.*, Schedule 156, 20 Dec. 1858; GH 8/38 Population Returns, 31 Dec. 1858. The Xhosa population of British Kaffraria (excluding the Crown Reserve, East London and King William's Town), which had numbered 37,697 at the end of 1857, fell to 25,916 by the end of 1858. The figure of 3,239 does not include Xhosa from the Ndlambe district, several hundreds of whom quit Kaffraria for Smith Mhala's settlement in the transKei during the same period.

91. PR 3624, Cory Library, Letterbook of Dr J. Fitzgerald, Report on the state of the gaol in King William's Town, 15 March 1858; GH 22/9 (?)-Civil Commissioner, Alice, 8 Nov. 1858; University of the Witwatersrand Library, Fairbairn Papers, J.A. Fairbairn-J. Fairbairn, 26 April 1858.

92. GH 8/34 Schedule 17, 4 Feb. 1858.

93. BK 89 Statement by Jonas, 18 Dec. 1858; BK 14 Memo by G. Pomeroy-Colley, 11 Nov. 1858.

94. W.W.Gqoba, 'Isizathu', Part 2, *Isigidimi*, 2 April 1888; BK 71 C. Brownlee-J. Maclean, 12 Dec. 1856, *Queenstown Free Press*, 19 Jan. 1859; 8/50 Statement by Umrweke, 22 Dec. 1858; GH 8/36 G. Colley-J. Maclean, 24 Dec. 1856.

95. CO 690 M. Jennings-J. Maclean, 7 Nov. 1857; CO 690 [Owner of the *Munster Lass*]-M. Jennings, 7 Nov. 1857; CO 692 C. Piers-Colonial Secretary 28, 31 Oct. 1857; *Cape Argus*, 8, 15 June 1858.

96. CO 692 C. Piers-Colonial Secretary, 28, 30 Sept., 31 Oct. 1857.

97. *Cape Argus*, 6 April 1858.

98. CO 715 Statement of Holo, 27 Feb. 1858.

99. *Cape Argus*, 6, 10, 13 Feb. 1857.

100. GH 28/73 J. Maclean-G. Grey, 5 April 1858; BK 386 J. Maclean-C. Piers, 28 Jan. 1858; 1/KWT (unsorted, old no. 1213) R. Taylor-J. Maclean, 26 Jan. 1859; *King William's Town Gazette*, 10 April 1858.
101. *Cape Argus*, 8 May 1858.
102. On the early history of Robben Island, S. de Villiers, *Robben Island* (Cape Town: Struik, 1971).
103. *Cape Argus*, 19 Dec. 1857; Hodgson (1980).
104. The best description of the Xhosa chiefs is 'A visit to Robben Island,' Part 2, *Cape Monthly Magazine*, 6 (1859). Also see CO 715, CO 724, CO 742, CO 779, CO 814.
105. A number of letters have been preserved in GH 17/3 and GH 17/4, for example GH 17/3 Delima-Governor, 23 March 1865. For Mhala's wives, GH 8/39, Schedule 68, 27 June 1859. For the leper woman, CO 779 J. Minto-Colonial Office, 26 Aug. 1861.
106. CO 814 W. Edmonds-R. Rawson, 3 Jan., 5 Dec. 1863; *Queenstown Free Press*, 9 Feb. 1859.
107. *Cape Monthly Magazine*, 6 (1859), p.231.
108. CO 724 J.F. Minto-Colonial Secretary, 1 Nov. 1858; CO 742 J.F. Minto-Colonial Secretary, 18 Jan. 1860; *Cape Argus*, 18 July 1857.
109. For Maqoma's brief return to Xhosaland, 1/KWT 5/1/2/2 T. Liefeldt-Magistrate of King William's Town, 27 Sept. 1869, 8 Sept. 1871, 19 Feb. 1872.
110. On Maqoma's last days, *Isigidimi samaXosa*, 1 Jan. 1872, 1 Oct. 1873; AB 1161 G2, University of the Witwatersrand, Anglican Church records.

CHAPTER 10

Everything You Always Wanted to Know About The Xhosa Cattle-Killing

You probably began this book with a number of questions in mind, and, as it draws to a close, you might be wondering whether any of these questions has really been answered. Analysis does, unfortunately, have a tendency to get in the way of narrative, and I have been forced to leave many of the answers implicit in the text. In this chapter, however, I am going to try to make amends by posing some of the major historical problems raised by the Cattle-Killing in the form of questions a reader might ask. Chapter and section references are given in brackets to locate more detailed treatment of these questions elsewhere in this book.

Who were Mhlakaza and Nongqawuse?

Mhlakaza's father, a councillor of Sarhili, killed Mhlakaza's mother. After this the future prophet entered the Cape Colony, where he adopted the name of Wilhelm Goliath and acquired the rudiments of Christianity. In 1848 he met Archdeacon N.J. Merriman, a man who was to change his life. He accompanied Merriman on various preaching expeditions around the Eastern Province, and came to perceive himself as a full partner in spreading the Gospel. However the Merriman family viewed him as a common servant and refused to take his religious experiences seriously. He left for Xhosaland about 1853 in order to become a 'Gospel Man', but he soon lost his Christian orthodoxy and began to preach the Cattle-Killing message instead (Chapter 1/4).

Nongqawuse's father was dead, and she viewed her uncle Mhlakaza as her guardian. It is possible that she was orphaned in the battles of the Waterkloof and witnessed for herself the horrors perpetrated by Colonel Eyre in the closing stages of the war.

The Cattle-Killing prophecies were uttered by Nongqawuse, who held conversations with spirits, whom she saw in the bush and in the sea. Mhlakaza then interpreted these prophecies to the believers and clarified the orders and instructions of the 'new people'. Evidence is lacking, but it seems likely that at first neither Nongqawuse nor Mhlakaza exercised any conscious control over when the 'new people' would appear or what they would say. They had devised no pre-conceived plan of action, but were as dependent as any other Xhosa on the next message from the spirits.

The prophets of the Gxarha were totally unprepared to deal with the crisis which their prophecies initiated. They were obviously unable to produce the 'new people' on demand, or to cope with the con-sequences of the failure of their prophecies. Rather than admit their limitations, they seem to have resorted to deliberate subterfuges such as 'showing' enquirers the black shapes of the 'new people' but forbidding them to approach close enough to get a proper look (Chapter 3/3). There is some evidence that the continual demands of Sarhili and the other believers eventually cracked the fantasy world of the prophets. Nongqawuse became too 'sick' to prophesy, and Mhlakaza began to deny responsibility for the sayings of his niece (Chapter 5/1).

That both Mhlakaza and Nongqawuse sincerely believed that the dead would rise seems beyond doubt. Mhlakaza certainly committed himself to the truth of the prophecies, to the extent of dying of starvation. For the fate of Nongqawuse, see Chapter 11.

Who were the strangers seen by Nongqawuse?

The strangers introduced themselves as messengers of Sifuba-Sibanzi (the Broad-Chested One) and Napakade (the Eternal One). Although these figures represented themselves as the indigenous gods of the Xhosa people, they were most probably more recent conceptions bred partly from Christian ideas and partly from the felt need of the Xhosa people for more powerful gods of their own (Chapter 4/4).

But did Nongqawuse really see any strangers at all? Many Xhosa believe that the strangers were the agents of Sir George Grey, or possibly even Grey himself in disguise. Other Xhosa believe that Nongqawuse's visions were the typical fantasies of a young girl, or, as one knowledgeable old man expressed it, 'She stared in the water and saw her own reflection.'[1]

It is not possible to prove this matter beyond doubt, but the weight of probability must be that the strangers seen by Nongqawuse never existed, except in her imagination. Nongqawuse was an orphan raised by an uncle who was himself a religious visionary. She had witnessed the horrors of war and the catastrophe of lungsickness, and she must have heard the prophecies of resurrection inspired by the supposed Russian victories in the Crimean War (Chapter 2/4). At the same time, as was indicated by her appearance ('has a silly look and appeared to me as if she was not right in her mind'),[2] she was undergoing an experience akin to the *thwasa* initiation of Xhosa doctors (Chapter 3/3). It is not to be wondered at if, given her history and her circumstances, the visions which she saw were not those of the normal *thwasa* initiate but others, inspired by rumours of the resurrection of the ancestors.

It would seem, then, that the mysterious strangers were nothing more tangible than the imaginary friends of Nongqawuse's day-dreams, and that the fatal prophecies originated in the fantasies of two young girls playing in a bush. As Nombanda, Nongqawuse's younger companion, related it, 'I frequently accompanied Nongqawuse to a certain bush where she spoke with people . . . I neither saw them nor did I hear them speak till after I had constantly visited the bush with her.' The little girls on the Mpongo River (Chapter 6/4), who built huts for their pet stranger to sleep in, were behaving in a similar fashion. Normal Xhosa parents living in normal times would have dismissed such childish games with a friendly laugh. But the times were not normal, and Nongqawuse's uncle, the frustrated Gospel Man Mhlakaza/Wilhelm Goliath, was a preacher in search of a prophecy. And so, instead of curbing Nongqawuse's talk of the two strangers, he actively encouraged it and brought it to the attention of Sarhili.

What did they tell the people?

Nongqawuse said that she had met with a 'new people' from over the sea, who were the ancestors of the living Xhosa. They told her that the dead were preparing to rise again, and wonderful new cattle too, but first the people must kill their cattle and destroy their corn which were contaminated and impure. They should also put away their witchcraft, which was the cause of all their afflictions.

They should not cultivate in the new season, but they should build great new cattle enclosures for the cattle which would rise, and dig deep grainpits for the corn which would miraculously appear. They should build new houses and wear new ornaments to greet a new and perfect world. On the appointed day, the sun would rise blood-red with a terrible heat until it turned back at midday to set again, turning the earth pitch-black. (An alternative version had two suns in the sky at once.) A terrible storm would follow complete with thunder, lightning and hurricanes. All this while, the believers were to wait in their newly built and carefully sealed houses, while the burning sun and the fearsome winds destroyed the unbelievers, their impure cattle, their tools of witchcraft, and all the other malevolent beings such as baboons and lizards which carried evil about the world.

After the storm would come the rising of the dead and the appearance of the new cattle and the new corn. All kinds of food and clothing and household goods would rise out of the ground. The blind would see, the deaf would hear, the cripples would walk, and the old would become young again. Peace, plenty and goodness would reign on earth. The ultimate goal of the Cattle-Killing movement was 'a happy state of things to all' (Chapters 3/1, 4/4, 5/2).

Why the emphasis on cattle-killing?

An important cause of the Cattle-Killing was the lungsickness epidemic which reached Xhosaland in 1855. Cattle mortality was as high as one half to two thirds in some places, and many Xhosa lost all their cattle. The great believer Chief Phatho, for example, lost 96 per cent of his 2,500 cattle. Even those who retained their cattle were fearful that these might yet be struck down. The Xhosa began to believe that their cattle were rotten and impure, and that they might as well kill them since they were probably going to die anyway (Chapter 2/4).

Nongqawuse's first instruction to the Xhosa was simply that they should 'get rid' of their cattle. Many sold their beasts to white traders, and when the first prophecies of the Cattle-Killing failed in August, this sale of cattle was blamed. It was said that the cattle should be slaughtered in a ritual manner, so that their spirits might also rise on the great day. This revised order to sacrifice their cattle fitted in very well with existing Xhosa ideas concerning the correct way to communicate with the ancestors, to please them, and to prove themselves worthy of the great benefits to come (Chapter 5/4).

Why did the people believe Nongqawuse?

The Cattle-Killing cannot be divorced from the colonial situation which was imposed on the Xhosa in 1847 by Sir Harry Smith. Although it has been necessary in this history to examine the personal role of Sir George Grey in detail, it should be remembered that the essential objectives of Grey were identical to those of Smith and of colonial rule generally: to destroy the political and economic independence of the Xhosa, to bring them under British law and administration, to make their land and their labour available to the white settlers, and to reshape their religious and cultural institutions on European and Christian models (Chapter 1/2).

The failure of Mlanjeni's efforts to shake off this domination left thousands of Xhosa dead and all their best land in settler hands. The one small concession wrung out of Governor Cathcart, the right to govern themselves in their own way, was rescinded by Sir George Grey, who sought to destroy the political and economic independence of the Xhosa chiefs by making them salaried adjuncts of British magistrates. The lungsickness epidemic finally pushed the people over the edge of despair — they would have clutched at any hope (Chapters 1/3, 2/3-4).

That hope was supplied by the supposed victories of the Russians in the Crimea and, in particular, the death in battle of ex-Governor Cathcart. No Xhosa had ever heard of these Russians before, and it was supposed that they were the ancestors of the Xhosa. Throughout Xhosaland prophets and prophetesses sprang up, who claimed to have seen the Russians or earlier prophets like Nxele and Mlanjeni (Chapter 2/4).

It is important to note that the idea of cattle-killing was widespread before Nongqawuse started to speak. This shows that the central beliefs of the movement were a logical development of existing Xhosa religious concepts, namely (1) that the dead do not really die, but live on; (2) that the cattle sickness was a sign from the ancestors that they were troubled and wished to communicate with the living; (3) that if all impure and evil things disappeared, the world would be a perfect place; (4) that all living things on earth originated from the uHlanga, and that the creative power of the uHlanga was not yet spent. The success of the movement also depended on the common belief in the Christian notion of the resurrection, which had been popularized by the prophet Nxele before 1820, and in the new Xhosa/Christian concept of Sifuba-Sibanzi (the Broad-Chested One), the expected redeemer (Chapter 4/4). Nongqawuse's ideas were thus not original. She succeeded where other prophetesses had failed because her claims were supported by King Sarhili, who was deceived by the little show which the prophetic group set up at the Gxarha River.

Sarhili was a man of religious inclination, who had all his life attended to the sayings of doctors and diviners. He was in great distress over the death of his Great Son, and haunted by guilt over the death of Bomela, whom he had allowed to be put to death. When

Nongqawuse 'showed' the King his lost son, Sarhili was captivated. From that time onwards, he was responsible for driving the movement forward, even when it was weak and flagging from its own failures. As one old councillor put it, 'the whole movement [was] Krieli's, and so resolute was he in carrying it out that he would permit no one to reason with him on the subject'.

One should not forget that most Xhosa did not have the time or the opportunity to visit the Gxarha and see for themselves. It was known by all that Sarhili had visited Nongqawuse and confirmed the truth of her prophecies. For most Xhosa, this was more than enough. The Ngqika Xhosa, for example, maintained that 'a chief in Kreli's position would not send the message he has sent unless he was fully convinced of Umhlakaza's assertions'.

But Sarhili was a victim himself. He was 'shown' a demonstration of some sort down at the Gxarha, and so were hundreds of other enquirers who flocked there. Unlike the other prophetesses, Nongqawuse did not simply proclaim the truth of her visions. She induced other people to share them. The enquirers were predisposed to do so by the remote situation and suggestive physical features of the Gxarha River area. Most of them had travelled several days to reach Mhlakaza's place, and when they did they found a locale redolent of mystery and awe: bush, cliffs, caves, river and, above all, the sea. Add mist and shadows and black shapes — dolphins or even seaweed — floating by, and any wishful thinker standing at a distance could easily be persuaded to believe that he was witnessing the magical forms of the new people, waiting and yearning to rise. On a clear day, with no mist or shadow, Nongqawuse either announced that the new people were not present that day, or contrived to satisfy her audience by inaudible conversations with spirits in her magic bush. Rumours, assurances, dreams and exhortations around the visitors' fire at night supplied any deficiency. Several of Nongqawuse's visitors — Nxito, Ngubo, Mjuza and Smith Mhala, for example — were thoroughly disillusioned and left the Gxarha as fierce unbelievers. But they were in a small minority.

But why didn't people get disillusioned when the prophecies failed to materialize?

Mhlakaza was always able to point to the disobedience of the un-believers as the cause of the failure, or rather the postponement, of the prophetic predictions. For example, he claimed after the December disappointment that Napakade had been about to rise with 600 cattle, until the ancestors of the unbelievers begged for a delay so as to give their descendants another chance.

Many believers were also guilty of only partial obedience to the cattle-killing command. They slaughtered some of their cattle immediately in the hope that these would suffice, but held others back just in case. As one of the Thembu believers put it, 'Many who have listened have only done so with one ear: the cattle are not all dead, and there is still a little corn left.' Even staunch believers like Phatho, Mhala and Sarhili himself did not kill their last head of cattle until eight days before the Great Disappointment. Thus there was always room for the 'new people' to say something like 'We said that all your cattle were to be killed, you have not done so — we leave you in disgust.'

The believers were naturally conscious of the 'stinginess' of the unbelievers, and of their own derelictions of duty. The disappointments did not therefore lessen their fervour; on the contrary, they increased the pressure on those who had not already fully complied with the orders of the prophet to destroy their last beast and their last grain of corn (Chapter 5/2).

Why did some Xhosa believe and others not?

So many factors affected the decision of a Xhosa homestead head whether or not to kill his cattle that it is impossible for any generalization to be absolutely valid. Certain distinguishable tendencies did operate. Chiefdoms which had been sorely afflicted by lungsickness were more likely to adopt the prophecies of the Cattle-Killing than chiefdoms which had not. Women, who performed the toilsome and socially unrewarding labour of cultivating the soil, were liable to be responsive to a message which promised them a future free of agricultural work. Those who had long collaborated with the colonial authorities were more likely to resist belief than those who had always been hostile. But there were significant exceptions even to these limited generalizations, and concerning factors such as age, status and religious belief it is impossible to generalize at all.

We should therefore adopt the distinction which the Xhosa themselves made between the 'soft' believers (*amathamba*) and the 'hard' unbelievers (*amagogotya*). The believers described themselves as 'soft' because they submitted themselves and their private interests entirely to the requirements of the national community as defined by Nongqawuse. By and large, they stood committed to the social ethos and the economic structure of the old, precolonial social formation which depended on reciprocal generosity and communal endeavour. The unbelievers were thought of as 'hard' because they stuck by their own conceptions of what was right and stingily exalted their private economic interests above the national well-being of the community at large. In as far as the personal lives of the leading unbelievers are known to us, it would seem that the backbone of the 'hard', *gogotya* party was made up of prosperous and wealthy men who were in a position to profit from the new economic opportunities created by the expansion of the colonial market. The 'soft', *thamba* party, on the other hand, was 'peculiarly . . . one of the common people', who stood or fell by the viability of the precolonial economy. The division between believers and unbelievers was not therefore a simple reaction to the crisis of the prophecies, but a reflection of the deeper communal tensions generated by the breakup of Xhosa society under colonial pressure (Chapter 5/4).

Wasn't the Cattle-Killing anti-white?

The Cattle-Killing was born partly out of Xhosa frustration at colonial domination and partly out of the hope awakened by the news that the Russians had beaten the English. Nongqawuse's promise of a perfect world in which 'no one would ever lead a troubled life' could hardly have accommodated a continued settler presence in Xhosaland. Among the many predictions that circulated at the time was one to the effect that the English, like all other evil things, would be swept away in the great storm which would precede the resurrection of the dead. It was said, at times, that the whites were doomed because they were responsible for the death of the Son of God. Such anti-white statements were naturally exaggerated among the settler community and played an important part in the genesis of the 'chiefs' plot' myth.

Nevertheless, one should not ignore the brief interlude following the First Disappointment (October 1856), when short-lived and ineffectual attempts were made to persuade the whites, too, to kill their cattle. It was said then that 'the people who have arrived have not come to make war on the white man, but to bring about a happy state of things to all', and this phrase seems to sum up the essentially optimistic orientation of the Cattle-Killing movement. It was not predominantly negative or hostile towards anything or anybody, but a movement driven by positive expectations, obliterating the evil past and looking towards a better future. The worst outbreaks of anti-white sentiment always occurred during the periods of disappointment. During the periods of hopeful expectation, the Xhosa always greeted their white visitors with a happy indifference (Chapter 4/1, 4).[3]

What was the role of Sir George Grey in all this?

Almost all Xhosa today hold Sir George Grey personally responsible for the Cattle-Killing, believing that in some way he manipulated Nongqawuse into prophesying as she did. This interpretation is very old and probably dates as far back as the Cattle-Killing period itself.[4] S.E.K. Mqhayi (d. 1945), the greatest of Xhosa historians, believed it, and the late Chief Ndumiso Bhotomane, in his time the leading Xhosa oral historian and himself the son of one of Sarhili's close advisers, repeated the story to me in 1975.

I have looked very closely into all the surviving documents, including the private correspondence between Grey and his chief subordinate Maclean,[5] and must state unequivocally that there is no documentary evidence whatsoever in support of this view. It is true — as I have frequently pointed out — that Grey was an exceptionally secretive and deceitful man, and that, barring a miracle, we shall never know exactly what really happened down there at the Gxarha. Clearly, many people are going to continue to believe that Grey was solely responsible for the whole thing. I am not going to quarrel with them. But I will say that anyone who thinks that blaming Grey absolves the Xhosa believers of their own part in this greatest of all Xhosa historical disasters is depriving himself of history's greatest gift: the opportunity of learning from the mistakes of the past.

Admirers of Grey cannot, however, complain or wonder if the Xhosa blame him for their misfortunes. His new system of administration, which broke the promises of the preceding Governor, was an important contributory factor. The threatening and bullying attitude which he adopted during the lifetime of the movement only strengthened the resolve of the believers, and the laughable disasters which befell his ship, the *Geyser*, encouraged them at a time when their faith was wavering (Chapter 4). After the Cattle-Killing was over, Grey did his best to turn this human tragedy to the political and economic profit of the Cape Colony. Instead of making food freely available to the hungry, he utilized the desperate starvation of the people to engineer their mass exodus via the colonial labour market, while filling their former lands with white settlers. Attempts by the Xhosa to find work independently of Grey's labour machine were countered by transport-ation, and the feeble efforts of the Kaffir Relief Committee to provide genuine charity were crushed (Chapter 8). On the pretence of the 'chiefs' plot,' petty charges were trumped up against the leading chiefs, who were tried by military courts and packed off to Robben Island (Chapter 7). Sarhili and his starving people were hounded out of their country, though Grey knew very well through his private spies that the Xhosa King was helpless and submissive (Chapter 9/2). The unbelievers, who had borne the brunt of the struggle against

Nongqawuse, were confined to small villages and loaded with hut tax (Chapter 9/3). By such means, a 'white corridor' stretching from East London to Queenstown was carved out of lands which had formerly been entirely Xhosa.

Even if Grey did not initiate the Cattle-Killing, he bears the responsibility for turning it into an irrevocable catastrophe.

But wasn't Grey a great friend of the black man?

Grey's reputation as a liberal depends largely on the fact that in his view non-European peoples like the Xhosa and the Maori were not 'irreclaimable savages' but 'as apt and intelligent as any race of men'. Whereas other Governors had been primarily concerned to erect military barriers shutting the Xhosa out of the Cape Colony, Grey wished, in his famous phrase, 'to make them a part of ourselves, with a common faith and common interests' (Chapter 2/2). The visionary language and the grand visible symbols (hospitals, schools, etc.) with which Grey cloaked his objectives should not blind us to the fact that the role which he envisaged for blacks in his new South Africa was essentially a subordinate one, as the continuation of the above phrase — 'useful servants, consumers of our goods, contributors to our revenue' — makes plain. Implicit in Grey's elevated ideals of civilization and Christianity was an unthinking dismissal of Xhosa culture and religion as wholly valueless. It is unlikely that the Xhosa viewed Grey, with his declared aim of destroying their legal, political and economic systems, as a better friend than Cathcart, who had conceded them the right to live according to their own laws and customs.

One should, in any case, beware of placing too much emphasis on Grey as an individual. He was first and foremost a colonial Governor, and like all colonial Governors his primary aim was to serve the British Empire, which in British Kaffraria meant to subjugate the Xhosa. Grey's policies were pretty much the same as Sir Harry Smith's, and even Cathcart's concessions were little more than a tactical retreat. In a very real sense, Grey's governorship was nothing more than the next logical step in the extension of British colonial domination of South Africa. We cannot imagine that the end result of the Cattle-Killing — the incorporation of Xhosaland into British South Africa — would have been very different, even if the individuals named Grey and Nongqawuse had never existed.

Grey's distinguishing feature as a colonial Governor was not his liberalism, but his extraordinary opportunism and ruthlessness. Whereas other colonial Governors were handicapped by the official rule book and by some sort of concern for the opinions of others, Grey was bound by no such scruples. As a young man of modest means, he had identified Australasia as a land of opportunity waiting for a great man, like himself, to set his stamp upon it. Inspired perhaps by Carlyle's vision of the hero, he aspired to an absolute dictatorship which he viewed as the just entitlement of his superior abilities. In his quest for absolute power he did not hesitate to lie, cheat and slander whoever stood in his way. Indigenous peoples like the Maori and the Xhosa were trampled down for convenient and imaginary treacheries and conspiracies. Grey's own behaviour, as described in this book and in the New Zealand literature, is the surest witness we have against him (Chapter 2/1-2).

What were the results of the Cattle-Killing?

The results of the Cattle-Killing are difficult to quantify. The only really reliable figure that we have is that the Xhosa population of British Kaffraria dropped by two thirds between January and December of 1857, from 105,000 to 37,500, and then again by another third to reach a low point of 25,916 by the end of 1858.[6] How many of these actually died is hard to say. Charles Brownlee estimated that an average of four persons had died per homestead by the end of September 1857, which would give us just over 15,000 dead in British Kaffraria alone. If we add in estimates for Sarhili's Gcaleka Xhosa and for the Thembu believers, and adjust fractionally upwards for deaths after September, we get a figure of 35,000. This is a very conservative estimate. The *Cape Argus*, quoting unnamed well-informed sources, published a figure of 50,000 and Bishop Gray of Cape Town suggested 40,000. This last estimate cannot be very far from the truth. Upwards of 150,000 more Xhosa were displaced, as many by Grey's attack on Sarhili in 1858 as by the Cattle-Killing itself. Cattle mortality figures are even more vague, but Brownlee's estimate of 400,000 slaughtered by January 1857 fits in well with what else we know, and is probably a conservative estimate of total cattle loss if we count in deaths from lungsickness as well.

Another measure of the disaster is the extent of land lost by the Xhosa. This amounted to more than 600,000 acres, not counting the land lost in the Crown Reserve following the War of Mlanjeni.[7] Map 5 tells its own story. Chiefs Mhala, Phatho and Maqoma lost all their lands, thus clearing the way for white settlement in the hinterland of East London. Sarhili was driven out of the whole of his territory and, although he was eventually (1865) allowed to reoccupy part of it, two thirds of the total was alienated permanently. Even in those areas,

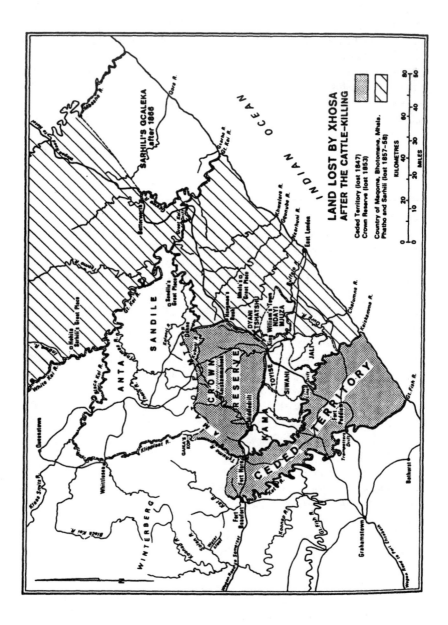

Map 5: Land Lost by the Xhosa as a Result of the Cattle-Killing

such as the chiefdoms of Sandile, Anta and Kama, where the unbelievers held sway, the amount of land effectively at their disposal was greatly curtailed by Grey's policy of concentrating them into villages. As more and more Xhosa returned home from their spell of forced labour in the Colony, so these tiny allocations became increasingly unable to support them and the whole of what is now the Ciskei degenerated into a vast rural slum and migrant labour pool.

British Kaffraria was transformed from an exclusively Xhosa territory ruled by Xhosa chiefs through Xhosa laws into a mixed territory populated by both blacks and whites. At the same time, most of the white towns of the eastern and midland Cape, from Somerset East to Beaufort West and beyond, acquired for the first time a substantial permanent black population. The 'whitening' of British Kaffraria and the 'blackening' of the Cape Colony eliminated the need to keep the two distinct. Once Kaffraria had ceased to be an alien and defiant territory held down by force, it was easily absorbed into the Colony as the districts of East London, King William's Town and Stutterheim (1866).

The impact on the Xhosa themselves is difficult to express in words. Their national, cultural and economic integrity, long penetrated and undermined by colonial pressure, finally collapsed. Sandile and some other traditionalist remnants clung on grimly to what remained of the old precolonial way of life, but they became increasingly irrelevant not only to the colonial authorities, but to the mass of the Xhosa population immersed in a world of which the chiefs and their cohorts knew nothing. When Sandile rose for the last time in the 1877 Frontier War, the occasion was of emotional significance only. Ethnically based resistance had long ceased to be a realistic strategy on the Eastern Frontier.

The majority of Xhosa accepted that the catastrophe of Nongqawuse was irreversible, and they took their places in the schools of Alice and the docks of Port Elizabeth to work out a new destiny inside the belly of the colonial beast. Grey had succeeded beyond his wildest dreams in turning them into 'useful servants, consumers of our goods, contributors to our revenue', and it was as an oppressed class within Cape society that they took up the continuing struggle for liberation. Independent Xhosaland was dead; Nongqawuse and Sir George Grey had irrevocably transformed the Xhosa nation into South Africans.

Is it likely that we shall ever know more about the Cattle-Killing?

This book is based on private and official papers, on interviews with elderly and knowledgeable Xhosa, and on a wide range of English and

Xhosa books and newspapers. The reader is referred to the bibliography for further details. But one cannot read every newspaper and one cannot interview every elderly person. It is altogether possible that further research will bring further information to light, though I doubt that we shall ever learn more about the inner history of the prophetic circle at the Gxarha River.

Even if no further information can be obtained, it must be possible to write histories of Nongqawuse from other perspectives than mine. It is now one hundred and thirty years since these dark and tragic events, and this book is the first detailed and informed account ever written on the subject. Let us hope that we do not have to wait another hundred and thirty years for the next.

Notes

1. Interview with B. Donga, Sigidi Location, Idutywa District, 1 Sept. 1983.
2. All quotations and information in this chapter are fully cited on their first appearance in this book.
3. For an example, see BK 70 C. Brownlee-J. Maclean, 19 Oct. 1856.
4. Burton (1950), p.70; 'Nzulu Lwazi' (S.E.K. Mqhayi), *Umteteli waBantu*, 5 Sept. 1931.
5. The private correspondence of Grey and Maclean may be found in the Cape Archives, Volumes GH 8/48-8/50.
6. These figures exclude the Mfengu population of the Crown Reserve, from which the Xhosa were strictly excluded, and the infinitesimal Xhosa populations of the white towns of East London and King William's Town. See the official population returns for British Kaffraria in Maclean (1858) and GH 8/38.

   Brownlee's estimate of four dead per homestead (BK 71 C. Brownlee-J. Maclean, 1 Oct. 1857) multiplied by the number of homesteads in British Kaffraria per census in Maclean (1858) gives a total 15,368. The population of Sarhili's Gcalekaland was usually estimated as roughly equal to that of British Kaffraria. Maclean (1858), p.151. According to the *King William's Town Gazette*, 2 May 1857, mortality in Sarhili's country was even higher than that in British Kaffraria. I have estimated Fadana's Thembu believers at 10 per cent of British Kaffraria, a figure which tallies with the estimated 300-400 fighting men at his disposal. CO 2949 W. Currie-R. Southey, 24 July 1857.

   The displacement figure was arrived at by subtracting the number of estimated dead from the total population lost by British Kaffraria (53,000) and adding the total population of Sarhili's country (90,000 after subtracting the estimated dead). If one adds in the Thembu believers and those who moved around inside British Kaffraria (for example, those who took shelter at the missions or with unbelieving relatives) the total should easily top 150,000.

Brownlee's estimate of 400,000 cattle killed is in GH 8/49 C. Brownlee-J. Maclean, 7 Jan. 1857. This is quite compatible with the figure of 130,300 dead of lungsickness and slaughtering up to the end of July 1856, at the very beginning of the movement. Imperial Blue Book 2352 of 1857, G. Grey-H. Labouchere, 3 Oct. 1856, p.35.

Bishop Gray's figure is quoted in Saunders (1978), p.11; The *Cape Argus* estimate appeared on 3 March 1858.

7. The figure of 600,000 is derived by multiplying 300+ white farms by 2,000 acres each. See Note 10 in Chapter 11 below.

And Last

The great three-decker novels of the Victorian era often used to end with a chapter summarizing what became of the principal characters in the story: their marriages, their subsequent careers, their eventual deaths. This history is not, unfortunately, a fiction but, having lived so long with these characters, I cannot bear to leave them without saying a few words as to their ultimate fate. Perhaps less sentimental readers will find these last pages interesting as a sort of biographical collage representing the remainder of the nineteenth century, by means of which some of the more important consequences of the Cattle-Killing may be more clearly perceived.

None of Sir George Grey's harsh and brutal measures with regard to the Xhosa raised an official eyebrow in London. Forced labour, arbitrary court-martial, unprovoked invasion and land theft on an unprecedented scale: all these were greeted by the Colonial Office with polite applause, as the apt and just measures of a man who truly understood the native mind. But Grey's other policies, the ones dealing with Imperial and settler matters that had a call on the heart of the Colonial Office and the purse of the Treasury, deeply embarrassed his superiors in London. Grey spent Imperial money with careless abandon. He disregarded direct orders as if they did not exist. When he was caught out in double dealing, he did not shrink from outright lies to justify his position. The affair of the German military settlers, whom Grey brought out to people the land he stole from the Xhosa, may serve as an example. The German settlement was an unmitigated disaster. The small plots allotted to the Germans were too small for settler-style farms, and the rough, undisciplined ex-soldiers were not prepared to work like Kaffirs, for other people or even for themselves. Their discontent was so obvious and so dangerous that Grey was forced to put them back on full army pay, which infuriated the War Office and removed any work incentive the Germans might previously have had. Most of them spent their entire incomes getting drunk until the next payday.[1] Rather than cutting back on so unsuccessful an experiment, Grey decided that the answer to the problem was yet more German settlers, and he contracted with a private firm, Cesar Godeffroy & Son of Hamburg, to send him 4,000 more immigrants at a minimum cost of £50,000. The Colonial Secretary in London was horrified by this extravagant and useless proposal, and sent Grey direct and unequivocal orders to stop the scheme immediately. Grey continued with his arrangements regardless, claiming that his deal with Godeffroy's had been finalized before he received these instructions. This was a downright lie. Some snappy detective work at the Colonial Office revealed that Grey had received the crucial dispatch on 27 July 1857, more than three weeks before he signed the contract with Godeffroy. Yet so great was the respect of the Colonial Office for the skill with which Grey had handled the Xhosa that they decided to grin and bear his little disobedience.[2]

Grey's pattern of behaviour in this matter was repeated over and over again. He failed to send Britain the troops it needed to deal with the Indian Mutiny. He failed to render proper accounts for the £40,000 a year he spent civilizing the Xhosa. He failed to publish the constitution which would have freed British Kaffraria from martial law. He insisted on appointing his own nominee as Attorney General, when he knew that the Colonial Office had another candidate. He even engaged the War Office in a long and ludicrous feud over expenditure on soldiers' boots.

But none of these indiscretions bothered the Governor's superiors half as much as Grey's attempts to resume British sovereignty over the Orange Free State, which the Colonial Office had given up with much relief in 1854. Grey made it clear soon after he arrived that he thought this was a mistake, and the war which erupted in 1858 between Moshoeshoe's Sotho and the Free State Boers, far from frightening him off, only confirmed his opinion. When the Free State, defeated by Moshoeshoe and thoroughly unable to defend itself any further, indicated an interest in rejoining the Cape, Grey immediately brought the matter before the colonial Parliament in defiance of his instructions from London. Bulwer-Lytton, the Colonial Secretary, was tired of Grey's continual disobedience and ordered him recalled. Not only the

Xhosa, but the Thembu, the Mpondo and all the other Xhosa-speaking peoples rejoiced at his departure 'to a man', for they realized that he aimed to steal the land and the independence of every black nation in the neighbourhood of the Cape.[3]

To Grey's surprise, he was greeted in London by the news that his old friend, the Duke of Newcastle, had taken over the Colonial Office and reinstated him in the Governorship he had lost. It was a glorious vindication for Grey, but it was also the high watermark of his career for, on the long voyage back to the Cape, nemesis struck him from a wholly unexpected source. His wife, Lady Lucy Grey, commenced an ardent flirtation with their fellow passenger, Admiral Henry Keppel. Estranged from her husband ever since his callous indifference to the loss of their only child way back in the Australian days, Lady Lucy attached herself to the dashing admiral, in her own words, 'like a creeping plant, clinging to a support that was unable to bear the strain'.[4] She sent him a note, asking him to unblock the interleading door between their cabins so that she could come to him in the night. This note was intercepted by Grey, who went quite mad with fury. He threatened to kill his wife or, alternatively, to kill himself. Lady Grey was disembarked at Rio, and remained separated from her husband for the next 36 years.

Most men might have been glad to hush up such an incident, but with Grey pride took second place to revenge. Even though he himself had been unfaithful on numerous occasions and once even kept a mistress in the house, he trumpeted his wrongs all over Cape society and the world at large, little caring how much this served to prolong and aggravate the scandal. He set spies on Lady Grey in London, he sold the house she lived in, and eventually he intercepted another letter from Keppel, which he sent on to the Colonial Secretary in the hope that it would ruin the admiral's career. He spent the remainder of his Cape governorship quite inactive from rage, pursuing his grand schemes for more annexations in the Free State and Natal half-heartedly if at all. An old missionary acquaintance, who met him by chance, was quite astonished when Grey greeted him by name: 'Otherwise I should not have discovered [recognised] him at all, I fear — as I had not done till he spoke — so broken down — so unlike himself.'[5]

Anxious to end the Governor's pursuit of Admiral Keppel, the Colonial Secretary offered Grey a second spell as Governor of New Zealand, where the Maori King movement now challenged British sovereignty over most of the North Island.[6] For a brief period, the old Grey flickered to life again. He proposed new self-governing institutions for the Maoris to pre-empt the King movement, and he instigated the invasion of the Maori territory of Waikato, complete with the usual Grey apparatus of false accusations, wholesale land confiscations and arbitrary court-martials. But Grey's spell was broken beyond repair. The Maoris were thoroughly disillusioned with British rule, and Grey was the last Governor on earth that they were prepared to trust.

Once the legend of his personal influence over the Maoris was exposed as a myth, Grey had nothing new to offer. The Dr Jekyll in him weakened, and the Mr Hyde burst ever more vigorously forth. His hands trembled, he lost his nerve, and he chickened out of important meetings with Maori chiefs. Most of his energy was consumed in endless petty bickering with his generals and his ministers, and the periods of inactivity and depression caused by his 'wound' multiplied in frequency and intensity. While New Zealand sank ever deeper into debt and civil war, Grey occupied his time plotting and scheming to outwit a colonial politician or get a general dismissed. The Colonial Office's disillusionment was slow in coming, but when it finally arrived, it was total and absolute. Only the fact that his term of office was nearly up saved him from the disgrace of a recall and, as it was, his replacement was sent out a few months early. On the express instructions of the relevant minister, the Colonial Office declined to send Grey the customary note of thanks, or even to admit that he had 'done his utmost' to promote the interests of New Zealand. 'I don't think [he] is likely to be re-employed,' was the Colonial Secretary's only comment on Grey's twenty-five years of devoted service.[7]

After a brief spell in England during which he agitated on the Irish land question, stood unsuccessfully for Parliament and utterly failed to find another job, Grey returned to New Zealand. He transformed his home at Kawau Island into a strange living fantasy world of exotic plants and animals. Peacocks, kookaburras and Chinese pheasants mixed with monkeys, wallabies, springbok and kangaroos against a background of cork, walnut, breadfruit, pomegranate and red gum trees, while New Zealand pohutukawa flourished alongside Brazilian palms, Indian deodars, Cape silver ferns and and Fijian spider lilies. Grey's favourite trick with visitors was to take them out into this jungle, provoke a wild bull to charge them, and then shoot it plumb between the eyes.[8]

In 1874 a quirk of New Zealand politics summoned Grey from this fantastic retreat to defend the provincial rights of Auckland against the powers of the New Zealand central government. Grey found this a convenient platform for his accumulated grievances against the

English landed aristocracy and their New Zealand counterparts. For five years he enjoyed an amazing Indian summer, including two years as Prime Minister, during which he stomped the country denouncing big landowners and corrupt businessmen, and advocating radical land taxes and universal manhood suffrage. Alas for Grey! He was born to dictate only to helpless, conquered Third World peoples, and he found he was unable to deal with fellow white settlers over whom he was granted neither the power to decree nor the might to coerce. He gave way, as usual, to petty jealousy and intrigues which culminated in his being dumped by his own supporters and confined to the backbenches.

There he continued, partly as a prophet but mostly as a harmless joke until his eighty-second year when, driven by a whim to see his beloved Queen Victoria once more before she died, he returned to England. He saw Her Majesty as he wished, but, totally unexpectedly, Lady Grey declared it her duty to return to him after 36 years of blissful separation, and descended on his small hotel in South Kensington. She was most put out, however, to discover how little money he still had left, and had to be hustled off to Bournemouth by friends. Grey never quite recovered from her visit, but died peacefully in her absence in September 1898, aged 86 years.[9]

It devolved upon Chief Commissioner John Maclean to put the finishing touches to the new British Kaffraria. We have already seen how the lands of Mhala, Maqoma, Phatho and the other unbelievers had been confiscated, and the unbelievers moved into villages to facilitate administration, taxation and white settlement. The lands thus made available were surveyed into 317 white farms of about 2,000 acres each. The white population increased sixfold (from 949 to 5388) in the two years of the Cattle-Killing, while the black population declined by nearly two thirds (105,000 to 38,500) during the same period. While this did not exactly equalize the racial mixture of the region to the extent that Grey had hoped, it did increase the white population from less than 1 per cent to a healthy 12.5 per cent.[10] Some sections of the district were kept open for government use, or for purchase by the anticipated class of Xhosa peasants in lots of between 10 and 80 acres. Grey wished to charge £1 an acre for land in British Kaffraria, a hefty price in view of the fact that established farms in the Cape Colony sold at less than half that amount, while unimproved land in the Colony was available at from 2 to 4 shillings an acre. Since white farmers were not interested in buying such expensive properties,[11] Grey was forced to virtually give it away to them at a quitrent of £2 per annum for 1,000 acres.

Potential black farmers were given no such concessions, however, but were required to pay the original £1 an acre. Even though there was much enthusiasm among both Xhosa and Mfengu for individual properties of this type, very few of them — mainly government interpreters and other salaried employees — were able to afford it.[12] Grey had, perhaps, achieved his ambition of creating a 'mixed community' in British Kaffraria, but economically speaking it was no contest. The majority of blacks were concentrated in villages with miserable little 4-acre plots, except for a tiny privileged minority who owned smallholdings of not more than 80 acres. The white settlers, on the other hand, received huge farms of 2,000 or so acres of better land, at a nominal rental and, literally, no capital outlay at all.[13] One consequence of this was that the most prosperous section of the community (the white farmers) paid virtually nothing into the Kaffrarian treasury, and the government's income depended on the 'hut tax' of 10 shillings per annum, which the downtrodden Xhosa (and Mfengu) were forced to contribute towards the costs of this unequal administration.[14]

Maclean had very little difficulty squeezing the people into villages or extorting their hut tax, but he dreaded the day when the Xhosa chiefs would be released from their island prison. 'I look forward with much apprehension to the time when the sentences passed on the [Xhosa] chiefs now confined in Robben Island shall have expired,' he confided to Grey. 'I fear they will find that in their absence their country has been divided amongst Europeans, and their tribes dispersed.' He suggested that the captive chiefs be outlawed for life, or, alternatively, that he be given sweeping and arbitrary powers over all Xhosa in British Kaffraria. Both Grey and his successor, Governor Wodehouse, resisted these demands, which they knew to be unnecessary. By the time that they were released from prison, the Xhosa chiefs were old and broken men, and the material basis of their former power was gone forever.

Nevertheless, Maclean was not taking any chances. He quite illegally told Phatho, the first of the chiefs to return, that if he ever attempted to rally his subjects round him, he would be sent back to Cape Town. Phatho pleaded 'that he had no wish to establish a chieftainship for himself . . . but that he wished that a location . . . should be laid out for his people'. Maclean replied in the most emphatic manner 'that it was a decided point that his [Phatho's] people should never be together again', and he again threatened the chief with a return to exile. He reminded Phatho that he was an old man who could not expect to live much longer, and advised him 'as a friend' to spend his few remaining years in peace and quietness.[15]

Maclean himself did not have much longer to live, though he did not know it. Some time in 1861 a gun went off by accident a little too near his right temple, and he began to suffer from acute neuralgia worsening into fits which rendered him wholly incapable. When, in 1864, it was decided to incorporate British Kaffraria into the Cape Colony, Maclean became something of an embarrassment and he was shipped off to be Lieutenant-Governor of Natal. There his condition deteriorated, as his old friend Gawler explained.

> [For five days, Maclean had been having a fit every twenty minutes.] During the intervals, he was perfectly rational and would do business though latterly much exhausted. At the end of the five days, the intervals diminished during twenty-four hours to a quarter of an hour, ten minutes, five, four, three, two, one, and then passed off into one continued one in which he lay for some hours with nothing but a quivering over his body, his eyes fixed and hands clenched.[16]

Maclean survived, but his left side was now completely paralysed. He strove to perform his official duties, but his mind would not answer the call of his will. When they brought him back from Natal to his little seaside cottage near Cove Rock, where the prophet Nxele had attempted to raise the dead in 1818, they discovered that he had completely mismanaged his finances and was hopelessly in debt. His sons were 'fine young fellows' and spoke Xhosa fluently, but he had paid so little attention to their education that they could scarcely read or write. Within a short five years, the Chief Commissioner had fallen from the heights of dictatorship to a state of utter physical, mental and financial destitution. He lingered on until 1874, then died almost forgotten by the British Kaffraria he had done so much to shape.

Charles Brownlee inherited Maclean's mantle as the European who best understood the 'native mind', and when the Cape attained Responsible Government, he was the natural choice as its first Minister of Native Affairs.[17] Brownlee was a great advocate of 'civilizing the Xhosa', and he looked on Grey's system of 1856 as the basis of Cape racial policy. But he paid surprisingly little attention to British Kaffraria and was content to leave Sandile and all his other Xhosa friends to the care of his drunken former clerk. Most of Brownlee's energies were devoted to bringing the benefits of Cape government to the independent black nations east of the Kei, and, one by one, the Thembu, the Bhaca and the Mpondomise signed away their freedom and accepted colonial magistrates and colonial control. One indirect effect of these changes was the encirclement of Sarhili and his diehard Gcaleka Xhosa who, unsurprisingly, were not inclined to volunteer for colonial domination. Partly due to Brownlee's mismanagement, clashes between Sarhili and the Colony's Mfengu clients finally escalated into the Ninth Frontier War (1877-8), and further bungling by Brownlee resulted in the involvement of Sandile and the Ngqika Xhosa on the side of their King. This discredited Brownlee in the eyes of his ministerial colleagues and Governor Frere, who called him 'fatally deficient' in nerve, promptitude and judgement.[18]

Although Brownlee undoubtedly was, as we have stressed, a humane man with a genuine liking for individual Xhosa, his paternalist conviction that he knew what was best for the black man led him into measures which were as harsh and dictatorial as those of Maclean and Grey. Thus he personally ordered all the Ngqika Xhosa into transKeian exile at the end of the Ninth Frontier War. He advised Sir Bartle Frere in his disastrous Natal policies, and he personally carried the unacceptable ultimatum to King Cetshwayo which provoked the Zulu War of 1879. As chief magistrate of East Griqualand, his last official post, he unwillingly assisted in the disarmament policies which led to the transKeian rebellions of 1880, and he consistently urged the subjugation of the Mpondo, the last independent black people on the southeastern coast of Africa.

Around the middle of the 1870s, Brownlee became afflicted by a rodent ulcer of the face which slowly ate away his nose. He visited London to seek medical assistance on a number of occasions, but even the famous surgeon, Sir Joseph Lister, was unable to effect a cure. He died at King William's Town in 1890.

Most of Grey's magistrates fought in the Indian Mutiny, but none of them did anything of note. George Colley, the first magistrate of the transKei, and Eustace Robertson, the magistrate with Anta, saw service in the Red River Rebellion led by the half-crazed Louis Riel, the prophet of the French-Canadian *metis*. Colley was killed by the Transvaal Boers at Majuba in 1881, and Frederick Reeve, the magistrate with Kama, fell in Sri Lanka in 1869. The health of Sir Walter Currie, the dashing commandant of the Frontier Armed and Mounted Police, collapsed after his campaign against the Korannas near Upington in 1878, and he returned to Grahamstown to find himself a bankrupt and his beautiful mansion of Oatlands sold over his head. Herbert Vigne, the magistrate with Phatho, was appointed Commissioner of the Crown Reserve but fell from grace on account of his polygamous relationships with a daughter of Stokwe and a granddaughter of Phatho. Dr Fitzgerald pottered about the great Native Hospital he built in King William's Town until he finally retired to Ramsgate in 1890.[19]

Major Gawler was appointed deputy adjutant-general to the troops in India, and commanded an expedition to Sikkim in 1861. He returned to South Africa in 1863 and spent a couple of years as military secretary in Grahamstown before returning to England. In 1872, he was appointed Keeper of the Crown Jewels at the Tower of London, a post which apparently left him too much time for reflection, for the middle-aged Gawler became an ardent millenarian and a leading exponent of the British Israel movement. The British, he believed, were descendants via the Scythians of the Israelite tribe of Dan, and the British Empire was God's successor to ancient Israel.

> Surely among the nations . . . there is no people or race in whom this wonderful doctrine of election is so specially manifest . . . as our own. . . . Thanks be to God, the sun never sets on the British Empire; and wherever the British flag flies, the Gospel of Christ is preached; and the Word of God is sent out from our island home in the language of every nation under heaven. . . .
>
> Israel we know to be a chosen race, but how comes it that, in this more blessed dispensation, the ark of the Covenant — now the testimony of Jesus — is, to speak soberly and practically, in the almost exclusive keeping of the British nation.[20]

In works such as *The Two Olive Trees* and *Our Scythian Ancestors*, Gawler painstakingly examined Greek and Hebrew texts, and proved by means of abstruse mathematical calculations from the dimensions of the tabernacles in the Biblical wilderness that the apocalyptical struggle between good (Britain) and evil (Russia) had commenced in the Middle East in 1875, and would continue until 'great Babylon' would 'come into rememberance before God', and 'Communism, Nihilism, infidelity and Popery' were obliterated. In addition to these eschatological speculations, Gawler wrote a pamphlet on military tactics and a book on his expedition to Sikkim. But of Nongqawuse, the real-life prophetess whom he had captured and who had lived in his house for several months, he never wrote a single word.

After the transKei invasion of February 1858, King Sarhili fled from Gawler and Currie and established himself in the forests just east of the Mbashe River, where he remained while the Cape Parliament and the British government squabbled over the future of his former territory. Both agreed that the transKei should be occupied by white settlers, but neither was prepared to shoulder the risk or the expense. Attempts were made by Sir Walter Currie to frighten Sarhili even further away, but the Xhosa King refused to abandon the hope of returning to his old country. 'Is the ground over the Umtata [River], the ground that [I] was born on?' he asked. 'Why does the Government point out that ground for my people to live upon?'

Eventually, Governor Wodehouse came up with a compromise which, like all compromises, satisfied nobody and made matters even worse. Sarhili was permitted to reoccupy the coastal strip between the Kei and Mbashe rivers, comprising perhaps a third of the total area of his former lands (1865). The Thembu of Glen Grey were encouraged to emigrate from their territory near Queenstown and to occupy the upper Kei aound Sarhili's old Great Place of Hohita. Sandile and the Ngqika Xhosa were urged to join in the great carve-up of Sarhili's territory, but they refused to betray their King by stealing his land. Instead, the colonial Mfengu, who were dissatisfied with the high taxes and small allotments of the Cape Colony, were induced to settle the central stretch of the transKei along the waggon road from Butterworth to Port Natal. The old rivalry between the Mfengu and the Gcaleka Xhosa was assiduously encouraged by the colonial officials, who argued that 'for many years, the [Xhosa] will require a watchful policy, and if they are to fight it is better that they should do so with the Fingo first'.[21]

The Cape government also supported the Thembu King Ngangelizwe as a counterweight to Sarhili's power, even though Ngangelizwe was a sadistic young man who crippled his Great Wife Nomkhafulo, Sarhili's daughter, by repeated beatings. Provoked by this brutally contemptuous behaviour, the Xhosa army swept through Thembuland, crushed the Thembu army and burned Ngangelizwe's Great Place to the ground. But the Cape authorities intervened and forced Sarhili to accept a miserly 40 head of cattle in compensation for the injuries to his daughter. Fortified by this display of colonial support, Ngangelizwe did not scruple to murder a female attendant of his ex-wife, who had foolishly remained behind in Thembuland. Again the colonial authorities, though acknowledging that Ngangelizwe was at fault, stepped in to protect him from the wrath of Sarhili. The Thembu were taken under colonial protection in 1875, which left Sarhili and his Gcaleka Xhosa surrounded and encircled, the only independent black nation west of the Umthatha River.[22]

In August 1877, a fight broke out at a beer drink between some Xhosa and some Mfengu. Although Gcaleka hostility was initially directed exclusively against the Mfengu, it soon escalated when it became clear that the colonial government intended to protect their Mfengu allies. Sarhili was unable to restrain all of his followers, but the essence of his attitude was that 'the [Gcaleka] did not want to fight the police but only the [Mfengu]'.[23] Militarily, the Gcaleka never had a hope, and they greatly diminished their chances by the insistence of their wardoctors that they attack in close formation, even when confronted by fortified positions equipped with artillery. The results of such misguided tactics were clearly demonstrated at the battle of Centane (February 1878) where nearly 400 Xhosa warriors died, but only two colonials. Sarhili offered to surrender in return for a guarantee of his life and liberty, but he was told that although his life would be spared, he would most likely be imprisoned. The colonial authorities put a price of £1,000 on Sarhili's head, but they never caught the old King. He took up residence in an impenetrable declivity in Bomvanaland, accessible only by clambering in single file across a series of ridges bounded by abrupt precipices hundreds of metres deep. There he skulked, in his own words, 'like a baboon in a hole'.[24] 'Where is my country?' he asked a visiting journalist. 'Where are my children? My country was over there — [his arm swept the horizon] — now I've no country.' In 1883 he was given a free pardon but he never emerged from this last retreat. He died there in 1893, 83 years old and eating thorns indeed.

The winds of war from Gcalekaland could not but rouse the Ngqika Xhosa west of the Kei. Crippled by the village system, impoverished by taxes and low wages, their location an open and treeless sourgrass plain, they were contemptuously neglected by the colonial government, which did not even bother to appoint efficient officers over them. Sandile, now grown very abject and drunken, was still their chief. His only response to the changing world about him was to draw in his horns like a snail and retreat into a shell of Xhosa customs and traditions which had long ceased to be relevant to the colonial situation.

When Khiva, Sarhili's fighting general, appeared in the Ngqika location to demand Ngqika Xhosa help for their King, many of Sandile's followers wanted to have nothing to do with him. But the chief himself, though he hesitated a little in deference to his councillors, never really doubted his course:

> How can I sit still when Rhili fights? If Rhili fights and bursts and is overpowered, then I too become nothing. No longer will I be a chief. Where Rhili dies there will I die, and where he wakes there will I wake.[25]

Sandile never had any illusions that he could survive this last war, and for the last few months of his life he strove to the utmost to make up for all the follies and mistakes of the past. Even after Sarhili had pulled out of the unequal struggle, Sandile fought on without any hope or any purpose, save never to surrender. They caught up with him at last in May 1878, and shot him dead in a skirmish in the Isidenge forests north of King William's Town. In the same bush lay his bodyguard Dukwana, the son of the Christian prophet Ntsikana, who went out to war saying that he was not fighting against Christianity or civilization but against the English who had robbed his people of their land.[26]

The Robben Island prisoners joined Sandile to a man. 'I would rather die in the field to be eaten by vultures than be carried out of my house on a board,' exclaimed the old chief Siyolo before he took to the Fish River bush, the scene of his greatest exploits during the War of Mlanjeni.[27] He got his wish. Phatho's son Dilima fought with him and was the last chief to surrender his arms. Xhoxho, Sandile's brother, was shot dead with his son by a police patrol. Tini, Maqoma's son, headed for the Waterkloof and eventually joined Siyolo in that old warrior's last stand on the mountain of Ntaba kaNdoda.

Kama, Siwani, Toyise and the other traditionally pro-government chiefs, together with Feni and Oba, stuck by the government. So did the people of Anta, who died just before the war began. Old Soga, the unbelieving councillor, opposed the war but refused to abandon his chief. He lurked about his village until the colonial Mfengu caught him and, granting his last request, killed him with his own spear. The only other noted unbelievers who fought with Sandile were his brother Matana and Chief Jali, who had been a young man at the time of the Cattle-Killing. Both were killed. Most of the Ngqika unbelievers, headed by the councillor Tyhala and Kona Maqoma, took refuge at Mgwali mission station and refused to fight, but their loyalty availed them nothing. In September 1878, their old friend and adviser Charles Brownlee appeared and personally ordered them to cross the Kei River, never again to return to their homeland. The loyal Ngqika were aghast and reproached themselves as cowards for their neutrality. Tyhala, for once, did not obey. He died the day before the removal, so it was said, 'of a broken heart'.[28]

Phatho and Mhala did not fight, for they had died in 1869 and 1875 respectively. Phatho never made it to Robben Island, but was detained for treatment at Somerset Hospital. There he encountered Prince Alfred, Queen Victoria's younger son, and Grey ordered him released as a gesture to please the young prince. As we have seen, Maclean refused him permission to resume his chieftainship or gather his people together, and he died in such utter obscurity that the clerk in charge of the district where he lived did not even bother to report his death, which occurred in October 1869. Mhala served out his full term and was released in 1863. He repeatedly asked permission to go to the Ndlambe settlement at Idutywa, but the colonial authorities were afraid that he would dominate his weak son Smith and link up with Sarhili. He was forbidden to possess land of his own and forbidden to reunite himself with his faithful Great Son Makinana, who lived in exile across the Kei. Eventually, he settled down with his son Ndimba, who lived in the Ngqika Location, and he died there on alien ground one rainy evening in April 1875. The Xhosa said that the heavens themselves were weeping for the passing of the old chief.[29]

And Nongqawuse? As we have already mentioned, Mhlakaza and most of the other residents of the prophetic homestead died of starvation, but the prophetess herself survived and was handed over to Major Gawler by the chief of the Bomvana. She stayed with the Gawlers for a while, and one day Mrs Gawler dressed her up together with Nonkosi, the Mpongo prophetess, and Dr Fitzgerald took them down to the photographer, where the stolid portrait reproduced in this book was taken. She also made several statements relative to the 'chiefs' plot' but even the prosecuting genius of Maclean could do nothing with them. In October 1858, she sailed with Nonkosi, Mhala and the Gawlers to Cape Town on board the schooner *Alice Smith*. The two prophetesses were taken to the defunct Paupers' Lodge, where the female prisoners and transportees were confined under the supervision of a Mrs Connelly.[30]

And there Nongqawuse vanishes from recorded history. When the prison at the Paupers' Lodge was broken up in August 1859, her name did not appear on the list of female prisoners. One 'Notaki' is listed, who must have been either Nongqawuse or Nonkosi, but it is absolutely certain that only one of the two prophetesses returned with the other female prisoners to East London. Sir Walter Stanford stated with assurance that she was still living on a farm in the Alexandria district near Port Elizabeth in 1905. The settler historian Cory was told in 1910 that she was alive somewhere under the name of Victoria Regina, but he failed to find her. In 1938, however, an itinerant journalist named D.R. d'Ewes stumbled across her tracks in Alexandria. Two elderly Xhosa of that neighbourhood informed him that she had settled down with relatives on a local farm, married and had two daughters. On one occasion, she had gone to live in Port Elizabeth, but when the Xhosa there discovered who she was, she had been forced to flee for her life. She was buried along with her daughters on the farm Glenthorn near Alexandria.[31]

I visited Alexandria myself in the hope of turning up something new, and was introduced to the great-nephew and great-niece of Nongqawuse. The great-niece insisted on telling me in English what she called 'the true story of Nongqawuse'. It began, 'Umhlakaza was a Kaffir witchdoctor,' and it was taken from a primary school reader. Her brother was a little more helpful. Speaking in Xhosa, he told me that his great-aunt Nongqawuse was 'a very nice lady', and that right up to the time of her death she would warn the people 'against the coming wrath of God'.[32] And so Nongqawuse departed this life as quietly and elusively as she entered it. But how great were the changes she wrought in between!

Notes

1. I intend no aspersions on the personal morality of the German settlers. The point is that Grey was trying to constitute a white rural working class in a country which lacked the material preconditions for it. For details, see Rutherford (1961), Chapter 25. For drunkenness and other misconduct, *Berlin Missionberichte*, Abt. III, Berlin Mission Archives, A. Briest-BMS, 22 May 1857, A. Kropf-BMS, 2 July 1857.
2. GH 1/264 Stanley-Grey, 4 May 1858.
3. Rutherford (1961), pp.297-8, 425. Grey ever after maintained that the reason he was recalled was his fearless refusal to submit to Lord Derby's nepotistic desire to appoint his kinsman, E.M. Cole. To believe this is to ignore all Grey's other derelictions of duty. See Rutherford (1961), Chapters 26-28, for the remainder of Grey's South African career. For black reaction, *King William's Town Gazette*, 1 Oct. 1859.
4. For the Keppel affair, see B.J. Dalton, 'Sir George Grey and the Keppel affair', *Historical Studies* (Melbourne) 16 (1974). Also the Newcastle papers, University of Nottingham, for example, NE 11031 H. Keppel-Lady Grey, 27 Feb. 1861.
5. MS 3030, Cory Library, Grahamstown, J. Ross-B. Ross, 13 Aug. 1860.
6. For Grey's second governorship of New Zealand, I have relied heavily on Dalton (1967), Chapters 6-8.
7. Rutherford (1961), pp.558-9.
8. Rutherford (1961), pp.504-6; Gorst (1908), pp.24-6.
9. Rutherford (1961), Chapters 38-42.
10. For the statistics, see Bergh and Visagie (1985), p.56. For the land regulations of British Kaffraria, see GH 8/35 Schedule 102, 15 July 1858; *King William's Town Gazette*, 26 June, 24 July, 11 Dec. 1858.
11. *King William's Town Gazette*, 27 March, 26 June 1858.
12. For a list of the first black applicants, Government Notice 3 of 1858, *King William's Town Gazette*, 30 Jan. 1858. In addition to these, Grey set aside considerable grants of land to the chiefs' children whom he had educated in Cape Town. See GH 8/39 J. Maclean-G. Grey, 15 Aug. 1859. For the desire of Xhosa and Mfengu to avail themselves of the Grey titles, see GH 8/34 Schedule 37, 11 March 1858. For a forceful comment on the differential treatment of whites and blacks with respect to land, see 'Anti-Humbug' in the *Cape Argus*, 13 Aug. 1859.
13. *King William's Town Gazette*, 26 July 1861.
14. For the hut tax, see BK 114 Circular to special magistrates, 15 July 1858.
15. GH 8/38 J. Maclean-G. Grey, 9 Aug. 1859; GH 8/38 Schedule 60, 13 June 1859; Du Toit (1954), pp.171-2; BK 83 Interview between the Chief

Commissioner and the Chief 'Pato', 11 Oct. 1860.

16. Grey letters, South African Library, Cape Town, J. Gawler-G. Grey, 6 July 1866, F. Travers-G. Grey, 14 May 1863.
17. The best overview of Brownlee's later career is Saunders (1977).
18. For Brownlee and the last Frontier War, see Spicer (1978), *passim*, esp. pp.74, 126-32, 214.
19. The reference to Vigne is to his relationships with a daughter and a granddaughter of chiefs captive on Robben Island. Stokwe and Phatho are the most probable, given their respective ages. GH 30/5 F. Travers-J. Maclean, 6 Oct. 1860. Grey letters, South African Library, Cape Town, R. Southey-G. Grey, 5 Oct. 1872 (Currie); *ibid.*, J. Fitzgerald, 26 Dec. 1890 (Fitzgerald); Black Watch Regimental Museum, Perth (Reeve).
20. J. Gawler, *The British Line in the Attack* (London: W. Mitchell, 1872); *Sikhim, with Hints on Mountain and Jungle Warfare* (London: E. Stanford, 1873); *The Two Olive Trees* (London: W.H. Guest, n.d.); *Our Scythian Ancestors* (London: W.H. Guest, n.d.).
21. Grey Letters, South African Library, W. Currie-G. Grey, 24 Dec. 1861. Saunders (1978), pp.9-15, is the most succinct guide to these complicated events.
22. Spicer (1978), pp.29-42. For a graphic description of the injuries inflicted on Sarhili's daughter by Ngangelizwe, see Chalmers (1878), pp.400-1.
23. On the Ninth Frontier War, see Spicer (1978), an excellent thesis which deserves to be published.
24. *Cape Times* correspondent, quoted by F. Dike in the programme notes to her excellent play, *The Sacrifice of Kreli* (1976).
25. For Sandile's last years, Brownlee (1916), pp.298, 301; CO 3090 C. Brownlee-R. Southey, 1 Oct. 1866. For the quote, Interview with Chief F. Mpangele, Mgwali Location, 26 Aug. 1975.
26. Spicer (1978), p.158.
27. Interview with S. Mgqala, Sittingbourne Location, King William's Town District, Aug. 1975.
28. Brownlee (1916), p.315.
29. Phatho: GH 30/5 F. Travers-J. Maclean, 2 Aug. 1860; CO 3146, 14 Oct. 1869. Mhala: for example, NA 173 T. Liefeldt-Sec. for Native Affairs, 16 April 1875; NA 841 C. Brownlee-J. Ayliff, 1 March 1875; CO 3140 J. Warner-Colonial Secretary, 12 June 1868 and marginal notes; CO 3090 C. Mills-J. Warner, 29 March 1866. For Mhala's death, *Kaffrarian Watchman*, 19 April 1875.
30. *South African Commercial Advertiser*, 3 Sept. 1859, 30 Oct. 1859. BK 111 C. Piers-J. Maclean gives a list of the women discharged from the Paupers' Lodge. The prisoners were given numbers according to their date of arrival. 'Notaki' is the only prisoner who arrived subsequent to April 1858.
31. W. Stanford, *The Reminiscences of Walter Stanford*, Vol. 1 (Cape Town: Van Riebeeck Society, 1958), p.5; G. Cory, 'I Tramp into Kaffirland in search of History', *South African Railways Magazine* (1927), p.2022; Burton (1950), p.96; *Eastern Province Herald*, 22 Nov. 1938. Both Burton and D'Ewes refer to 1898 as the year of Nongqawuse's death, but I am disposed to think that their Xhosa informants simply said that she died 'about the time of the rinderpest', which would leave Stanford's date as a clear possibility.
32. Interview with Wallace Sukutu and sister, Alexandria, 27 Feb. 1976.

Select Bibliography

1. Primary Sources

A. Cape Archives, Cape Town

Acc 611/7 Southey Papers.
Acc 793 Letterbook of Major Gawler.
BK 14 President, Criminal Court Commission, British Kaffraria, 1856-60.
BK 69-71 Gaika Commissioner (Brownlee).
BK 81 Magistrate with Umhala (Gawler).
BK 82 Magistrate with Macomo (Lucas).
BK 83 Magistrate with Pato (Vigne).
BK 85 Magistrate with Anta (Robertson).
BK 86 Magistrate with Kama (Reeve).
BK 89 Secret Information.
BK 100 Health (Fitzgerald).
BK 373 Letters dispatched to the High Commissioner.
CO 2949-2952 Tambookie Agent (J. Warner).
GH 8/16-43 Dispatches received from Chief Commissioner, British Kaffraria.
GH 8/48-50 Unofficial Correspondence, Maclean-Grey.
GH 19/8 Chiefs Sandilli, Kreli, Pato etc.
GH 20/2/1 Papers relative to British Kaffraria, 1853-8.
GH 23/26-7 Letters dispatched to Colonial Office, London.
GH 30/4-5 Letters dispatched by High Commissioner.

B. Cory Library, Grahamstown

Sir George Cory Interviews.
John Ross Papers.
MIC 172/2 United Society for the Propagation of the Gospel (microfilm).
MS 7113 R.J. Mullins Diary.
MS 575-588 Miscellaneous Letters relating to 8th Frontier War.
MS 15,899 Methodist Church Records.
MS 16,713 Grahamstown Diocese Archives.
PR 3664 E.G. Sihele Ibali labaTembu.
PR 3624 J. Fitzgerald Letterbook.
PR 3563 H. Halse Autobiography.

C. South African Library, Cape Town

MSB 139 Cumming Papers.
Grey Collection.

D. Great Britain

Bramston, T.R. Diary. Greenjackets Regimental Museum, Winchester.
Elwes, V.D.C. Letters. Lincolnshire Archives, Lincoln.
Fisher, J. Letters. Greenjackets Regimental Museum, Winchester.
Graham, L. Diary. National Army Museum, London.
Grey, Earl. Papers. University of Durham.
Holdich, E.A. Diary. Staffordshire Regimental Museum, Whittington.
Kingsley, J.C.G. Journal. National Army Museum, London.
Mellish of Hodsock. Papers. University of Nottingham.
Rich, J. Diary. Black Watch Regimental Museum, Perth.
Robinson, H. Letters. Humberside County Record Office, Beverley.
Seymour of Ragley. Papers. Warwickshire County Record Office, Warwick.
St. John, W.J. Journal. National Army Museum, London.

E. Germany

Berlin Mission Archives, Abt. III. Reports of A. Kropf, 1857-9.

F. Oral Sources

B.F. Anta, Teko Location, Kentani District, 8 Jan. 1976.
N. Bhotomane, Ramntswana Location, Kentani District, 16 Dec. 1975.
N. Bhotomane, Interview with H. Scheub, 1968. Courtesy of Professor Scheub of the University of Wisconsin.
W. Dwaba, Tshabo Location, Berlin District, Aug. 1975.
M. Kantolo, Kantolo Location, Kentani District, 22 Aug. 1983.
M. Ngovane, Mahlahlane Location, Willowvale District, 15 Nov. 1975.
W. Nkabi, Bulembu Location, King William's Town District, 24 Aug. 1975.
A. Nkonki, Ngcizele Location, Kentani District, 7 Jan. 1976.
N. Qeqe, Shixini Location, Willowvale District, Oct.-Nov. 1975.
M. Soga, Kobonqaba Location, Kentani District, 25 Aug. 1983.
W. Sukutu, Alexandria (Cape), 27 Feb. 1976.
R. Tshisela, Mncotsho Location, Berlin District, 23 Aug. 1982.

G. Journals and Newspapers

Anglo-African, 1855.
Anglo-Germania, 1858.
Berlin Missionberichte, 1850-60.
Cape Argus, 1857-9.
Cape Church Monthly, 1856.
Cape Frontier Times, 1853.
Cape Mercury, 1859.
Cape Monitor, 1856.
Church Chronicle of the Diocese of Grahamstown, 1881-4.
Edinburgh Evening Courant, 1851-2.
Graaff-Reinet Herald, 1856-8.
Grahamstown Journal, 1845-65.
King William's Town Gazette, 1856-66.
Illustrated London News, 1851-2.
Journal des Missions Evangeliques, 1850-2.
Home and Foreign Record of the Free Church of Scotland, 1850-3.

Nottingham Journal, 1851-2.
South African Commercial Advertiser, 1856-8.
Umteteli waBantu, 1927-40.
United Services Magazine, 1852.

H. Printed Official Sources

A. IMPERIAL BLUE BOOKS

311 of 1841 Correspondence respecting the Colonization of New Zealand.
635 of 1851 Select Committee on the Kaffir Tribes.
949 of 1848; 1056 of 1849; 1288 of 1850; 1334 of 1851; 1428 of 1852; 1635 of 1853; 1969 of 1855; 2096 of 1856; 2202 of 1857; 2352 of 1857; Papers re State of the Kaffir Tribes.

B. CAPE PARLIAMENTARY PAPERS

G 4 of 1858 Proceedings and findings of the court . . . and sentence . . . upon Macomo and other Kafirs.
G 5 of 1858 Papers indicating the Nature of the Plans formed by the Kafir Chiefs.
G 36 of 1858 Deposition made by Nongquase, a Kafir Prophetess.
Select Committee on Frontier Defence, 1855.

I. Other Printed Sources

Adams, B. 1941. *The Narrative of Private Buck Adams*. Cape Town: Van Riebeeck Society.
Alberti, L. 1810. *Account of the Xhosa in 1807*. Trans. W. Fehr. Cape Town: Balkema (1968).
Appleyard, J. 1971. *The War of the Axe and the Xhosa Bible*. Cape Town: Struik.
Backhouse, J. 1844. *Narrative of a Visit to the Mauritius and South Africa*. London: Hamilton Adams.
Black, W.T. 1901. *The Fish River Bush*. Edinburgh: Young J. Pentland.
Brownlee, C. 1916. *Reminiscences of Kaffir Life and History*. 2nd ed. Lovedale: Lovedale Press.
Campbell, P.S. n.d. *Reminiscences of the Kaffir Wars*. London: Buck Brothers.
Chalmers, J. 1878. *Tiyo Soga*. 2nd ed. Edinburgh: Elliot.
Cathcart, G. 1857. *Correspondence of Sir George Cathcart*. London: John Murray.
C.W.N. 1900. *George Gawler*. Privately printed: Australia (?). Copy in British Museum.
Currey, J.B. 1986. *John Blades Currey, 1850-1900*. Ed. P.B. Simons. Johannesburg: Brenthurst Press.
Dugmore, H.H. 1858. 'Papers', in J. Maclean (ed.), *Compendium of Kafir Laws and Customs*. Reprinted Grahamstown: J. Slater (1906).
Godlonton, R. and Irving, E. 1851. *Narrative of the Kaffir War of 1850-51*. London: Pelham Richardson.
Goldswain, J. 1946-9. *The Chronicle of Jeremiah Goldswain*. Ed. U. Long. 2 vols. Cape Town: Van Riebeeck Society.
Gorst, J. 1908. *New Zealand Revisited*. London: Pitman.

Gqoba, W.W. 1888. 'Isizatu Sokuxelwa Kwe Nkomo Ngo Nongqause', *Isigidimi SamaXosa.*

Grey, G. 1841. *Journals of Two Expeditions of Discovery in . . . Australia.* London: Boone.

Grey, G. 1855. *Polynesian Mythology.* London: John Murray.

Hutcheon, D. 1905. 'Lungsickness of Cattle', *Agricultural Journal* (Cape Town), 27.

Kay, S. 1833. *Travels and Researches in Caffraria.* London: John Mason.

King, W.R. 1853. *Campaigning in Kaffirland.* London: Saunders and Otley.

Kropf, A. 1891. *Der Lugenprofeten Kafferlands.* Berlin: Berlin Evangelischen Missions-Gesellschaft.

Kropf, A. and Godfrey, R. 1915. *Kaffir-English Dictionary.* 2nd ed. Lovedale: Lovedale Press.

Lakeman, S. 1880. *What I Saw in Kaffirland.* Edinburgh: Blackwood.

Le Cordeur, B. and Saunders, C. 1981. *The War of the Axe.* Johannesburg: Brenthurst Press.

Lichtenstein, H. 1812-15. *Travels in Southern Africa.* Trans. A. Plumptre. 2 vols. Cape Town: Van Riebeeck Society (1928-30).

Mackay, J. 1871. *Reminiscences of the Last Kafir War.* Reprinted Cape Town: Struik (1970).

Maclean, J. 1858. *Compendium of Kaffir Laws and Customs.* Reprinted Grahamstown: J. Slater (1906).

Merriman, N.J. 1957. *The Cape Journals of Archdeacon Merriman.* Eds D.H. Varley and H.M. Matthew. Cape Town: Van Riebeeck Society.

Milne, J. 1899. *The Romance of a Proconsul.* London: Chatto and Windus.

Mitra, S.M. 1911. *Life and Letters of Sir John Hall.* London: Longman.

Moodie, J.W.D. 1835. *Ten Years in South Africa.* 2 vols. London: Bentley.

Mqhayi, S.E.K. n.d. *Ityala lamaWele.* 7th impression. Lovedale: Lovedale Press.

Pearse, H. 1898. 'The Kaffir and Basuto Campaigns of 1852 and 1853', *United Services Magazine.*

Read, J. 1818. 'Narrative of the journey of Mr Read and others to Caffraria', *Transactions of the London Missionary Society,* 4.

Rubusana, W.B. 1906. *Zemk'iinkomo Magwalandini.* London: Butler and Tanner.

Scully, W. 1913. *Further Reminiscences of a South African Pioneer.* London: T. Fisher Unwin.

Shaw, W. 1860. *The Story of my Mission in South-eastern Africa.* London: Hamilton Adams.

Smith, H. 1901. *The Autobiography of Sir Harry Smith.* London: Murray.

Smith of St Cyrus, A. 1895. *A Contribution to South African Materia Medica.* 3rd ed. Lovedale: Lovedale Press.

Soga, J.H. n.d. *The Ama-Xhosa: Life and Customs.* Lovedale: Lovedale Press.

Soga, Tiyo. n.d. [1983]. *The Journal and Selected Writings.* Ed. D. Williams. Cape Town: Balkema.

Soga, T.B. n.d. *Intlalo kaXhosa.* Lovedale: Lovedale Press.

Steinbart, G. 1975. *The Letters of Gustav Steinbart.* Port Elizabeth: University of Port Elizabeth.

Stretch, C.L. 1876. 'Makana and the attack on Graham's Town', *Cape*

Monthly Magazine, New Series, 12.

Stubbs, T. 1978. *The Reminiscences of Thomas Stubbs*. Eds W. Maxwell and R. McGeogh. Cape Town: Balkema.

Theal, G.M. 1876. *Compendium of South African History and Geography*. 2nd ed. Lovedale: Lovedale Press.

Ward, H. 1851. *The Cape and the Kaffirs*. London: Bohn.

Wilmot, R. 1856. *A Cape Traveller's Diary, 1856*. Johannesburg: Donker.

2. Secondary Sources

Australian Dictionary of Biography, Vol. 1. Melbourne: Melbourne University Press, 1966.

Berglund, A-I. 1976. *Zulu Thought-Patterns and Symbolism*. London: Hurst.

Bergh, J.S. 1984. 'Die lewe van Charles Pacalt Brownlee tot 1857', *Archives Yearbook for South African History*.

Bergh, J.S. and Visagie, J. 1985. *The Eastern Cape Frontier Zone, 1660-1980*. Durban: Butterworths.

Clark, C.M.H. 1973. *A History of Australia*, Vol. 3. Melbourne: Melbourne University Press.

Cook, P.A.W. n.d. *Social Organisation and Ceremonial Institutions of the Bomvana*. Cape Town: Juta.

Cory, G. 1965. *The Rise of South Africa*. 6 vols. 1910-39. Reprinted Cape Town: Struik.

Crowther, M. 1981. *The Workhouse System, 1834-1929*. London: Batsford.

Dalton, B.J. 1967. *War and Politics in New Zealand 1855-1870*. Sydney: Sydney University Press.

Dodd, A.D. 1938. *Native Vocational Training*. Lovedale: Lovedale Press.

Du Toit, A.E. 1954. 'The Cape Frontier, 1847-1866', *Archives Yearbook for South African History*.

Festinger, L., Riecken, H.W. and Schachter, S. 1964. *When Prophecy Fails*. New York: Harper and Row.

Finer, S.E. 1952. *The Life and Times of Sir Edwin Chadwick*. London: Methuen.

Goedhals, M. 1979. 'Anglican missionary policy in the diocese of Grahamstown under the first two bishops', M.A. thesis, Rhodes University.

Harington, A. 1980. *Sir Harry Smith: Bungling Hero*. Cape Town: Tafelberg.

Horton, R. 1967. 'African traditional thought and Western science', *Africa*, 37.

Hodgson, J. 1979. 'Zonnebloem College and Cape Town: 1858-1870', in C. (ed.), *Studies in the History of Cape Town*, Vol. 2. Cape Town: University of Cape Town.

Hodgson, J. 1982. *The God of the Xhosa*. Cape Town: Oxford University Press.

Hodgson, J. 1987. *Princess Emma*. Johannesburg: Donker.

Houghton, W.E. 1957. *The Victorian Frame of Mind, 1830-1870*. New Haven: Yale University Press.

Hunter, M. 1936. *Reaction to Conquest*. Oxford: Oxford University Press.

Jordan, A.C. 1973. *Towards an African Literature*. Berkeley: University of California Press.

Kirk, T. 1980. 'The Cape economy and the expropriation of the Kat River

Settlement, 1846-53', in S. Marks and A. Atmore (eds), *Economy and Society in Pre-Industrial South Africa*. London: Longman.

Lehmann, J. 1977. *Remember You Are an Englishman*. London: Jonathan Cape.

Milton, J. 1983. *The Edges of War*. Cape Town: Juta.

Marincowitz, J. 1985. 'Proletarians, privatisers and private property rights: mission land regulations in the Western Cape'. Unpublished seminar paper, Institute of Commonwealth Studies, London.

Ngubane, H.S. 1977. *Body and Mind in Zulu Medicine*. London: Academic Press.

Peires, J.B. 1981. *The House of Phalo*. Johannesburg: Ravan Press.

Peires, J.B. 1985. 'The late great plot: the official delusion concerning the Xhosa Cattle-Killing', *History in Africa*, 12.

Poynter, J.R. 1969. *Society and Pauperism: English Ideas on Poor Relief*. London: Routledge Kegan Paul.

Ray, B. 1976. *African Religions*. Englewood Cliffs: Prentice-Hall.

Rutherford, J. 1961. *Sir George Grey, K.C.B.* London: Cassell.

Saunders, C.C. 1978. 'The annexation of the Transkeian territories', *Archives Yearbook for South African History*.

Schnell, E.L.G. 1954. *For Men Must Work*. Cape Town: Maskew Miller.

Spicer, M. 1978. 'The war of Ngcayechibi'. M.A. thesis, Rhodes University.

Stokes, E. 1959. *The English Utilitarians and India*. Oxford: Oxford University Press.

Thornton, R. 1983. 'The elusive unity of Sir George Grey's library', *African Studies*, 42.

Ward, A. 1974. *A Show of Justice*. Canberra: Australian National University Press.

Wards, I. 1968. *The Shadow of the Land*. Wellington: Department of Internal Affairs.

Wilson, M. 1969. 'Co-operation and conflict: the Eastern Cape frontier', in M. Wilson and L. Thompson (eds), *Oxford History of South Africa*, Vol. 1. Oxford: Oxford University Press.

Wilson, M. 1977. 'Mhlakaza' in C-A. Julien et al, *Les Africains*, Vol. 5. Paris: Edition J.A.

Zarwan, J. n.d. 'The Xhosa cattle-killings, 1856-57', *Cahiers d'Etudes Africaines*, 63-4.

Index